t Southern, the name coming from a winter creek running alongside the vineyard, and a view of The Abbey in the S.
eslings have had significant show success. Accad, Guy came to prominence in Burgundy in the mid-1980s, advocatin
e onset of fermentation, which in turn gave rise to the concept of pre-fermen
Oregon for the International Pinot Noir Celebration. In Australia cold soak i
in liberating colour (which has particular relevance for pinot noir), and the
ome winemakers in fact use both pre- and post-fermentation techniques. ac
cessarily part of table wine, but at high concentrations it is a major fault. The
dition of appropriate sulphur dioxide. acetic acid is present in all table win
gal limit is 0.8 mg/l for white wine and rosé, 1.2 mg/l for red wine and 1.5 mg/l for botrytised wine. acid is present
amounts of citric acid. Where the acid is too low, any one of the three acids may legally be added to wine to bring
nises the chance of oxidation. additives to wine are controlled by the Australia New Zealand Food Standards Cod
cannot be added, even if it is in no way harmful. One example of the latter is sorbitol. It is widely used in the frui
ere is the curious situation that as one travels north across the equator, acid becomes the work of the devil; as one c
r substance if they believe the quality of the wine will be improved by the addition. On the other hand, they shou
us. For a full list of permitted additives see Standard 4.5.1 of the Australia New Zealand Foods Standards Code.
dissolve additives such as fining agents including casein and bentonite. It is also recognised that small amounts of
er simply to reduce the alcohol level; Californian winemakers, by contrast, are able to add up to 10 per cent of wat
Mount Lofty Ranges Zone, yet is a bare 30 minutes' drive from the CBD of Adelaide. A flourishing region in the
in 1971, but the arrival of Brian Croser and his founding of Petaluma in 1976 were the pivotal events. If there is a
emost producers in the region are Ashton Hills, Bird in Hand, Deviation Road, Fox Gordon, Geoff Weaver, Hah
na, Pike & Joyce, Romney Park, Setanta, Shaw & Smith, Tilbrook and Wicks Estate. The common themes of the
netre contour line, but the ever-twisting and turning hills, valleys and rivers within the region provide a large rai
climate to that of Adelaide throughout much of the summer has to be experienced to be believed. The veritable m
Adelaide Hills has an unequivocally cool climate; it is not until one reaches the northern extremity of the region, ar
and sauvignon blanc, and into terrain which satisfactorily ripens cabernet sauvignon and shiraz. The Adelaide Hill
ly structured soils of lesser quality. Fertility varies, tending to be higher in the southern and central areas. Lat 34°
le Plains, gazetted 25 March 2002, is the most dramatic proof of the lack of meaning to the grouping of regions v
nt Gulf of St Vincent is unable to provide any significant cooling. It is warmer than the Hunter Valley and its gre
Vale, leaving Ceravolo, Diloreto and Domenic Versace to provide some respectability. Shiraz, cabernet sauvigno
of southeastern Australia, with alkaline subsoils and free limestone at deeper levels. These are excellent viticultura
clay soils which are strikingly different in structure, but once again tend to be alkaline rather than acidic, and once
h; Chief vit. hazard Nil Adelaide Zone is a so-called super zone which encompasses the Mount Lofty Ranges, Fle
s and regions in its purview, and simply label them 'Adelaide'. The only problem is that very few winemakers have
th a back label affirmation of 'Wine made in Australia'. aftertaste is experienced after the wine has been swallowe
ncipal variety used in Falernian, the most famous of all Roman wines). Its current champion in Italy is Mastrobera
ry late ripening variety will surely be more widely commercially propagated if temperatures continue to rise. Albar
curiosities of history that, when Great Britain formally claimed ownership of the western part of Australia on Chris
t and west was used for grazing and wheat farming, Albany became famous for whaling, which continued until 197
perhaps Vancouver – itself named by Captain George Vancouver, the 1791 explorer of Albany and thereafter of B
planted by the Sippe family at Redmond Vineyard in 1975, using cuttings of riesling supplied by Forest Hill Vine
h were made at Plantagenet; for some time thereafter the vineyard was neglected, but now it forms the core of Pl
n. Self-evidently, Albany's climate is maritime, strongly shaped and moderated by the Southern Ocean; the sta
l, and moderate humidity in summer assists ripening by reducing stress on the vines. The hills and valleys make th
of an infallible guide to the best soils for grape vines: lateritic gravelly, sandy loams or sandy loams derived directly
, cabernet sauvignon and merlot do best further away from the coast. The principal wineries are Kalgan River W
19°C; Harv Mid-March to end April; Chief vit. hazard Birds albarino is a native white grape of Spain, and seen
Its source, so it appeared, was impeccable: the nursery vineyards of the CSIRO at Merbein, Victoria. Doubts en
e of gewurztraminer grown in the Jura region of France. It is small wonder that misidentification of grape variet

reek Vineyard (est. 1990) is the family business of Mike and Mary Dilworth in the Forongup subregion of the G

he 1.6 ha vineyard is equally split among riesling, pinot noir and cabernet sauvignon planted in 1990 and '93. The

ry high levels of SO2 in red must prior to the commencement of fermentation. The effect was to significantly delay

spoke at two major conferences, one in 1987 and one in 1990, one in the UK for the Masters of Wine, the other in

is chilled below 10°C, and it is this temperature which prevents the onset of fermentation. It is extremely effecti

is quite different from that in an alcoholic environment. Thus, post-fermentation maceration has a different role

compounds known as aldehydes, which are produced at the last stages of fermentation. At low concentrations it is

fruit aroma and flavour not unlike the effect of oxidation. In barrel or tank, the problem is easily treated with the

olatile acidity, which results in a pungent, sharp odour and flavour when present at levels of 0.6 mg/l or above. The

various forms. The most important is tartaric acid, followed by malic acid at slightly lower concentration, with tr

The other acid added to white wines (though not red) is ascorbic, which, in conjunction with sulphur dioxide, min

ations thereunder. The regulations list a series of substances which may be added, and any substance not on that

, and gives the wine a softer and (arguably) more pleasant taste and mouthfeel – but it is an illegal additive. Finally,

pposite direction, sugar becomes the work of the devil. Good winemakers anywhere should not hesitate to add eit

he herd, seeking to rely instead on achieving balance in the vineyard so that the addition of either becomes superf

has been legal to add up to 7 per cent of water to either the must or the finished wine, chiefly where water is neede

ncorporated with wine during bulk transfer by pump from one vessel to another. However, it is not legal to add

tion of fermentation problems. Adelaide Hills, gazetted 9 February 1998, is the coolest of the three regions in the

ha of vines, it declined into obscurity before the last vines disappeared, which was in the 1930s. Planting began ag

which marks the region, it is sauvignon blanc, however important chardonnay, pinot noir and shiraz may be. The

by Geoff Hardy, Longview Vineyard, Mount Torrens Vineyard, New Era Vineyards, Ngeringa, Paracombe, Peta

d are elegance and clarity of varietal expression. The southern and eastern boundaries are determined by the 40

nates. Altitude is the key to the climate: Mount Lofty and the Piccadilly Valley are at 500 metres, and the contras

nd sub-valleys means there is much mesoclimatic variation, making generalisations hazardous. However, most of t

ing slopes, that one moves out of a climate suited principally to early-ripening varieties such as chardonnay, pinot n

nantly grey, grey-brown or brown loamy sands and clay loams; there are also patches of much sandier and more w

–500 m; hdd 1270; Gsr 310 mm; Mjt 19.1°C; Harv Mid-March to late April; Chief vit. hazard Poor fruit set Ade

this case the Mount Lofty Ranges Zone. This is a dead flat and hot region with an altitude of 20 metres; the ad

ainfall is on a par with that of the Swan Valley. Its most highly rated winery, Primo Estate, has moved to McLa

are the main varieties. There are two soil types. First, the ubiquitous red-brown loamy sands found through so m

adily support the typically high yields of the region. Then there are also smaller patches of heavier loam and crack

vigorous vine growth. Lat 34°41'S; Alt 20 m; Hdd 2081; Gsr 130 mm; Mjt 23°C; Harv Mid-February to early M

ossa zones. One of the ostensible reasons for this larger zone was to allow the blending of wines from the quality z

ge of this somewhat dubious proposition. Even Penfolds Magill Estate is content with the vineyard name, coupled

breath thereafter has been taken. aglianico is a red grape much admired by the Greeks and the Romans (it was the

aurasi is based on aglianico. It is propagated by Chalmers Nurseries at Mildura, with two clones available, and as

n of the Great Southern region of Western Australia, its focal point being the town of the same name. It is one of t

826, the point of possession relied on was Albany rather than Perth. While the surrounding country to the north,

ed bays and granite outcrops make this beautiful region (and, in parts, atmospheric town) seem like a mini Seattle

ia. Albany's whaling museum is the largest in the world and is justifiably a major tourist attraction. The first vines

et sauvignon was also planted.) The first two crops of grapes were sold, but in 1981 a riesling and cabernet Sauvi

state. However, the present emphasis is more on chardonnay and pinot noir than on riesling and cabernet sauv

ion is that it is Mediterranean, with moist, cool winters and warm, dry summers. Diurnal temperature range is mi

e enough, but when ocean views are added, and huge marri or karri eucalypts soar skywards, it takes on the chara

and gneissic rocks. The region is best suited to chardonnay. Sauvignon blanc and (in some vintages) pinot noir, sl

mery's Hill, Oranje Tractor, Phillips Brook Estate and Wignalls. Lat 35°02'S; Alt 75 m; Hdd 1495; Gsr 303 mm

ny advantages in the Australian climate; its small plantings proliferated rapidly in the opening decade of this cen

s true identity, and in April 2009 it was officially announced that DNA testing had revealed it to be savagnin vert

# The
# Australian Wine
# Encyclopedia

# The Australian Wine Encyclopedia

## JAMES HALLIDAY

Hardie Grant Books

# Contents

# Foreword

If the author and publisher had asked me to come up with a name for this book, I would have volunteered, 'Remind me, James'. That's the way it feels, like having the guru at your elbow. 'Hell, James, can you remember about ascorbic acid?' 'What happened to Buring's?' 'Are you allowed to add water?'

Of course he can remember. If anyone on earth can provide the answer it is Mr Halliday, who has been talking, tasting and occasionally swallowing wine since he was an articled clerk. Yes, that's how he started – by training his brain. He mastered law before he started on anything more complicated.

I met James Halliday with Len Evans, his boon companion, at memorable parties (we called them 'tastings') in the 1970s. I was always impressed with the depth and scope of Australians' specialist wine knowledge in general, but with James I was overawed. In due course, and many tastings later, he convinced me (and others) that the Yarra Valley had as much potential for cool-climate grapes as anywhere in Australia – or indeed France. I had a small hand in his triumphant venture at Coldstream Hills (and still have some bottles of the early releases, still drinking well). But Australian business doesn't allow brilliant private enterprises to remain private for long.

He may not like being called a technocrat, but that's the part James played in the book we eventually co-authored, *The Art & Science of Wine*. What sort of crat I was I don't recall, but I do refer to the book constantly for its clear exposition of stuff outside my field – and so do bright wine students everywhere.

James is indefatigable and uncatchoutable; terse or talkative – it's not hard to tell how he's feeling. He is the man to brief us all. A river of books has flowed out of him, including his indispensable annual *Australian Wine Companion*. 'Remind me, James' has a different role to fill: the nearest thing to a constant personal briefing. Now you can be uncatchoutable too.

*Hugh Johnson*

# Introduction

This encyclopedia is a distillation of the knowledge I have accumulated over the past 40 or so years. That said, the memory of a 70-year-old male is much less reliable than that of a 30-year-old, or any age in between. So I have had recourse not only to books, papers and articles written by others with far greater expertise than mine on given subjects, but also to books I have written over the decades.

This, I suppose, is a form of living history, and I have variously been surprised, confused and delighted by what I have found. I am acutely aware of the fact that merely having written something (say) 30 years ago about a then recent event, or a recently researched event, does not in any way guarantee its truth. Moreover, the truth or relevance may have been undermined by the intervening period.

These ruminations reflect the underlying purpose of this book. I have tried to write it in an easily accessible fashion, rather than in the precise, didactic and compressed language more commonly found in encyclopedias. Even the spelling of the word 'encyclopedia' gives an early warning sign of my approach.

So I have included generous helpings of background history, and might rightly be charged with self-indulgence on this score. When writing about Australia's wine regions, I have endeavoured to convey a sense of the physical presence, the beauty, which many of those regions have. I have been slightly more circumspect when writing about the people, past and present, who have contributed so much to the Australian wine industry.

Space constraints mean that the profiles of important wineries established over the past 40 years tend to be short and to the point (websites can provide vast amounts of detail), but where the wineries have a history stretching back two centuries, I have dwelt on it.

The transition from this type of content to the scientific is bridged by explanations of tasting terms and information on all the grape varieties being commercially grown in Australia as at 2009. (This will become ever more incomplete with each passing vintage.)

Once I move into wine science, I have tried to be more disciplined, but also to explain the particular subject using as much lay language as possible. I must emphasise that I have no first-hand scientific knowledge – I have no tertiary qualifications in any aspect of wine science – and can only hope that I have accurately summarised what I have gleaned over the years from qualified winemakers, conferences, scientific papers and, most importantly of all, from the academic staff of the Australian Wine Research Institute.

I am also acutely aware that when I proudly open the encyclopedia for the first time, and scan its pages, a sudden chill will come over me as I realise that I have neglected to deal with a subject of obvious importance. Equally certainly, reviewers and other readers will helpfully add to the list. If they do their job well, I will be able to write an indispensable second, much expanded, edition.

It remains for me to thank the many people who have answered my questions without complaint: Beth Anthony, who devised an index of possible subjects as a framework to begin with, and shepherded the manuscript through to the stage where it could be sent to Sarah Shrubb, who edited it with rare commonsense; and to the team at Hardie Grant, headed by Sandy Grant and Fran Berry, who had sufficient faith in the project to back it in the face of the dismal financial world of 2009.

# Alphabetical
# entries

a b c d e f g h i
j k l m n o p q
r s t u v w x y z

**Abbey Creek Vineyard** (est. 1990) is the family business of Mike and Mary Dilworth in the Porongurup subregion of the Great Southern, the name coming from a winter creek running alongside the vineyard, and a view of The Abbey in the Stirling Range. The 1.6 ha vineyard is equally split among riesling, pinot noir and cabernet sauvignon planted in 1990 and '93. The rieslings have had significant show success.

**Accad, Guy** came to prominence in Burgundy in the mid-1980s, advocating the use of very high levels of $SO_2$ in red must prior to the commencement of fermentation. The effect was to significantly delay the onset of fermentation, which in turn gave rise to the concept of pre-fermentation maceration, commonly known as cold soak. He spoke at two major conferences, one in 1987 and one in 1990, one in the UK for the Masters of Wine, the other in Oregon for the International Pinot Noir Celebration. In Australia cold soak is often used, but in lieu of high levels of $SO_2$ the must is chilled below 10°C, and it is this temperature which prevents the onset of fermentation. It is extremely effective in liberating colour (which has particular relevance for pinot noir), and the extraction of all anthocyanins in an aqueous solution is quite different from that in an alcoholic environment. Thus, post-fermentation maceration has a different role; some winemakers in fact use both pre- and post-fermentation techniques.

**acetaldehyde** is the most common form of the chemical compounds known as aldehydes, which are produced at the last stages of fermentation. At low concentrations it is necessarily part of table wine, but at high concentrations it is a major fault. The wine will be described as aldehydic, denoting a loss of fruit aroma and flavour not unlike the effect of oxidation. In barrel or tank, the problem is easily treated with the addition of appropriate sulphur dioxide.

**acetic acid** is present in all table wines, but normally at low levels. It is this which creates volatile acidity, which results in a pungent, sharp odour and flavour when present at levels of 0.6 mg/l or above. The legal limit is 0.8 mg/l for white wine and rosé, 1.2 mg/l for red wine and 1.5 mg/l for botrytised wine.

**acid** is present in all grapes in various forms. The most important is tartaric acid, followed by malic acid at slightly lower concentration, with trace amounts of citric acid. Where the acid is too low, any one of the three acids may legally be added to wine to bring it into balance. The other acid added to white wines (though not red) is ascorbic, which, in conjunction with sulphur dioxide, minimises the chance of oxidation.

**additives** to wine are controlled by the Australia New Zealand Food Standards Code, and by regulations thereunder. The regulations list a series of substances which may be added, and any substance not on that list cannot be added, even if it is in no way harmful. One example of the latter is sorbitol. It is widely used in the fruit juice industry, and gives the wine a softer and (arguably) more pleasant taste and mouthfeel – but it is an illegal additive.

Finally, there is the curious situation that

as one travels north across the equator, acid becomes the work of the devil; as one crosses in the opposite direction, sugar becomes the work of the devil. Good winemakers anywhere should not hesitate to add either substance if they believe the quality of the wine will be improved by the addition. On the other hand, they should not follow the herd, seeking to rely instead on achieving balance in the vineyard so that the addition of either becomes superfluous. For a full list of permitted additives see Standard 4.5.1 of the Australia New Zealand Foods Standards Code.

Since 2007 it has been legal to add up to 7 per cent of water to either the must or the finished wine, chiefly where water is needed to dissolve additives such as fining agents including casein and bentonite. It is also recognised that small amounts of water may be incorporated with wine during bulk transfer by pump from one vessel to another. However, it is not legal to add water simply to reduce the alcohol level; Californian winemakers, by contrast, are able to add up to 10 per cent of water for amelioration of fermentation problems.

**Adelaide Hills**, gazetted 9 February 1998, is the coolest of the three regions in the Mount Lofty Ranges Zone, yet is a bare 30 minutes' drive from the CBD of Adelaide. A flourishing region in the 1870s, with 530 ha of vines, it declined into obscurity before the last vines disappeared, which was in the 1930s. Planting began again in 1971, but the arrival of Brian Croser and his founding of Petaluma in 1976 were the pivotal events. If there is a single variety which marks the region, it is sauvignon blanc, however important chardonnay,

pinot noir and shiraz may be. The foremost producers in the region are Ashton Hills, Bird in Hand, Deviation Road, Fox Gordon, Geoff Weaver, Hahndorf Hill, K1 by Geoff Hardy, Longview Vineyard, Mount Torrens Vineyard, New Era Vineyards, Ngeringa, Paracombe, Petaluma, Pike & Joyce, Romney Park, Setanta, Shaw & Smith, Tilbrook and Wicks Estate. The common themes of the wines produced are elegance and clarity of varietal expression.

The southern and eastern boundaries are determined by the 400-metre contour line, but the ever-twisting and turning hills, valleys and rivers within the region provide a large range of mesoclimates. Altitude is the key to the climate: Mount Lofty and the Piccadilly Valley are at 500 metres, and the contrast in climate to that of Adelaide throughout much of the summer has to be experienced to be believed. The veritable maze of valleys and sub-valleys means there is much mesoclimatic variation, making generalisations hazardous. However, most of the Adelaide Hills has an unequivocally cool climate; it is not until one reaches the northern extremity of the region, and the west-facing slopes, that one moves out of a climate suited principally to early-ripening varieties such as chardonnay, pinot noir and sauvignon blanc, and into terrain which satisfactorily ripens cabernet sauvignon and shiraz.

The Adelaide Hills have predominantly grey, grey-brown or brown loamy sands and clay loams; there are also patches of much sandier and more weakly structured soils of lesser quality. Fertility varies, tending to be higher in the southern and central areas.

**LAT** 34°50'S; **ALT** 400–500 m; **HDD** 1270; **GSR** 310 mm; **MJT** 19.1°C; **HARV** Mid-March to late April; **CHIEF VIT. HAZARD** Poor fruit set

**Adelaide Plains**, gazetted 25 March 2002, is the most dramatic proof of the lack of meaning to the grouping of regions within zones, in this case the Mount Lofty Ranges Zone. This is a dead flat and hot region with an altitude of 20 metres; the adjacent Gulf of St Vincent is unable to provide any significant cooling. It is warmer than the Hunter Valley and its growing season rainfall is on a par with that of the Swan Valley. Its most highly rated winery, Primo Estate, has moved to McLaren Vale, leaving Ceravolo, Diloreto and Domenic Versace to provide some respectability. Shiraz, cabernet sauvignon and grenache are the main varieties.

There are two soil types. First, the ubiquitous red-brown loamy sands found through so much of southeastern Australia, with alkaline subsoils and free limestone at deeper levels. These are excellent viticultural soils which readily support the typically high yields of the region. Then there are also smaller patches of heavier loam and cracking clay soils which are strikingly different in structure, but once again tend to be alkaline rather than acidic, and once again promote vigorous vine growth.

LAT 34°41'S; ALT 20 m; HDD 2081; GSR 130 mm; MJT 23°C; HARV Mid-February to early March; CHIEF VIT. HAZARD Nil

**Adelaide Zone** is a so-called super zone which encompasses the Mount Lofty Ranges, Fleurieu and Barossa zones. One of the ostensible reasons for this larger zone was to allow the blending of wines from the quality zones and regions in its purview, and simply label them 'Adelaide'. The only problem is that very few winemakers have taken advantage of this somewhat dubious proposition. Even

Penfolds Magill Estate is content with the vineyard name, coupled with a back label affirmation of 'Wine made in Australia'.

**aftertaste** is experienced after the wine has been swallowed and the first breath thereafter has been taken.

**aglianico** is a red grape much admired by the Greeks and the Romans (it was the principal variety used in Falernian, the most famous of all Roman wines). Its current champion in Italy is Mastroberardino, whose Taurasi is based on aglianico. It is propagated by Chalmers Nurseries at Mildura, with two clones available, and as a very late ripening variety will surely be more widely commercially propagated if temperatures continue to rise.

**Albany** is a subregion of the Great Southern region of Western Australia, its focal point being the town of the same name. It is one of the curiosities of history that, when Great Britain formally claimed ownership of the western part of Australia on Christmas Day in 1826, the point of possession relied on was Albany rather than Perth. While the surrounding country to the north, east and west was used for grazing and wheat farming, Albany became famous for whaling, which continued until 1978. Its convoluted bays and granite outcrops make this beautiful region (and, in parts, atmospheric town) seem like a mini Seattle, or perhaps Vancouver – itself named by Captain George Vancouver, the 1791 explorer of Albany and thereafter of British Columbia. Albany's whaling museum is the largest in the world and is justifiably a major tourist attraction.

The first vines were planted by the Sippe family at Redmond Vineyard in 1975, using cuttings of riesling supplied by Forest Hill Vineyard. (Cabernet sauvignon was also planted.) The first two crops of grapes were sold, but in 1981 a riesling and cabernet Sauvignon were made at Plantagenet; for some time thereafter the vineyard was neglected, but now it forms the core of Phillips Brook Estate. However, the present emphasis is more on chardonnay and pinot noir than on riesling and cabernet sauvignon.

Self-evidently, Albany's climate is maritime, strongly shaped and moderated by the Southern Ocean; the standard description is that it is Mediterranean, with moist, cool winters and warm, dry summers. Diurnal temperature range is minimal, and moderate humidity in summer assists ripening by reducing stress on the vines. The hills and valleys make the area attractive enough, but when ocean views are added, and huge marri or karri eucalypts soar skywards, it takes on the character of an infallible guide to the best soils for grape vines: lateritic gravelly, sandy loams or sandy loams derived directly from granite and gneissic rocks.

The region is best suited to chardonnay. Sauvignon blanc and (in some vintages) pinot noir, shiraz, cabernet sauvignon and merlot do best further away from the coast. The principal wineries are Kalgan River Wines, Montgomery's Hill, Oranje Tractor, Phillips Brook Estate and Wignalls.

LAT 35°02'S; ALT 75 m; HDD 1495; GSR 303 mm; MJT 19°C; HARV Mid-March to end April; CHIEF VIT. HAZARD Birds

**albarino** is a native white grape of Spain, and seemed to offer many advantages in the Australian climate; its small plantings proliferated rapidly in the opening decade of this century. Its source, so it appeared, was impeccable: the nursery vineyards of the CSIRO at Merbein, Victoria. Doubts emerged about its true identity, and in April 2009 it was officially announced that DNA testing had revealed it to be savagnin blanc, a clone of gewurztraminer grown in the Jura region of France. It is small wonder that misidentification of grape varieties was common in the 19th century.

**alcohol**, the common name for ethanol, is variously expressed as 'abv' (alcohol by volume), or '% alc/vol', or, most briefly, by the degree sign, '°'. Since the latter part of the 1990s, the alcohol content in wine has become a much discussed subject in Australia, most particularly in the context of chardonnay and red wines other than pinot noir. On the subject of chardonnay, there is in fact little debate: all winemakers seeking to produce high-quality chardonnay are doing their utmost to keep alcohol below 14% alc/vol, in most instances simply by picking earlier. Shiraz, on the other hand, causes the major divide, nowhere more obvious than in the Barossa Valley and McLaren Vale. Influential critics in the US market give glowing praise and maximum points to shiraz which can be as high as 16.5% alc/vol, close to the upper limit to which normal yeasts can produce without being killed by the alcohol. Quite apart from the fact that the EU does not allow unfortified wines to have higher than 15% alc/vol, the majority of critics and consumers both in Australia and in Europe do not enjoy high-alcohol red wines. In 2008 moves were afoot in Australia to change the long-existing tolerance of the alcohol disclosure on wine labels of plus or minus 1.5% alc/vol (the same as EU-produced wines): in other words, a wine labelled 14.5% alc/vol could in reality be as low as 13% alc/vol or as high as 16% alc/vol. Wines exported to the EU must show the alcohol rounded to whole or half numbers, but be within 0.5% of the official analysis of the alcohol.

In bygone years, famous winemakers such as Maurice O'Shea and Colin Preece relied on ice blocks to cool the ferment (or so they said) or simply watered the wine back, using what was termed the long black snake. These days alcohol can be (legally) reduced by the addition of low-alcohol juice to the must before fermentation (juice from which alcohol has been stripped out by reverse osmosis), which is still legally classed as grape juice and thus not prohibited, or by using techniques such as reverse osmosis (the most widely used) after the wine has fermented.

**aldehydic oxidation** is a particular form of oxidation which takes place when fortified wines are held in barrel for many years. It can quickly appear with table wine, and is wholly undesirable; it is treated by the addition of sulphur dioxide. In the context of fortified wines, it is part of the ageing process and is desirable, ultimately resulting in the formation of esters and flavours called rancio.

**aleatico** has been described by Jancis Robinson as a 'bizarre Italian red grape variety' because it makes a red wine with many of the characteristics of muscat à petits grains, normally a sweet white wine. Producers growing small amounts include di Lusso (Mudgee), Rimfire Vineyards (Queensland),

Riversands Vineyards (Queensland) and Tizzana (South Coast Zone).

**alicante bouschet** is a cross bred in France between 1865 and 1885 by Henri Bouschet, and is a 'teinturier', a rare grape type which has not only red skin, but also red flesh, and even when cropped to extreme levels can still produce a deeply coloured, if somewhat flavourless, wine. Rockford is the principal grower and producer, using it to make a super-charged rosé.

**aligoté** is the white grape equivalent to gamay, its highest expression reached in the town of Bouzeron, France, where Aubert de Villaine, co-owner and director of Domaine de la Romanée-Conti, makes the family wine (in no way connected to Domaine de la Romanée-Conti). DNA profiling has shown it to be a member of the pinot family, but it has limited traction in Australia. Hickinbotham Family Winemakers on the Mornington Peninsula grow it and often blend it with chardonnay.

**Alkoomi** (est. 1971) is a high-quality producer in the Frankland River subregion of the Great Southern. Its 90,000-case production is anchored around more than 100 ha of estate vineyards; both white and red wines show precisely defined varietal character, and an uncommon degree of elegance. Exports to all major markets.

**All Saints Estate** (est. 1864) is located in Rutherglen, in the northeast of Victoria. A first-time visitor might well wonder how a turreted castle, erected around an internal quadrangle, came to be built at a place like Wahgunyah and, for that matter, why a flag flies proudly from the corner tower with its castellated parapet. The answer lies in family tradition. The first George Sutherland Smith arrived in Australia in the 1850s. His family had worked for generations as carpenters and joiners at the castle of Mey at Caithness, Scotland, in the parish of All Saints. This ancient building was owned and tenanted by Queen Elizabeth the Queen Mother until her death, in 2002.

It barely needs saying that, having made some capital with his brother-in-law John Banks plying the river trade on the Murray in the 1860s, and having in 1864 purchased a large river-front block at Wahgunyah on which they planted the vines, George Sutherland Smith would want to build his own castle. This he literally did: a clay pit was dug on the river bank, and the kiln that he used to fire the bricks still stands today. First of all he built stables with an incongruous Spanish-style façade, and then in 1880 he commenced building the immense cellars and winery which – along with Fairfield, Mount Prior and the Tuilleries – are the great landmarks of the northeast today.

The vineyards flourished on the sandy loam of the Murray, and George Sutherland Smith and John Banks quickly learnt the art of winemaking, it would seem. In the manner of the day they were active exhibitors in overseas competitions and, while not challenging Morris at Fairfield, had many successes. The story goes that in 1876 a wine entered in a major competition at Brussels in Belgium was rejected because of its alcohol content, which the judges declared would not have occurred naturally and was due to the addition of fortifying spirit. (This was a fate which befell many Australian wines, and led to a furious debate in England, where

the consequence was not the withholding of prizes but the imposition of a higher rate of duty.) The Australian ambassador in Brussels became involved, and after due enquiries and assurances the wine was once again (grudgingly) admitted to the competition as being one naturally high in alcohol.

The sandy soils of the vineyard did not stop phylloxera (even though other similar vineyards across the region were spared), and in the 1890s David Banks Smith, George's son, had to replant all the vineyards with grafted phylloxera-resistant rootstocks. Notwithstanding the cost and disruption involved, the turn of the century was a time of expansion for the Sutherland Smith business. The winery capacity was extended on several occasions to feed the growing market, which had been served by the establishment of a Melbourne warehouse and bottling facilities at Selborne Chambers some 20 years earlier. All Saints remained at Selborne Chambers for over 80 years, finally moving to new premises in North Melbourne in 1960.

The business continued in the ownership of the Sutherland Smith family for well over 100 years, before being acquired by an investment syndicate in the late 1980s. The sudden death of the CEO of the syndicate led to the appointment of a receiver, and the sale of considerable quantities of the large stocks of old fortified wines, leading to the (incorrect) belief at the time that all the best aged wines had been sold. In 1991 Brown Brothers acquired All Saints and set about restoring all aspects of the business. A few years later, and as part of an amicable rearrangement of the Brown Brothers family interests, Peter R Brown sold his share in Brown Brothers and acquired All Saints Estate (and St Leonards Vineyard) from the family. In November 2005, his three children (the fourth generation of the Brown family) – Eliza, Angela and Nicholas – took over management. Eliza became a youthful but energetic CEO, Angela taking responsibility for brand development and export markets, and Nicholas going down the viticulture and winemaking path. All Saints is an outstanding tourist destination, and has a wide range of venues for everything from weddings to one-on-one visits.

The quality of the fortified wines is equal to the best of Rutherglen, and the increasing range of table wines makes maximum use of the available resources.

**Alpine Valleys,** gazetted 29 November 1999, is a well-named region nestling in the Great Dividing Range as it ceases travelling south, and swings to the west in northeast Victoria. Mount Buffalo guards one side, Mount Beauty the other, but in between lie the Buckland, Ovens and Kiewa valleys. The word picture is completed by towns such as Myrtleford and Bright, and wineries such as Annapurna, its vines snow-covered in winter. Annapurna Estate, Boynton's, Gapsted and Michelini are the leaders of a select population. Altitude rises from 150 metres to over 320 metres, with the highest sites having significantly cooler growing seasons and much higher rainfall. Coupled with the risk of spring frost (and occasional autumn frosts), this makes site selection of prime importance. Harvest begins in February for sparkling wine base and continues to mid-April.

The soils in the four major valleys are all formed on river deposits from similar rocks, mostly granite; all have good structure, ranging from sandy loams to red-brown duplex soils. The common feature is their above-average fertility, which imposes the need for vigour control in most sites.

LAT 36°31'S; ALT 150–320 m; HDD 1482; GSR 425 mm; MJT 21.3°C; HARV February to mid-April; CHIEF VIT. HAZARD Spring frost

**alternative varieties** is a strictly non-scientific name given by wine writers to obscure and/or recently introduced (into Australia) *Vitis vinifera* varieties from Portugal, Spain, Italy, Georgia and elsewhere. These include aglianico, albarino, aleatico, alicante bouschet, arneis, barbera, bianco, biancone, carmenère, carnelian, cienna, cortese, corvina, fiano, furmint, garganega, hárslevelü, kerner, lagrein, lemberger, malvasia istriana, marzemino, muller thurgau, nebbiolo, orange muscat, petit manseng, picolit, prosecco, rondinella, sagrantino, saperavi, schönburger, siegerrebe, sylvaner, taminga, tannat, tempranillo, tinta negra, tinto cao, touriga nacional, verduzzo, vermentino, zibbibo (a synonym for muscat of alexandria) and zinfandel.

**amontillado sherry** will have been phased out as a permitted term by 31 December 2009. It is created when the flor yeast on fino sherry dies, and the wine is exposed to oxygen. The best amontillados have a rich and nutty palate, but finish dry or near dry, and the outstanding maker is Seppelt. The new name will incorporate the words medium-dry in conjunction with the generic word apera.

**amoroso** is a very old, luscious, wood-matured apera, which has a sweet finish. It has all but disappeared from the scene. Lindemans in bygone decades was one of the last producers. Its new name is apera cream.

**ampelography** is the science of the identification and classification of grape vines, much enhanced in recent years by ever-expanding knowledge and use of DNA profiling.

**Angove Family Winemakers** (est. 1886) was established by Dr William Angove, a general practitioner and surgeon who emigrated from Cornwall in 1886 with his wife and young family. He shared with Dr Henry Lindeman and Dr Christopher Rawson Penfold the firm belief that wine had a wide range of medicinal benefits, and his experimentation with vines, winemaking and distilling soon led to the establishment of a vineyard at Tea Tree Gully in the Adelaide foothills of the Mount Lofty Ranges. The business grew, and by the end of the 19th century production reached 300 tonnes of grapes from 20 ha of vineyard. William Angove's eldest son, Thomas 'Skipper' Angove, branched out from the family home in Tea Tree Gully while completing studies in oenology at Roseworthy Agricultural College, and set up a distillery at Renmark in the Riverland in 1910. Urban sprawl saw the end of the Tea Tree Gully vineyard, and the progressive development of the massive Nanya Vineyard at Renmark. Thomas (Tom) Angove, Skipper's son, joined the business after graduating as dux in oenology at Roseworthy, and began the planting of the Nanya Vineyard, at that time the largest single vineyard in the southern hemisphere. He also planned the massive expansion of the winery to cope with the grapes from Nanya. Fourth-generation John Carlyon Angove took over the CEO role in 1983, and in the latter part of the 1990s began a complete redevelopment of the 480-ha Nanya Vineyard, which involved the progressive removal of all the blocks and turning the rows 90°, so that they now run east–west, and replacing overhead irrigation sprinklers with drip irrigation controlled by moisture measures via gypsum blocks at different depths. Individual rows in the reorganised vineyard are up to 5 kilometres in length.

Well in advance of the problems confronting the Murray Darling at the end of the first decade of the current century, Angove's began to source grapes from other regions, including Coonawarra, Adelaide Hills, Wrattonbully, Clare Valley, Padthaway, Mount Benson, Cape Jaffa and the Southern Flinders Ranges. The company also has a small holding of vines more than 60 years old in McLaren Vale.

**Annie's Lane** (est. 1852) has an immense amount of history within its stone walls and extensive surrounding vineyards. The passing parade commenced with a gold and copper miner, Francis Treloar, who acquired a 47-ha property which he named Springvale in 1852, planting vines the following year. He was succeeded by an even more successful prospector and miner, Walter Hughes, who acquired the neighbouring property in 1862, naming it Prospect Farm. In 1868 Hughes employed Carl Sobels, who, in partnership with Hermann Buring, acquired the properties in 1890. In 1898 Hermann's son Leo Buring returned from studies in Geisenheim and Montpellier, briefly joining his elder brother Rudi, but thereafter moving away to pursue other oenological interests (there were too many Burings and Sobels already in the business). Leo retained a consultancy role, though. In the late 1920s he brought back (in his handkerchief) flor yeast spores, which were the source of Quelltaler's (as it by then was known) best-selling Gran Fiesta Sherry. In the 1990s the property was acquired by Foster's, the name changed to Annie's Lane (coming from Annie Wayman, a local identity at the turn of the 20th century) and winemaking was moved to the Barossa Valley. This may have ended a major chapter in the proud history, but the buildings remain, and the quality of the wines (particularly under the super premium Copper Trail label) put it firmly in the upper echelon of Clare Valley wines. Exports to the UK, the US and Europe.

**Antcliff, Allan** (1923–85) was the senior principal research scientist at the then CSIRO division of horticultural research at Merbein, Victoria. He was the first Australian researcher in the 20th century to systematically study, record and describe the wine grape varieties being grown in Australia. In 1976 he was responsible for the publication of *Some Wine Grape Varieties for Australia*, followed by *Major Wine Grape Varieties of Australia* (1979) and *Minor Grape Varieties of Australia* (1983). He was also responsible for several French ampelographers visiting Australia, including M Paul Truel in 1982.

**anthocyanins** are responsible for the colour of black and red grapes, and of the wines made from them, both as wine components and as a precursors of pigmented tannins. They play a significant role in the keeping qualities of a red wine, although their physical nature changes as the wine ages, leading to the progression from bright red/purple to brick red, and to the deposit of sediments.

**anthracnose** is a fungal disease which preceded the far more dangerous downy mildew and powdery mildew diseases, and was responsible for the failure of the first vines planted in Sydney Cove, shortly after the arrival of the First Fleet. The colloquial name 'black spot' describes the symptoms very well.

**antioxidant** is a term which is frequently found on labels of Australian wines, and denotes the addition of sulphur dioxide (220), sodium metabisulphite (223) or ascorbic acid (300), these numbers simply substituting for the chemical names.

**apera** was adopted by Australia as the generic name for sherry in January 2009. The change was necessitated by the terms of the Wine Agreement reached with the EU, which requires the removal of the word 'sherry' from bottles by the end of 2009. See also topaque.

**Appellation Contrôlée** is the French system of laws which guarantees the authenticity of a wine with a given label, extending to region, grape variety, methods of viticulture and (occasionally) methods of vinification. In Australia the equivalent term is Geographic Indications.

**arneis** is a white grape variety native to Piedmont in Italy. It underwent a near-death experience there in the 1970s (only two producers were making the wine) but has had a major recovery since that time and has spread to Australia. It is best suited to cool climates, which has not restricted its planting in regions as unsuited as the Riverland, where the naturally low acidity means massive acid additions need to be made. It is not unkind to suggest that it has an aroma and flavour profile only marginally higher than that of pinot gris.

**aroma** is a notoriously imprecise term denoting the scent or smell of a wine early in its life, when the varietal expression of the grape or grapes is at its maximum. The secondary characters which develop with barrel and/or bottle age are said to constitute the bouquet, but writers such as the author tend to see aroma simply as part of the bouquet.

**aroma wheel** was developed by Professor Anne Noble at the University of California, Davis, in the early 1980s. It groups aromas into three circles, the innermost circle with 12 groups, the next circle with twice that number, and the outer circle with many more times. It is an extremely useful tool for inexperienced tasters wishing to master the arcane language of tasting notes, its limitation being that it does not attempt to describe texture, body or mouthfeel.

**Arrowfield** (est. 1968) in the Upper Hunter Valley continues in the ownership of the Inagaki family, which has been involved in the Japanese liquor industry for over a century. It has 47 ha of low-yielding old vines in the Upper Hunter, and also buys grapes from other parts of Australia, making varietal wines appropriate to those regions. In 2007 it merged with Mornington Peninsula winery Red Hill Estate, the subsequent company trading as InWine Group Australia. Exports to all major markets.

**ascorbic acid** is none other than vitamin C, which was one of the first vitamins to be discovered, and is part of a normal daily diet (as well as being sold in tablet form). Unripe grapes contain significant levels of vitamin C, but most is lost during the ripening process and thereafter in winemaking operations. When added to white wine after the end of fermentation, it reacts directly with any dissolved oxygen in the wine. It is generally accepted that an addition of $SO_2$ needs to be made at the same time to optimise the antioxidant properties of ascorbic acid. Some questions remain about the mechanisms of the chemistry involved, and there is ongoing research in Australia.

**Ashbrook Estate** (est. 1975) was established in the Margaret River region by the Devitt family, variously known for their viticultural, winemaking and cricket skills, beanpole Tony Devitt being a fast bowler of considerable note. The estate is a fastidious maker of consistently excellent estate-grown table wines recognised for their elegance, but is content to keep a low profile, selling much of its wine to loyal mailing list customers and through the cellar door. Exports to the UK, Canada, Denmark, Germany, Indonesia, Japan, Singapore and Hong Kong.

**Ashton Hills** (est. 1982) may only produce around 1500 cases of wine a year from its fully mature estate vineyards but it deservedly enjoys a very high reputation for its pinot noir, chardonnay and riesling, departing from the usual Adelaide Hills pattern by eschewing sauvignon blanc, which some may think is a very laudable decision. In lieu of that it offers Three, a blend of pinot gris, gewurztraminer and riesling which succeeds in spite of itself.

**assemblage** is a French word which in its most basic expression simply means the blending of parcels of wine. Its highest expression occurs in the blending used for Champagne or sparkling wine (in Australia and elsewhere) but its meaning extends to any form of blending, to produce an icon wine and a lesser priced wine of a single variety, blending oaked and unoaked wines within a single variety, blending different varieties or blending wines from different regions (witness Penfolds Grange). It is one of the most skilled and important winemaking practices.

**astringency** is the mouth-puckering result of tannins; in small doses with young wines (especially cabernet sauvignon) it is not a fault if there is sufficient fruit to balance the astringency.

**aucerot** is the incorrect name for montils.

**Australian Society of Viticulture and Oenology** was founded in 1980 as a non-profit organisation to serve the interests of practising winemakers and viticulturists by encouraging the exchange of technical information. Since that time it has organised and conducted numerous one-day seminars on specialised topics in viticulture and oenology, and, in conjunction with the Australian Wine Research Institute, organises and conducts the Australian wine industry technical conferences held every three years since 1983. It publishes its own scientific journal, the *Australian Journal of Grape and Wine Research*, which covers a wide variety of research topics, many of vital practical interest to the industry.

**Australian Wine and Brandy Corporation** is a statutory body created under its own Commonwealth Act (and regulations thereunder) which has the responsibility of enhancing the operating environment for the Australian wine industry through market development, quality and integrity controls, and knowledge development. It promotes and develops markets for Australian wine, licenses exporters and issues export permits for wines destined for overseas markets. It is primarily funded by wine sector levies, market program membership fees, sponsorships and charges for compliance services and information products.

**Australian Wine Research Institute (AWRI)** had its origins in 1934, when the Wine Overseas Marketing Board (which in due course became the Australian Wine Board) asked the University of Adelaide to investigate the causes of bacterial spoilage in Australian fortified wines, which then constituted almost all of the country's very substantial export trade. With financial support from the board, the university appointed John Fornachon as its investigating officer in November 1934. Fornachon was a microbiologist and graduate of both the university and Roseworthy; he remained an employee of the university until 1945, when he transferred to the CSIR, but continued research work for the wine industry.

His early success in solving the problem of spoilage, his subsequent research into the sherry flor process, his early evaluation (in 1954) of ion-exchange for pH control, and his work on the role of malolactic fermentation in table wine (the latter an area in which Ray Beckwith and Alan Hickinbotham also carried out much pioneering research) was convincing evidence to the wine industry of the value of research. Progress reports, contained in the annual reports of the Australian Wine Board, ran through to the early 1950s, at which time Fornachon's work on flor sherry production was continuing.

After five years of argument about funding (there was in fact over £1 million in the Wine Export Encouragement Trust Fund which had accumulated during World War II) the AWRI was ultimately incorporated under the Companies Act of South Australia on 27 April 1955 as a company limited by guarantee. John Fornachon was appointed Foundation Director. It became and remains the major centre of wine research in Australia, and enjoys an excellent reputation worldwide.

Its ongoing services are funded by the Grape and Wine Research and Development Corporation and fee-for-service activities. It has played a pivotal role in the rapid development of the industry since 1955, and, in particular, in the increase of the overall quality of Australian wines. This has been achieved because, in large measure, the activities of the AWRI have been guided by consultation with the industry, thus directed to issues of both short-term and long-term relevance.

The AWRI states that it has four basic functions. The first is to undertake research into wine composition, quality and sensory characteristics, identifying improvements in red and white winemaking through innovative improvement to viticultural and winemaking practices, and communicating the results to the industry at large. In 2007 the AWRI research chemists identified the hitherto unknown trace compound rotundone, which gives shiraz its distinctive black pepper aroma. In 2008 the minty, eucalypt character often found in Australian red wines, particularly shiraz, was traced to cineol, a volatile monoterpene (chemical compound) that can originate from a number of sources, including eucalypt trees. More important was the world-first sequencing of the whole genome of a wine yeast strain of *Saccharomyces cerevisiae*, enabling the comparison with other, non-wine strains of *S. cerevisiae*. It will provide a powerful resource for wine yeast strain development programs, such as the prior development of the so-called sauvignon blanc yeast. Over 40 per cent of the total staff of around 100 people are in this sector of the business.

The second function of the AWRI is industry development and support, providing winemaking, viticultural, environmental, health, nutritional and regulatory advice, plus a problem-solving service. This also extends to developing advanced analytical technologies while educating through extension activities. A particularly important example of this function has been the dissemination of knowledge about and treatment of *Bretannomyces*. Equally importantly, the AWRI has long been a leader in research into the causes of cork taint or failure, and has run extensive research programs over a number of years evaluating the performance of all the commercially available wine closures. This led to the first understanding of the phenomenon known as random oxidation. Between 2003 and 2008 research into the causes of smoke taint led to the discovery that the contaminants are in the grape skins, not on them, nor in the pulp of the grapes. All of these advisory services are provided free of charge to the Australian industry.

The third function is to provide an analytical service, which offers a range of fee-for-service routine and advanced analytical testing, including export certificates. A by-product, as it were, is that it facilitates the practical use of research in the industry. It builds a large database of information which is legitimately used to provide overviews of issues or trends without breaching client confidentiality. Coupled with contract research for individual businesses, it raises over 15 per cent of all source income.

The fourth leg is the coordination of technical and regulatory information for Australian grapegrowers and winemakers, providing the collection, collation and dissemination of oenology and viticultural research for the benefit of the whole Australian wine industry. When Australia was producing 2 per cent of the world's wine, the AWRI was publishing 20 per cent of its research papers into oenology and viticulture. This interlocks with the triennial four-day Australian Wine Industry Technical Conference, a world-scale event which gives rise to important research papers and to extensive poster presentations. There is a vast amount of information on all four functions available on the AWRI website (www.awri.com.au).

**autolysis** is an essential process in the making of quality sparkling wines; it is the destruction of yeast cells by naturally occurring enzymes. It greatly enhances mouthfeel and what are often described as biscuity or bready notes in the aroma and flavour of the wine.

a b c d e f g h i
j k l m n o p q
r s t u v w x y z

**back-blending** is little different in meaning from blending (or assemblage), but normally carries with it the connotation of reducing some excessive character in the base portion of the wine, be it oak, tannins, alcohol or (uncommonly) acidity.

**Baileys of Glenrowan** (est. 1866) was established by Richard Bailey, who, with his family, left Manchester in England in the 1830s and moved to Glenrowan, Victoria, in the 1840s, not to mine for gold, but to run the first general store in the town. When the gold ran out, and the miners dwindled, the Baileys used their accumulated profits to buy a grazing property; it was left to son Varley Bailey to plant vines in 1866 to supplement the grazing activities on the farm. He chose the rich, red granite soil found on part of the property. The first vintage was made in 1870, and demand for the wines – particularly for the fortified wines – led to significant expansion of the plantings. By 1892 the wines were sold locally, in Melbourne and exported to England.

Varley Bailey replaced the old slab cellar with concrete cellars which are still in use today. He died in 1931. His son Alan Bailey ran the winery, using the same techniques as his father and grandfather, until 1972, when it was sold to David Gelatine (a story in itself); it is now part of Foster's Wine Estates.

Baileys is the one notable fortified wine producer in the region, its new winery also facilitating the making of high-quality shiraz from the oldest vines: the 1904 Block Shiraz – planted immediately after the onset of phylloxera, and the oldest in northeast Victoria – and the 1920s Block Shiraz. Exports to the UK and NZ.

**balance** is the harmony or equilibrium between the different components of wine, including alcohol, acidity, sweetness, tannins, oak (where used) and fruit flavour.

**Balgownie Estate** (est. 1969) was established by Bendigo pharmacist Stuart Anderson, who was at the forefront of the boutique winemakers who began to make their appearance (albeit in small numbers) across Australia in the 1960s and '70s. His 1974, 1975 and 1976 cabernet sauvignons were benchmarks of the highest quality, throwing down the challenge for others to emulate. He learnt much about making cabernet from Louis Vialard of Chateau Cissac in Bordeaux, and spent a number of vintages there. Not surprisingly, he established a great wine cellar, and never tired of sharing bottles with his friends, while still finding time to play the bassoon and collect vintage Bugattis and Ferraris. It came as a shock to the wine industry when Anderson decided to sell Balgownie to Mildara in 1984 after it became clear that there would be no family succession. Balgownie passed back out of corporate ownership in 1999 when it was acquired by the Forrester family. This led to a $3 million upgrade of the winery and a doubling of the size of the vineyard to 35 ha. In 2004 the company established a second vineyard and winery in the Yarra Valley, the 7 ha of estate vines producing fine chardonnay and pinot noir to complement the cabernet sauvignon and shiraz from Bendigo. Exports to the UK, the US and other major markets.

**Ballarat** lies at the southwestern corner of the Central Victoria Zone, and has by far the coolest climate of any part of that zone. While the plantings of pinot noir and chardonnay are quite numerous, they are small, and the area does not yet have the critical mass to enable it to apply for registration as a Geographic Indication. In the warmer years it produces exciting wines, and would welcome any onset of continuing climate change. Tomboy Hill is the leading winery.

**Balnaves of Coonawarra** (est. 1975) is based upon the pick of the crop from 52 ha of estate vineyards dating back to its establishment. Owner–viticulturist Doug Balnaves and winemaker Pete Bissell join forces to produce outstanding cabernet sauvignon, shiraz and cabernet blends, with one of the best Coonawarra chardonnays thrown in for good measure. It is also a contract winemaker for Parker Coonawarra Estate and other Coonawarra wineries. Exports to the UK, the US and other major markets.

**Bannockburn Vineyards** (est. 1974) was founded by Stuart Hooper and can fairly claim to be the most important winery in Geelong, notwithstanding the departure of long-term winemaker Gary Farr. The close-planted Serre Pinot Noir can rise to exceptional heights – the 1994 wine is one of the greatest pinots made in Australia – and the SRH Chardonnay has exceptional complexity. The Serre and SRH are made in small quantities in the best vintages; the principal releases of these two varieties are simply named 'pinor noir' and 'chardonnay' respectively. The wines come from 25 ha of 35-year-old low-yielding estate plantings. Exports to Canada, Dubai, Korea, China, Singapore and Hong Kong.

**Banrock Station** (est. 1994) in the Riverland features a $1 million eco-friendly visitor centre which is a major tourist destination. Owned by CWA, the Banrock Station property covers over 1700 ha, with 240 ha of vineyard and the remainder a wildlife and wetland preservation area. Recycling of all waste water and use of solar energy build on the preservation image. Each bottle of Banrock Station wine sold generates funds for wildlife preservation. The wines have consistently offered excellent value. Exports to all major markets.

**barbera** is an important red-grape workhorse in Italy's Piedmont region, capable of producing very good wine if the yields are kept low and appropriate oak is used, but thin and acidulous wine if overcropped. The 159 ha given to it in Australia are spread across New South Wales, Victoria and South Australia, with no single significant plantings, and with moderately successful outcomes for the wineries which make it.

**Barossa Valley,** gazetted 15 August 1997, is the most internationally recognised region in Australia, its shiraz the focus of most attention. Johann Gramp was the first to plant vines there, at Rowland Flat in 1847. Two years later English brewer Samuel Smith settled at Angaston and founded Yalumba, but it was George Fyffe Angas who played a crucial role in the development of the valley. (Angas Town, later Angaston, was named after him in 1841.) Needing labour for his large holdings, he financed the immigration of three shiploads of German Lutheran farmers from Silesia who were suffering religious oppression from King Frederick III. It was thus that Germans (or, more correctly, Silesians) became by far the most important group of vignerons in the valley. The impact of their culture extends to this day: their stone houses, their Lutheran faith and their cuisine all symbols of the valley. Running more or less due south to north, with Williamstown in the most southerly part, thence north through Lyndoch, Tanunda and Angaston on the eastern border, Nuriootpa northwest of Angaston (and the last town travelling north), the terrain varies from dead flat to rolling hills and yet steeper slopes on the eastern side, bordering the Mount Lofty Ranges. Soils differ markedly, the best still succouring shiraz, mourvedre and grenache reaching 160 years of age, but every decade for the past 150 years is also represented, which, in total, constitutes a priceless heritage. As at 2008 there were 147 wineries sharing 10,312 ha of vines. The large wineries are household names: Orlando, Penfolds, Peter Lehmann, Wolf Blass and Yalumba, the number of top-quality smaller makers including but by no means limited to Charles Melton, Dutschke, Grant Burge, Haan, John Duval, Kaesler, Kalleske, Langmeil, Spinifex, Thorn-Clarke, Torbreck and Turkey Flat, with Seppeltsfield occupying a very special position.

The climate is warm and dry, with low relative humidity and rainfall in the growing season. It is continental in nature, with cool to cold nights and hot summer daytime temperatures. Taken with long daily sunshine hours, the biologically effective temperature summation is (surprisingly) only slightly warmer than that of Bordeaux and Margaret River. The complex system of transverse subvalleys and twisting hills results in a multiplicity of varying slopes, aspects and sites. The soils vary widely, but fall in an overall family of relatively low-fertility clay loam through to more sandy varieties, ranging through grey to brown to red. As in so much of southeast Australia, acidity increases in the subsoils, restricting root growth and vigour.

LAT 34°29′S; ALT 250–370 m; HDD 1710; GSR 160 mm; MJT 21.4°C; HARV End February to late April; CHIEF VIT. HAZARD Drought

**Barossa Valley Estate** (est. 1985) is owned by CWA, marking the end of a period during which it was one of the last significant co-operative-owned wineries in Australia. Across the board, the wines are full flavoured and honest. E&E Black Pepper Shiraz is an upmarket label with a strong reputation and following; the Ebenezer range likewise. Exports to all major markets.

**Barossa Zone** is the most used zonal Geographic Indication, as it comprises the abutting Barossa Valley and Eden Valley regions. This is useful for blended red wines from both regions, and also for wineries with vineyards in both camps. On the label, it will simply appear as 'Barossa', without the word 'Valley' appended.

**barrel** is most commonly used to encompass a barrique (225 l) or a hogshead (300 l). The latter was once the most widely used size in Australia, but is increasingly being replaced by either barriques or puncheons (500 l).

**barrel fermentation** has been the method of fermenting white burgundy (chardonnay) since time immemorial, but it did not become common in the New World until the mid-1980s, and, even then, its use was largely limited at first to small producers. In Australia, chardonnay (and to a lesser extent semillon and sauvignon blanc, particularly where blended) can either be pressed and taken straight to barrel, or transferred to a stainless-steel fermentation tank, inoculated with yeast, and taken to barrel only once the fermentation has started. Wild yeast fermentation, by contrast, will almost always start in barrel.

There is an infinite number of permutations and combinations of yeast selection and fermentation temperature, and then the choice of new or previously used oak. Thus used, barrel fermentation will give rise to lees in the barrel, which may then be stirred over an indeterminate period, and with varying frequency. Barrel fermentation of red wines almost invariably refers to red wine which has been pressed before the fermentation has been completely finished, typically with somewhere between 2 baumé and 4 baumé; once again, this offers the prospect of lees in the barrel, which act as an antioxidant and also enrich the palate. Malolactic fermentation will most likely accompany the end of fermentation or the early stages of maturation.

**Barringwood Park** (est. 1993) in Northern Tasmania is owned by Judy and Ian Robinson, who operate a sawmill at Lower Barrington, 15 minutes south of Devonport on the main tourist trail to Cradle Mountain; when they planted 500 vines in 1993 the aim was to do a bit of home winemaking. In a thoroughly familiar story, the urge to expand the vineyard and make wine on a commercial scale came almost immediately, and they embarked on a six-year plan, planting 1 ha per year in the first four years and building the cellar and tasting

rooms during the following two years. The pinot noirs have had exceptional success in wine shows, winning innumerable trophies.

**Barwang Vineyard** (est. 1969) was the first planting in the 20th century in the Hilltops region of New South Wales. It was established as part of a diversification program for Peter Robertson's 400 ha grazing property. When McWilliam's acquired Barwang in 1989, the vineyard amounted to 13 ha; today the plantings exceed 100 ha. Wine quality has been exemplary from the word go: always elegant, with precise varietal definition to the chardonnay, shiraz and cabernet sauvignon, in each instance reflecting the moderately cool climate.

**Bass Phillip** (est. 1979) has often been described as the foremost producer of pinot noir in Australia, although it has to be said that style and quality are as unpredictable as the moods and movements of proprietor and vigneron Phillip Jones. Jones did not follow in the footsteps of others when he chose the land for his vineyard, but did follow Burgundian practice with the close spacing and low trellis of his 16 ha of pinot noir (out of a total of 23.5 ha on four vineyard sites). It is no real surprise that at their best these Gippsland wines are eerily Burgundian in character, or that there are now several satellite vineyards which also supply him with pinot noir.

**bastardo** is a red grape variety from Spain, incorrectly called cabernet gros in the Barossa Valley, and of minimal importance other than to temporarily inflate the statistics for cabernet sauvignon in the 1960s.

**baumé** is the scale for the measurement of grape sugar; 1 degree baumé equals 1.8 per cent sugar, or 1.8 degrees brix. It is baumé, rather than brix, which has long been preferred in Australia as the measurement of ripeness. However, when baumé levels typically ranged between 10 and 12, it was easy to assume that 1 degree baumé would produce 1% alc/vol, a conversion in fact accurate for white wine at 10 baumé, but increasingly inaccurate thereafter. Thus 13 baumé is most likely to produce 13.9% alc/vol; 14 baumé, 15.2% alc/vol; and 15 baumé, 16.5% alc/vol. The situation with red wines is quite different: 10 baumé produces 8.8% alc/vol; and 15 baumé, 14.9% alc/vol. The reason for the difference is that white wines are typically fermented cool in closed vessels, and red wines are fermented at higher temperatures in open fermenters or with vigorous aeration via pump overs during fermentation, which causes some of the alcohol to evaporate.

**Bay of Fires** (est. 2001) is one of the foremost quality producers in the Pipers River area of Northern Tasmania. It has seen an unusual number of owners since the vineyard's first grapes were planted in 1985 by Swiss-born Bernard and Brigitte Roche. A succession of devastating spring frosts led to its sale to the JAC Group, led by beef magnate Joe Chromy; it was then on-sold to Pipers Brook and called Ninth Island, before finally passing into the ownership of the Hardy Wine Company in 2001, when it was renamed Bay of Fires. All the base wine for Arras, Australia's foremost sparkling wine, is fermented at Bay of Fires, along with base wines for a number of top-end Hardys sparkling wines. But it is also an outstanding producer of riesling, pinot noir, chardonnay and of encouraging sauvignon blanc. It has 20 ha of estate vineyards; grape purchases provide much of the annual crush. Exports to all major markets.

**Beckwith, Ray, OAM** (1912–) received the highest honour the wine industry can confer on one of its members when, in July 2006, he was given the McWilliam's Wines Maurice O'Shea Award. He was 94 when he received the award, but his acceptance speech had the precision, grace and fluidity of a man in his intellectual prime.

Beckwith graduated from Roseworthy Agricultural College in 1932 with an Honours Diploma in Agriculture (including oenology) and the Haselgrove Prize for Viticulture and Oenology. He was almost immediately offered a cadetship back at Roseworthy working alongside Australia's first wine science lecturer, Alan Hickinbotham. It was during this time that he began his work on cultured yeasts, researching the cause and possible solutions of bacterial spoilage in wine (which was causing up to 30 per cent of wine to be rendered undrinkable). The following year he was offered a role working with wine industry legends Colin Haselgrove and Roger Warren at Hardys while continuing his work at Roseworthy. He published a paper on his yeast researches in the *Australian Wine and Brewing Journal* in 1934. It was this paper which brought Beckwith's work to the attention of Lesley Penfold Hyland, who offered him a role at Penfolds commencing in 1935. Here Beckwith continued to study fortified wine spoilage, running trials at the University of Adelaide. It was during this time that he discovered pH could be used to control wine spoilage and convinced Penfold Hyland to purchase a pH meter (at a cost equal to 20 weeks of Beckwith's salary). With the addition of tartaric acid to control pH, he solved one of the industry's most frustrating problems and reduced fortified wine bacterial spoilage to zero.

Over the decades, as Penfolds' chief chemist until his retirement in 1973, Beckwith made several more scientific discoveries, designed Australia's first yeast propagation machine, and did pioneering work with the use of atomic absorption spectrophotometry in winemaking circa 1962. He worked closely with Max Schubert, and was responsible for recommending that Schubert be given the role of Penfolds winemaker. He is a University of Adelaide Doctor of the University (*honoris causa*), an inaugural life member of the Winemakers' Federation of Australia, and an honorary life member of the American Society of Oenology and Viticulture.

**Beechworth**, gazetted 8 December 2000, is one of the smallest regions with Geographic Indication status, sandwiched between Rutherglen to the north and the Alpine Valleys to the south. The town which gives the region its name was built on the back of gold, which was discovered in March 1852. The first land sale followed in 1855. The town is perched precariously on a steep hillside with streets plunging at unexpected angles, flanked by stone buildings. It retains much of the charm born of its 19th-century heritage, and is especially beautiful in autumn, when the numerous European trees blaze yellow, orange and gold. It had a 19th-century background of viticulture on a small scale, and when Rick Kinzbrunner arrived in 1985 to establish

Giaconda by planting 2.8 ha of chardonnay, pinot noir and cabernet sauvignon, he began a career as tantalisingly brilliant yet as elusive as that of Phillip Jones of Bass Phillip.

The climate is inextricably linked to altitude, with a wide range in all components between the lower and higher parts of the region. Frost risk is site-specific; most of the vineyards are planted on slopes with free air drainage taking the frost downhill. The major climatic limitation is restricted water availability, forcing most developments to be dry-grown. The precise soil patterns are as complex as the hilly topography, but there are two major soil types: very old sandstone gravel and clay derived from marine sediments, and granitic soil overlying clay derived from volcanic deposits.

There are 16 wineries in the region, with the 40 ha vineyard affiliated with Brokenwood being the largest single planting. It is thus not the least surprising that chardonnay, shiraz, pinot noir, cabernet sauvignon, merlot, sangiovese, sauvignon blanc, nebbiolo and gamay all compete for a foothold. The most notable wineries are Castagna Vineyard, Giaconda, Golden Ball and Sorrenberg.

**LAT** 36°21'S; **ALT** 300–720 m; **HDD** 1240–1687; **GSR** 370–550 mm; **MJT** 19.9°C–20.4°C; **HARV** Mid-March to end April; **CHIEF VIT. HAZARD** Drought

**Belgravia** (est. 2003) is an 1800-ha mixed farming property (sheep, cattle and vines) 20 kilometres north of Orange. There are 190 ha of vineyard with 10 ha devoted to the Belgravia brand. In 2006 Belgravia opened its cellar door at the heritage-listed former Union Bank building in Orange, which also operates as a wine bar and restaurant. Exports to the UK and Denmark.

**Bellarmine Wines** (est. 2000) in the Pemberton region is owned by German residents Dr Willi and Gudrun Schumacher. Long-term wine lovers, the Schumachers decided to establish a vineyard and winery of their own, using Australia partly because of its stable political climate. There are 20 ha of chardonnay, riesling, sauvignon blanc, pinot noir, shiraz, merlot and petit verdot; the rieslings are especially commendable. Exports to Germany.

**Bendigo**, gazetted 27 June 2001, and nearby Ballarat rivalled Ararat as the epicentres for the discovery of gold in the early 1850s. There are conflicting accounts of the timing of the discovery of gold and the planting of the first vineyards, but it is certain that vineyards and primitive wineries proliferated rapidly in the gold rush days. The 1873 Vienna Exhibition brought brief fame to the region; Henry Vizetelly, in his book *The Wines of the World* (published in 1875), recounts that a jury, including a number of French experts as well as Vizetelly, gave particular praise to several wines made from hermitage (shiraz). When it was discovered that the wines were from Bendigo, the French jurors withdrew in protest, claiming that the wines must be French. Only after a substantial delay, and much reassurance, did they consent to resume judging. (It's far from certain that much has changed in the ensuing 105 years.)

By 1880 there were more than 100 wineries in operation, although total plantings of 216 ha demonstrates that many of these were just another form of subsistence farming, the wine either to be consumed by the family or bartered for other products. Be that as it may, 1893 heralded the arrival of phylloxera and the bank crash which threatened the very fabric of the national economy – and the end of viticulture. When Bendigo pharmacist Stuart Anderson planted the first vines at his Balgownie Estate vineyard in 1969, it signalled the rebirth of viticulture in the region, and he attracted much praise and attention for his early vintages of cabernet sauvignon and hermitage (1973, '74 and '75).

The climate is strongly continental, with warm to hot days and cool to cold nights in summer, the diurnal differential diminishing in autumn. It is ideally suited to the making of full-bodied reds, the principal limitation being the shortage of water for irrigation. The modest annual rainfall (500 mm) falls mainly in winter and spring, and supplementary water (particularly in drought years) in summer is important if excessive vine stress is to be avoided. The majority of the soils are those found in much of southeastern Australia: brownish loamy sand over a relatively acidic stony clay base, needing additions of lime and gypsum if reasonable yields are to be obtained. Other than the lower slopes of the Great Dividing Range, on which most of the vineyards nestle, the two geographic features are Mount Alexander (744 metres) and Mount Tarrangower (570 metres).

Bendigo is first, foremost and last a red wine–producing region, in turn dominated by shiraz and cabernet sauvignon. The warm days and cold nights are ideally suited to these varieties, with absence of water a pre-existing problem which may well be exacerbated in the future. There are 48 wineries, with Balgownie Estate, BlackJack Vineyards, Bress, Chateau Leamon, Passing Clouds, Pondalowie

Vineyards, Sandhurst Ridge and Water Wheel to the fore.

LAT 36°45'S; ALT 240–390 m; HDD 1579; GSR 267 mm; MJT 21°C; HARV Mid-March to end April; CHIEF VIT. HAZARDS Frost; drought

**Best's Wines** (est. 1867), in the Great Western subregion of the Grampians, oozes history from every pore. In the 1850s brothers Joseph and Henry Best set up a business as butchers at Ararat, and miners being by nature hungry, the business flourished. Joseph began planting a vineyard in 1862; Henry took up a 30-ha property on nearby Concongella Creek and started planting in 1866. It was this property which ultimately came into the ownership of the Thomson family in 1920.

Today it is a particularly successful producer of exemplary shiraz at three quality/price levels, headed by the Thomson Family label. Many would say its most unique asset is a 1.02-ha block of 2400 vines comprising 32 varieties – this was planted as a nursery by Henry Best in 1866. Some of the varieties no longer exist in France, and several others have defied all attempts at identification by French experts. Others are well-known varieties which have produced cuttings of mainstream varieties (pinot meunier and pinot noir, for example), which have in turn provided plantings of exceptional quality. Exports to the UK and other major markets.

**biancone**, an important white grape in Corsica, was grown in the Riverland in the late 1970s, producing prodigious yields of 30 tonnes per hectare, the wine headed for distillation. There are one or two tiny plantings treated with more respect, but its chief value would lie in a game of ampelographical scrabble.

**Big Rivers Zone** covers the Riverina (on the Murrumbidgee River), Perricoota (on the NSW side of the Murray River, but extending well north of the river) and the Swan Hill and Murray Darling regions, both of which straddle the Murray River, thus falling partly in New South Wales and partly in Victoria.

**Bindi Wine Growers** (est. 1988), perched high in the Macedon Ranges, takes terroir to its ultimate conclusion. Owned by the Dhillon family, with Michael Dhillon as winemaker and viticulturist, Bindi has divided the relatively small estate plantings into even smaller vineyard lots, producing three pinot noirs, two chardonnays and a long lees-aged NV Chardonnay Pinot Noir, all made with unequalled precision and transparency. The total production of 1500 cases means that the quite exceptional wines are sold either by mail order or through restaurants, with only a tiny fraction reaching the specialist retail market.

**biodynamic viticulture** yields only to climate change in terms of the discussion, in all forms of media, it is generating in the 21st century. Its concept and practices were developed and codified by the Austrian philosopher Rudolf Steiner, who died in 1925. The core of his belief and teachings is that the earth is a living organism with diurnal and seasonal rhythms which depend on, and are influenced by, cosmic cycles. Vines have four components – root, leaf or shoot, flower and fruit – and these are linked to the four elements of earth, water, air and fire (heat). Each component is favoured during particular points of the moon's cycle, when it is positioned in front of one of the 12 signs of the zodiac. So there are leaf days, root days and so forth, most with only a two- or three-day duration, thus requiring split-second timing.

Also central to the practice are the preparations, with numbers such as 501, 502 and so on. The two most important are cow manure (501) and silica (502), placed in cow horns and buried in the soil for six months over winter (manure) or summer (silica). Horn manure is sprayed in the afternoon as the sun sets, stimulating microbial life in the soil. Horn silica is sprayed over the soil in the morning as the sun rises, with the consequence of stronger, more upright vine growth, to improve fruit quality and to discourage fungal growth. One of the problems for sceptics is that only a few grams of each are required per hectare. Scepticism increases with the instruction that the preparations have to be created in animal organs, which act as containers for, but not ingredients in, the preparations. The organs are chosen for the properties they possessed in their former function within the animal. If there is a mouse plague, Steiner says a mouse should be skinned, the skin burnt, and the ashes scattered (again in minute amounts), which will immediately end the plague. The same applies to vine pests, which should be collected, burnt and ashes scattered on the vines. (One wonders how efficacious it might be with cane toads.)

Work in the cellar should also be controlled by the lunar calendar; it is said a wine destined for long ageing should be bottled under the Leo star sign, because the fruit force will be most concentrated in the wine at this time, and bottling will capture and seal it.

Some of the greatest producers in France have adopted biodynamic viticulture, most notably Domaine Leflaive of Puligny Montrachet, Domaine Leroy of Vogne Romanee, Comtes Lafon of Meursault, Domaine Huet of Vouvray, and the arch high priest of biodynamic practices, Nicolas Joly of Clos de la Coulée Serrant in Savennieres, Loire Valley. In Australia one of the most passionate adherents is Vanya Cullen of Cullen Wines, and one of the most pragmatic is David Paxton, a major grower in McLaren Vale and a highly respected viticultural consultant. California also has a number of very well known producers.

Biodynamic farming has to be regarded (and respected) as a religion. While the leading soil scientist Claude Bourguignon has found high levels of microbial life on the roots of vines managed biodynamically, there has been no satisfactory demonstration of the superiority of wine made from biodynamically grown vines. Most observers believe that the more significant move is to organic viticulture, where Bordeaux mixture and elemental rock sulphur are approved sprays to control mildew (and are likewise approved for biodynamic farming) but all conventional chemicals and fertilisers are forbidden.

Both organic and biodynamic viticulture require constant close attention to the vines, and a much increased level of hand labour. The add-on cost of biodynamic preparations and practices is relatively small, so it can be said that there is no significant downside when compared with organic viticulture, and both practices will become more common in a drier, warmer world.

**bitterness** is, properly speaking, not the same as astringency, and is detectable on the back of the tongue (rather than the gums or cheeks). It is chiefly caused by lack of grape ripeness and associated green acidity.

**Blackwood Valley,** gazetted 10 December 1998, is a substantial region in the South West Australia Zone, noticeably larger than Margaret River; both are on the same latitude, Margaret River on the coast, and Blackwood Valley to the east, its centre (Bridgetown) 120 kilometres from the coast. It has many of the same climatic characteristics as Margaret River (relatively cool, dry summers and relatively warm, wet winters) but does have a higher diurnal temperature range because of its greater continentality.

The soils are part of the Darling Plateau system, with moderately incised valleys providing gravel and gravelly soils on the divides, and yellow soils and red earths on valley slopes. Overall, the result is well-drained gravelly loam soils perfectly suited to viticulture.

Around 70 per cent of the plantings are of red varieties; in descending order of area the overall plantings are cabernet sauvignon, shiraz, chardonnay, merlot, sauvignon blanc and semillon. None of Blackwood Valley's 12 wineries is particularly well known, and a significant part of the region's grape production is sold to wineries outside the region or converted to bulk wine and similarly disposed of.

LAT 34°00'S; **ALT** 100–340 m; **HDD** 1578; **GSR** 219 mm; **MJT** 20.7°C; **HARV** Late February to early April; **CHIEF VIT. HAZARD** Spring frost

**Blass, Wolf, AM** (1934–) was born in Germany and almost immediately showed he was a boy-man in a hurry, running away from

home when only 15. He was retrieved and apprenticed to a wine business in Rheinhessen, before undertaking an oenology degree course. He became the youngest student to graduate (in October 1957) with a Kellermeister Diploma, emblazoned on every bottle of Blass wine until 2001, whereafter he was described as 'Wolf Blass AM – Founder'. After two years with Avery's of Bristol, he arrived in the Barossa Valley in 1961 with a three-year contract to make sparkling wine. By 1966 he was making his own red wines, in 1974 winning the first of three successive Jimmy Watson Trophies, with John Glaetzer his trusted executive winemaker. He had already made a fortune when his company and Mildara merged in 1991, thereby adding another dimension to that fortune. He was then able to establish the Wolf Blass Foundation, which supports the wine industry in a wide variety of ways. It is hard to say whether it has been his winemaking or his wine marketing skills which have been most important in driving his business success. He has been brilliant in both.

**Bleasdale** (est. 1850) in the Langhorne Creek region is one of the most historic wineries in Australia, drawing upon 61 ha of vineyards that were once flooded every winter by diversion of the Bremer River, which provided moisture throughout the dry, cool growing season. The wines show that particular softness which is the hallmark of Langhorne Creek. Exports to all major markets.

**Blickling Estate** (est. 1999), in the New England region, has 10 ha of riesling, chardonnay, sauvignon blanc, pinot noir, cabernet sauvignon and shiraz, at an elevation of 950 metres. Frosts in spring and April underline how cool the climate is, necessitating careful site selection. The use of contract winemaker Monarch Winemaking Services in the Hunter Valley has put Blickling Estate in first position, the quality of the 7000-case production above all other wineries in the region.

**Bloodwood** (est. 1983) is the venture of Rhonda and Stephen Doyle, two of the pioneers of the Orange district. The 4000-case production is sold mainly through the cellar door and by an energetically run and informative mailing list. It has an impressive track record across the full gamut of varietal (and other) wine styles. Big Men in Tights has long been the name for its very good rosé, the name enlivened by recent changes to the ingredient labelling laws which have led to the addition of 'Caution: may contain traces of nuts' on the back label. Exports to the UK.

blue imperial  **see** cinsaut.

**Blue Metal Vineyard** (est. 1999) in the Southern Highlands is an 11-ha vineyard situated on part of a cattle station at an elevation of 790 metres; the name comes from the rich red soil that overlies the cap of basalt rock. A wide range of grape varieties are planted, including sauvignon blanc, pinot gris, merlot, cabernet sauvignon, sangiovese and petit verdot. The wines have been very competently made. Exports to the UK.

**body** is a term used to describe the weight or substance of a wine in the mouth, principally deriving from alcohol and tannin. Australian

wine-show usage once divided classes into light-bodied, medium-bodied and full-bodied, but has moved away from these descriptors because of the absence of clear demarcation: for example, wines described as light- to medium-bodied, medium- to full-bodied, and so on.

**Boireann** (est. 1998) is a micro boutique winery in the Granite Belt region of Queensland, producing slightly less than 1000 cases of beautifully made and balanced red wines from the 2 ha of immaculately maintained vineyards. Owner–winemaker Peter Stark is self-trained, but makes wines in the same league as Australia's best, with styles as disparate as shiraz viognier and The Lurnea, a blend of petit verdot, cabernet franc and merlot.

**Bordeaux mixture** was invented in 1885 by Alexis Millardet, professor of botany at Bordeaux University. A mix of lime, copper sulphate and water, it was the first effective control of downy mildew, and is one of the few preparations permitted in organic viticulture and biodynamic viticulture. There is now a wide range of other sprays to contain downy mildew: in particular, systemic sprays which can halt the outbreak after it has become established. Bordeaux mixture, on the other hand, is effective only as a prophylactic measure.

**Borrodell on the Mt** (est. 1995) is owned by Borry Gartrell and Gaye Stuart-Nairne, who have planted 5.25 ha of pinot noir, sauvignon blanc, pinot meunier, traminer and chardonnay adjacent to a cherry, plum and heritage apple orchard and truffière. It is a 10-minute drive from Orange, and adjacent to Lake Canobolas, at an altitude of 1000 metres. The wines have been consistent medal winners at regional and small winemaker shows.

**botrytis** is the enemy of dry table wines, white or red, but is the essential driver for the making of sweet table wines. *Botrytis cinerea* (called *pourriture noble* in France and *Edelfäule* in Germany) is a microscopic fungus or mould that attacks first the skin and then the pulp of grapes in certain very specific climatic conditions, causing the skin to perforate and the pulp to lose its water. The grape then softens and shrinks, with a corresponding concentration of its remaining components, notably sugar and acid. The grey-brown grapes look extremely unattractive, and the juice first pressed from them equally so, but juice settling and subsequent fermentation produce the great sweet wines of the world. In every case, however, it is essential that botrytis develops once the grapes have fully ripened; if it attacks too early, unwelcome moulds join the party.

Lindemans Porphyrys from 1923, 1937, 1949 and 1956 (all tasted in the 1970s) were great wines, but the contribution of botrytis was not easy to determine. In 1958 McWilliam's made a magnificent Pedro Sauterne from heavily botrytised Riverina grapes back-blended with Hunter Valley semillon. However, it has been the De Bortoli botrytised semillons which, since 1982, have been the greatest examples in the sauternes mould, winning many hundreds of gold medals, and a very large number of trophies, over the years. Botrytis rieslings of considerable quality have also been made, with Yalumba (courtesy of Heggies Vineyard) a major practitioner.

**bouquet** is, strictly speaking, the smell of the wine (as opposed to simply the aroma of the grape), which is produced by the volatile esters present in any wine. The bouquet becomes more complex during the time taken for the wine to reach full maturity and finally softens and dissipates with extreme age. Much work still remains to be done to fully understand the chemical changes which take place in a wine as it matures and which contribute to the changing bouquet. There is also the practical problem for wine writers of determining when the smell of a wine stops being its aroma and becomes its bouquet.

**Brand's Laira Coonawarra** (est. 1966) was founded by Eric and Nancy Brand, although Eric had become a grapegrower when (in 1950) he purchased a 24 ha block from the Redman family. It had been taken up by a former ship captain named Stentiford during the establishment of the Penola Fruit Colony (renamed Coonawarra in 1897) by John Riddoch in the 1890s, and 2 ha had been planted to grapes (the major part was an orchard). The plantings had been much increased by the time McWilliam's, following the pattern of Mount Pleasant, acquired a 50 per cent share. This ultimately moved to 100 per cent ownership, initially leaving the Brand family in place. The move to full ownership marked a further major expansion of the vineyards, with the purchase of 100 ha of additional land. The two flagships are Stentiford's Reserve Old Vines Shiraz (from the 2 ha, 100-year-old plantings, of course) and The Patron (97 per cent cabernet sauvignon, 3 per cent merlot). It has also produced some remarkable riesling over the years, fitting naturally into a group of wines which are notable for their elegance rather than oak, extract or alcohol.

**Brangayne of Orange** (est. 1994) is the venture of orchardists Don and Pamela Hoskins, who decided to diversify into grapegrowing and have progressively established 25.7 ha of high-quality vineyards. Right from the outset, Brangayne has produced high-quality wines across all mainstream varieties, remarkably ranging from pinot noir to cabernet sauvignon. Exports to the UK, Canada and Spain.

**Bream Creek** (est. 1975) stands in splendid isolation on the east coast of Tasmania, but at the same latitude as Hobart, rather than further to the north where the five well-known east coast wineries are situated. The vines were first planted in 1975, and the grapes sold to Moorilla Estate. The problem was inconsistent and often desperately low yields. In 1990, Fred Peacock, the Moorilla Estate viticulturist, purchased the problem vineyard and quickly put matters aright. In 1996 Peacock acquired a second vineyard in the Tamar Valley, lifting production significantly, to 3500 cases. The wines are made at Winemaking Tasmania by Julian Alcorso, the pinot noir typically outstanding, and some very attractive sauvignon blanc (from the Tamar Valley property) in support.

**breathing**, strictly speaking, results from the removal of the seal from the bottle some hours before the wine is poured. It will have little or no impact on a young wine, but can, on occasion, remove the so-called bottle-stink from old wines.

**Bremerton** (est. 1988) in Langhorne Creek is owned by the Willson family, who began grapegrowing before adding winemaking into the mix. Their vineyards have more than doubled to over 100 ha (predominantly cabernet sauvignon, shiraz and merlot), as has their production of wine under the Bremerton label. In 2004 sisters Rebecca (winemaking) and Lucy (marketing) took control of the business, marking the event with (guess what?) revamped label designs. It can fairly claim to be the best producer in Langhorne Creek. Exports to all major markets.

*Bretannomyces*, commonly shortened to 'brett', is a genus of yeast, closely related to, but different from, dekkera. The most widely encountered of the five species of *Bretannomyces* is *B. bruxellensis*. Research work by Dr Pascal Chatonnet between 1992 and 1995 showed that *Bretannomyces* was common in the best French wines, with one-third having levels above the taste threshold. Brett creates volatile phenols and fatty acids with strong, unpleasant olfactory characters. The principal culprit is 4-ethyl-phenol, the presence of which can be readily analysed and which is accepted as the prime marker for brett activity. The descriptors most frequently used for 4-ethyl-phenol (colloquially called 4EP) are wet bandaid, game and/or horse stable aromas, typically coupled with a metallic, sour finish to the taste. The second phenol is 4-ethyl-guaiacol, typically present in concentrations one-tenth of 4EP. The third is isovaleric acid; all three interact.

While brett has always been part of the wine scenery, levels in Australia prior to the 1990s were not significant. However, many

Australian winemakers were then intent on reducing the amount of sulphur dioxide in their wines – at the very time that alcohol levels (and hence pH levels) were rising (decreasing the effectiveness of any given $SO_2$ level). It was a problem that caught many winemakers by surprise, and by 1997 the mean concentration of 4EP in all red wines tested by the Australian Wine Research Institute was over 1200 micrograms per litre (commonly cited as parts per billion, or ppb). This was almost three times the accepted sensory detection level of 425 ppb. The institute recommended various courses of action to minimise the problem, the most important being to add $SO_2$ once only in a concentration of 50–60 ppb, rather than in repeated small doses. By 2002 the mean concentration had fallen to under 400 ppb, and has fallen further since (2008) to 224 ppb, well below the commonly accepted level for sensory detection. This mean concentration is in fact distorted by a few rogue wines with very high concentrations of up to 4660 ppb. Thus almost half have levels below 60 ppb, and the trend is still downwards as at the start of 2009.

**brine** is a general description of the fluid used in refrigeration systems in wineries; it is not simply salty water, and may be either ammonia or an ethanol-saline mix.

**brix** is a method of gauging the potential alcohol content of a wine by measuring the approximate concentration of grape sugars in solution using either a refractometer or hydrometer: 1% alc/vol corresponds to approximately 16.8 g/l sugar in white wines, and 18 g/l in red wines.

**broad** is a somewhat imprecise term used to describe wine which is softly coarse, lacking in refinement and/or focus.

**Brokenwood** (est. 1970 by three lawyers, including the author, who deserted ship in 1983 to move to Melbourne) in the Lower Hunter Valley is a deservedly fashionable winery producing consistently excellent wines. It has kept Graveyard Shiraz as its ultimate flagship wine, while extending its reach through many of the best eastern regions for its selection of varietal wine styles. Its big-selling Hunter semillon remains alongside Graveyard, and there is then a range of wines from regions including Orange, Central Ranges, Beechworth, McLaren Vale and Cowra. Exports to all major markets.

**Brookland Valley** (est. 1984), in the Margaret River region, has an idyllic setting, plus a café and its Gallery of Wine Arts, which houses an eclectic collection of wine, food-related art and wine accessories. After acquiring a 50 per cent share of Brookland Valley in 1997, CWA moved to full ownership in 2004. The quality and consistency of the wines is, quite literally, awesome. Exports to the UK, the US and other major markets.

**Brown Brothers** (est. 1885) stands alongside Tyrrell's and Yalumba, sharing with those wineries a history dating back to the mid-19th century, an unbroken line of family ownership, and commercial success on a significant scale. The rich Brown Brothers story commences in 1852 when 18-year-old law clerk George Harry Brown arrived in Melbourne. Like so many others, he found the lure of gold irresistible and went to Bendigo to join the search. He was unsuccessful, and joined with four others to travel further north and buy a property at Hurdle Creek near Milawa. Known locally as the 'Farmers Five', they prospered sufficiently for each to soon acquire his own property. George Brown stayed at Hurdle Creek and that property remains in the Brown family, with 18 ha under vine. In 1857 a Scot named John Graham arrived at Milawa and purchased 50 ha at the first land sale at Oxley Plains. George Brown met and married Graham's schoolteacher daughter, and on her father's death the couple moved to the Milawa property.

John Graham had planted table grapes, and George Harry Brown extended the plantings with wine varieties. His son John Francis Brown (born in 1867) made the first wine on the property, using an old Canadian-style barn which John Graham had built. It still stands and is used for maturing the fortified wines of Browns. In 1900 an additional winery was built, part of which remains. It was incorporated into the winemaking complex which has grown, Topsy-like, over the ensuing 100-plus years.

In 1915 phylloxera finally made its way from Rutherglen to the Milawa area of the King Valley. The beginning of World War I had meant the end of the export trade and had taken many young Australians to the battlefield. Of the numerous vineyards around Milawa destroyed by phylloxera, only the Brown vineyard of 16 ha was replanted. John Charles Brown, eldest son of John Francis, left school in 1933 and made his first vintage in 1934. It was due to the extraordinary foresight of this gentle, kind

and compassionate man that Brown Brothers was transformed from a quiet and sleepy family winery at the end of the 1950s to one of Australia's leading mid-sized wineries, with a production of over 1 million cases.

Following the retirement of John Charles, elder son John Graham Brown took on the senior winemaking role, and younger son Ross Brown the marketing. When John Graham retired, Ross became CEO, guiding the business with a sure hand.

Brown Brothers was always in the vanguard of trialling new varieties, and this has not changed. It has 24 varieties planted, moving from mainstream to sangiovese, tempranillo, barbera, dolcetto, durif, orange muscat, flora, tarrango, cienna and vermentino. It has developed substantial vineyards in diverse locations: 80 ha at the Milawa vineyard (King Valley); 312 ha at Mystic Park (on the Murray River); 69 ha at the high-altitude Whitlands vineyard (King Valley); 122 ha at Banksdale (King Valley); and, most recently, 164 ha in Heathcote. Its cellar door has the greatest turnover of any in Australia, helped by the fact that exclusive cellar door releases feature some of the most unusual varieties. Across the board, the wines over-deliver at their price points, with the Patricia range of wines (named in honour of the late Patricia Brown, who outlived husband John Charles) invariably excellent. Exports to all major markets.

**brown frontignac, brown muscat** are synonyms for muscat à petits grains.

**brut** is in theory the driest of the sparkling wine styles, though in almost all instances it contains some residual sugar that is masked by the high acidity of the wine. There are no technical rules in Australia as there are in Champagne for the use of the term.

**Buller** (est. 1921) is a family-owned winery in Rutherglen, best known for its superb releases of Museum fortified wines. Limited releases of Calliope Shiraz and Shiraz Mondeuse can also be good. Exports to the UK and the US.

**bunch-thinning** refers to the removal of whole bunches of grapes to reduce the crop, normally undertaken at the time of veraison. The two criteria for removal will be bunches which are still green and showing no colour change, or to reduce the number of bunches on a given shoot, regardless of ripeness.

**bung** is the stopper in a wine barrel, once fashioned from wood, but increasingly made from silicon, which guarantees an airtight seal.

**Buring, Leo** (1876–1961) was the son of TG Hermann Buring, who became one of the founding partners of Buring & Sobels, the original owners of Quelltaler Estate. He studied first at Roseworthy Agricultural College (where he graduated as dux and gold medallist) then continued his studies in Geisenheim in Germany and Montpellier in France. In 1898 he returned to Australia to work for several vintages at Buring & Sobels before moving to Penfolds' Minchinbury Cellars in 1902. He stayed with Penfolds until 1919, leaving to become one of Australia's first wine consultants. It was in this capacity that the Commercial Banking Company of Sydney appointed him as governing director of Lindemans Wines in 1923. It was a de

facto receivership, the fate which formally befell the company when Buring was removed by the bank in 1930, having failed to trade Lindemans out of its financial problems.

The following year Buring went into partnership with Reginald Mowatt of Great Western to form Leo Buring & Company, and began the Sydney-based wine merchant business which built its success on the first semi-sweet white wine to be commercialised actively in Australia. Rhinegolde became a household name; produced from Hunter Valley semillon vintaged by the Phillips family, and bottled in a distinctive German flask-shaped bottle, its already substantial success grew further during World War II.

In 1941 Buring took over the long-established Melbourne wine merchant Matthew Lang & Company, and in 1945 he moved to the Barossa Valley to purchase a small winery which had been built by Gottlieb Hoffman in 1897. This became Chateau Leonay, an extraordinary amalgam of architectural styles which stands as one of the more striking landmarks of the Barossa Valley today. Buring expanded the winery substantially and took the opportunity to add strange turrets to the corners of the building. In 1955 John Vickery, then recently graduated from Roseworthy, joined Buring as an assistant winemaker. The re-equipping of the winery was still proceeding and the grand schemes for its façade were incomplete when Buring died in 1961, at the age of 85.

In 1962 the wheel turned full circle with Lindemans' acquisition of Buring's business. Lindemans immediately spent large sums in upgrading the winemaking equipment and substantially extending the winemaking facilities and storage capacity of the winery. Refrigeration was installed prior to the 1963 vintage, and from 1964 John Vickery and Reg Shipster began making rieslings of unequalled quality. No other company in Australia could produce a range of rieslings of remotely comparable quality between 1964 and 1975.

Leo Buring's image in the marketplace was immeasurably damaged by corporate ownership and the usual succession of brand managers, as all sorts of wines of variable quality and provenance were made and released under the Leo Buring label. Instead of increasing sales, this steadily eroded the brand to the point where it was a mere shadow of its former self. Happily, it has been repositioned as a high-quality producer of riesling, principally from the Eden and Clare valleys, but justifiably taking in Tasmanian and Great Southern grapes to establish a legitimate point of difference.

**Busby, James** (1801–71) is generally recognised as the father of Australian viticulture, although Governor Phillip, noted explorer Gregory Blaxland and Captain John Macarthur, best known for establishing the Australian wool industry by importing Merino sheep, all obtained and planted vine cuttings before him.

Busby was 23 when he arrived in Australia in 1824. With an agricultural background gained only in Ireland and Scotland, he had convinced himself before he left Europe that viticulture had a great future in New South Wales. Therefore, he spent several months studying viticulture and winemaking in France.

He published two books in New South Wales: *Treatise on the Culture of the Vine* (1825) and *A Manual of Plain Directions for Planting and Cultivating Vineyards and for Making Wine in New South Wales* (1830). The second book in particular was of considerable practical use, but Busby's lasting contribution was his three-month trip in 1831, starting in Cadiz on 28 September and ending in Champagne on 21 December. While he brought back 433 varieties from the botanic gardens at Montpellier, 110 from the Luxembourg Garden and 44 from Sion House near Kew Gardens in England (362 of these survived the trip to Sydney), the most important were the 52 varieties he collected from vineyards on his journey. From Rousillon he obtained (using Busby's spelling for all the following varieties) carignan, grenache, mataro, blanquette, muscat and grenache blanche; from Hill of Hermitage siraz/scyras, roussette/roussanne and marsan; from Clos Vougeot pineau blanc, or chaudeny, 'the only variety of white grape planted in the best vineyards', and pineau noir; and from the region of Ay in Champagne pineau dore – black, pineau vert – black, 'the variety most commonly cultivated in Champagne', and plant blanc or white pineau: 'This variety and the two preceding are exclusively cultivated in the vineyards, which produce the wines of Champagne of the first quality.'

From the Luxembourg Garden he obtained and specially catalogued the varieties grown in the Medoc: 'carbenet, or carmenet a petits grains – de la Gironde – black, carbenet sauvignen – black, malbek – black, verdot – black, sauvignen – white, semilion – white', and five other wines, commenting that 'Sauvignen and semilion yield the best white wines of this department, including Vin de Grave, Barsac and Sauterne.' He arranged for the successful transportation of his vast collection to Sydney, where the cuttings were initially planted out in the Botanic Gardens, with distributions made to his Kirkton Vineyard in the Hunter Valley (run by brother-in-law James Kelman), to Macarthur's property at Camden and to the Adelaide Botanic Gardens, from where thousands of clippings were taken and spread through South Australia. Not long thereafter, the collections in both the Sydney and Adelaide botanic gardens became neglected; they ultimately disappeared.

**bush-pruned vines** see canopy management.

**buttery** is a term encompassing the aroma, taste and texture of a white wine, usually oak-matured, but which can also develop from long bottle age. It is typically found in semillon and chardonnay. In the latter case, it is sometimes attributable to a particular type of malolactic bacteria.

**By Farr** (est. 1999), and Farr Rising (est. 2001), are the father-and-son enterprises of Gary and Nick Farr in Geelong. The focus is on chardonnay, pinot noir and shiraz, all of which are profoundly influenced by both men's experience of making wine in Burgundy, notably at Domaine Dujac. Ultra-close-planted vineyards for pinot noir are very important; while the pinot noirs of each winemaker are not greatly different, father Gary makes more opulent and complex chardonnay, with son Nick following a restrained, minerally path, with more than a passing nod to chablis. Exports to the UK, the US, Denmark, Japan, India, Malaysia, Hong Kong and Singapore.

a b c d e f g h i
j k l m n o p q
r s t u v w x y z

**cabernet franc** is a relatively recent red grape arrival in Australia, first making the statistical records in the middle of the 1980s. At that time misidentification of cabernet franc as merlot probably led to the figures being understated. However that may be, after hitting a peak of 834 ha in 2004, cabernet franc is now on the slide, as it is in Bordeaux, plantings having decreased to 693 ha in 2008. For reasons which are not clear, the only regions in which it consistently produces wine of good quality, either as a straight varietal or in a blend, are the Margaret River and Great Southern regions of Western Australia.

**cabernet gros** see bastardo.

**cabernet sauvignon**, a spontaneous crossing of interplanted cabernet franc and sauvignon blanc vines, is often described as the most noble red grape, although those besotted by pinot noir would strongly disagree; shiraz is altogether too compliant to mount a meaningful challenge. Jancis Robinson has pointed out that in Bordeaux it emerged from the shadows only in the late 18th century, and did not become the dominant variety until phylloxera led to wholesale replanting and to the fall from grace of malbec and carmenère. As the James Busby journal makes clear, the grape arrived in Australia early in the piece, and was planted in the Hunter Valley, at Tahbilk in the Goulburn Valley, in the Yarra Valley and in many places in South Australia. However, its relatively low yield and alcohol and its physical toughness caused planting to dwindle to near zero as fortified wine swept all before it. In 1966 the official Australian Bureau of Statistics figures showed a crush of 621 tonnes,

compared with 12,400 tonnes of shiraz and 32,000 tonnes of grenache. The growth from that point on was spectacular, and for some time it looked certain that it would overtake shiraz as the most widely planted variety in Australia. But it stalled as the new millennium arrived, while shiraz continued to increase: as at 2008 there were 27,553 ha of cabernet sauvignon compared with 43,997 ha of shiraz. That said, there is almost three times as much cabernet sauvignon as the third-placed merlot, at 10,764 ha. It has made Coonawarra its home away from home, each feeding on the reputation of the other. Not surprisingly, it does very well in maritime regions, most notably Margaret River, Yarra Valley, McLaren Vale and all the regions in the Limestone Coast Zone.

The oldest planting in Australia is Block 42 in the Kalimna Vineyard of Penfolds, planted in the 1880s; there are no known plantings older than this in the world. Block 42 produces magnificent wines in cooler vintages, giving birth to Grange Cabernet Sauvignon (1953), Penfold Show Bin 58 (1961) and Bin 54 (1963), the first vintage of Bin 707 (1964), and in 1996, Block 42 Cabernet Sauvignon, followed in due course by 2004's Block 42 Cabernet Sauvignon.

**Caledonia Australis** (est. 1995) is a pinot noir and chardonnay specialist, with 33 ha across two vineyard locations in the Leongatha area of Gippsland. The vines have been established on red, free-draining, high-ironstone soils over a limestone or marl base. The slopes are east- to northeast-facing, resulting in full ripening in most vintages. Small-batch winemaking has resulted in consistently high-quality production of 6000 cases. Exports to the US, Singapore, Hong Kong and Japan.

**Campbells** (est. 1870) quietly gets on with producing the full range of Rutherglen fortifieds, starting with the varietal, thence Classic, next Grand and, at the top, Isabella Rare Tokay (henceforth Topaque) and Merchant Prince Rare Muscat. All show clear-cut varietal character, and all share a degree of elegance which puts Campbells apart from the full-on mainstream styles. The topaques are especially commendable, and elegance is not achieved at the expense of intensity or complexity as one moves into Grand and Rare territory. Exports to the UK, the US and other major markets.

**Canberra District**, gazetted 9 February 1998, took a long time to grow from adolescence into adulthood. Some of the early vineyards were planted in places where frost was virtually certain to cause havoc in spring, and, even where this was avoided, marginal growing season rainfall, and subsoils which are not particularly water-retentive, slowed growth for the majority of vineyards without irrigation. With its extremely continental climate, the Canberra District shows just how inadequate a single index of climate can be. It is a mix of warm and cool factors, compounded by different site climates. A very warm, dry summer (but with cold nights) gives way to a cool autumn, with harvest not infrequently interrupted by significant rain. The major viticultural limitation lies in the very dry spring and summer months.

There was also considerable uncertainty in the choice of varieties; even though most of the 40 wineries are in the Murrumbateman area, with outliers north of Lake George, and a few scattered south of Murrumbateman closer to the New South Wales/ACT border, matching site and variety took time. Two wineries have done more than most to shape and enhance the reputation of the region. Clonakilla (est. 1971) was one of the pioneers, and the fiercely committed Tim Kirk has taken the company to national prominence with its shiraz viognier, generally regarded as the best in Australia. The indefatigable Ken Helm established his eponymous winery in 1973, and has sent more press releases than any other small winery in Australia promoting his business, riesling, and the region in general. Dr Roger Harris at Brindabella Hills (est. 1986) does not hesitate to source grapes from elsewhere in the Southern New South Wales Zone when conditions at his estate vineyard demand it, and has a broader portfolio than most in the region. Dr David and Sue Carpenter at Lark Hill (est. 1978) have shown that its elevation (860 metres) offers special opportunities for pinot noir when the conditions are right. Hardys' initiative in 2000 in building Kamberra, the largest winery in the region, in 2000 was relatively short-lived: it was sold well before the 2008 rationalisation of its regional wineries by CWA (four were put on the market, along with their vineyards).

The soils are principally in the hard red duplex group, with brownish clay loam surface soils which are usually shallow. The subsoils are not particularly water-retentive, adding to the need for irrigation. It is not surprising that, while the plantings are overall 60 per cent red, and 40 per cent white, there should be such a wide spread: in descending order of amount planted they are shiraz, cabernet sauvignon, merlot, chardonnay, sauvignon blanc, riesling, semillon and pinot noir, with Italian and Spanish varieties also grown.

LAT 35°0'S; ALT 500–850 m; HDD 1410; GSR 360 mm; MJT 20.2°C; HARV Mid-March to end April; CHIEF VIT. HAZARDS Spring frost; drought

**canopy management** is an expression which came into use in Australia (and elsewhere in the New World) in the 1980s, and covers the way the annual spring and summer vine growth is controlled. It is by no means a new concept, dating back to Roman times, and is deeply embedded in the way the best vineyards of Europe are managed.

The systems used range from ultra-traditional and simple through to highly complex. The common aim is to achieve a correct balance between the number of functioning leaves and the number and size of bunches on each vine. Inherent in this is allowing dappled sunlight into the canopy, and onto the bunches.

The most traditional in New World and Old World vineyards alike are free-standing bush-pruned vines, which have no trellis, simply a very short trunk from which the canes grow each year, originally perpendicularly, and, once the bunches are fully formed, bending over and outwards. The management here involves the removal of excess shoots early in spring, but little else.

The other traditional and widely used system in Australia is called cane pruning in the vernacular, or double Guyot more technically. Each year two canes, one on each side of the crown of the trunk, are selected from the previous year's growth, and wrapped around the lower of two wires of the trellis.

The second wire (the catchwire) is used to restrain the canopy, and can be raised as the canopy grows. This catchwire may have a second wire on the opposite side of the canopy.

Other than cane pruning, the most widely used method is Vertical Spur Positioning (VSP). This involves two permanent arms affixed to the cordon wire with two bud spurs created from the previous season's new growth, the spurs ideally a hand span (or 10 cm) apart. As the canopy grows in spring, several pairs of moveable catchwires, each having one wire on either side of the canopy, are lifted vertically and attached to predetermined positions on the intermediate posts in the vineyard. There may be up to three positions, resulting in a thin vertical wall of canopy.

Scott Henry is one of the recently developed and more elaborate systems, in which the canopy is effectively split in two, half trained upwards (held in place by two moveable catchwires) and the other half trained downwards (again in a vertical plane, again with catchwires). It is typically used in high-vigour situations with generous yields. The downside is the very narrow window of time during which the soft canes must be manipulated into their positions.

Other less commonly used systems are the Smart Dyson, developed by Dr Richard Smart, and achieving the same result as Scott Henry, but with less work in springtime, and the Lyre trellis, an open V trellis with the canopy split along the sloping arms of the V.

Geneva Double Curtain, where the permanent cordon is affixed at the top of the trellis, results in all the canes falling towards the ground, thus ensuring good fruit exposure. Once in fashion, it has fallen out of favour.

**cap**  is the layer of red grape skins which rise to the top of the vat as fermentation gets underway. It sinks after a lapse of one to two weeks after the end of fermentation. (Many red wines are in fact pressed before the cap falls.)

**Capel Vale**  (est. 1974) was established by Perth-based former radiologist Dr Peter Pratten. The first vineyard, adjacent to the winery, was planted on the banks of the quiet waters of Capel River in the Geographe region. The very fertile soil there gave rise to extravagant vine growth, and until the mid-1980s provided 95 per cent of the winery's intake. Since that time the viticultural empire has been expanded to 175 ha, spread across Capel (30 ha), Mount Barker (25 ha), Manjimup (80 ha) and Margaret River (40 ha), with 18 varieties planted, the most recent arrivals being petit verdot, sangiovese, tempranillo and nebbiolo. Production is in excess of 100,000 cases, and every aspect of the business is subject to Pratten's close scrutiny. Exports to all major markets.

**Cape Mentelle**  (est. 1970) was one of the first movers in the Margaret River, and has been long regarded as one of its pre-eminent wineries. Founded by David Hohnen, it won lasting fame by capturing the Jimmy Watson Trophy in 1983 and 1984 with its strongly structured cabernet sauvignon. Hohnen went on to establish Cloudy Bay in New Zealand, and the two wineries were a temptation that Louis Vuitton Moet Hennessy could not resist, although one is left to speculate which winery was most highly prized by LVMH (or, more precisely, Veuve Clicquot, which has always exercised a certain degree of independence). It is ironic that the cabernet sauvignon should have had various technical problems over the years, first mercaptan and much later on *Bretannomyces* (both now vanquished), while the chardonnay, semillon and sauvignon blanc have always been among Australia's very best, the potent shiraz going from strength to strength, and the red berry zinfandel curiously left marooned as the best example of this difficult variety in Australia. Exports to all major markets.

**Capercaillie**  (est. 1995), the reincarnation of the former Dawson Estate, has been emblematic of the best boutique wineries in the Hunter Valley, unhesitatingly going outside the Hunter to regions such as Hilltops, Mudgee and McLaren Vale to build red wines like The Clan, a Bordeaux blend. On the other hand, it also produces Hunter Valley semillon, chardonnay and shiraz of the highest quality. Production may be only 6000 cases, but it punches well above its weight. Exports to the UK, Japan, Singapore and Dubai.

**carbonic maceration**  is the (partial) fermentation of whole berries due to the action of enzymes within the fruit rather than yeast. It is a complex process, but suffice it to say that once the alcohol inside the berry reaches 2% alc/vol, the process stops. The most obvious application in Australia is the whole bunch inclusion in pinot noir, and, to a lesser degree, in shiraz.

**carignan**  is a late-ripening red grape variety which has yet to gain a commercial foothold in Australia, but it is one of the red grapes which may well come into favour if global warming is as extreme as the Jeremiahs would have us believe.

**Carlei Estate and Carlei Green Vineyards** (est. 1994) is the hydra-headed winery and contract winemaking business of the perpetually mobile Sergio Carlei, whose head keeps popping up here, there and everywhere. Most of his attention is focused on the Yarra Valley (pinot noir and chardonnay) and Heathcote (shiraz), but he also dances with Tre Rossi, a blend of shiraz, barbera and nebbiolo. Exports to the US, Canada, China, Singapore and Malaysia.

**carmenère** was an important red grape variety in Bordeaux before the onset of oidium and phylloxera, but was not replanted after that. It is grown in Chile and California, and, as part of the incessant search for 'new' varieties, is making an appearance in Australia in a small way.

**Casella Wines** (est. 1969) is a modern fairy story, a series of events propelling it to the front of the international stage. It was just one of a number of flourishing Riverina wineries on the Murrumbidgee River, shown as making 650,000 cases in 2000, significantly less than De Bortoli and McWilliam's. In a seemingly unconnected event, Rosemount Estate management took control of Southcorp in the wake of its reverse takeover. Newly installed CEO Keith Lambert, with a beer background, came up with the master plan of having two distributors in each country around the world for the Southcorp brands. The first distributor would have Penfolds and Rosemount; the second distributor would have all the other brands. In the US the choice of the second distributor meant that WJ Deutsch, which had been spectacularly successful in the development of the market for Lindemans Bin 65 Chardonnay, with representatives spread throughout the US to support the local sales teams (necessary under the arcane US three-tier sales system), was informed that it would henceforth no longer distribute Lindemans wines. History does not relate how much Southcorp had to pay to terminate the distribution arrangement, but the result was that WJ Deutsch needed to find a substitute, big-volume brand. Fate's fickle finger led to John Casella meeting WJ Deutsch, and assuring it that he could meet its needs. Time was short, and Casella walked into Adelaide-based graphic designer Barbara Harkness' office, knowing that she had trademarked names and label designs available for sale in precisely the same way that lawyers provide shelf companies. A short time later, and for a tiny fraction of the amount which would normally be spent in developing a label for a major new brand, John Casella walked out of Harkness' office with [yellow tail] safely in his pocket.

[yellow tail] has broken both preconceptions and sales records ever since, and has the ultimate good fortune of being based in the Riverina, with much more secure water access for its growers than is available to those on the Murray Darling. Moreover, it can pick and choose (in the short term, at least) from the fluctuating lake of surplus wine which has characterised the second half of the first decade of the 21st century. The fact that [yellow tail] has managed to secure dominant sales positions in numerous countries outside the US shows that it is a great deal more than a pretty face. To further confound the critics, some of its limited production wines have had conspicuous show success in that toughest arena of all, the Australian wine show system. It matters not that the base wines cater for base wine tastes: wine at this level is a fast-moving consumer good, sold on price, store position and an ever-present hint of sweetness.

**Cassegrain** (est. 1980), under the ownership and winemaking direction of John Cassegrain, has benefited greatly from the development of the New England region, which has provided a far more reliable source of grapes than the estate vineyards or elsewhere in the Hastings River region. While part of the 60,000-case production comes from the Hunter Valley and elsewhere, most comes from the Granite Belt and New England regions. Contract winemaking is also part of the business, with an upgraded winery and a temperature-controlled bottle maturation facility. Exports to the UK and other major markets.

**cassis** is French for blackcurrant, although many use it as a separate tasting term, simply because cassis juice in a bottle tastes much sweeter than the grape from which it comes. Its use is common in describing the taste of cabernet sauvignon.

**Castagna** (est. 1997) was established by Julian and Carolann Castagna, the family involvement completed with son Adam Castagna as assistant winemaker. This 4 ha biodynamically managed estate at Beechworth, Victoria, produces 2000 cases of highly regarded wines, with Genesis Syrah leading the way.

**Castle Rock Estate** (est. 1983), established by Angelo Diletti and family, is the foremost of the 13 wineries of Porongurup, a subregion of the Great Southern in Western Australia. Its gently sloping vineyards have a panoramic view second to none, stretching away to the far-distant coast. The two-level winery, set on the natural slope, maximises gravity flow, in particular for crushed must feeding into the press. Son Rob Diletti is the talented winemaker, producing finely crafted and utterly deceptive rieslings, which in their youth can often look light and unconvincing to the uninitiated, but which invariably grow and develop with age, without ever losing that purity and finesse which marks the style. As the pinot noir vines at Castle Rock have gained maturity, so has the quality of the wine, reaching the point where it is now among the best from the entire southwestern corner of Western Australia, albeit in the reserved house style which marks all the wines of the estate. Rob Diletti has also built up an impressive contract winemaking business for other wineries in the Great Southern region. Exports to Japan and Singapore.

**Centennial Vineyards** (est. 2002) is a substantial development in the Southern Highlands of New South Wales jointly owned by wine professional John Large and investor Mark Dowling, covering 133 ha of beautiful grazing land, with 29 ha planted to pinot noir, chardonnay, sauvignon blanc, tempranillo, pinot gris, albarino, riesling and pinot meunier. Production from the estate vineyards is supplemented by purchases of grapes from other regions, notably Orange. The consistency of the quality of the wines is wholly commendable, and reflects the skilled touch of winemaker Tony Cosgriff in a region which often throws up climatic challenges. Exports to the US, Denmark, Singapore, China and Korea.

**Central Ranges Zone** of New South Wales encompasses Mudgee, Orange (the two briefly kissing at their southwest/northeast corners) and Cowra, which stands apart from Orange. A considerable part of the zone remains to be blessed as regions, even though wineries are scattered throughout.

**Central Western Australia Zone** has roughly half of the Peel region in its compass, with another handful of vineyards randomly scattered over its 500-kilometre north to south range.

**cepage** is a French term for a blended wine (or its constituents), from time to time used by Australian wine writers.

**Chaffey, George** (1848–1932) and William (1856–1926) were lured to Victoria by future prime minister Alfred Deakin, who had seen the irrigation systems engineered by the brothers in California in the 1880s. Bumbling and uncomprehending bureaucracy in Victoria caused the Chaffeys to move to Renmark in South Australia, where all their (logical and far-sighted) conditions were quickly agreed to, leading to the wide streets and parklands which remain features of Renmark to this day, not to mention the establishment of the infrastructure for viticulture. This caused Victoria to think again, and the Chaffeys were invited back to develop Mildura on

precisely the terms and conditions they had laid out in the first instance. Were it not for the drought-induced near collapse of the Murray Darling system in the first decade of the new millennium, their achievements would still underwrite more than 50 per cent of Australian wine production.

**Chalkers Crossing** (est. 2000) is a newcomer in a relatively unknown region (Hilltops, New South Wales). It is owned by Ted and Wendy Ambler, who had the good fortune to employ French-born and -trained winemaker Celine Rousseau, who broke all speed records in becoming an Australian citizen once she moved here. Rousseau's elegant wines have been consistently excellent, spanning riesling, chardonnay, semillon, shiraz, cabernet sauvignon (all from Hilltops), pinot noir and sauvignon blanc (from Tumbarumba). The wines are significantly underpriced, and it is small wonder that exports to a number of major markets are in place.

**Chambers Rosewood** (est. 1858) is one of the oldest wineries of Rutherglen, established by German-born vigneron Anthony Ruche. Charles Hubert de Castella, in *Notes of an Australian Vine Grower*, first published in 1882, tells the story of Ruche, who, 20 years earlier, had established a 1-ha vineyard. In 1880 he was persuaded to sell his entire stock to an enterprising Melbourne wine merchant. De Castella takes up the tale:

Ruche, the wine grower, until then had clung to his casks like a hen to her chickens, and had never sold until his back was to the wall, in a few cases only because he was forced by the few creditors who supplied his humble needs. It was his mania. Selling his wine was a heartbreak for him. Consequently when one of his barrels was put up for sale it used to fetch a good price, even when other vine growers could not sell theirs. Besides, the man was an expert, and if he was so keen on keeping his wine it was because he rightly had a very good opinion of it.

Having cost the merchant 4 shillings and 9 pence a gallon (4.5 litres), the wine brought in 6 shillings per gallon at auction. To what extent the ensuing publicity was responsible will never be known, but in the following six years plantings in the Shire of Rutherglen trebled, rising from 2770 ha in 1880 to 7410 ha in 1886. Apparently heartbroken by the sale of his treasured wine, Ruche sold the winery and vineyard to the grandfather of present incumbent, William (Bill) Chambers. The area of the vineyard was increased significantly, but much had to be replanted after phylloxera arrived in 1899; between 1890 and 1910 virtually every vineyard was destroyed, and a number of vignerons left the region for good. The Chambers family replanted, and a significant part of the present 48 ha is 100 years old.

Bill Chambers (born 1933) has handed over some of the winemaking responsibilities to son Stephen, but continues to protect the business. Not only did the printed portion of sales invoices even in the late 1980s show the business of WH Chambers & Company as 'incorporating Anthony Ruche', but Bill had a similar reluctance to part with his oldest and best muscat and tokay: it seemed that each time someone bought a bottle, the price would go up. The quality of the oldest fortified wines is beyond compare, and requires no marketing effort. They now use the rare classification in conjunction with muscat or topaque (formerly tokay). The table wines are in a different category altogether, principally sold through the cellar door at low prices. Exports to all major markets.

**chambourcin** is a red grape hybrid (not to be confused with a cross) which first appeared in France in 1963, briefly becoming popular in the cooler and wetter parts of Muscadet; it is now on the wane there. Like all hybrids, it is strongly resistant to the mildews. It has high yields and produces a remarkably intensely coloured wine. For the coastal regions of New South Wales, notably the Hastings River, propagating it makes sense; why wineries in 'normal' climates should plant it, and use it for vintage port, is beyond me. The Achilles heel of the variety is a marked lack of structure on the back palate and a very short finish.

**chaptalisation** involves the addition of sugar to fermenting wine to increase its alcohol level. At one time there was a push towards legalising it in Australia, but no more.

**character** is a tasting term usually linked to a given grape variety (that is, varietal character), or terroir (regional character).

**chardonnay** is by far the most important white grape/white wine in Australia, and will always be so. In terms of both hectares planted and tonnes produced, it accounts for around 45 per cent of all white grape/wine production. It has been demonised by wine writers and the café set shrilling 'Anything But Chardonnay' (the ABC Club), but in truth, the real ABC Club is 'Always Brings Cash'. There is a gulf between Australia's chardonnay styles. There is the 'sunshine in a bottle' style, which was the chief weapon in Australia's armoury as it raced from the rear of the field to fourth place in the world exporters league, and those who continue to buy it have no interest in the barbs increasingly thrown at it by UK journalists. At the other end of the scale, the best Australian chardonnays are among the best in the world, the foremost regions being the Margaret River, Yarra Valley, Mornington Peninsula and Adelaide Hills. The contrast between the richness, texture, depth and complexity of Margaret River chardonnays and the elegant, intense and very long palate of Yarra Valley chardonnays neatly demonstrates the impact of terroir. Winemakers are also having their say, some veering towards the flinty, minerally, low-oaked chablis style, others towards the more opulent, layered and complex Burgundian style, with a degree of funkiness part of the picture; in the middle is what might be the new classic Australian style, the apparent contradiction in these words denoting the style midpoint and the wonderful balance and mouthfeel of these wines. All three styles should be in any serious Australian wine cellar.

**Charles Melton** (est. 1984) was established by Charlie Melton, one of the Barossa Valley's great characters, who made a particular name for himself with his Chateau Neuf du Pape–inspired Nine Popes; he was also one of three voices crying in the wilderness (the other two being Turkey Flat and Geoff

Merrill), producing beautiful rosés which no one wanted to know about. Within a blink of an eye, rosé was on everyone's lips, one of the rare cases in which fashion and substance act synergistically, for chilled rosé is an ideal Australian summer drink for the widest possible range of food. Charlie's shiraz and cabernet sauvignon do not let him down. Exports to all major markets.

**Charles Sturt University Winery** (est. 1977) is the only commercially successful student winery (under the direction of a full-time, experienced winemaker). The now-defunct Roseworthy campus winery is the most obvious failure, not to mention the University of Sydney's campus in Orange, which Charles Sturt University acquired. Thus a new $2.5 million commercial winery was opened in 2002, complementing the $1 million experimental winery opened the previous year. (Between 1977 and 2001 a much smaller winery had been used.) Charles Sturt University regularly produces wines which are infinitely better than their price point would suggest, making full use of the 11 ha of vineyard at Wagga Wagga and 18 ha in Orange, and supplemented to a small degree by grapes purchased from other regions in the Southern New South Wales Zone.

**chasselas** has one claim to fame – it is France's most common white table grape – but in Switzerland (where it is known as *fendant*) it is regarded as a high-quality wine grape. Elsewhere in Europe its high yield denies any claim to high quality. Intriguingly, there is some evidence that it may have been the first variety cultivated by man. There were around

100 ha in production in Australia in 1976, with the Grampians in Victoria its principal base, and Seppelt (up to the 1960s) its most distinguished producer. Since then it has spread (in very small quantities) to the Swan District and the Northern Rivers Zone.

**Chatto Wines** (est. 2000) has always been a lesser part of Jim Chatto's winemaking responsibilities. His early years were spent as winemaker at Rosevears Estate in Tasmania, after which he moved to the Hunter Valley to become one of the two senior winemakers at Monarch Winemaking Services, and thereafter at Pepper Tree Wines. He has a quite exceptional palate, and is a deadly accurate wine show judge, which explains why his wines (pinot noir from Tasmania, semillon and shiraz from the Hunter Valley, and riesling from the Canberra District) are so consistently excellent. Exports to the US and Canada.

**chenin blanc** is a white grape variety which has produced magnificent wines in the Loire Valley for over 500 years. The wines are noted for their extreme longevity (examples over 100 years old the author has tasted have been awe-inspiring); 1921 and 1947 produced wines of similar quality, and potential longevity, if properly cellared and periodically recorked. Everywhere else in the world, most notably in the Napa Valley and Australia, the grape produces a bland wine with many similarities to verdelho. Only in South Africa and Western Australia (mainly the Swan District but also Margaret River) does it produce a wine with minor pretensions to quality: lightly oaked wines can gain complexity for up to 10 years. Its plantings have remained roughly constant

over the last 10 years, in no small measure due to its position as the highest yielding variety of the recognised quality grapes.

**Cheviot Bridge** (est. 1998) brings together a highly experienced team of wine industry professionals and investors who provided the $10 million–plus required to purchase the Long Flat range of wines from Tyrrell's in 2003. Most of the business activity is that of a virtual winery, acquiring bulk and/or bottled wine from various third-party suppliers. The brands include Cheviot Bridge Yea Valley, Cheviot Bridge CB, Kissing Bridge, Thirsty Lizard, Long Flat and Terrace Vale. Exports to all major markets.

**cinsaut** was a once-popular red grape variety (mainly for its high yield) but is now in fast retreat around the world. Its stronghold was the Languedoc in the south of France, followed by South Africa, where it was the most important red variety until the end of the 1960s. There, crossed with pinot noir, it produced the country's ubiquitous pinotage. Its cause in Australia has not been helped by the fact that it was known as oeillade in Langhorne Creek (a name used by Lindemans) and blue imperial in Rutherglen. In this context it is of small moment that it is often spelt 'cinsault'. There are no more than eight growers in Australia, Chambers Rosewood and Morris being the most notable.

**citric acid** is abundant in citrus fruits (hardly surprising) but rare in grapes. In Australia, if acidification is required, it will be mainly achieved through the addition of tartaric acid, but minor, last-minute adjustments can involve the addition of citric acid, particularly in white wines.

**clairette**  (incorrectly known as blanquette) is a white grape variety which was once widely planted in the Hunter Valley, but its naturally low acidity has led to all but one grower (Honeytree Estate) abandoning it. Ironically, Honeytree's plantings are increasing, and there are scattered, small plantings elsewhere in Australia.

**Clare riesling**  see crouchen.

**Clare Valley,**  gazetted 25 March 1999, can best be seen through the eyes of the legendary Mick Knappstein, who said, 'There are only two kinds of people: those who were born in Clare, and those who wished they were born in Clare.' As you enter the valley from the south, and proceed due north through the towns of Auburn, Leasingham, Watervale and Penwortham, in the pinched valley through which the Main North Road runs, the sense of history is almost claustrophobic. If you seek release by deviating to the west or east, and follow the roads which, in both instances, run parallel to the Main North Road, history becomes even more palpable. Inevitably, albeit somewhat sadly, the town of Clare itself has been largely emasculated by 20th-century changes.

The region was first settled by John Horrocks in 1840, who arrived one year after it had been explored by Edward John Eyre on his way north. Horrocks established a 400-ha property which he named Hope Farm, and directed his manservant, James Green, to plant some vines. In 1842 Horrocks returned briefly to England and, while passing through the Cape of Good Hope, arranged for a further consignment of vine cuttings to be sent to Hope Farm. He died prematurely in 1846, aged 28, from an accidental gunshot wound sustained while exploring the country north of Spencer Gulf; thus ended a life very full of promise. Clare became a thriving frontier town, successfully supported by copper, wheat, silver and processed fruit booms before viticulture moved to centre stage.

In the 19th century shiraz, cabernet sauvignon and malbec dominated plantings, but in the first 60 years of the 20th century those varieties were largely replaced by high-yielding grenache, pedro ximinez, crouchen, mourvedre, doradillo, muscadelle, muscat gordo blanco and frontignac, all headed to end use in fortified wine. The only survivors from the 19th century were shiraz and cabernet sauvignon with 12 ha, while malbec disappeared into the category 'mixed red'.

The Clare Valley of the 21st century started to take shape from the mid-1960s. Its climate remains as challenging as ever, with derisory growing season rainfall of only 200 millimetres, and an extreme diurnal temperature range in mid-summer and early autumn as the grapes ripen. It ought to be exclusively red wine country, but in fact makes some of Australia's finest and longest lived riesling, the answer to the paradox lying in the cold nights. Nonetheless, extreme vine stress and defoliation by the time the grapes are picked is common.

With the exception of the open expanses of the Polish Hill River to the west, and Auburn to the south, the region is broken into a series of subvalleys running in every direction, with numerous creeks or creek beds. The higher altitude or west-facing slopes often produce the best vineyard sites in this very beautiful region. The soils vary, but are by and large excellent, red to brown-grey in colour, and with a significant limestone content, particularly in the more southerly subregions. That the region can be sustained without irrigation is a testament to the quality of the soil; shiraz, cabernet sauvignon and riesling provide the best grapes and hence the best wines; for inscrutable reasons, the Clare Valley is just about the only region where chardonnay struggles to express itself. The best wineries are Annie's Lane, Grosset, Jim Barry, Kilikanoon, Knappstein, Leasingham, Mount Horrocks, O'Leary Walker, Pikes, Sevenhill Cellars, Stringy Brae of Sevenhill, Taylors, Wendouree and Wilson Vineyard. Wendouree is one of the living national treasures of Australia, fiercely and single-mindedly guarded by the reclusive Tony and Lita Brady.

LAT 33°50′S; ALT 400–500 m; HDD 1770; GSR 200 mm; MJT 21.9°C; HARV Early March to late April; CHIEF VIT. HAZARDS Frost; drought

**clarification** can be used both in the treatment of white juice prior to fermentation, and in both red and white wines after fermentation. Bentonite is the most common form of product used to clarify white grape juice, and egg whites are the most gentle form of clarification of red wines (but lead to the need for disclosure on the back label).

**classic** is a word used with enthusiasm by wine writers (the author included) seeking to describe a wine conforming exactly to style and of very high quality, but it does have oxymoronic overtones.

**clean** sounds somewhat banal, but means the absence of any foreign or 'off' odour or flavour, which is an important aspect of a wine of quality.

**climate** is, in the final analysis, regarded by the majority of Australian winemakers as the most important factor in determining wine quality, effectively relegating terroir to second place; this is the opposite view to that held by French (conspicuously) and other European winemakers. The broadest definition of terroir does in fact include some, but not all, of the elements of climate.

Scientific or mathematical measurement of climate affecting the growth of the vine dates back to 1735 and thence to the observation by de Candolle in the mid-19th century that there is little vegetative growth in the vine at temperatures below 10°C. Professors Amerine and Winkler took this as a starting point, by taking the difference between 10°C and the mean temperature of the month, multiplying that difference by the number of days in the month, and then adding the resultant figures for each of the seven growing season months. The result was described as heat degree days.

The first adaptation and expansion of the Amerine and Winkler system was that of Dr Richard Smart and Dr Peter Dry, in 'A Climatic Classification for Australian Viticultural Regions' (*Australian Grapevines and Winemakers*, April 1980, pp. 8–16), in which they proposed that the mean January temperature was as important as, if not more important than, heat degree days, but also added measures of annual rainfall, growing season rainfall, relative humidity, sunshine hours per day, continentality and an aridity index (the gap between the growing season water requirements of the vine and growing season rainfall). The one measure they did not cover was wind, which has a profound influence (most vividly exposed by Carneros and the Salinas Valley in California).

**climate change**  will have different implications for the wine industry than for other Australian businesses. At the outset, and perhaps continuously, it will be important to understand to what degree changed rainfall patterns are part of long-term drought cycles rather than being due to climate change. Permanent loss of water from the Murray Darling system would have a greater impact on viticulture than increased temperatures. Likewise, increasing salinity will progressively reduce the value of water, ultimately to the point where it would kill the vines if used for irrigation.

That said, there are many measures which will probably be used to combat drier, hotter growing conditions. If suitable water is available, it will be applied through underground drip systems with sophisticated moisture measurement devices. Heavy mulching will be established along the vine rows, and as much leaf canopy as possible will be retained. At the present time, north-facing slopes with maximum sun interception are considered the best. In the future, south-facing slopes may be preferred if the object is to retain the same varietal plantings. Likewise, cooler and wetter vintages may give better outcomes than warmer, drier years.

A premium will be placed on regions or subregions that are within 30 kilometres of the coast (especially the Southern Ocean) and have an average rainfall of 700 millimetres, or are at elevations of 1000 metres. In the most extreme scenario, the varietal mix will change, with a shift to later-ripening varieties.

The foregoing is based on the premise that the 'settled science' propagated by the Intergovernmental Panel on Climate Change is indeed settled. A considerable number of scientists, and others interested in the topic, believe the science is far from settled, and challenge the anthropogenic, carbon-based global warming thesis. The recipient of the 2008 Maurice O'Shea Award for outstanding contribution to the wine industry was Dr John Gladstones. He has long been a sceptic of the IPCC's 'settled science', and robustly challenges the idea that rising temperatures and increased $CO_2$ spell doom for the planet. His thesis is that if there were to be a 1°C warming of the earth over, say, the next 50 years, and this warming were coupled with a continuing increase in $CO_2$ levels in the atmosphere, vines (and all other plants and trees) would benefit from those changed conditions. In the case of vines, sugar surplus to the vines' requirement for ripening the grapes would become available, and would be partly or wholly converted into enzymes within the grape, which would increase varietal flavour. He thus suggests that for at least some varieties, this scenario could favour a shift to warmer areas, not cooler areas. However, once the rise in temperature were significantly above 1°C, a tipping point would be reached, and thereafter the more conventional scenario for future plantings and vineyard management would prevail. For further information see Ian Plimer's *Heaven and Earth – Global Warming: The Missing Science.*

**Clonakilla** (est. 1971) was founded at Murrumbateman in the Canberra District by scientist Dr John Kirk. Winemaker son Tim Kirk has since taken Clonakilla to the top of the small winery (6500 cases) quality tree in Australia, pioneering the structured use of viognier co-fermented with shiraz. He has a worldview of wine style and quality, and has been exceptionally generous in making his wines (and those Rhône Valley wines which he most admires) available for educational purposes. Exports to all major markets.

**clonal selection** is the propagation of a superior vine, with several generations ultimately producing a very large number of vines of the same clone. The antithesis of this is the deliberate selection of vines with different physical characteristics (in Europe called *sélection massale*). The aim of the latter is twofold: to guard against any single factor which may impact on one (presumed) clone among several in the vineyard, and in the winery to give greater complexity to the finished wine.

**clone** is a single vine or a population of vines all sharing a single mother vine, and theoretically identical to each other. Propagation is by cuttings or buds, not by seed germination. The term is often loosely used to describe vines of a given variety which appear physically distinct from others. However, until DNA profiling takes the next step it is not possible to say with absolute certainty whether those apparent differences are due to the physical circumstances in which the vine has been growing over a protracted period of time, or the action of viruses, or genetic mutation.

**Clovely Estate** (est. 1998) has the largest vineyards in Queensland, having established 174 ha of immaculately maintained vines at two locations just to the east of Murgon in the South Burnett. There are 127 ha of red grapes (including 74 ha of shiraz) and 47 ha of white grapes. The 30,000-case production is released under a number of labels at various price points, some primarily designed for the export market to the UK and other major destinations.

**Clover Hill** (est. 1986) was established by Taltarni in Northern Tasmania with the sole purpose of making a premium sparkling wine. It has 21.7 ha of vineyards: 13.1 ha of chardonnay, 7.3 ha of pinot noir and 1.24 ha of pinot meunier. The sparkling wine quality is excellent, combining finesse with power and length. The 6-ha Lalla Gully property is situated in a sheltered amphitheatre, with a site climate 1°–2°C warmer than Clover Hill, and thus the fruit ripening a week or so earlier. Exports to the UK, the US and other major markets.

**cloying** describes the palate and finish of a sweet wine with insufficient acidity to provide balance.

**coarse** indicates a wine with excessive extract of solids, particularly tannins, and which may have been affected by oxidation during the making process.

**cold-settle** is a technique used to clarify white grape juice prior to fermentation. It relies purely on taking the temperature of the juice in tank to below 5°C, and then racking the juice off the solids which fall to the bottom of the tank. It is a natural alternative to filtration.

**cold soak** see pre-fermentation maceration.

**Coldstream Hills** (est. 1985) was founded by the author, who continues to be involved as a consultant. It was acquired by Southcorp in mid-1996, and is thus now a small part of Foster's Wine Estates. It has 100 ha of owned or managed Yarra Valley estate vineyards as the base. Chardonnay and pinot noir are the principal focus; merlot came on-stream in 1997, sauvignon blanc around the same time, reserve shiraz later still. Vintage conditions permitting, chardonnay, pinot noir and cabernet sauvignon are made in both varietal and reserve form, the latter in restricted quantities. It has been a prolific winner of trophies and gold medals over the decades. Exports to the UK, the US and Singapore.

**colombard** is the third most important grape variety in the Charente (Cognac) area of France, and has the ability to retain high levels of natural acidity even when grown in warm climates and heavily cropped. Brown Brothers pioneered its use in Australia, and it remains an important component of 'bag in box' wines; its average yield is higher than all other white varieties, which propels it into third place behind chardonnay and semillon. The only producer continuing to make quality colombard is Primo Estate, albeit with the judicious inclusion of some sauvignon blanc.

**condition** is a technical term to describe the clarity of the wine; a cloudy wine is described as being out of condition.

**Constellation Wines Australia** see CWA.

**continental, continentality** of a region is the measure of the difference between the average mean temperature of its hottest month and that of its coldest month, with a high diurnal range also making its presence felt. Climates with a wide range are called continental; those with a narrow range, maritime. Continental climates tend to be in the interiors of larger continents, while maritime climates are near oceans or large bodies of water. The split between continental and maritime climates in Australia is roughly equal. The possibility of frost needs to be met by careful site selection (for example, steep slopes).

**Coonawarra** (an Aboriginal word meaning honeysuckle), gazetted 6 January 2003, in the Limestone Coast Zone, can be grouped with the Haut Medoc of Bordeaux to prove the exception to the rule that almost all of the foremost wine regions of the world have landscapes of great beauty. Coonawarra is Australia's outstanding cabernet sauvignon region, once again placing it alongside the Haut Medoc; when you then consider the aristocratic and often austere nature of cabernet sauvignon the two regions' essentially bleak landscapes actually seem appropriate. The Haut Medoc, at least, has its chateaux to provide some relief; Coonawarra only has Wynns Coonawarra Estate, a lasting testimonial to Coonawarra's founder, John Riddoch. In 1890 Riddoch set up the Penola Fruit Colony, based on the subdivision of the area into 4-ha blocks, and built the large winery (now Wynns) to vinify the grapes.

With a heat degree summation of

1430, Coonawarra was the first cool-climate viticultural region to gain national prominence. Due to limited maritime influence, the winters are cold, wet and windy, and throughout much of the growing season the night-time temperatures are low. In almost all vintages Coonawarra receives intermittent bursts of very hot weather in February and March; the other problems in a basically favourable climate are wind and rain during flowering, and spring frosts.

Australian wine writer Dr WS Benwell observed that Coonawarra 'lies between Melbourne and Adelaide, but is never quite on the way between the two cities, no matter which way one goes'. Bill Redman, every bit as much a father of Coonawarra as John Riddoch, once wrote that 'From 1890 to 1945 you can write failure across the face of Coonawarra.' In the first half of the 20th century it very nearly succumbed to a vine pull scheme, and to the near purchase of what is now Wynns Coonawarra Estate by the Woods and Forest Department of South Australia. By the time the Geographic Indications legislation was put in place, Coonawarra's terra rossa (limestone-based soils turned red by the oxidation of iron impurities in the topsoil) had been universally recognised as the greatest terroir for cabernet sauvignon in Australia. The soil is extremely friable and well drained; the adjoining soils to the west and east are far less suited to viticulture. If one were cynical, it should have come as no surprise to find that a long drawn-out, incredibly expensive and ultimately futile war erupted over the region's boundaries; it was finally determined by the court of appeal to extend from the South Australian/Victorian border on the east to a similar north–south line

on the west, with a couple of odd protrusions. The court took the view that the broadest possible boundaries should be drawn, but chose to exclude St Mary's to the west of Penola.

While the area may be dead flat and devoid of obvious beauty, it is ideally suited – many would argue altogether too suited – to low-cost, broadacre viticulture with a high degree of mechanisation. Happily, the ugly spectre of what were euphemistically called minimally pruned vines (giving rise to a blackened jumble of canes looking rather like porcupines in winter) is no longer typical. The vast majority (90 per cent) of the plantings are red, with cabernet sauvignon, shiraz and merlot leading the way; riesling is the most important white variety, followed by chardonnay. There are 35 wineries in the region, led by Balnaves of Coonawarra, Brand's Laira, Jamiesons Run, Katnook Estate, Ladbroke Grove, Leconfield, Lindemans, Majella, Murdock, Parker Coonawarra Estate, Penley Estate, Punters Corner, Wynns Coonawarra Estate and Zema Estate.

LAT 37˚18'S; ALT 60 m; HDD 1430; GSR 220 mm; MJT 19.6˚C; HARV Early March to early May; CHIEF VIT. HAZARDS Spring frost; poor fruit set

cordon cut  wines are made from grapes which have partially dessicated (becoming significantly sweeter) on the vine. This is achieved by cutting either the individual cane with bunches attached, or one of the main growing arms (cordons) with multiple canes attached. The part of the vine that is detached seeks to sustain itself by absorbing water from the bunches.

Coriole  (est. 1967), established by Mark Lloyd, is one of the foremost producers of shiraz in McLaren Vale. Shiraz may be its major wine, particularly the Lloyd Reserve, but it was one of the first wineries to seriously tackle sangiovese, more recently adding barbera and nebbiolo (from the Adelaide Hills) to its portfolio. Exports to the UK, the US and other major markets.

**corked** is a generic term used to describe a wine adversely affected by cork taint. In most instances the cause is a mould formed when chlorine in the environment interacts with organic phenols to create 2, 4, 6-trichloranisole (or TCA). The TCA may have its origins in the forest, in the cork manufacture process, in the shipment, or in the winery, the second being by far the most common. The mouldy character it gives to the wine can be detected by humans in minute concentrations, measured in parts per trillion. Cork producers, led by Portuguese companies, have radically changed all the handling processes of cork bark from the time it is stripped from the trees, having previously long denied that TCA was a significant problem. It was this denial which led Australia and New Zealand to follow the path of Switzerland and move en masse from one-piece cork to other closures, principally screwcaps. Ironically, the move was driven more by issues of random oxidation, seen as far more damaging and widespread than TCA taint, the incidence of which has been reduced by the changes in production protocol.

**corks**, obviously enough, are made from the bark of the cork tree, *Quercus suber*. Natural cork is a quite extraordinary substance, with around 40 million gas-filled hexagonal cells per cubic centimetre, which explains why

it has proved very difficult to create a man-made equivalent using plastic/polymers. Its longevity is demonstrated by fishermen's floats for nets still bobbing in the Dead Sea several thousand years after their initial immersion; its resilience and toughness are exemplified by industrial uses from cork floor tiles to women's shoes to car engine gaskets. Nonetheless, the fact remains that the union of cork and glass is a 350-year-old technology, and it is hardly surprising that alternative closures have been developed. The most common is the screwcap; it has the huge advantage of being affixed to the exterior of the bottle neck, not the interior. The interior is in a molten stage in the mould, while the exterior is formed by direct contact with the mould. Thus the specifications for the exterior can be precisely determined to extremely fine tolerances, the screwcap likewise. A number of products have been developed as halfway houses between natural one-piece cork and synthetics. The most common of these has involved granulating cork, binding it with a special glue and placing discs of normal cork at each end of the agglomerate body. This Twin Top® was developed by Amorim, the largest cork producer. An Australian invention places a complex but very thin multi-layer membrane on the outside of the cork, designed to trap any TCA (see corked) within the membrane barrier (ProCork®).

The most promising, although still without a long-term track record, is Diam®; here the cork bark is ground to the consistency of flour, subjected to super-critical $CO_2$ at a temperature of $-31°C$ and under enormous (72-bar) pressure – in this state it has the penetration power of a gas and the extraction power of a liquid. When the pressure returns to normal, the $CO_2$ has removed any taint from the cork, leaving no trace behind. The process was developed by the French Atomic Energy Commission on behalf of Oeneo, then the second-largest cork producer, which has since sold its traditional cork manufacturing business, and put all its eggs in the Diam basket.

The most recent closure is Vin-o-Lok®, a clear glass stopper with a small silicon O-ring at the upper end which fits into the bottle, and locks with a very fine rim on the inside. It is visually elegant, and can be replaced as easily and quickly as a screwcap, but its long-term seal capacity has yet to be demonstrated. Both screwcaps and Diams can be (and are) made with differing levels of oxygen permeability, giving rise to the 21st-century possibility of making wine in the bottle. While most of the changes of age are anaerobic, the greater amount of oxygen finding its way past or through the closure, the more rapid that change will be.

**cortese** is a relatively obscure Italian white grape, mainly associated with Piedmont, but also grown elsewhere; the modesty of its quality is even greater than its rarity. Produced by Lost Valley Winery, Upper Goulburn.

**Cowra**, gazetted 16 October 1998, is the southernmost region in the Central Ranges Zone (the other two regions are Mudgee and Orange), which might suggest that it is the coolest; in fact, it is the warmest, due to its lower altitude and by and large flat landscape.

The first vines were planted in 1973 by Cowra Estate, and the region grew rapidly on the back of chardonnay, which remains its dominant variety. The climate is hot and dry,

with the mean January temperature between 23.5°C and 24.4°C, significantly above that of Cessnock (Hunter Valley) or Mudgee. Growing season rainfall is relatively high, but relative humidity is low, reflecting the continental nature of the climate. Spring frosts mean appropriate site selection is required. The soils are those most commonly found throughout southeast Australia: brownish loamy sand to clay loam on the surface, with red clay subsoils. They are moderately acidic, and moderately fertile. Overall wine quality is adequate, but no more, and a considerable proportion of the grape production is sold either as grapes or bulk wine to wineries in other parts of Australia. Of the 17 wineries, Cowra Estate (the largest), Hamiltons Bluff, Mulyan, Wallington and Windowrie Estate (with the highest quality wines) are the best known.

LAT 33°57'S; ALT 300–380 m; HDD 2130; GSR 370 mm; MJT 23.5°C; HARV Early March to early April; CHIEF VIT. HAZARD Spring frost

**Craiglee** (est. 1864), in Sunbury, was established by James S Johnston, a member of the Victorian Parliament and one of the founders of the *Argus* newspaper. He planted 7 ha, initially to a large number of varieties, but he ultimately rationalised these to concentrate on shiraz and riesling. In common with most of the cool-climate regions of Australia, it went out of production in the late 1920s, but the four-storey bluestone winery (using gravity wherever possible) is still in immaculate condition, although the ever-vigilant Department of Health has decreed that the Carmody family (who purchased the property from the Johnstons in 1961) cannot use it for winemaking as (strange though it may seem) it does not conform to present-day health regulations.

The 1872 Hermitage (10.5% alc/vol) won an award in Vienna, and a cache of the wine was discovered in the winery in the 1950s. It was sold by the leading wine merchant of the day, Tom Seabrook. Tasting by the author of a number of bottles over the decades showed some to be remarkably fresh and wonderful to taste, others (unsurprisingly) tired and oxidised.

Son Pat Carmody persuaded the family to re-establish the vineyard in 1976, and has made a succession of quite beautiful cool-climate shirazs, with a mix of intense red and black berry fruits plus generous amounts of licorice and spice. While shiraz dominates the 10 ha vineyards, sauvignon blanc, chardonnay, viognier, pinot noir and cabernet sauvignon are also planted, the most significant being chardonnay. Exports to the UK, the US, Hong Kong and Italy.

**Craigow**  (est. 1989) was established by Barry and Cathy Edwards in the Coal River area of southern Tasmania, northeast of Hobart. It has 10 ha of vineyards, selling part of the grapes, and has gradually extended the range of varieties to encompass riesling, chardonnay, pinot noir, sauvignon blanc and late-harvest gewurztraminer. Back vintages of riesling are usually available, demonstrating exceptional cellaring capacity.

**Crawford River Wines**  (est. 1975) was the first winery to follow Seppelt's Drumborg Vineyard in the region now officially known as Henty; Seppelt planted its first vines in 1964, and local grazier John Thomson began the development of Crawford River in 1975. He undertook the external winemaking course at what was then called Riverina College of Advanced Education (now Charles Sturt University), and right from the outset demonstrated exceptional talent, most obviously in the winery, but also in coming to grips with the at times very challenging climate. His rieslings are always among the best in Australia, particularly in those years when a reserve version is released, though this should not be seen to demean the standard riesling, nor the Young Vines Riesling. An excellent sauvignon blanc semillon seldom misses, but cabernet merlot is dependent on warmer vintages for success. Finally, the Nektar is a glorious late-harvest style. Exports to the UK, Ireland, Canada, Japan and Southeast Asia.

**Croser, Brian, AO**  (1949–) has had what can only be described as a stellar career in the Australian wine industry. Having obtained a Bachelor of Agricultural Science degree from the University of Adelaide (in 1969) he was employed by Thomas Hardy, who sponsored his postgraduate degree at the University of California, Davis (the nearby town of Petaluma providing him with the name for his future winery). He returned to become chief winemaker at Thomas Hardy, making a benchmark Siegersdorf Riesling in 1975. He moved again in 1976, to set up the former Riverina College of Advanced Education (now Charles Sturt University) course in wine science and viticulture. That year also saw his establishment of Petaluma. In 1985 he set up a separately owned vineyard and winery (Argyle) in Oregon, which he and his family still own. In 2002 he joined with Jean-Michel Cazes of

Chateau Lynch-Bages in Pauillac, Bordeaux, and Société Jacques Bollinger, the parent company of Champagne Bollinger, to establish Tapanappa.

Throughout his adult life he has been a wine show judge and educator; he is a past president of the Winemakers' Federation of Australia, the Australian Winemaker's Forum, and the Australian Society of Viticulture and Oenology. He received the prestigious Maurice O'Shea Award in 1997 for his outstanding contribution to the Australian wine industry; he was made an Officer of the Order of Australia in 2000; and he served as deputy chancellor of the University of Adelaide from 1999 to 2008, receiving an Honorary Doctorate in 2007, having much earlier received the same award from Charles Sturt University.

**cross, cross-breeding, or crossing,** is used to describe a new variety made by crossing two *Vitis vinifera* species. The CSIRO has developed several such crosses, the foremost being tarrango (touriga/sultana), commercially used by Brown Brothers to produce a light, fresh red wine. Tyrian (cabernet sauvignon/sumoll) has been used by McWilliam's to make a vintage port style; and cienna (sumoll/cabernet sauvignon) by Brown Brothers and Yalumba for light-bodied wines.

**cross-flow filtration** encompasses reverse osmosis, ultra-filtration and micro-filtration; the last is the technique under discussion here. The wine or juice to be filtered flows across the membrane filter surface, which consists of many fine-bore tubes. Some of the stream will pass through the pores of the membrane as filtrate, while the remainder flows back to the vessel holding the unfiltered liquid, and is termed 'retentate'. The continual cross-flow helps to prevent the build-up of particulate matter, with consequent blockage of the filtration surface. Because the liquid is not forced through the filter membrane, it is in fact very gentle, and is now used with high-quality wines. See filtration.

**crouchen,** incorrectly called Clare riesling in the Clare Valley, where it happened to be quite widely planted, produces there (as anywhere) a somewhat coarse wine given to rapid oxidation.

**crusher** is a basic piece of winery equipment which removes the stalks from the grape bunches and splits the berries, resulting in a mix of juice, skins and pips (collectively known as must).

**crusher-destemmer** removes the stalks but, theoretically, does not split or break the berries. Most crusher-destemmers can be set in either mode, and the use of the destemmer is normally restricted to red wines. An alternative for white grapes is to bypass the crusher/crusher-destemmer altogether, and be taken directly to the press for whole bunch pressing.

**crust,** strictly speaking, is the heavy sediment which forms in vintage port over a period of several years. However, it can also be produced by red table wines thanks to the continuing polymerisation of tannins. It can either adhere to the sides of the bottle or fall to the bottom, in which case the wine should be decanted. Although it does not diminish the flavour, crust alters the texture of the wine in the mouth. Over decades, it may in some circumstances strip the wine of its essential character.

**Cullen Wines** (est. 1971) is one of the leading wineries of the Margaret River region, established by Dr Kevin Cullen and wife Diana. When Kevin died in 1994, Diana took over as chief winemaker, before passing the baton on (many years before her death in 2003) to her immensely talented daughter Vanya. Under Vanya's care, the vineyard gained certified organic status before moving on to biodynamic certification, and, subsequent to that, became the first vineyard and winery in Australia to be certified as carbon neutral. While Cullen Wines makes the greatest cabernet merlots in Australia, the quality of its chardonnay and sauvignon blanc semillon is also quite exceptional. The more recently introduced Mangan Vineyard wines have seamlessly fed into the portfolio. The 20,000-case production means that limited quantities of Cullen wines are exported to all the major markets, and are likewise to be found on the wine lists of Australia's best restaurants.

**Cumulus Wines** (est. 1995), in the Orange region, began life with a complicated tax investment scheme supporting the establishment of its vineyards, which proved its undoing when the commissioner of taxation denied the expected tax advantages. It has over 500 ha of vineyards planted at various altitudes, and a 14,000-tonne capacity winery. The acquisition of a 51 per cent share by the large Berardo Group of Portugal (with numerous world-size wine investments in Portugal, Canada and Madeira)

should see long-term stability, and underpin the strong export focus for the 200,000-case production. The quality of the pinot gris, chardonnay, shiraz, merlot and cabernet sauvignon has been good, but one has the feeling that there is more to come as the vines mature. Exports to the UK and the US.

**Curlewis Winery** (est. 1998) is among the foremost producers in the Geelong region. Owners Rainer Brett and Wendy Oliver purchased the property in 1996, with 1.6 ha of pinot noir that had been planted in 1985. Those plantings have since been extended, mainly by pinot noir, but also with chardonnay and some shiraz. Self-confessed 'pinotphile', Brett uses all the tricks of the pinot trade: cold soaking, hot fermentation, post-fermentation maceration, part inoculated and part wild yeasts, prolonged lees contact and bottling neither fined nor filtered. It is a high-risk game to produce wines of exceptional complexity, but so far the winery has achieved precisely what was desired. Exports to Canada, Sweden, Malaysia, Singapore and Hong Kong.

**Curly Flat** (est. 1991) stands shoulder to shoulder with Bindi Wine Growers in making the finest chardonnay and pinot noir in the Macedon Ranges region. Phillip and Jeni Moraghan have painstakingly established 8.5 ha of pinot noir, 3.4 ha of chardonnay and 0.6 ha of pinot gris, with the same fanatical attention to the vines as that of Bindi. A multi-level gravity-flow winery handles the 5000-case production with minimum impact on the immaculately made wines. The second label of Williams Crossing can also be of great quality. Exports to the UK, Japan and Hong Kong.

**Currency Creek**, gazetted 9 October 2001, is a strongly maritime region in South Australia contiguous on its northern border with the much better known Langhorne Creek. The eastern border is defined by Lake Alexandrina and the south faces Encounter Bay; a substantial area of the region is taken up by the Finniss River, the Goolwa or Lower Murray, and the Goolwa Channel, theoretically the mouth of the Murray River – theoretically because the water level is now below that of Encounter Bay, and the mouth is blocked.

The region was first explored by Captain Charles Sturt, who travelled down the Murray River in 1829–30, and whose last campsite was near the present town of Goolwa, which was the first (or last, depending on which way you were travelling) port on the Murray River. In 1837 Hindmarsh Island and the town of Currency Creek were officially named, and an elaborate town plan for the latter was laid out in 1840.

Agriculture, river transport and recreation developed over the next 50 years, but it was not until 1969 that the first vines were planted, by Wally and Rosemary Tonkin: 0.4 ha each of riesling, grenache, shiraz and cabernet sauvignon. Despite local cynicism, the vines flourished and the first vintage followed in 1972, for what was then called Santa Rosa Winery (now Currency Creek Estate). In that same year the first vines (2.6 ha) were planted at what is now Middleton Winery; they were likewise successful.

Hindmarsh Island constitutes a significant part of the region and was the subject of a celebrated and long-running battle over Aboriginal 'secret women's business' which opposed the idea of a bridge linking the island to the mainland. The bridge was ultimately constructed.

Towards the end of the first decade of the 21st century, Currency Creek is gripped by the well-known near collapse of the Murray Darling River system, and is at the very end of the aquatic food chain. Unless and until Lake Alexandrina returns to somewhere near its original size, or the pipeline from the Murray River above the lowest weir which is bringing some water to Langhorne Creek, is extended, the outlook for the region is very uncertain.

The climate of Currency Creek is slightly warmer than that of Langhorne Creek and Coonawarra, on a par with that of Margaret River and California's Carneros. The region's very low growing season rainfall means that irrigation is essential. Dominant rolling sandy slopes (which allow easy infiltration of water) overlay friable cracking clays, which are easily accessed by the vines' roots. The other suitable soils are loams with red alkaline clayey subsoils.

The principal grape varieties, in descending order, are cabernet sauvignon, shiraz, merlot, sauvignon blanc, chardonnay and semillon. The principal wineries are Ballast Stone Estate, Currency Creek Estate, Middleton Wines and Salomon Estate.

LAT 35°29'S; ALT 50–70 m; HDD 1525; GSR 155 mm; MJT 18.5°C; HARV Early March to mid-April; CHIEF VIT. HAZARD Drought

**Cuttaway Hill Estate** (est. 1998) is one of the largest vineyard properties in the Southern Highlands, with a total of 38 ha on three vineyard sites. The original Cuttaway Hill vineyard at Mittagong has 17 ha of chardonnay, merlot, cabernet sauvignon and shiraz. The Allambie vineyard of 6.9 ha, on the light sandy loam soils of Ninety Acre Hill, is planted to sauvignon blanc, pinot gris and pinot noir. The third and newest vineyard is 14.2 ha at Maytree, west of Moss Vale, in a relatively drier and warmer mesoclimate. Here cabernet sauvignon, merlot and pinot noir (and a small amount of chardonnay) have been planted. The standard of both viticulture and contract winemaking is evident in the quality of the wines. Exports to the UK, the US, Canada and Ireland.

CWA is the Australian arm of the world's biggest wine group (Constellation Wines), encompassing the brands Banrock Station, Barossa Valley Estate, Bay of Fires, Brookland Valley, Chateau Reynella, Goundrey, Hardys, Houghton, Leasingham, Moondah Brook, Starvedog Lane, Stonehaven, Tintara and Yarra Burn.

a b c d e f g h i

j k l m n o p q

r s t u v w x y z

**Dalrymple** (est. 1987) was established by Dr Bertel Sundstrup after a long search for 'the perfect site', and over the next 20 years produced some excellent wines. The 12.3-ha Northern Tasmania vineyard and winery were purchased by Yalumba in 2007, and continue to produce high-quality sauvignon blanc and pinot noir.

**Dalwhinnie** (est. 1976) is, by some margin, the best winery in the Pyrenees. The estate-grown production of 4500 cases provides compelling chardonnay, shiraz and cabernet sauvignon, the quality underwritten by the erection of a 50-tonne high-tech winery in 2001. David and Jenny Jones are the proprietors; David is the winemaker, with some consultancy advice. The wines are represented in all the most important export markets.

**d'Arenberg** (est. 1912), in McLaren Vale, has reinvented itself on several occasions, with major changes in direction, but has always been in the ownership of the Osborn family. In 1912 Francis Osborn purchased the first vineyard; some of the vines had been planted in the 1890s. He was originally a grapegrower, before moving to make a vintage port and a massive dry red, with all the pressings returned, and sold to the Emu Wine Company for export to the UK. Francis's son d'Arenberg (universally known as d'Arry) joined his father in 1943, and had progressively taken over responsibility for the business before Francis' death in 1957. He decided the time had come for the winery to establish its own brand; he was determined to have a label which would make a statement, and with the Houghton White Burgundy label and its diagonal blue stripe as an influence, the striking d'Arenberg label, with a diagonal red stripe, was developed. However, it was not until 1965 that the first release appeared under the d'Arenberg label. It wasn't long before it became famous, thanks to the 1967 d'Arenberg Burgundy (mainly grenache) winning seven trophies and 25 gold medals. That might have been enough, but the 1968 cabernet sauvignon won the Jimmy Watson Trophy at Melbourne in 1969. d'Arenberg had well and truly arrived.

By 1983 production had risen to the then-significant level of around 38,000 cases, and d'Arry's son Chester, a Roseworthy graduate, had arrived. He progressively took over winemaking and management responsibilities. With the combined impact of continuing show success, energetic marketing (giving rise to the War and Peace back labels which, in time, became almost as important as the front label), a proliferation of clever names long before most of the competitors took notice, and ongoing marketing spin, d'Arenberg has reached the position where (with a 250,000-case production) it is among the most financially successful and high-profile family wineries in Australia, with exports to every conceivable market.

**dead fruit**, a term said to have been coined by Brian Croser, describes red grapes which have become overripe, often as a conscious decision by the viticultural/winemaking team seeking extra flavour, but losing freshness as a consequence.

**Deakin Estate** (est. 1980) in the Murray Darling is part of the Katnook Estate, Riddoch and Deakin Estate triumvirate, which constitutes the Wingara Wine Group, now 60 per cent owned by Freixenet of Spain. Deakin Estate draws on over 300 ha of its own vineyards, making it largely self-sufficient, and produces wines of consistent quality and impressive value. Exports to the UK, the US, Canada, NZ and Asia.

**De Bortoli**  (est. 1928) is one of the largest and most successful family companies in Australia. Vittorio De Bortoli left the Treviso region of northern Italy in 1924, at the age of 24, arriving at Griffith later the same year. He found his way to McWilliam's and worked at their Beelbangera winery until 1927, when he purchased a 22 ha farm at Bilbul, in the Riverina region, which remains De Bortoli's home property to this day. It included 3 ha of shiraz, but the market for grapes had collapsed after the removal of trade preferences with the UK. With nothing else to do, he made wine and established a market with Italian cane cutters returning from Queensland in the off-season, and managed to survive the Depression. It was still a minor business when Vittorio's son Deen took over management in 1959, a position he held until his death in 2003. By that year his reputation had grown beyond measure, as had production, rising from 436,000 litres in 1959 to 3.6 million litres in 1984, and to 27 million litres (3 million cases) by the turn of the century.

Success came as a result of the sheer hard work and total commitment of the De Bortoli family, including a constant watch on new winemaking developments (it was the first winery to install a Potter fermenter in Australia). By the early 1980s De Bortoli was making 60 different wines, using all of the varieties then available, including such relative rarities at the time as colombard and sauvignon blanc. The arrival of grandson Darren De Bortoli fresh from Roseworthy Agricultural College in 1982 saw the development of the highly botrytised semillon now known as Noble One, which, although produced in modest quantities, made the De Bortoli name famous in fine wine markets around the world. In 1987 De Bortoli moved into Victoria's Yarra Valley (see below) and in 2002 to the Hunter Valley.

**De Bortoli, Yarra Valley**  (est. 1987) has been run since its establishment by Leanne De Bortoli and husband Steve Webber, and has been every bit as successful in its own way as the parent company. Viewed with a certain amount of suspicion by some of the local wineries when it purchased Chateau Yarrinya, it has proved to be a model business in every way: scrupulous in its labelling; exceptionally diligent in rapidly expanding its estate vineyard holdings (by planting and acquisition); working tirelessly to promote the Yarra Valley as a whole as well as its own business; and forever thinking laterally about the development of appropriate wine styles in a cool environment. It offers varietal wines across four levels: at the bottom, Windy Peak, which is Victorian labelled, although it does often contain Yarra Valley components; Gulf Station, 100 per cent Yarra Valley, produced in part from contract-grown grapes and in part from estate-grown; estate varietals; and, at the top, reserve varietals. It is hard to choose between its chardonnay, pinot noir, shiraz and shiraz viognier at the top, as all are made with a deliberately gentle hand in the winery, and all offer value for money at their respective impressive price points. It is small wonder the winery's production has grown from less than 30,000 cases to 350,000 cases, penetrating all major export markets, but with particular success in the hardest market of all, the UK.

decant means to pour a bottle of wine into another vessel (usually, but not always, a specifically designed and made decanter) with several objects in mind. If it is an aged red wine, or an aged, barrel-matured white, it will separate the clear wine from sediment at the bottom of the bottle. This is particularly true when the bottle to be decanted has been stood upright for some days before the decanting process takes place, and where the process is a continuous one, not involving any interruption to the flow of the wine, and – in particular – not bringing the bottle back to a vertical position until all the wine has been poured out. A torch or candle placed directly underneath the neck of the bottle being decanted is highly desirable, allowing the process to stop immediately the first sediments are seen to start making their way towards the neck of the bottle. The second purpose of decanting is to deliberately introduce oxygen into the wine, albeit in limited quantities, particularly when the wine is old and may have developed reduced or other similar characteristics. The younger the wine, the more robust it is, and the more likely it will be to withstand the downside of aeration, notably oxidation.

There are three schools of thought on the timing of decanting. At the most extreme is the view of many Burgundian winemakers (and of Professor Emil Peynaud) that no wine should be decanted, because it necessarily results in the diffusion (via subtle oxidation) of some of the elements of the bouquet. The middle position says that decanting should be undertaken only when necessary, and then immediately before pouring the decanted wine into glasses. This view is summarised in the expression 'You can wait for wine, but the wine won't wait for you.' The third school of thought says that decanting should be undertaken several hours before the wine is poured into glasses. The legendary English wine merchant Ronald Avery (died 1976) believed in double decanting pre-phylloxera clarets the day prior to service, filling up the air space in the bottle with small marbles. Double decanting is pouring a wine into a decanter, rinsing out the bottle whence the wine came to remove sediment, and then pouring the contents back into the bottle.

de Castella, Charles Hubert (1825–1907), invariably called Hubert, is best known as the founder of St Huberts, and the author of two books, the first written and originally published in French in 1882 (and later translated into English), entitled *Notes of an Australian Wine Grower*, the second written in English and published in 1886, entitled *John Bull's Vineyard*.

Born of a wealthy family, and like younger brother Paul de Castella, Hubert had no viticultural experience before arriving in Victoria. Moreover, it was Paul who was the first to arrive (November 1849) and who persuaded Hubert that he should emigrate to Australia. For all his prominence, Hubert returned to Switzerland on several occasions, the first between 1856 and 1862, the second between 1886 and 1906. It was his return to Australia in 1862 which was pivotal; he had decided to establish a vineyard and winery, and he was able to purchase 1170 ha from Paul's creditors. The land was situated just to the east of the Yering homestead and he named the property St Huberts. He and his wife had 10 children, and St Huberts flourished. By 1875 it was an 80 ha vineyard with wine cellars able to hold two or three vintages.

The continuing need for capital to fund the expansion led to a decision to float the St Huberts Vineyard Company, with Hubert retaining a majority interest and wealthy Melburnians providing the rest of the capital. It was not a success, and in 1879 Hubert, in partnership with Irishman Andrew Rowan, repurchased the company.

In 1886, aged 61, Hubert returned once again to Switzerland, leaving his son François, then only 19 years old, to watch over the family interests. However, continuing needs for capital meant that by 1890 St Huberts had liabilities of £60,000, and when Andrew Rowan offered Hubert £30,000 for his share, he accepted the offer, leaving the property in Rowan's hands. He did not return to Victoria until one year before his death in 1907.

de Castella, François (1866–1953) was the son of Hubert de Castella. When the de Castella viticultural empire in the Yarra Valley came to an end, François went on to become Australia's best known viticultural authority. He joined the Victorian Department of Agriculture as its viticultural expert, and after the discovery of phylloxera at Geelong and elsewhere in Victoria, he travelled overseas to look for phylloxera-resistant rootstock. He was held in such esteem that he was commissioned by the government of South Australia to undertake a survey of the viticultural industry of that state between 1941

and 1942, and to formally report to the South Australian Phylloxera Board with advice on the appropriate responses to the threat of the pest. In the course of preparing that report, he visited all the major plantings in South Australia, discovering that many varieties were misnamed. He may not have been solely responsible for preventing the movement of phylloxera to South Australia, but he certainly played his part.

de Castella, Paul Frederick (1827–1903) was the entrepreneur in the de Castella family. At the age of 23 he formed a partnership with Adolphe de Meuron and purchased Yering Run (more than 4000 ha) from William and James Ryrie – the first settlers in the Yarra Valley, having travelled overland from southern New South Wales – and set about establishing a large cattle business. In 1852 Frederic Guillaume de Pury (see Yeringberg) joined the business, lending de Castella £2000; not long thereafter de Meuron sold de Castella his share in Yering. In 1854 de Castella began a major vineyard planting program of 40 ha; lacking viticultural expertise, he engaged Joseph Clement Deschamps, who carried out the land drainage in preparation for the planting of 20,000 vines, imported mostly from Chateau Lafite, in Bordeaux.

De Castella continued his ever-diversifying investment activities (one disaster was the manufacture of bitumen-covered cardboard pipes) and land dealings (these extended as far north as Swan Hill). By 1862 his partnership was £200,000 in debt, and it was this which gave Hubert de Castella the chance to buy the land (separate from Yering) which became St Huberts.

**deep** indicates both complexity and profundity of a wine when applied to the bouquet or the palate; it also indicates the intensity of the hue when applied to a wine's colour.

**De Iuliis** (est. 1990), in the Pokolbin district of the Hunter Valley, has involved three generations of the family in its development, initially selling grapes to Tyrrell's, but now focusing on the 10,000-case production of its own brand. Third-generation winemaker Michael De Iuliis, with postgraduate studies in oenology at the University of Adelaide, and a Len Evans Tutorial scholar, has made a series of exemplary shirazs and pure semillons in the mainstream of Hunter style.

**Delatite** (est. 1982) is the foremost winery in the Upper Goulburn; with its sweeping views across to the snow-clad Alps, it necessarily practises uncompromising cool-climate viticulture, and the wines naturally reflect that. Light but intense riesling and spicy gewurztraminer flower with a year or two in bottle, and in the warmer vintages the red wines achieve flavour and mouthfeel.

In 2002 David Ritchie (the viticulturist in the family) embarked on a program to adopt biodynamic viticulture, commencing with the sauvignon blanc and gewurztraminer. He says, 'It will take time for us to convert the vineyard and change our mindset and practices, but I am fully convinced it will lead to healthier soil and vines.' Exports to Japan and Malaysia.

**Denmark** is a coastal neighbour of Albany and is one of the five subregions of Great Southern. It is marginally wetter and cooler than Albany, but the differences are not of any significant magnitude. As one moves north away from the coast, the ocean influence lessens; there is also a series of steep hills and valleys before you emerge onto the rolling slopes of the Great Southern region proper. The pretty town of Denmark is a magnet for visitors, and some of the more remote wineries from other subregions have set up cellar doors there.

While there is some north–south variation, the climate is broadly similar to Albany; the varieties being grown and the wine styles are also similar. Once again, the soils are similar to Albany's, the native eucalypts the equivalent of a water diviner for finding the best. The principal grape varieties are chardonnay, sauvignon blanc, cabernet sauvignon, merlot, shiraz, riesling and pinot noir.

It has a number of important wineries, notably Harewood Estate, Howard Park and West Cape Howe. The significance of Harewood Estate and West Cape Howe has in part been driven by their contract winemaking activities, and in part from grape sources extending outside the somewhat restrictive climate of Denmark.

LAT 31°56'S; ALT 50–150 m; HDD 1471; GSR 354 mm; MJT 18.7°C; HARV Early March to late April; CHIEF VIT. HAZARD Birds

**destemmer** see crusher-destemmer.

**developed** has a number of meanings, ranging from pejorative (such as 'prematurely developed') to laudatory (such as 'beautifully developed') when used to describe an aged wine.

**Devil's Lair** (est. 1981) was established by former brewer and perennial marketer Phil Sexton in the Margaret River region. It was acquired by Southcorp in late 1996, and has been an outstanding success under that ownership (now Foster's), protecting the high quality of its chardonnay and cabernet sauvignon, while building the volume of the cleverly named Fifth Leg Red and Fifth Leg White to the point where production has increased from 40,000 to 220,000 cases. The striking label designs and the printing of the email address on the cork (a first) are legacies of Phil Sexton, now owner of Giant Steps in the Yarra Valley. Exports to the UK, the US and other major markets.

**Diam®** is a new form of closure which came into use in Australia in the early years of the 21st century. The process was developed by the French Atomic Energy Commission. Large pieces of cork are ground to the consistency of flour, and are then treated to super-critical $CO_2$ held at very low temperatures and under extreme pressure – in this state, the $CO_2$'s penetration has the solvent capacity of a liquid. When the pressure is released, the $CO_2$, and hence the cork dust, returns to ambient conditions, and all the trichloranisole, and any other taint compound, has been captured by the $CO_2$. The 'flour' is then compressed and bound with a natural glue, forming the shape of a conventional cork. It is available in two densities, the lighter density guaranteed against oxidation for five years, the heavier density for 10 years. The former can be used for wines which the maker wishes to evolve and develop more quickly, with a controlled amount of oxygen able to pass through the closure. The guarantees may well prove to be conservative; the only question that some winemakers have is the possible taint from the glue.

The winemakers of the Mornington Peninsula in particular (although they are far from alone) have enthusiastically adopted the closure, and report no problems. A striking feature of the Diam when removed from the bottle is the perfect circle of colour on the bottom face (when the wine is red) and no wine transfer or streaking up the side of the cork. This is doubtless due to the fact that Diam regains 97 per cent of its full shape and elasticity within 30 seconds of insertion. By 2020 Diam will be judged either an unqualified success, or to have inherited at least some of the problems of natural cork.

**Diamond Valley Vineyards** (est. 1976) was established by David and Cathie Lance, and quickly made a name for itself as one of the best producers of pinot noir in the Yarra Valley, the style always notable for its elegance. The chardonnay, too, has been first class. In a complicated arrangement, the Lances sold the brand and stock, and leased the winery and most of the vineyard, to Graeme Rathbone (brother of Doug Rathbone of Yering Station), leaving son James Lance as winemaker. Exports to the UK.

**di Lusso Wines** (est. 1998) was established by Rob Fairall and partner Luanne Hill, with the aim of creating an Italian enoteca operation, offering Italian varietal wines and foods. The plantings of 2.5 ha of barbera and 2 ha of sangiovese are supported by 0.5 ha each of nebbiolo, picolit, lagrein and aleatico. The estate also produces olives for the table and for oil. The decision to focus on Italian varieties has been a major success; the wines are of very good quality.

**disgorgement** is the last phase of the making of bottle-fermented sparkling wine. The lees from the second stage of fermentation are taken to the neck of the bottle in a vertical or near vertical position, the wine inside the neck is frozen, and the resulting pellet of ice is ejected when the crown capsule is removed. The bottle is then returned to an upright position and topped up with what is usually termed 'reserve wine' before being finally corked.

**Ditter, Don, OAM** (1926–) was raised in the Barossa Valley, and joined Penfolds as a laboratory assistant at the Magill winery near Adelaide in December 1942. He served with the RAAF from 1944 to 1945, returning to undertake winemaking studies at Roseworthy Agricultural College in 1946. He graduated in 1950 with first class honours, and returned to Penfolds. After several years at the Nuriootpa winery he was transferred to Sydney in 1953, and in 1963 was promoted to New South Wales production manager responsible for Penfolds operations in the Hunter Valley, Minchinbury, Riverina and Sydney production centre. In 1973 he was appointed national production manager, effectively national chief winemaker, a title created in 1975 (and accorded to Ditter) following the retirement of Max Schubert. From 1973 until his retirement in 1986 he was responsible for the making of, *inter alia*, Grange; he continued as a consultant thereafter.

**DNA profiling** (or fingerprinting, or testing) allows the unequivocal identification of any living individual or organism. It was first used in 1985 for forensic identification, and on grape varieties in 1993 by Australian researchers. Initially, it was used to identify synonyms, such as zinfandel and primitivo, and likewise to show that petite syrah and durif were one and the same. The next phase was the tracking of parentage; in 1997 Professor Carole Meredith and John Bowers of the University of California, Davis, found that the parents of cabernet sauvignon were cabernet franc and sauvignon blanc, in a spontaneous crossing of interplanted vines in the early days of viticulture in Bordeaux. In 2000 they showed that shiraz/syrah was the offspring of mondeuse blanche and dureza, again due to a spontaneous crossing that took place just to the east of the northern Rhône Valley around 100 AD. So far, DNA profiling has not allowed the positive identification (and hence differentiation) of clones of a given variety.

**dolcetto**, a red grape variety, has been grown in Australia for more than 100 years (by Best's Wines in the Grampians), but neither there nor anywhere else in any significant quantity. Given the interest in all things Italian, the number of wineries with dolcetto in their portfolio may well increase in years to come. Thus far, most Australian wineries produce a brightly coloured wine with soft, red berry fruits on the palate, avoiding any tannin-related astringency on the finish.

**Domaine A** (est. 1973) was a micro vineyard established in Tasmania by George Park, an engineer with the Tasmanian Hydro Electric Commission. Ludicrous bureaucratic requirements by the Tasmanian Department of Health, which had no understanding of appropriate winery hygiene standards, forced him to abandon the idea of establishing his own winery, and led to his sale of the property to Swiss businessman Peter Althaus and wife Ruth. They built a multi-level concrete winery with immensely thick walls and floors, and expanded the vineyard to the point where it now produces 5000 cases of finely crafted, long barrel-aged wines headed by the Lady A Fumé Blanc, Pinot Noir and Cabernet Sauvignon. All are made with a marked degree of discipline, and all repay extended cellaring. Exports to the UK, Denmark, Switzerland, Germany, France, Belgium, Canada, NZ, China, Japan and Singapore.

**Domaine Chandon** (est. 1986) is and always has been the wholly owned Australian subsidiary of Moet et Chandon. Dr Tony Jordan was appointed its first chief winemaker and CEO on its foundation, and guided the business even when travelling the world with other responsibilities as Moet et Chandon's international technical director. In 2008 he retired from full-time employment, but remained a consultant – which, ironically, was his occupation before joining Domaine Chandon. The winery, too, has changed, initially producing only sparkling wine, but thereafter developing table wines under the now-discontinued Green Point label (all the wines now appear under the Domaine Chandon brand). The sparkling wines cover the full gamut from Zero Dosage (Z*D) to Blanc de Blancs, Tasmanian Cuvee, Non

Vintage Rosé and Vintage Brut. The table wines are centred around chardonnay and pinot noir grown in the Yarra Valley, and shiraz from either the Yarra Valley or Heathcote. Exports to all major markets.

**Dominique Portet** (est. 2000) is at once the name of the Yarra Valley winery and the name of its owner/winemaker. The latter was bred in the purple, spending his early years at Chateau Lafite (where his father was *regisseur*), and was one of the very first flying winemakers, commuting to Clos du Val in the Napa Valley, where his brother is winemaker. Since 1976 Portet has lived in Australia, spending more than 20 years as managing director of Taltarni, and also developing the Clover Hill vineyard in Tasmania. After retiring from Taltarni, he moved to the Yarra Valley, a region he had been closely observing since the mid-1980s. In 2000 he found the site he had long looked for, and in the twinkling of an eye built his winery and cellar door, and planted a quixotic mix of viognier, sauvignon blanc and merlot next to the winery. These are supplemented in the wines by shiraz and cabernet sauvignon purchased from Heathcote. Portet also undertakes contract winemaking for others. Exports to the UK, the US and other major markets.

**doradillo**, colloquially known as dora, is a once-important but now rapidly disappearing white variety – in 1981 with 1900 ha producing 33,300 tonnes, diminishing to 145 ha in 2004 and 96 ha in 2007. The wine is now chiefly headed to distillation.

**double pruning** was developed by viticultural researcher and academic Dr Peter Dry in 1987.

The vine is conventionally pruned in winter, and pruned again after flowering in spring. This forces base buds which would otherwise have provided the growth for the next growing season to shoot. They will be less fruitful, thus significantly reducing the ultimate yield. More importantly, the growing season will be effectively retarded by two months; thus, grapes which would normally ripen and be picked in February, in hot weather, will be harvested in the much milder temperatures of April or, possibly, May.

**downy mildew** is the most significant fungal disease affecting vines, introduced to Europe from North America around the same time as phylloxera. It attacks all the green parts of the vine, damaging its photosynthetic capacity, and hence its ability to ripen the grapes. It is particularly common in cooler and wetter regions of Australia, where Bordeaux mixture (a mix of lime and copper sulphate) is sprayed as a prophylactic measure every 10 days – an expensive practice. If an outbreak is not prevented or controlled, systemic chemical sprays can be used which will stop the disease developing further. While the copper sulphate sprays are permitted under the organic or biodynamic regimes in Australia, systemic sprays are not.

**dry** is a generic term, mainly applied to table wines (but also sherry), denoting the apparent absence of sweetness, with a normal technical cut-off of 7 grams per litre of unfermented sugar in a table wine.

**Duke's Vineyard** (est. 1998) is a relatively small (2500 cases) winery in the Porongurup

subregion of Western Australia's Great Southern. When Hilde and Ian (Duke) Ranson sold their clothing manufacturing business in 1998, they were able to fulfil a long-held dream of establishing a vineyard with the acquisition of a 65-ha farm at the foot of the Porongurup Range. They planted 3 ha each of shiraz and cabernet sauvignon and 4 ha of riesling. It is with the last of these that Duke's has had exceptional success, although the shiraz is a classic spicy, cool-climate style. Exports to the UK.

**dull** denotes a wine that is either cloudy or hazy in colour (often associated with high pH levels in red wines) or that has a muted/oxidised bouquet or palate.

**durif** is a red cross, bred in France in the 1880s by Dr Durif from parents syrah and peloursin. In California, and elsewhere in both North and South America, it is incorrectly called petite syrah. In Australia its traditional base was Rutherglen in North East Victoria (with Morris cultivating the variety since 1923), but it has spread to the Riverina and Riverland regions thanks to its ability to provide high yields of strongly flavoured and coloured wine.

**Dutschke Wines** (est. 1998) is the venture of Wayne Dutschke and uncle Ken Semmler, the former having spent over 20 years working in Australia and around the world as a winemaker, and the latter a long-term grapegrower of note in the Barossa Valley. They brought their talents together in 1998, and now produce 6000 cases of high-quality red wines, led by the St Jakobi, Oscar Semmler and Single Barrel Shiraz labels. While having generous levels of alcohol, the wines do not heat up on the finish, seemingly carrying their alcohol with ease. Exports to the UK, the US and other major markets.

abcdefghi
jklmnopq
rstuvwxyz

**earthy** is a frequently used tasting term, one of a trio (the other two being fruity and savoury) which has as much to do with mouthfeel as it has to do with flavour, and it denotes a spectrum of characters which are not the least unpleasant, ranging from fresh earth to the smell of litter on a forest floor.

**Eastern Plains, Inlands and North of Western Australia Zone** serves mainly to cover this vast expanse of land, many times greater than the area covered by the other zones and regions in the state, that extends east to the border with South Australia, and is terminated on the west by the coastline. It is almost perverse that two wineries have chosen to locate themselves in the far southern portion of the zone, both making shiraz, and both having significant show success with at least one of their wines. They are Across the Lake and WJ Walker Wines, situated on opposite sides of Lake Grace.

**Eden Hall** (est. 2002) was established in the Eden Valley following the 1996 purchase by David and Mardi Hall of the historic 120-ha Avon Brae property. They have planted 32 ha, with cabernet sauvignon and riesling accounting for over 22 ha, the remainder planted to shiraz, merlot, cabernet franc and viognier. Most of the grapes are sold to other wineries, although 10 per cent of the best grapes have been held back for the Eden Hall label since 2002, excellent riesling, shiraz viognier and cabernet sauvignon leading the way. Exports to the UK, the US and Asia.

**Eden Valley,** gazetted 18 August 1997, in the Barossa Zone, has a particularly rich history.

Captain Joseph Gilbert planted vines at his Pewsey Vale vineyard in 1847, the same year that Johann Gramp planted the first vines in the Barossa Valley at Rowland Flat. A detailed description of the vineyards and wineries in 1862 appears in journalist Ebenezer Ward's book, *The Vineyards and Orchards of Australia*, and readily explains why Gilbert's riesling, shiraz and cabernet sauvignon were so highly regarded.

While the Eden Valley of today has a symbiotic relationship with the Barossa Valley (much of Eden Valley's grape production finds its way to the Barossa), it is a high-quality and important region in its own right. It is not always recognised that while Heggies Vineyard, Hill Smith Estate and Pewsey Vale are all in the Eden Valley, so is Yalumba itself, for the northwestern boundary of the region skirts the town of Angaston. Henschke is the other famous maker in the region, supported by Thorn-Clarke (which has dual residence here and in the Barossa Valley), Mountadam, Eden Hall, Poonawatta Estate, Poverty Hill, Radford and Torzi Matthews Vintners, which are among the best of the total of 28 producers in the region.

Altitude is all-important in determining mesoclimate, although aspect and slope are also significant in the varied, hilly terrain. Thus the Pewsey Vale and Heggies vineyards, at an altitude of about 500 metres at the southern end of the Eden Valley, are appreciably cooler than the Henschke vineyards around Keyneton, at an elevation of 380–400 metres. Overall, growing season temperatures are significantly lower than those of the Barossa Valley, and the final stages of ripening (and harvesting) take place in cooler conditions. As one might expect, given the terrain, there are a number of soil types, but the most common range is grey to brown in colour and from loamy sand to clay loams, with subsoils deriving from weathered rock. Ironstone gravels, quartz gravels and rock fragments are present in both the surface and subsurface. Water resources are strictly limited, with dams the main source.

LAT 34°35'S; ALT 380–550 m; HDD 1390; GSR 280 mm; MJT 19.4°C; HARV Mid-March to early May; CHIEF VIT. HAZARD Autumn rain

**Elderton** (est. 1984) is a distinguished, family-owned business in the heart of the Barossa Valley. Mother Lorraine Ashmead, and sons Allister and Cameron, guide the fortunes of the business, based on 75 ha of old, high-quality Barossa Valley floor estate vineyards. A move away from American to French oak has added lustre to the red wines. Command Shiraz is at the peak, with a worldwide reputation. Exports to all major markets.

**Eldridge Estate of Red Hill** (est. 1985) is a Mornington Peninsula winery situated in the eponymous Red Hill area. Winemaker/owner David Lloyd (with wife Wendy in support) is focusing on clonally selected chardonnay and pinot noir, with a cross-hatch of single-block wines. Their interest in all things Burgundian has also led to the planting and making of one of the best gamays in Australia, however oxymoronic that may seem to some.

**esparte** was the (incorrect) name for mourvedre used by Colin Preece at Seppelt's Great Western.

**esters** are compounds formed by the reaction of acid and alcohol during fermentation, the most common in fermenting or recently fermented wines being ethyl acetate; it is joined by numerous other esters as wine ages in barrel or bottle.

**Evans & Tate** (est. 1970), in the Margaret River region, was a very important winery until an expensive and ill-timed foray into the eastern states caused it to go into a prolonged receivership. In the end, the winery and vineyards were sold, the brand name becoming the property of McWilliam's, reducing it to the status of a virtual winery.

**Evans, Leonard Paul, OBE, AO** (1930–2006) made a contribution to the cause of Australian wine which will never be equalled, let alone exceeded, by any other person. Born in England, but of Welsh extraction, he migrated to New Zealand in 1953, moving to Australia in 1955. He had become a golf professional in England prior to his decision to migrate, saying afterwards that there was money to be made as a professional golfer, but not as a golf professional. His almost profligate talents and quick mind resulted in his move into the food and wine industry via a first job as a glass washer at a Circular Quay hotel. Within a few short years he was the food and beverage manager of what was then Sydney's leading hotel, The Chevron at King's Cross, its Silver Spade Room famous for its extravagant food and wine. In 1965 he became the first national promotions executive for the Australian Wine Board, immediately insisting that the promotion should be for table wine, and not, as the board wished, for fortified wine. Within a few more years he had moved on to co-author the *Galloping Gourmets* with Graham Kerr, the nickname coming from a 35-day worldwide dash through the finest restaurants around the world. He had also moved to set up his restaurant and wine retail complex in Bulletin Place, and wrote scripts for a highly successful commercial television program called *The Mavis Bramston Show*, appearing in person in another comedy show, as part of a panel called on to decide the identity of mystery objects.

The intellectual wanderlust ended with the founding of The Rothbury Estate in 1969, and because of the level of activity in Bulletin Place. These linked seamlessly with Evans' immense promotional talents and exceptional tasting ability, which inspired so many people within or around the wine industry. He invented The Options Game in 1968; in 1973 he wrote the first major encyclopedia of Australian wine; he continued to write prolifically for magazines (notably *The Bulletin*), for newspapers and for his own monthly wine journal. He took the wine show judging process onto an immeasurably higher plane, thereby broadening the skill base of the judges from pure winemaking to what he termed style judges, those without formal training, but who had naturally gifted palates. Wine writers, retailers and sommeliers all fell within that category. He also instituted lavish wine dinners during the wine shows, producing with abandon great wines from Europe (which in the early days very few senior winemakers in Australia had ever tasted) and adding impetus to the flying winemakers.

Throughout his life Evans was a compulsive builder and collector, and an enthusiastic sculptor. These three facets led to the building of the family house in the Hunter Valley which he called Loggerheads, saying he and wife Trish were always at loggerheads (which wasn't true). He finally won building approval for the home by agreeing to describe it as a motel, which had an element of truth, except that all his numerous friends who were its sole patrons never paid a solitary cent for their stay.

By 1979 the company he owned jointly with financier and close friend Peter Fox had bought Chateau Rahoul in Graves, and Chateau Padouen in Sauternes, and was well advanced in discussions to purchase Chateau Lascombes in 1981, negotiations which were brought to an end by Fox's death in a car accident. Others might have spent their life grieving over the absolute certainty that the purchase price would have been paid out of the profits from the 1982 and 1983 vintages; Evans instead thought only of his departed friend. He had already become chairman of Petaluma and this, coupled with Rothbury Estate, kept him occupied when he was not being a master of ceremonies at charity events, a brilliant (and eventually highly paid) after-dinner speaker, a motivator or anything else he chose to do. His many awards included the Epicurean Award for services to the wine and food industry, the Charles Heidsieck award for wine writing, an Order of the British Empire (OBE) in 1982, Personnalitée de l'Année (1986) Paris (Oenology section – Gastronomy), Chevalier de l'Ordre Mérite Agricole (French government), Maurice O'Shea Award (1991), first life member of the Society of Wine Educators (1995), elected member of the College of Patrons of the Australian Wine Industry, Restaurant Association Hall of Fame, *Decanter Magazine* International Award for 'Man of the Year' (1997), and Officer in the General Division of the Order of Australia (1999).

For those lucky enough to be part of the inner circle of wine lovers, Evans started the Single Bottle Club in 1977 (on that occasion attended by Michael Broadbent from the UK and prime minister of the day, Malcolm Fraser), featuring what seemed to be an extraordinary array of old wines, which were magically repeated at every Single Bottle Club Dinner (held annually) thereafter. Following his death in 2006, the Single Bottle Club Dinner became the Len Evans Memorial Single Bottle Club Dinner.

In 1999, following the sale of Rothbury Estate, Evans formed a syndicate of wealthy (and high profile) friends to build and operate Tower Estate, the most luxurious accommodation (with 12 guestrooms) in the Hunter Valley. As with Loggerheads, he was the designer (employing an architect only because he had to) and decorator, furnishing the rooms with objects he had collected or procured for the estate. Despite pleas and complaints from management he resolutely refused to install bar fridges, regarding them as beneath the dignity of the class of customer he sought for the estate. Finally, and most importantly in his eyes, he created the Len Evans Foundation, which stages intensive five-day masterclasses for 12 scholars, known as the Len Evans Tutorial.

**extract** is, in the strict sense of the term, the measurable amount of non-volatile solids in a given wine: these include sugar, acids, minerals, phenolics, glycerol, glycol and traces of other substances. Paradoxically, a wine high in extract does not have to be high in alcohol or body; thus, German rieslings which are low in alcohol and light-bodied can have high levels of extract.

**extraction** is a term increasingly associated with over-extraction, although it simply refers to the extraction of desirable phenolics and other characters during and after fermentation. Over-extraction denotes excessive processing and pressing of the must, typically by leaving the wine in contact with the skins for an excessive period, or by pressing the skins too hard and incorporating the pressings with the free-run wine. Thus the term has most relevance to red wines, not white.

a b c d e f g h i
j k l m n o p q
r s t u v w x y z

**Faber Vineyard** (est. 1997) in the Swan Valley subregion of the Swan District, itself part of the Greater Perth Zone, brings together the winemaking duo of John Griffiths and wife Jane Micallef. Griffiths spent some time as a senior winemaker with Houghton Wines, and has an excellent palate, which has led to the making of rich Swan Valley shiraz, elegant Frankland River cabernet sauvignon and similarly elegant chardonnay from southern regions.

**fading** describes a wine which is past its best, and is slowly losing both complexity and fruit flavour.

**Far North Zone** of South Australia covers a vast area, but has only one region, the Flinders Ranges.

**fault,** in its most basic meaning, is self-explanatory; the devil is in the detail of innumerable types of faults. They fall into three basic groups: sight, smell and taste.

### Sight

All wines, red or white, should have a bright colour, free from haze or cloudiness. In deeply coloured red wines, it may be necessary to tilt the glass and look at the colour grading from the centre to the rim of the wine. Modern wineries have the capacity to measure what is called turbidity; this analytical tool is particularly useful for determining whether or not red wines need to be filtered prior to bottling. Cloudiness or haze can derive from bacterial infection, the remnants of yeast, or proteins (particularly in white wines), giving rise to protein haze. This haze appears in white wines which have not been cold-stabilised,

and is triggered by warm transport or storage conditions. While posing no threat to health, it is an unacceptable fault.

Crystalline deposits are harmless, though they may look like fine pieces of glass. They are normally the result of excess potassium or calcium in the wine coming out of solution. German riesling makers call them 'wine diamonds'.

A small amount of gas, normally evident in the form of small bubbles around the rim, can have several causes. In white wines it is more likely than not to be caused by $CO_2$, very often introduced or left in the wine to keep it fresh. This spritz, as it is called, is viewed by many as quite acceptable in a young wine, but not in a mature white wine. Nonetheless, it is at best a minor fault. On the other hand, gas on the rim of a red wine may simply be $CO_2$ (strictly speaking unacceptable) or, worse, an indication of partial malolactic fermentation in bottle.

Lastly, there is the question of colour. The colour of white wines sealed with a traditional cork may, over time, darken significantly in some bottles in a given batch, while others remain much paler. This is a sure sign of random oxidation, and is easily detected by passing the bottles in front of a light-box or by spectrographic analysis.

### Smell

Smell covers a multitude of sins. The most common fault in a wine made by an otherwise good producer is the mouldy, bitter smell caused by the formation of trichloranisole in the cork (see corked). This fault is especially annoying for winemakers, as it is beyond their control, and there are no sure safeguards against it.

Next in importance is *Bretannomyces* and the wet bandaid or farmyard characters it gives rise to. Closely associated with this, but different, is what is termed mousyness. A consequence of the activity of lactic acid bacteria, this is an insidious fault which is not immediately apparent in the bouquet of the wine, and which builds up in normal tasting circumstances in the delayed aftertaste. Moving quickly from one wine to the next may hide the fault. Experienced tasters, suspecting its presence, rub a small amount of the wine on the back of their hand, which increases the alkalinity/pH of the wine, immediately making the unpleasant smell evident.

Mercaptans are the next major group, giving a range of unpleasant smells, and are caused by the presence of hydrogen sulphide in the wine. In Australia, it is a once-prevalent wine fault now in fast retreat.

All wines have a proportion of volatile acidity; it is only when the level of acetic acid rises significantly that the sharp, faintly vinegary smell of volatility will make its present felt, more commonly in red wines than in white wines (other than sweet white wines).

*Taste*
The majority of off characters on the palate are simply extensions of those detected in the bouquet. This gives rise to an acronym used on wine show tasting sheets: DNPIM, which stands for 'Do Not Put In Mouth'. One of the exceptions is an excessively astringent or tannic wine, although some experienced tasters will sense the presence of excessive tannins, and blame themselves for failing to observe the DNPIM rule.

**fermentation**, at its most simple, is the process of converting grape sugar to ethanol (ethyl alcohol) and $CO_2$ through the action of yeast. The exact chemistry of fermentation is complex, and is best found in technical wine books or manuals.

Complicated though it may be, the archaeology of wine (which falls within the compass of palaeoethnobotany) continues to narrow down the places where the vine has been domesticated and likewise where the first wine residues have been found in clay pots. A site in Georgia, Transcaucasia, has yielded the earliest finds of pips from domesticated grapes and the earliest residue of resinated wine in a pot. It seems nothing more than a matter of commonsense to suggest that grapes, picked in autumn, would have been stored in clay pots to provide a food source during winter, and that spontaneous fermentation would have resulted in the first de facto winemaking. One has to come forward almost 8000 years before Louis Pasteur ended the argument running through to the middle of the 19th century on the cause and process of fermentation by showing that yeasts were the initiating mechanisms. One and a half centuries later, the move back from cultured yeasts to what are variously termed native, indigenous or wild yeasts (three words for the same thing) has taken fermentation back into the mists of time.

Because fermentation is the cornerstone of turning grapes into wine, it is best understood in the context of the processes leading up to it and those immediately following it. This in turn leads to the necessity of describing the fermentation of white grapes and red grapes separately. Likewise, the central role of yeast is discussed under that heading, with compressed references to it at this point.

*White wine fermentation*

The ever-present choice between hand-picking or machine-harvesting grapes is of critical importance with white wines. If the grapes are hand-picked, it is possible to place them as whole bunches direct into the press, which will almost certainly be an airbag press, with an internal bladder that is inflated, pushing the bunches against a perforated screen which completely encircles the bladder. The screen in turn may be wholly encased in an outer jacket, with a single draining point; this is known as a tank press, and it is specifically designed to prevent oxidation of white grape juice. Where there is a perforated exit strip running the length of the tank, it is called a universal press: it is suited to pressing either white or red grapes. Whichever type is used, it will result in juice with a low percentage of solids, particularly if the automated pressure is not set too high, or where the free-run juice is separated from the pressings. Juice obtained this way can be taken direct to barrel (particularly with chardonnay) for fermentation without prior clarification, or, if the wine is to be tank-fermented in stainless steel, direct to tank. Whether or not it is clarified at this stage will depend on the variety and the type of wine being made.

If the grapes have been machine-harvested (and crushed or destemmed), they will normally be taken through a heat exchanger, taking the temperature down to 10°C, and then pressed. The content of solids here will be significantly higher than in the case of whole bunch pressed juice, and the juice will normally undergo at least partial clarification before being taken to barrel or to another tank.

Where cultivated yeast is added, the temperature of the juice will be taken up to 15°C to help initiate the fermentation; where wild yeasts are used, it is improbable that fermentation will start at temperatures much below 15°C. Unlike with red wine, there is nothing to be gained by delaying the onset of fermentation. With barrel-fermented white wine, the yeast can be either added direct to the juice in each barrel, or added in tank, and the temperature lifted to 15°C or more. When the fermentation has converted around 1 baumé of sugar to alcohol, the fermenting juice is taken to barrel. Aromatic white wines fermented in stainless steel will be held at significantly lower temperatures than barrel-fermented wines, with the aim of converting approximately 0.5 baumé a day into alcohol, giving rise to a fermentation period of between two and three weeks. To achieve this, the temperatures will need to be held at 10°–12°C.

In a typical coolroom situation, an ambient temperature of 10°–12°C will see the wine in barrel fermenting at 15°C. In the case of both tank-fermented and barrel-fermented wines, it is prudent to ensure that the temperature rises towards the end of fermentation to avoid stuck fermentation. In the case of barrels, they will be taken out of the coolroom; in the case of wine in tank, it is even easier: the temperature will simply be raised to 15°–17°C.

If the wine has been barrel-fermented, at the end of fermentation all that is needed is a topping-up of the barrels with the same wine (foaming during the early stages of fermentation means the barrels cannot be completely filled) because the lees are highly prized, and will be stirred (see lees stirring). Tank-fermented wines which have neither been taken to barrel nor had oak chips or oak staves will normally (but not invariably) be racked off the lees soon after fermentation.

## Red wine fermentation

The critical difference between white and red wine fermentation is that, in the case of the latter, pressing takes place after the wine has fermented, rather than before fermentation commences.

The choice between hand- and machine-picking is important; apart from the use of whole bunches in the fermenter, one of several advantages with hand-picked grapes is the ability to move them along a sorting table before they pass through the crusher or the destemmer, giving the option of further sorting of the individual berries. If the grapes have been machine-harvested, they will usually be passed through the crusher-destemmer, simply to remove fragments of leaves, stalks and canes which always find their way into mechanically harvested bins.

For pinot noir in particular, and to a lesser degree for other mainstream red varietals, the must may be passed through a heat exchanger to chill it to 10°C or below for a period (up to seven days) of pre-fermentation maceration (cold soak, for short). Again for pinot noir, but not uncommonly for shiraz, the chilled must will be pumped into an open tank which already has a percentage (25 per cent would be common) of whole bunches. Cold soak was first used by Lebanese oenologist Guy Accad in Burgundy in the latter part of the 1980s; he delayed the onset of fermentation with large additions of $SO_2$, but Australian practitioners rely on the cold must to prevent the onset of fermentation, particularly if it is not intended to add cultured yeast.

More conventional ferments for varieties such as shiraz or cabernet sauvignon will usually involve crushing of 100 per cent of the grapes, not chilling the must unless it is very warm (as the consequence of picking on a hot day), and then relying on one of three methods: manual or hydraulic punch-down of the cap; pumping juice over the cap, possibly taking all the juice out of the tank into another receptacle before returning it to the fermenter (rack and return); or using header boards which are fixed to the interior of the tank and hold the cap permanently submerged. This method will see temperatures rise to 25°–28°C. Pinot noir makers will normally seek to have fermentation temperatures reach 33°–35°C.

Where whole bunches form part of the must in the vat, and indeed where there is no crushed component, simply whole bunches, the aim is to encourage intracellular fermentation (carbonic maceration), involving enzymes in the living berry attacking the stored reserves of $CO_2$, thus creating 2–2½ degrees of alcohol inside the berry. At that point the alcohol kills the berry, and the only way fermentation can proceed is by the progressive fracturing of the skins, allowing yeast to do its work. In this scenario, punch-down (manual or hydraulic) will be used. When most of the apparent sugar in the must has been converted to alcohol, with around 1 baumé of sugar remaining, the winemaker may deliberately take the must (including significant remnants of whole bunches) to the press, and see the baumé rise to 2–3 degrees, then transfer the quite actively fermenting juice straight to barrel. In developing Grange, Max Schubert pressed the must (no whole bunches) at 3–4 degrees baumé, very briefly settling the fermenting must, then taking it to barrel to finish its fermentation. Thus for Grange and other wines in the Penfolds stable, it was a technique developed over 50 years ago; Wolf Blass was the first to copy it in Australia, Brokenwood the first of the small wineries, on the first occasion entirely by accident. It has only been since the advent of shiraz plantings around the world, stimulated by Australian shiraz, that winemakers in other countries have been tempted to finish the fermentation in barrel. The great advantage of this is that it integrates new oak with the wine in much the same way that barrel fermentation does with white wines.

Regardless of the variety, some makers use both pre-fermentation and post-fermentation maceration, the former involving extraction of colour and flavour in an aqueous medium, the latter in an alcoholic medium. The mechanisms involved are quite different.

The three additions which may be made to fermenting red wine are diammonium phosphate (DAP), used where there is a question mark over the sufficiency of the nutrient for the yeasts to feed on, thus avoiding stress and the production of hydrogen sulphide as a consequence of that stress; acid, where the pH is rising either in the lead-up to or during the onset of malolactic fermentation (which in Australia not infrequently accompanies primary fermentation, and does so without the problem of formation of excessive volatile acidity, so feared by European winemakers); and cultured yeast to ensure that the fermentation converts all the available sugar to alcohol.

Finally, many of these techniques are used in the context of fine winemaking, but not commercial wine. In the latter case, fermentation will be managed in large vessels, with cultured yeast, and the most simple handling techniques will be used throughout. Malolactic fermentation will be completed in tank, and the wine completely clarified before it is taken to barrel.

**Ferngrove** (est. 1997), in the Frankland River subregion of Great Southern, did not arrive on the scene until the late 1990s, but has made its present felt since then in no uncertain fashion. It started life as a grapegrower, with 414 ha of grapes spread across three vineyards in the Frankland River, and a fourth in the Mount Barker subregion. Initially, winemaking under its own label was seen as a means of advertising the quality of its grapes (some sold as grapes, some sold as bulk wine). Both of these facets of the business continue, but so has the growth in the 50,000 cases of Ferngrove branded wines. What is more, it consistently outperforms expectations at the various price points, with the wines released in three tiers. Riesling, sauvignon blanc semillon, chardonnay, cabernet sauvignon, shiraz, shiraz viognier, malbec and shiraz cabernet fill a very impressive product range. Exports to the UK, the US and other major markets.

**fiano** is an ancient Italian grape variety dating back to Roman times, when it made apianum, the celebrated white counterpart to the red falernian. It is suited to hot and dry growing conditions, and soils which are not too fertile; it may well come into its own in the years ahead. It is propagated by Chalmers Nurseries at Mildura.

filtration raises passions around the world. The very distinguished French oenologist Professor Emil Peynaud once wrote that he had never seen a wine which was not improved by appropriate filtration, continuing:

> The more a wine is clarified, the finer the filtration, the smoother and more supple the wine will taste. Filtration properly carried out does not strip or attenuate a wine; it clears it of internal impurities and improves it. To deny this is to say that a wine's quality is due above all to foreign substances in suspension.

The notable Californian wine importer Kermit Lynch describes wines that have been filtered thus:

> Squeezed through the sterile pads, the poor wine expressed sterility and cardboard … three or four times I have seen an unfiltered wine go bad … it may be unrealistic, but I believe customers who have such a wine should accept the loss and shut up about it … if one loves natural wines, one accepts an occasional calamity. We would not castrate all men because some of them go haywire and commit rape.

Robert Parker Jnr holds similar views; it is perhaps no coincidence that neither he nor Lynch has made wine, yet fearlessly express strong views on highly technical issues.

New World winemakers, especially those of Australia and New Zealand, do not hesitate to filter a wine if they believe the process will improve and/or protect it. The advent of modern cross-flow filtration machines makes the case for filtration (where needed) absolute, for the process is extremely gentle, and has no downside other than cost. That said, Australian winemakers will not filter a wine if they are satisfied it has no active bacteria, and that it is of appropriate clarity and brilliance (in colour).

finesse is an important wine-tasting term, even if it is decidedly subjective. It is the consequence of precisely chosen and calibrated winemaking techniques which place maximum emphasis on preserving the innate flavour and structure of a wine.

fining has the same opprobrium attached to it by the likes of US-based Kermit Lynch and Robert Parker Jnr as filtration, but is used where the winemaker believes the wine will be improved by the addition of a fining agent. Before coming to a conclusion one way or the other, a conscientious winemaker will conduct fining trials in the laboratory, aiming to determine the most appropriate type and amount of fining.

The three most commonly used fining agents for white wines are bentonite clay, which is added to wine to remove protein which may cause the wine to become slightly cloudy when exposed to heat; skim milk (or lactic casein, a milk component) to remove phenolic bitterness; and polyvinyl-polypyrrolidone (PVPP), which removes unwanted phenolic compounds, particularly those which cause pinking, browning or premature yellowing in young white wines. Despite its threatening name, PVPP is in fact a gentle fining aid with no downsides (residues) for the treated wine. Egg whites are the most commonly used fining agent for red wines, to clarify the colour and (depending on the amount used) to reduce tannin levels. Isinglass, obtained from the bladders of kingfish and some other freshwater fish, is a traditional fining agent, mainly for red wines, but also for white wines as a final treatment prior to bottling. Its use in Australia is not widespread. The most brutal fining agent is activated carbon, or charcoal, which is used to strip colour of red wines (even to the point of turning them white). It is only used on low-quality wines. The most outlandish fining agent is potassium ferrocyanide (or blue fining). It is used to remove copper and iron, and remains on the list of permitted additives in Australia, even though it is seldom, if ever, used. See also labels.

**finish** is the flavour or taste remaining in the last seconds before or after the wine leaves the mouth, and is a critical factor in determining the quality of a wine. Sometimes there will be a distinct delay before other characters emerge (on the downside, notably mousyness) in what is termed the aftertaste by some writers.

**firm** is a term usually applied to the finish of a wine, denoting the impact of tannin and possibly acid. It has no negative implications for quality, and is an important part of the flavour profile of a young red wine other (normally) than pinot noir.

**flabby** describes a wine without sufficient acid and freshness, triggered in most instances by excess alcohol deriving from grapes grown in a warm to hot climate … or simply poor winemaking.

**flat** is similar to dull and/or flabby, indicating a lack of freshness, varietal character or acidity; oxidation will normally be the underlying cause.

**fleshy** is used to describe a young wine with plenty of fresh, supple fruit flavour on the mid-palate, there expressed without obvious oak or tannins.

**Fleurieu Zone** of South Australia encompasses the Currency Creek, Kangaroo Island, Langhorne Creek, McLaren Vale and Southern Fleurieu regions.

**flora** is a white cross between gewurztraminer and semillon bred by Professor Harold Olmo at the University of California, Davis. Brown Brothers has grown the variety for many years, and blended it with orange muscat to make a highly aromatic off-dry white wine of some appeal.

**flowery** describes an aroma reminiscent of flowers or fruit tree blossom most commonly found with riesling and other aromatic varieties. The term is often qualified by specifying the blossom involved (such as cherry blossom, apple blossom and so forth).

**flying winemakers** was a term first used by (and thereafter registered by) Tony Laithwaite of the Sunday Times Wine Club. Laithwaite employed Australian winemakers during the 1987 vintage to work at French co-operative wineries and produce wines for the club. The scheme proved hugely successful, and while Laithwaite continued with it, it led to ever more young Australian winemakers (independently of Laithwaite) working in regions right across France, and ultimately elsewhere in Europe, gaining experience while significantly enhancing the quality of the wines they had total or partial responsibility for. Their reputation for attention to detail, strict winery hygiene, knowledge of a wide variety of fermentation techniques for both white and red wines, and familiarity with analysis of grape sugar, acidity and pH (all taken for granted in Australia) opened up increasing opportunities to work at all levels, including at some of the most famous wineries of France. A handful never came back, securing perm-anent employment and thereafter direct equity in European wineries. Viticulturists, too, had their place.

There were those who were opposed to the whole idea, arguing that Australian winemakers were passing on invaluable technology and know-how to countries in direct competition with Australia in export markets. Whether or not this was true, it was impossible to stop Australians heading north for the European vintage. The reality is that they returned with knowledge they could never have otherwise gained, of the limitations and the potential of the areas in which they worked, of their social and economic climate, and, quite often, of the places to which the wines they made were exported. Other than New Zealand, none of the other southern hemisphere countries has either been able or wanted to participate in meaningful numbers, (the latter applies notably to South Africa, Chile and Argentina). In Chile and Argentina the traffic has been going the other way, with high-profile French winemakers such as Michel Rolland and Jacques Lurton (of The Islander Estate Vineyard) arriving in South America.

**Fonty's Pool Vineyards** (est. 1989) in the Pemberton region are part of the original farm owned by pioneer settler Archie Fontanini, who was granted land by the government in 1907. In the early 1920s a large dam was created to provide water for the intensive vegetable farming which was part of the farm's activities. The dam became known as Fonty's Pool, and to this day remains a famous local landmark and recreational facility. The first grapes were planted in 1989, and at 110 ha the vineyard is now one of the region's largest, supplying grapes to a number of leading Western Australian wineries. However, an increasing amount of the production is used for Fonty's Pool. Exports to all major markets.

**Forest Hill Vineyard** (est. 1965) is one of the oldest 'new' family-owned winemaking operations in Western Australia, and was the site for the first grape plantings in Great Southern, in 1965. The Forest Hill brand became well known, aided by the fact that a 1975 riesling made by Sandalford from Forest Hill grapes won nine trophies. In 1997 a program of renovation and expansion of the vineyards commenced; the quality of the wines made from the oldest vines on the property is outstanding (released under the numbered vineyard block labels). Exports to the UK and China.

**Fornachon, John** (1905–68) came into prominence in November 1934, when the Wine Overseas Marketing Board asked the University of Adelaide to investigate the causes of bacterial spoilage in Australian fortified wines, which then constituted almost all of the country's very substantial export trade. With financial support from the board, the university appointed Fornachon as its investigating officer. His subsequent pioneering research solved the problems and ultimately led to his appointment as the foundation director of the Australian Wine Research Institute in 1955 (see this entry for further details of his career).

**fortified wine** is made by the addition of grape-derived spirit to partly fermented juice (occasionally unfermented). The addition prevents further fermentation taking place, and leaves the wine with not less than 18% alc/vol. It represented approximately 85 per cent of total wine production in Australia up to 1960. Approximately, because detailed industry statistics segmenting wines into the various fortified types on the one side and table wines on the other were not kept. What is known is that between 1927 and 1940 Australia exported more wine to the UK than did France, and that virtually all of it was fortified wine, sent in barrel. As at 2008, fortified wine sales in Australia constituted 3.7 per cent of total market value. The fortified wine market is split in the same two fundamentally different categories as table wine: high-quality, limited production wines and commercial, larger volume wines, the latter still sold in flagons as well as bottles. High levels of consumption of these wines by Australia's Indigenous peoples is an ongoing matter of concern to the industry.

A transitional agreement between Australia and the European Community on trade in wine came into force on 1 March 1994. It involved a two-stage process: first, an agreement to agree on phase-out dates for the use of various descriptive terms that were then in common use in Australia, but which conflicted with EU use, and second, having reached that point, to agree on a phase-out date. Despite the fact that, strictly speaking, an agreement to agree on something has no legal efficacy, the intention of the wine agreement has been fulfilled. The last areas to be agreed were the use of the terms 'port', 'sherry' and 'tokay'. In December 2008 an agreement covering fortified wine nomenclature was signed by the relevant ministers, and a phase-out period of 12 months for sherry, port and other fortified wines was agreed; in the case of tokay, the phase-out period is 10 years. Agreement on these details led to finalisation of all aspects of the wine agreement, and to its signing by both parties on 14 February 2009 in Brussels.

The categories of port have been specified in a code of practice which will allow the continued usage of the terms 'tawny', 'vintage' and 'ruby', though without the word 'port' appended. However, the region can be specified. Tawny can be classified as Australian (or by region – Barossa Valley, Rutherglen, et cetera) classic, grand or rare in a similar fashion to muscat.

The word 'sherry' will have to be discontinued by December 2009, and in January 2009 Australia announced that it had adopted (and registered) the name 'apera' to replace 'sherry'. Once that generic description has been determined, the code of practice defines pale dry, medium dry, medium sweet, sweet and cream as more or less corresponding to the fino, amontillado, oloroso and cream terms used by Spain, and which are no longer available.

The fortified muscat wines of northeast Victoria are unaffected by the agreement, as muscat is the name of the grape used. Tokay, however, is not (the grape is muscadelle) and Hungary objected to the continued use of the name, even though its sweet wines are not fortified (simply botrytised) and the spelling (tokaji) is different. The compromise of a 10-year phase-out was ultimately agreed, but, once again, Australia has moved pre-emptively, and has registered the name 'topaque', which will gradually replace 'tokay'.

In future, tawny, muscat and topaque will fall into four categories: Australian (simply the name tawny, muscat or topaque as the case may be), classic, grand and rare.

**Foster's Wine Estates**, as at 2009, had two main streams of brands: those which it had prior to the amalgamation with Southcorp, and those which came with Southcorp. Alphabetically, in the former category are: Andrew Garrett, Annie's Lane, Baileys of Glenrowan, Cartwheel, Early Harvest, Eye Spy, Half Mile Creek, Ingoldby, Jamiesons Run, Maglieri Lambrusco, Maglieri of McLaren Vale, Metala, Mildara, Mount Ida, Pepperjack, Robertson's Well, Saltram, Shadowood, St Huberts, T'Gallant, The Rothbury Estate, Wolf Blass, Yarra Ridge and Yellowglen. The Southcorp-originated brands are: Blues Point, Coldstream Hills, Devil's Lair, Edwards & Chaffey, Fisher's Circle, Glass Mountain, Kaiser Stuhl, Killawarra, Kirralaa, Leo Buring, Lindemans, Matthew Lang, Minchinbury, Penfolds, Queen Adelaide, Rosemount Estate, Rouge Homme, Seaview, Seppelt, The Little Penguin, Tollana and Wynns Coonawarra. Those which have dedicated vineyards wholly or partially within their control and/or have separate winemaking facilities will be found under their separate entries. Heemskerk is a later addition. Exports to all major markets.

**Frankland Estate** (est. 1988), in the Frankland River region, was established by Barry Smith and wife Judi Cullam on their large sheep property. Over the ensuing years, 29 ha of vineyard have been planted, predominantly to riesling, with lesser quantities of chardonnay, shiraz and cabernet sauvignon, and small amounts of merlot, malbec and cabernet franc. The major focus has always been on riesling, the quality reaching new highs since 2005, with a series of individual vineyard wines. Cullam is a relentless advocate for riesling in its broadest sense, and also for Frankland Estate, and to this end she has established the Biennial Frankland Estate International Riesling Conference. Exports to the UK, the US and other major markets.

**Frankland River** is one of the five subregions of the Great Southern in Western Australia. It is situated in the northwestern corner of the region, its western boundary touching the eastern side of the Blackwood Valley, and close to the eastern side of Manjimup. For the pedantic cartographers, the boundaries of the South West Australia Zone, and of many of the regions within it (Geographe, Blackwood Valley and Great Southern) have utterly illogical discrepancies and gaps. Frankland River is in good company when it comes to these discrepancies.

The first vineyard in the Frankland River was planted in 1968 on a property owned by the wealthy Roche family of Perth. Originally called Westfield, it is now owned by Houghton and known as Netley Brook Vineyard (a locality name). It is a major and important vineyard, giving Houghton some ultra-premium grapes. Then, in 1971, Merv and Judy Lange began the development of the now highly rated and substantial Alkoomi vineyard and winery. This is open, and at times sparse, country, without the forests which populate the south, although the controversial Tasmanian blue gum plantings are to be found here as elsewhere (headed to wood pulp, but with no one certain about the recovery or future use of the land).

It is the most northerly, inland subregion of Great Southern, still Mediterranean in terms of dominant winter–spring rainfall, but with greater continentality, thus favouring riesling (in particular), shiraz and cabernet sauvignon. A unique feature is a sea breeze which finds its way inland and cools the late afternoon temperature by about 2°C. Total rainfall decreases from west to east, and salinity in the soil and surface water makes irrigation very difficult. The answer is a complex and extensive system of very long collection channels and drains on slopes, plus holding dams and long-distance pumping.

The gently rolling hill country is catchment for the Frankland, Gordon, Kent and Tone rivers. The soils are chiefly derived from granite or gneiss outcrops, and so are typically rich, red in colour and of uniform depth. The principal grape varieties in descending order of importance are shiraz, riesling, chardonnay, cabernet sauvignon and sauvignon blanc, with the usual scattering of other varieties, including some notable

malbec. The leading wineries are Alkoomi, Ferngrove Vineyards, Frankland Estate and Old Kent River.

LAT 34°39'S; ALT 200–300 m; HDD 1441; GSR 310 mm; MJT 19°C; HARV Mid-March to mid-April; CHIEF VIT. HAZARDS Drought; birds

**free-run** is the juice of white grapes which drains without pressing from freshly crushed must prior to fermentation, or the red wine which runs from the fermentation vessel or press, once again without any pressure other than the weight of the must. If it is white grape juice it will be lower in solids and phenolics than the portion which is pressed, and if it is red wine it will be lower in tannins. As a very rough rule of thumb, 60–70 per cent will be free-run. The term is occasionally used for red wine prior to, or at the first stages of, pressing the must at the end of fermentation.

**fresh** describes an aroma or taste free from any fault or bottle-developed characters, usually found in young wine, but is occasionally a component in older wines.

**Freycinet** (est. 1980) is one of Tasmania's most impressive wineries, founded on the east coast, south of the town of Bicheno. Its principal vineyard is an elongated amphitheatre which traps a lot of the daytime warmth and provides a near-perfect environment for chardonnay, riesling and pinot noir. All three of these wines, and the Radenti sparkling wine (from pinot noir and chardonnay) are consistently of high quality. Claudio Radenti and Lindy Bull have taken the business founded by Lindy's father, Geoff Bull, to another level, yet are almost painfully modest about their achievements, likewise their exceptional generosity. Exports to the UK and Sweden.

**Frogmore Creek** (est. 1997) is a Pacific Rim joint venture, the owners being Tony Scherer of Tasmania and Jack Kidwiler of California. They have developed a substantial organic vineyard, and have acquired the Hood/Wellington wine business previously owned by Andrew Hood, who continues his involvement as a consultant. Winemaking has been consolidated at Cambridge, where the Frogmore Creek and 42° South brands are made; there is also a thriving contract winemaking business there. Its rieslings, made either dry or as FGR (40 grams residual sugar), are of very high quality. Exports to the US, Japan and Korea.

**Frog Rock** (est. 1973) was established by leading Sydney chartered accountant Rick Turner; it is now one of the larger vineyards in the Mudgee region, with 60 ha under vine, led by 22 ha each of shiraz and cabernet sauvignon, and smaller plantings of chardonnay, semillon, merlot, petit verdot and chambourcin. Exports to Canada, Singapore, Hong Kong and Fiji.

**frontignac**, sometimes with the words 'white', 'red' or 'brown' appended, is an alternative and widely used name for muscat à petits grains. The term is often applied to table wines made from the variety; fortified wines use the abbreviated nomenclature of muscat. It is a superior grape to muscat gordo blanco.

**fruity** describes the aroma and taste of a well-made young wine, and is not necessarily linked to the amount of residual sugar.

**fumé blanc** does not have any legislative meaning in Australia, or, for that matter, California. It was first coined by Robert Mondavi, who chose not to protect the use of the name by registering a trademark. In most instances, however, it applies to a barrel-fermented and mature wine with a preponderance of sauvignon blanc.

**fungicides** have come into widespread use since the introduction of downy and powdery mildew from North America in the second half of the 19th century. They now fall into three groups: protectants, eradicants and systemics. Bordeaux mixture is typically used as a protectant, sprayed before downy mildew appears; powdery mildew can be similarly prevented (or controlled) by sulphur-based sprays. Despite the length of time for which these sprays have been used, resistance has not developed. Eradicant fungicides are applied after infection appears. They inhibit or kill fungi thanks to their ability to penetrate plant tissue. The best can be applied seven days after infection has first occurred and still be effective. Systemic fungicides move within a plant's system, and are highly effective in bringing major outbreaks of downy mildew under control. However, resistant strains quickly develop, and it is thus essential to rotate different systemic sprays to minimise resistance. Bordeaux mixture and sulphur are contingently permitted under organic and biodynamic regimes, but systemics are not. The qualifications for use of Bordeaux mixture under these regimes are that: it can contain copper hydroxide and copper sulphates, but not copper oxychloride; it cannot be used as a herbicide; and it can be used at rates of up to 8 kilograms per hectare but in a manner that prevents excessive copper accumulation in the soil. Sulphur can be used, but must be derived from soil or rock, not from petroleum.

**furmint** is the major white grape partner of the great dessert wine of Hungary, tokaji; the junior partner is hárslevelü. The two varieties have been grown for some years by Eling Forest winery in the Southern Highlands region, and in the Perth Hills of Western Australia. In both cases dry table wines have been made, rather than botrytised sweet wines.

a b c d e f g h i
j k l m n o p q
r s t u v w x y z

**gamay** is the red grape of Beaujolais, notoriously high yielding, causing Phillip the Good, at the end of the 14th century, to describe it as a bastard and order its destruction and removal from Burgundy. However, not only did it survive in Beaujolais; it now accounts for all but 1 per cent of the plantings in that region. In Australia it has gained limited traction, partly because some of the plantings are in regions which are far too warm. The four serious producers to emerge at the start of the new millennium are Bass Phillip, Eldridge Estate of Red Hill, Roundstone and Sorrenberg.

**garganega**, a white grape, is the chief contributor to the oceans of soave made in Italy's Veneto region every year. It grows vigorously, and yields generously. The first (and perhaps only) Australian producer is Robin Day, with an estate planting at his Mount Crawford property high in the Barossa Valley hills.

**Garlands** (est. 1996) in Mount Barker is a partnership between Michael and Julie Garland and their vigneron neighbours Craig and Caroline Drummond and Patrick and Christine Gresswell. Michael Garland came to grapegrowing and winemaking with a varied background (in biological research, computer sales and retail clothing) and has a Charles Sturt University degree in oenology. The winery has a capacity of 150 tonnes, and will continue contract winemaking for other small producers in the region as well as making wine from the 9.25 ha of estate vineyards (planted to shiraz, riesling, cabernet sauvignon, cabernet franc, chardonnay, sauvignon blanc and semillon). Cabernet franc is the winery specialty. Exports to the UK, Switzerland, Trinidad, Hong Kong and Singapore.

**gassy** describes wine containing small bubbles of $CO_2$ which may indicate secondary fermentation in the bottle, but more likely (especially with white wines) is deliberately left in solution by winemakers to add freshness. Regardless of the source, it should not be evident in red wines.

**Geelong,** gazetted 11 June 1996, was, like the Yarra Valley, dominated by Swiss vignerons in the early years. Ebenezer Ward opens his book *The Vineyards of Victoria in 1864* with a description of the Neuchatel (or Pollock's Ford) Vineyard as

> being, in fact, if not the oldest vineyard in the colony, at all events, the oldest in the western district … the present lessee of the property is Mr Brequet, sen., of Geelong; but Mr D Pettavel was associated with him in the establishment of the vineyard. Planting was commenced there as early as 1842.

Ward was wrong in suggesting this was the oldest vineyard in Victoria. William Ryrie, who travelled overland from the New South Wales Monaro with his sheep, planted the first vines in the Yarra Valley in 1838. However, the Swiss-viticultural connection (via Charles La Trobe's Neuchatel-born wife) was first made in Geelong, and production grew apace, making Geelong the most important region in the state by 1861. It had around 300 ha planted to vines by the end of that decade, reaching the peak of its success in 1874. Disaster struck in 1875 when phylloxera was discovered at Fyansford, not far from the town of Geelong, and not much later than its discovery in France. The Victorian government reacted to public pressure by ordering the removal of 220 ha of vines, leaving 100 ha to be dealt with later, and indeed only a tiny patch of vineyard survived the turn of the century, the last small blocks surviving until World War II.

Viticulture returned to the region in 1966, when local veterinary surgeon Daryl Sefton and wife Nini began planting. They planted 7 ha each of cabernet sauvignon and shiraz, 4 ha of gewurztraminer and 2 ha of chardonnay over the ensuing 15 years. Ken and Peter Caldwell commenced planting the Rebenberg Vineyard at Mount Duneed in the early 1970s, followed closely by Stuart Hooper at Bannockburn Vineyards in 1973, focusing on pinot noir and chardonnay. The greatest historical resonance came with the re-establishment of the pinot noir–only Prince Albert vineyard at Waurn Ponds, when Bruce and Susan Hyatt commenced the replanting on the exact location of the picture-postcard vineyard of DL Pettavel, one of the most influential Swiss vignerons of the time. (It would seem Prince Albert was originally exempted from the destruction order, but it had long ceased production when revived by the Hyatts.)

The principal soil type is one of the commonest to be found in viticultural regions in Australia: red-brown clay loam over a hard clay base, ranging from mildly acidic to mildly alkaline. There are also patches of a similar-looking group of dark black cracking clays. Almost all the vineyards are established on gentle to moderate slopes. This open and strongly maritime-influenced region has a climate roughly halfway between that of Bordeaux and Burgundy in terms of ripening temperatures and sunshine hours. The long, cool and usually dry autumn means that chardonnay and pinot noir achieve optimum ripeness almost every year, but the later-ripening cabernet sauvignon can struggle in cooler, wetter vintages. Yields are low to moderate, with both wind and lack of rainfall inhibiting vigour, particularly on the more exposed slopes and hardened soils. The region is planted to two-thirds red, and one-third white, with pinot noir, shiraz, chardonnay and sauvignon blanc leading the way, all the wines showing the uncompromisingly cool climate of Geelong.

Today there are 70 wineries in the region, foremost among them Bannockburn Vineyards, by Farr, Clyde Park Vineyard, Curlewis, Farr Rising, Grassy Point Wines, Scotchmans Hill and Shadowfax.

LAT 38°07′S; ALT 20–150 m; HDD 1470; GSR 250 mm; MJT 19°C; HARV Early March to end April; CHIEF VIT. HAZARD Drought

**Gemtree Vineyards** (est. 1998) is the highly successful venture of the Buttery family, who have been prominent grapegrowers in McLaren Vale for over 25 years, with 130 ha of vines under their control.

In 1998 they made the decision to start producing wine under the Gemtree Vineyards name, and have had striking success with high-quality shiraz under the Obsidian, Uncut and White Lees labels, backed up at the other end of the spectrum with albarino, petit verdot and tempranillo, as well as other mainstream varieties. Exports to the UK, the US and other major markets.

**genetic modification** occurs when a gene or genes foreign to a particular organism is/are inserted into the normal genetic structure of that organism. It is, and will remain for the foreseeable future, highly controversial, and until such time as there is greater consensus, the attitude of the Australian wine industry is that it will not use genetically modified organisms (GMOs) in the wines it produces. This is very frustrating for scientists and for those who stand to benefit from the use of GMOs, simply because the opposition comes from a highly vocal minority, many of whom have no scientific training, effectively demanding that its proponents prove a negative. It is similar to the hysterical opposition to the radical idea of pasteurising milk proposed by Louis Pasteur over a century ago; it took several decades before it was accepted across the world.

On the positive side are the spin-offs which come from molecular biochemistry, including genetic modification on an experimental level. New insights into grape vines, grapes, yeasts and wines allow choices (and desirable consequences) previously undreamt of. It is ironic that a country which needed the election of a new president, Barack Obama, to remove obstacles to stem cell research had for many years supported the growing of genetically modified crops. The US regulations flow from the approach that there is no *a priori* reason to assume that the use of GMOs is more risky than conventional methods of introgressing new genes into organisms and products. Accordingly, the regulations require each GMO to be considered on its own merit, albeit with lengthy trials to establish that it poses no threat to human health or the environment.

The European Union takes the view that GMOs have an intrinsic level of risk above that of non–genetically modified products, with a consequent moratorium on all GMOs. In 2003, the US, Canada and Argentina instigated dispute proceedings with the EU; whether this will result in a breakthrough is hard to predict.

GMOs are inextricably linked to globalisation issues; it is certain that those who oppose one will also oppose the other. Supporters of the technology argue that natural diversity in the characteristics of wine is augmented by the appropriate use of technology, not through its withdrawal. As the team at the Australian Wine Research Institute, headed by its director Professor Isak Pretorius, says, the concerns that GM wines will become 'standardised and McDonaldised' are without foundation; indeed, the reverse is more likely to be the case.

The opportunities to improve grape vines are threefold. First, the improvement of disease and pest resistance: specifically, to make vines immune to downy and powdery mildew, thus negating the need for sprays; to eliminate botrytis (where desired); and to increase resistance to viral attack. Second, the improvement of vine stress tolerance: specifically, resistance to water stress. Third, the improvement of quality factors through better colour development and sugar accumulation and transport. The one major caveat is that (quite apart from other GM issues) there is no change in the varietal characteristics of the grapes: this means the development timeline would need to be 10 to 20 years.

In the winery there are numerous opportunities for improving fermentation performance, wine processing, wine wholesomeness and wine sensory attributes through the use of GMOs. Some of the specific objectives are: to increase levels of resveratrol in red wine (highly cardiovascular-protective); to decrease levels of alcohol (especially for New World chardonnay and warm-grown shiraz); to reduce sulphite and sulphide production; and to make biologically based reductions in acidity levels (previously 'plastering' was used, involving high-pH calcium materials). The ultimate goal is the incorporation of all relevant antimicrobial agents into selected strains of wine yeast and malolactic bacteria, thus eliminating all contaminating spoilage bacteria (notable *Acetobacter*), yeasts (notably *Bretannomyces* and *Dekkera*) and moulds (including *Aspergillus* and *Trichoderma*) in winemaking.

The advent of equipment enabling reverse osmosis, micro-oxygenation and cross-flow filtration results in the winemaker being able to reduce or increase alcohol levels in wines, accelerate the softening of tannins in red wine, remove unwanted substances, particularly taints, and so forth. Similar changes can be achieved by the use of genetic modification, and it is strongly arguable that the outcome should be the determinant, not the process. That said, these issues have given rise to the concept of natural wine, which eschews all but the most basic procedures in winemaking, even fining and filtration of any kind. There are, as yet, no codified requirements for the use of the term, but a priori that the only additive which might be permitted is SO$_2$.

In conclusion, the underlying thrust of all except natural wine precepts is to increase choice for the winemaker. It will in no way standardise or industrialise winemaking or wines. It will be every bit as useful – arguably more so – for the smallest low-tech wineries as for the biggest high-tech producers. In many instances, there will be incontestable benefits for the ecosystems of vineyards and wineries alike.

**Geoff Merrill Wines**  (est. 1980), in McLaren Vale, was established by Geoff Merrill, achieving immediate recognition thanks to his extreme marketing skills and zest for life. It would not be unkind to suggest that the quality of the wines did not always measure up to the marketing standard in the early years, notwithstanding some conspicuous show success for older bottle-matured semillon chardonnay and chardonnay. On the other side of the coin, his grenache rosé was always near the top of the tree, long before the style gained overnight popularity all around the world, and the three-tiered shiraz releases, together with the Reserve Coonawarra McLaren Vale Cabernet Sauvignon, manage to combine flavour and length on the palate with considerable elegance. Production of 75,000 cases speaks for itself. Exports to all major markets.

**Geoff Weaver**  (est. 1982) crafts wines of uncommon finesse and elegance for his eponymous winery in the Adelaide Hills. All are long-lived, thanks to the quality of the grapes coming from his 11-ha estate vineyard (planted between 1982 and 1988) and to his low-key intervention in the winery. Low key with one remarkable exception: an intermittent release of sauvignon blanc which breaks all the rules, barrel-fermented in French oak, with 12 months on lees, and released only with 18 months bottle age (Ferrous Lenswood Sauvignon Blanc). Exports to the UK and the US.

**Geographe**, gazetted 25 March 1999, has the Indian Ocean as its western border, Margaret River as its extreme southwestern corner, then the Blackwood Valley heading diagonally east, thence heading north until it turns at right angles west, its northern boundary coinciding with the southern edge of Peel. It is a relatively small region, and it might be assumed that the boundaries drawn in this fashion result in a logical and coherent area. However, there are in truth three quite distinct parts. The first is the true coastal sector, stretching from Busselton to Bunbury, with the lush, peaceful Capel River (and the town of Capel) at its centre. Wholly maritime-influenced by the warm Indian Ocean, its climate is similar to that of the northern part of the Margaret River, although the soil types vary considerably – the richer alluvial soils around Capel lead to exceptionally vigorous vine growth. Next is the Donnybrook area, which has a quite different climate, as it is cut off from the maritime influence by the Darling and Whicher ranges. The net result is a climate which Dr John Gladstones describes as closely resembling that of Bendigo and Rutherglen in Victoria, with considerable diurnal temperature fluctuation. The third area is the Ferguson Valley; here, early success with sauvignon blanc, shiraz, merlot and cabernet sauvignon has led to rapid expansion in plantings. The largest venture in this subregion is Willow Bridge Estate, with a 100 ha vineyard and a 2000-tonne capacity winery. The major Geographe winery is, and has been from the start, Capel Vale, driven by the energy and passion of Perth-based former radiologist Dr Peter Pratten, and producing 100,000 cases a year. However, Hackersley, Harvey River Bridge Estate and Willow Bridge Estate are all important producers by any standards.

Geographe is an area of considerable beauty and great variation in its topography and scenery. The unifying force is the West Australian flora: magnificent gum trees, ranging from the tuarts of the coastal sands of the same name through to marri and karri further inland, and the spectacular, omnipresent native shrubs and flowers.

The climate of the coastal portion is warm, sunny and dry (in the growing season), with minimal diurnal temperature fluctuations. It shares with the Bunbury Hills the tempering effect of sea breezes which take hold relatively early in the day, and high afternoon relative humidity which alleviates the stress that the warm climate might otherwise induce. While frost presents no threat on the coast, site selection within Donnybrook is important if frosts are to be avoided. The coastal tuart sands have limestone as their parent material, and overlie limestone; a permanent watertable at a depth of 3–15 metres is a further aid to viticulture. However, low natural fertility and ready leaching of nutrients mean care has to be taken to achieve the best results. The soils of the traditional farming and orchard land at Donnybrook are richer, being either gravelly sandy loams or heavier soils derived from the gneissic country rock in the valleys. Those of the Ferguson Valley are gravelly loam, usually on good slopes.

A little over 62 per cent of the production is of red grapes; in descending order of importance the principal varieties are shiraz, cabernet sauvignon, chardonnay, merlot, sauvignon blanc and semillon.

**LAT** 33°18'S; **ALT** 5–70 m; **HDD** 1700; **GSR** 185–220 mm; **MJT** 22°C; **HARV** Early February to mid-March; **CHIEF VIT. HAZARD** Birds

**Geographic Indications**  is the term for the officially recognised super zones, zones, regions and subregions of Australia which have been entered in the Register of Protected Names by the Geographic Indications Committee (GIC), constituted under Sections 40N to 40Z of the *Australian Wine and Brandy Corporation Act 1980* (Cth). At its most general, registration is based on state boundaries or an aggregation of states or part thereof. The broadest is South Eastern Australia, which takes in the whole of New South Wales, Victoria and Tasmania and those sectors of Queensland and South Australia in which grapes are (or may conceivably be in the future) grown. Next come individual states, designations which need no explanation. Each state is then divided into zones; securing agreement on the names and boundaries of the zones (through the State Viticulture Associations) proved to be far more difficult than anyone had imagined, but was completed in 1996. The regulations provide that a zone is simply an area of land, without any particular qualifying attributes. The one super zone is Adelaide, which includes the Mount Lofty Ranges, Fleurieu and Barossa zones.

Each zone is then subdivided into regions, and each region into subregions. A region must be a single tract of land, comprising at least five independently owned wine grape vineyards of at least 5 ha each, and usually producing at least 500 tonnes of wine grapes a year. A region is required to be *measurably* discrete

from adjoining regions and have *measurable* homogeneity in grapegrowing attributes over its area. A subregion must also be a single tract of land, comprising at least five independently owned wine grape vineyards of at least 5 ha each, and usually producing at least 500 tonnes of wine grapes annually. However, a subregion is required to be *substantially* discrete within the region and have *substantial* homogeneity in grapegrowing attributes over the area. As is obvious, the legislation is vague, and the difference between a region and a subregion is extremely subtle. Once registered, however, it is the end of the matter; the relevant decision is written in unalterable stone (see below).

A minor and little-known anomaly is that a region can extend across zonal boundaries. Thus the Peel region of Western Australia lies partly in the Greater Perth Zone and partly in the Central Western Australia Zone; and the Southern Flinders Ranges region of South Australia is mainly in the Far North Zone, but its southern extremity extends into the Mount Lofty Ranges Zone. Indeed, close inspection of the state maps showing zones and regions will reveal a number of other minor instances of overlap.

The procedures for registration were and are inevitably tortuous and slow. First, the application for registration (and the detailed supporting material) must come from the region's vignerons. This presumes the will, the ability and the mutual agreement of those vignerons; there have been prolonged internal disagreements about both names and boundary lines which have delayed applications. In other instances, no one has been prepared to undertake the unpaid work which is involved in preparing an application. Moreover, if regional boundaries abut, there has to be interregional agreement, as the committee has decided that there cannot be regional overlap of the kind one finds under comparable legislation in the US.

Then the committee has to determine whether the application meets the statutory criteria; if it is so satisfied, it will publish an interim determination in the *Government Gazette*. It must then consider any objections, and, having done so, publish its final determination. However, that determination can be challenged by anyone with a demonstrable interest; the appeal is to the Administrative Appeals Tribunal, with the possibility of further appeal to the High Court. The six-year battle over the boundaries of Coonawarra, costing many millions of dollars in legal and experts' fees, showed just how drawn-out the process can be. Moreover, the outcome was neither advocated nor anticipated by any of the initial protagonists, the boundaries ultimately decided being wider than anyone imagined, and still having illogical sections at various points along the way.

As the number of Australian wineries continues to increase, and their geographic spread likewise, the process of mapping will continue. The one limiting factor is the absence of any power of the Geographic Indications Committee to change either the name or the boundaries of any registered Geographic Indications, presumably an oversight in drafting the regulations. The process has been, and will continue to be, painstakingly slow and bureaucratic, but this in no way diminishes its importance for the future.

**gewurztraminer**  (a white grape variety often shortened to traminer) might at first sight appear to be at a standstill in Australia, its annual crush having increased only marginally since 1987. This obscures the fact that plantings in unsuitably warm regions have been removed, and that the focus of activity is now centred on Tasmania, the Yarra Valley, Macedon Ranges, Adelaide Hills, Eden Valley and Upper Goulburn. That said, the Australian wines still do not deliver any of the spicy pungency of the grape's home ground in Alsace, France. It may well be that Australia has poor clonal stock to choose from.

**Giaconda**  (est. 1985) is the creation of Rick Kinzbrunner, who moved to Beechworth to pursue the holy grails of pinot noir, chardonnay and cabernet sauvignon (the last now largely replaced by shiraz). He is as elusive as are his wines, which are made in small quantities using techniques he has uniquely devised, building on the back of an international winemaking career. The unpredictable climate of Beechworth adds a degree of difficulty to the equation, but when Kinzbrunner gets chardonnay exactly right, it is a superb wine. Exports to the UK and the US.

**Giant Steps**  (est. 1997), which also includes the Innocent Bystander label in its portfolio, was established by Phil Sexton a year after he sold Devil's Lair to Southcorp, and while he was a flying beermaker commuting between Oregon (on behalf of Corona of Mexico) and Australia. The name Giant Steps comes in part from his love of jazz and John Coltrane's album of that name, and in part from the rise and fall of the property (in the Yarra Valley) across a series of ridges ranging from 120 metres to 360 metres. The 35-ha vineyard is predominantly planted to pinot noir and chardonnay, but with significant quantities of cabernet sauvignon, plus small plantings of merlot, cabernet franc and petit verdot. The quality of the strongly structured and flavoured wines made by Steve Flamsteed is consistently high. Exports to the UK, the US and other major markets.

**Gibson BarossaVale**  (est. 1996) is the venture of Rob Gibson, who spent much of his working life as a senior viticulturist for Penfolds, with particular involvement in research tracing the characters that specific parcels of grapes give to a wine; this left him with a passion for identifying and protecting old vine plantings. His Old Vine Collection shiraz and grenache are especially meritorious, though quite expensive, but lower priced varietal bottlings also merit high points. Exports to the UK and Hong Kong.

**Gilberts**  (est. 1980) was once a part-time occupation for sheep and beef farmers Jim and Beverly Gilbert, but is now a full-time and very successful one. The mature Mount Barker vineyard (shiraz, chardonnay, riesling and cabernet sauvignon), coupled with contract winemaking at Plantagenet, has long produced very high-class riesling, and now also makes excellent shiraz. In 2000 a new red wine was introduced into the range: the Three Devils Shiraz, named in honour of their young sons. Exports to Hong Kong and Switzerland.

**Gippsland Zone**  stretches from Melbourne to the southeast coast of Australia. The distance between its westernmost winery, Phillip Island Vineyard, and its easternmost, Wyanga Park (at Lakes Entrance), is 240

kilometres as the crow flies, much more by road. There are plantings dotted all over the zone, with significant populations around the Bairnsdale and Lakes Entrance area in the east, and around Leongatha towards the western end. The threshold requirement for registration under the Geographic Indications legislation has so far precluded any attempt to register regions, but the large distances involved and the number of wineries spread across hundreds of kilometres mean that were plantings to increase sufficiently there would in all probability be three regions: South Gippsland, West Gippsland and East Gippsland. Even then, the most distinguished of the Gippsland winemakers, Phillip Jones (of Bass Phillip) would take the process further via subregions, for he asserts that there are six distinct climatic areas.

East Gippsland was the focus of wine-making in the 19th century, with a number of vineyards. The most important were those of the Costellos and Louis Wuillemin in the Maffra-Bairnsdale region. The remains of the Wuillemin cellars are still visible, although winemaking ceased prior to World War I. East Gippsland was also the area in which viticulture resumed when Pauline and Dacre Stubbs began planting Lulgra in 1970, followed by Robert and Anne Guy in 1971 with Golvinda. Both ventures resulted in wines being commercially sold in the 1970s, but the labels are no more. Pioneers whose vineyards and wineries have survived are Peter Edwards of McAlister Vineyards (est. 1977) and Ken Eckersley at Nicholson River (est. 1979).

The zone has complex weather patterns, some moving south from the New South Wales coast, others driven by the high and low pressure cells which sweep from Western Australia across to Victoria and thence to the Tasman Sea. At times these may block each other, and the region has highly unpredictable rainfall, summer drought and floods making grapegrowing difficult in some seasons.

West Gippsland is at roughly the same latitude as East Gippsland, but over 200 kilometres (as the crow flies) to the west, its western boundary abutting the southeastern boundary of the Yarra Valley. Its climate is distinctly less Mediterranean, as it is up to 100 kilometres from the coast, and it is by a small margin the warmest part, with overall climate slightly more predictable. Coolest of all – though only by comparison – is South Gippsland, where the influence of the Bass Strait (and onshore winds) is marked. Rainfall, too, is higher, and the dark loam soils around Leongatha make this first-class dairy country. All in all, an unlikely environment for one of Australia's foremost pinot noir producers, Bass Phillip.

There are now 56 wineries in the zone, the four most distinguished being Bass Phillip, Caledonia Australis, Narkoojee and Phillip Island Vineyard, with Ken Eckersley's Nicholson River producing wines which often have a massive impact, those of Ada River being more genteel. Chardonnay, pinot noir, shiraz and cabernet sauvignon are the principal varieties, sauvignon blanc gaining ground.

LAT 37°30′S; ALT 20–50 m; HDD 1300–1470; GSR 420–530 mm; MJT 18.1°–19°C; HARV Early March to end April; CHIEF VIT. HAZARDS Drought; flood

**Gladstones, Dr John** is, in the view of many, Australia's foremost viticultural research scientist, even though his professional background was in lupins, and he has not

chosen to become a viticultural consultant for individuals. His book *Viticulture and Environment* (Winetitles, Adelaide, 2002) is the most detailed and comprehensive study of the climate and soil of Australia either presently or prospectively planted with vines. He has in publication a book looking at viticulture in the 21st century, with particular reference to climate change; it will challenge some commonly accepted views and conclusions. His importance as a viticultural researcher was recognised in 2008 when he received the Maurice O'Shea Award for outstanding contribution to the wine industry.

A particular area of interest for Gladstones has been the Margaret River region, and it was a paper he wrote in the mid-1960s which said:

Being virtually frost-free, and having a much lower ripening period, cloudiness, rainfall and hail risk than Manjimup and Mount Barker, it has distinct advantages over both those areas, and indeed over all other Australian vine districts with comparable temperature summations … Not only should excellent quality be obtainable with choice grape varieties, but the district might also be very suitable because of its equable climate for higher-yielding, but still good quality varieties, such as shiraz and semillon.

The report was read by Perth heart specialist Dr Tom Cullity, and led directly to his establishment of Vasse Felix in 1967. In August 1999 Gladstones proposed six subregions for Margaret River, based purely on distinguishing climate and soil characteristics, not on satisfying the requirements of the Geographic

Indications legislation. The names chosen were Yallingup, Carbunup, Wilyabrup, Treeton, Wallcliffe and Karridale (on a north to south progression). Notwithstanding this focus, Gladstones' interest in and knowledge of regions as far afield as the east coast of Tasmania and southern Queensland is second to none.

**Glaetzer Wines** (est. 1996), in the Barossa Valley, is the impressive tip of the Ben Glaetzer iceberg; as well as making the marquee reds for his own label (led by Amon Ra, Bishop, Godolphin and Anaperenna), he has one of Australia's most successful contract winemaking businesses at his Barossa Vintners base.

The Glaetzer trademark is sumptuous, rippling fruit, with none of the overt oak reliance of the wines of his uncle John Glaetzer, and they are all the better for that. It is hardly surprising that the wines have a devoted following in the US, but they are exported to all major markets, spreading the 15,000-case production thinly, particularly given the relatively modest prices of all but the Amon Ra, and even that is within bounds.

**Glenrowan**, gazetted 14 October 2003, is little more than 20 kilometres to the west of Wangaratta, in the North East Victoria zone, but the Warby Range State Park collars the wineries in a north–south line on the foothills of the range; Lake Mokoan is an equally dominant part of the landscape to the west of Baileys of Glenrowan. In an oft-repeated story, vines here followed in the footsteps of gold. Richard Bailey and family settled near Glenrowan in the early 1860s, operating the first store in the town to supply the Beechworth and Ovens gold miners. When the gold ran out, the Baileys turned to farming and viticulture on their property Bundarra (Aboriginal for 'meeting of the hills') at the southern foot of the Warby Range.

Its other most famous (albeit transient) citizen will never be forgotten: Ned Kelly still resonates with all Australians, whether in books, plays or Sidney Nolan's *Ned Kelly* paintings. There is something special about the atmosphere of the region, the savage and the romantic equally balanced.

The climate is somewhat warmer than that of Rutherglen, but has less extremes. Thus spring and autumn are warmer (reducing though not eliminating the risk of frost) but the mean January temperature is lower. This is due in part to the moderating influence of Lake Mokoan, which also supplies irrigation to those vineyards which require it. The rainfall pattern (drought permitting) is excellent, and the best soils have good water-holding capacity, so most of the older plantings are in fact not irrigated. The soil at the foot of the Warby Range is well drained, fertile, deep red clay and loamy clay, derived from granitic material washed down from the range. The soils around Lake Mokoan are dark clays, loams and silty sands.

Only negligible quantities of white grapes are planted; shiraz, cabernet sauvignon, durif, muscadelle and muscat à petits grains provide 95 per cent of the grapes, the last two used for fortified wines. There are six wineries in the region: Baileys (by far the most important), Auldstone, Goorambath, Granite Range, Judds Warby Range Estate and Taminick.

LAT 36°27'S; ALT 190 m; HDD 1750; GSR 310 mm; MJT 22.2°C; HARV End March to end April; CHIEF VIT. HAZARD Frost

**glycerol**, or glycerine, is present in most table wines at concentrations ranging from 5 to 12 grams per litre, rising to 25 grams per litre in botrytised white wines. It imparts a moderately sweet taste, but does not contribute to viscosity, and thus has no role in the tears apparent on the inside of the wine glass after it has been swirled. It is only when the level rises above 28 grams per litre that it will start contributing to viscosity.

**gouais**, or gouais blanc, has been described as the Casanova of grapes for its suspected role as one of the parents of a number of varieties, its partner in many instances being one of the four main clones of pinot: pinot blanc, pinot gris, pinot meunier and pinot noir. The most famous offspring is chardonnay (a cross with pinot noir); aligoté and gamay are the next best known. Recent research indicates that gouais may also be a parent of riesling and furmint; the other parents are not yet identified. In Australia a small, 100-year-old planting of gouais is at Chambers Rosewood (Bill Chambers nicknamed the wine 'gooey') in Rutherglen; there are one or two other producers, none able to coax anything more than an ordinary white wine from the variety. Nonetheless, its parentage role will certainly save it from extinction.

**Goulburn Valley**, gazetted 29 November 1999, and its Nagambie Lakes subregion are situated in the Central Victoria Zone, stretching from the New South Wales border down to a spindly tail in the south terminating at Broadford, to the south of Seymour. It is in the southern funnel, which includes the Nagambie Lakes subregion, that most of the wineries are concentrated; there are only nine scattered throughout the central and northern parts. The Goulburn Valley wineries are Cape Horn Vineyard on the Murray River in the extreme northwestern corner of the region; Monichino Wines, halfway between Cobram and Numerka in the far north; Goulburn Valley Estate, northeast of Shepparton, close to the Goulburn River; Tallis Wine and Gentle Annie, just inside the eastern boundary, and directly east of Shepparton; Murchison Wines, not far north of Nagambie Lakes; 12 Acres on the western side of the subregion; and Hankin Estate and Sugarloaf Creek Estate to the south.

**Goundrey** (est. 1976) is part of the CWA empire. In 2008 the Mount Barker winery was put on the market by CWA, together with its 237 ha of estate vineyards, and in 2009 it was purchased by comparative minnow West Cape Howe Wines. However, the brand name has been retained by CWA, and significant quantities of wine will continue to be made from its West Australian base, with 100 per cent of the grapes sold back to CWA pursuant to a contract with West Cape Howe. Exports to all markets.

**graciano** was once an important red grape contributor to the Rioja wines of Spain, providing aromatic and rich wine, but its low yield has led to a significant decline in plantings there. Small plantings are scattered across Australia. Brown Brothers is one of its pioneers; Cascabel in McLaren Vale uses its Spanish synonym, monastrell.

**Gralyn Estate** (est. 1975) was established in the Margaret River region by the Hutton farming family, led by Graham and wife Merilyn. They had the foresight to plant shiraz as well as cabernet sauvignon, and the good fortune to have some of the best viticultural land in the region. Now well past their 30th birthday, the vines regularly produce some of the best grapes in Margaret River, directed in part to Gralyn Estate's label, with the remainder sold to eager producers willing to pay high prices per tonne. Son Dr Bradley Hutton has taken over winemaking responsibilities, and the sumptuous style, these days supported by French oak, is as good as ever.

Grampians, gazetted 16 June 1997 and long called Great Western (the latter now a subregion of the Grampians), is the most important of the three regions in the Western Victoria zone, the other two being Pyrenees to the east and Henty to the southwest. The region was at the very centre of the gold rush which so altered the fabric of Victorian society. The lure of gold attracted hopefuls from all corners of the globe, and from all social strata. The human amalgam which resulted brought a multitude of skills to the goldfields; while all were intent on amassing a fortune in the least possible time, not all sought to do so by digging for gold. Others realised that there was ample money to be made in filling the miners' stomachs and, above all, slaking their considerable thirst. Thus, while French immigrants were noticeably absent from the early years of most Australian wine regions, 20-year-old Anne-Marie Blampied and her 15-year-old brother Emile left Lorraine in France in 1853 to seek their fortune in Victoria. They went first to Beechworth, where Anne-Marie met and married Jean-Pierre Trouette, a Frenchman from Tarbes, and the three formed a partnership transporting supplies and provisions for the miners. A few years later they moved to Great Western, where they acquired land and commenced a market garden. Around the same time brothers Joseph and Henry Best moved to nearby Ararat, setting up business as butchers, but also buying land to plant vines.

The Melbourne Intercolonial Exhibition of 1870 suggests that Trouette and Blampied were the first to plant vines (in 1858), followed by Best's in 1862. Indeed, the most probable chain of events was that Blampied and Trouette obtained cuttings from Geelong to establish their St Peters Vineyard, and that Joseph Best in turn obtained his cuttings from St Peters. Henry Best acquired his 30-ha property near Concongella Creek in 1866 and established the vineyard (including the precious nursery block). It was purchased by Frederick Pichon Thomson in 1920.

After the gold ran out, Joseph built a substantial winery, and employed out-of-work miners to tunnel through the seams of soft decomposed granite under the winery to create the famous cellars of the Seppelt Great Western winery of today. When he died intestate, his estate was auctioned, and the winery and vineyards were purchased by Hans Irvine for the considerable sum of £12,000. In the 1890s Irvine lured Charles Pierlot, who had learnt champagne-making in Rheims in France, to become his chief winemaker; then in 1918 Irvine sold his vineyard and winery to Seppelt.

For 30 years (1932 to 1963) Great Western was the home base for one of Australia's three greatest winemakers of the 20th century:

Colin Preece of Seppelt. (The other two were Maurice O'Shea and Max Schubert.) Preece had an uncanny ability to blend small parcels of various red varieties from up to three or four vintages to make as little as 500 cases of the wine in question. The vintage ascribed would normally be the youngest component: wine labelling laws were all but non-existent prior to 1963. His other winemaking practice was to wait until he was satisfied that the grapes had achieved the flavour he was looking for (typically with a potential of 15% alc/vol), and then use either water or blocks of ice to pull the alcohol back to between 12.5% and 13% alc/vol, simultaneously lowering the pH. Some would argue that it is a great shame that this type of adjustment is now illegal, particularly those who have had the opportunity of recently tasting Preece's superlative red wines from the 1940s and 1950s. However, it is true that reverse osmosis can now (legally) achieve a similar result.

This is red wine country, with shiraz firmly in control: 75 per cent of the plantings are red, dominated by shiraz and cabernet sauvignon; chardonnay, sauvignon blanc, pinot noir, pinot meunier, riesling and merlot give variable results depending on their location. Grey-brown loamy sands and clay loam surface soils which are quite acid need lime adjustment; the subsoils are less permeable than the surface soil, and can lead to drainage problems. Unless the pH is significantly increased by liming both the surface and the subsoil, it will militate against vine vigour and restrict crop levels.

In part due to its location on the fringes of the Great Dividing Range, which provides altitude, the region has a significantly cooler climate than areas to its east. The low heat summation is, however, offset by high ratios of growing season sunshine hours, and to a lesser degree by moderate relative humidity. Growing season rainfall is particularly low, and the disappearance of old, low-yielding vineyards throughout the region has been due in large part to lack of available water. The big three producers are, of course, Best's, Mount Langi Ghiran and Seppelt Great Western, but Clayfield, Grampians Estate and Westgate Vineyard produce wines of the highest quality (but in small quantities), standing out from the 18 wineries in the region.

LAT 37°09'S; ALT 240–440 m; HDD 1460; GSR 240 mm; MJT 20.2°C; HARV Mid-March to mid-May; CHIEF VIT. HAZARDS Spring frost; drought

**Grampians Estate** (est. 1989) is the venture of graziers Sarah and Tom Guthrie, who began their diversification into wine in 1989; their core business continues to be fat lamb and wool production. Both activities were ravaged by the 2006 bushfires, but each has recovered, that of their grapegrowing and winemaking rising like a phoenix from the ashes. They have acquired the Garden Gully winery at Great Western, giving them a cellar door presence and a vineyard of 2.4 ha of 60-year-old shiraz, and 3 ha of 45-year-old riesling vines. During 2008 Grampians Estate wines continued to excel, winning seven trophies. A feature of the cellar door will be wine education sessions during school holidays. It will offer not only the full range of Grampians Estate wines but also specially chosen wines from smaller local boutique wineries.

**Grange** stands alone at the top of the pyramid of Australian wine, the extraordinary creation of an extraordinary winemaker, Max Schubert.

Moreover, its genesis was totally unplanned. In 1950 Penfolds did something it had never done before: it sent someone who was not a member of the family on an overseas trip. Schubert's mission was to travel to Jerez de la Frontera and Sanluca de Barrameda in the south of Spain, there to improve his already considerable knowledge about making sherry. He passed through London on the way, and stayed for some weeks as he evaluated stocks of Penfolds sherry sitting in warehouses on the London docks, much of it unsaleable as a result of bacterial contamination. During his time he impressed Penfolds' London agent, who arranged for him to return north through France (Bordeaux, Paris and Champagne), finishing in Germany, after he had absorbed all there was to learn in Spain and Portugal. When he reached Bordeaux, he was taken under the wing of Christian Cruse, then in his 70s, who shared with him 30-year-old Bordeaux wines which, in Schubert's words 'had the typical violet, cranberry bouquet and character which is missing entirely from our wines. In comparison our wines are thin, harsh, dead and characterless. They are without the freshness and life which are two of the main characteristics of the Bordeaux wines.' Chance would have it that he also tasted the great 1949 vintage wines out of barrel, and saw the still-fermenting wines from the 1950 vintage being transferred to new oak casks. (It seems Schubert was unaware that this was not usual practice, but simply had been necessitated by the large vintage in 1950, which meant that fermentation vats had to be emptied much earlier than usual.)

Schubert came back to Australia determined to make a red wine which would age for at least 20 years, using new small oak barrels and high-quality grapes. With Bordeaux chemistry in his mind, he precisely specified that the juice should be not less than 11.5 and not more than 12 degrees baumé, with a total acidity of not less than 6.5 and not more than 7 grams per litre. He also determined that the fermentation would last for 12 days, converting 1 degree baumé to 1% alc/vol each day, this to be achieved by lowering the fermentation temperature in the early stages of fermentation, and raising it as necessary at the tail end. A rare heat exchanger was employed for this purpose, and it was necessary to hold the must under header boards (which prevent the cap from rising to the top) and to use rack and return techniques.

The 1951 vintage was Schubert's first opportunity to experiment with his ideas, and he used five new oak hogsheads (a total of 1500 litres) and a single 4550-litre old oak dry red cask as a control. He recounted that 'After 12 months, both wines were crystal clear, with superb dark, full, rich colour and body – but there the similarity ended. The experimental wine was bigger in all respects, better in bouquet, flavour and balance.' He went on to say that it was almost as if the new wood had acted as a catalyst to release previously unsuspected flavours and aromas from the hermitage (as shiraz was then called) grape. By contrast, 'several hundred dozen bottles of the control wine were kept, and while it developed into an exceptionally good wine in the orthodox manner, it never reached the heights of the first experimental Grange Hermitage'.

The 1952 vintage was made entirely with new oak hogsheads, and in 1953 two wines were made: one, as usual, from hermitage, the other from 100 per cent cabernet sauvignon from the Penfolds Kalimna vineyard in the Barossa Valley, then 70 years old. Schubert had decided from the outset that there was insufficient cabernet to make a high-quality vintage wine every year, and in that year made the one and only Grange Cabernet, because the composition of the grapes was perfect. The author has been privileged to taste the wine on a number of occasions (usually in the context of vertical tastings of all of the Granges extant) and it has always been one of the very greatest Granges.

Schubert watched the development of the first six vintages (1951–1956) with enormous satisfaction: the wines improved continuously. However, Penfolds' head office in Sydney became concerned at the amount of wine accumulating, and arranged a wine tasting for well-known wine identities in Sydney, personal friends of the board and the top management. Schubert recounted: 'The result was absolutely disastrous. Simply, no one liked Grange Hermitage. It was unbelievable, and I must confess that for the first time, I had misgivings about my own assessment of Grange.' Tastings organised around Adelaide (with the help and support of Jeffrey Penfold Hyland) were, with some notable exceptions, equally dire. The exceptions included Jeffrey Penfold Hyland, George Fairbrother, the most senior wine judge in Australia at the time, Douglas Lamb, a well-known Sydney wine merchant, and the late Dr Max Lake, who, said Schubert, 'either purchased for a song or consumed most of the 1953 experimental Cabernet himself'. On the other side of the fence were individuals who variously said, 'A concoction of wild fruits and sundry berries with crushed ants

predominating' and (this by another leading wine person), 'Schubert, I congratulate you. A very good, dry port, which no one in their right mind will buy – let alone drink.'

Prior to the 1957 vintage Schubert received written instructions from head office to stop production of Grange Hermitage. The reason given was the accumulation of large stocks of wine which to all intents and purposes were unsaleable, and that the adverse criticism directed at the wine was harmful to the company image as a whole.

While he was deprived of the funds to buy new oak barrels, with Jeffrey Penfold Hyland's connivance he continued to make Grange as best he could using second- and third-use barrels. Neither Schubert himself nor anyone since has suggested that the secret Granges made over the 1957–59 vintages were great wines. The irony was that at the very time when he was prevented from making the wine with new oak, opinions were changing, and just before the 1960 vintage he was instructed officially to start making Grange Hermitage again. In 1962, after many years' absence from Australian wine shows, the company decided to re-enter the ring, and at its first showing in the open claret class in the Sydney Wine Show of that year the 1955 Grange won its first of more than 50 gold medals.

It was much later (September 1979), six years after Max Schubert had gone into retirement and handed the mantle of chief winemaker over to Don Ditter, that he delivered a lengthy paper chronicling the development of Grange, and also disclosing for the first time that the wine came from various vineyards, and that the 1953 Grange Hermitage had 13 per cent cabernet sauvignon, the 1954 had 2 per cent cabernet sauvignon, and the much-lauded 1955 had 10 per cent cabernet sauvignon. Indeed, decades passed before a wine was produced without at least some cabernet sauvignon, although never more than 15 per cent.

Grange has only had four winemakers: Max Schubert up to 1973, Don Ditter between 1974 and 1985, John Duval between 1986 and 2001, and Peter Gago since 2002. All of these winemakers have jealously guarded the quality of Grange, and refused point blank to produce more wine than their quality standards dictate. The style has changed slightly, with the level of volatile acidity decreased, and alcohol increased. The former change was very much by design, the latter somewhat less welcome, reflecting changed growing conditions. However, none has exceeded 14.5% alc/vol. The wine is, in the slightly archaic words of the great English wine writer Hugh Johnson, 'Australia's one true First Growth Claret'.

**Granite Belt**, gazetted 25 March 2002, is the foremost Geographic Indication in Queensland. Its southern and eastern boundaries mark the border between New South Wales and Queensland; the west and north are straight lines of convenience. It is in fact the northernmost extension of the New England Tableland, and is a massive granite protrusion approximately 200 million years old. The hardness of the rock has guaranteed that this landscape stands out above the surrounding country (600–1000 metres). The most spectacular scenery is in the southern end of the Granite Belt, where streams have dissected the rock to produce dramatic boulder-strewn landscapes. It is certainly worth a detour; indeed, it is worth a single-purpose trip.

While the region was registered as a Geographic Indication well before the other recognised region (South Burnett) and some of the southern regions, its history prior to 1965 revolved around production of table grapes and the making of moderately lethal home brews from them. It was not until 1965 that the first *vinifera* plantings were made, 1 ha of shiraz, a fortuitous choice because it has proved the mainstay over the following 40-plus years.

It took a long time, but by the start of the new millennium the region had conclusively proved that it was and is capable of producing grapes and wines of high quality, judged by any standards. Excuses and/or reliance on the tourist trade were no longer necessary; success in national wine shows against all comers and national distribution provide objective proof of quality.

The climate of the region is the product of its high altitude and continentality. These two factors explain how a region so far north is able to produce high-quality table wines. That said, its northern location places it within the reach of summer monsoons moving down from the tropics (and, hence, vintage rain), while its continentality exposes it to the risk of spring frosts. The frost risk can be minimised by careful site selection, but vintage rain (while significantly less than in coastal regions) knows no boundaries.

The two principal soil types are different from those encountered in most Australian wine regions. One is a highly permeable, speckled (from granite), sandy, grey-black soil; the other is a light brownish-grey soil, also speckled. The subsoils are a bleached sand passing into clay at depth, and while the drainage is good, this increases the need for irrigation. Overall, 55 per cent of the plantings are red, and 45 per cent white, the principal varieties (in descending order of amount produced) being shiraz, cabernet sauvignon, chardonnay, semillon, merlot, sauvignon blanc and verdelho. Alternative varieties are also making inroads in the first decade of the 21st century.

There are 48 wineries in the region. The largest, Sirromet, has an absentee landlord – its winery is on the coast, and its vineyards (bar an unimportant patch of chambourcin surrounding the winery) are all in the Granite Belt. The foremost resident wineries are Boireann and Symphony Hill, which are out on their own in quality terms, followed by Back Pocket, Bungawarra, Golden Grove Estate, Kominos, Lucas Estate, Pyramids Road, Ravens Croft, Robert Channon, Whiskey Gully Wines and Witches Falls.

LAT 28°40'S; ALT 810 m; HDD 1602; GSR 519 mm; MJT 20.6°C; HARV End February to mid-April; CHIEF VIT. HAZARD Spring frost

**Granite Hills**  (est. 1970) was the second winery to arrive in the Macedon Ranges (two years after Virgin Hills). Gordon and Heather Knight had been graziers on the high, windswept hills for many years before successive booms and busts in the cattle and wool industries led to the somewhat unlikely decision to plant grapes in 1970. Unlikely, because the Knights had no previous connection with viticulture and did not even drink wine, and because of substantial doubts as to whether the grapes would ripen at the vineyard height of 550 metres. The first plantings were of shiraz and cabernet sauvignon, and the grapes from the first three vintages (1973–75 inclusive) were sold to Virgin Hills, and contributed a substantial part of the excellent Virgin Hills wines of those vintages.

The first Granite Hills wine was made in 1976, with son Llew taking over winemaking shortly thereafter, spurred by Brian Croser (his lecturer at the Riverina College of Advanced Education) into planting riesling. Granite Hills has lived in the shadows of Bindi and Curly Flat, partly because of its low marketing profile, but also because its two best wines are riesling and shiraz, not chardonnay and pinot noir. Exports to Ireland, Canada, China and NZ.

**Grant Burge**  (est. 1988) had very considerable industry experience before he established his eponymous winery in the Barossa Valley. Right from the outset, he has demonstrated a Kerry Packer–like ability to know when to sell assets and when to buy them. He has built a chequerboard of 440 ha of high-quality grapes across the Barossa Valley and Eden Valley, and has taken production to 400,000 cases. While the winery has had occasional outstanding success with chardonnay, sauvignon blanc and semillon, the heart of the high-quality portfolio lies with shiraz and cabernet sauvignon, plus the Rhône varieties. Exports to all major markets.

**Grape and Wine Research and Development Corporation (GWRDC)**  was established in 1991 under the *Primary Industries and Energy Research and Development Act 1989* (Cth). It is an Australian Government statutory authority, governed by a board of directors, and situated in Adelaide. Its stated function is to support the development of the Australian wine and grape industry by planning and funding collective research and development programs, and then facilitating the dissemination, adoption and commercialisation of the results throughout the industry. However, the GWRDC does not undertake research and development itself. Rather, it funds particular research and development programs run by the Australian Wine Research Institute, the CSIRO, and Australian universities. The program must be approved by the GWRDC and a budget agreed before commencement of the project.

The corporation is funded by a levy of $5 per tonne of grapes crushed by winemakers, and $2 per tonne for grapes delivered by growers to winemakers. These industry contributions are matched by the Australian Government, giving rise to funding of between $20 million and $25 million per annum, depending on the size of the crush. Typically, these funds will support research into 45 to 50 projects at any one time.

**Greater Perth Zone**  runs parallel with the coast of Western Australia, stretching over 200 kilometres north of Perth a little over 100 kilometres to the south. It includes the Swan District, most of the Perth Hills and roughly half of Peel, the last of these stretching well into the adjoining Western Australia Zone.

**Great Southern,**  gazetted 30 October 1996, in Western Australia, is Australia's largest region, a rectangle 200 kilometres from east to west and over 100 kilometres from north to south. It is thus not surprising that it moved quickly to establish five subregions under the

Geographic Indications legislation – more than any other region. While these encompass most of the wineries, they leave at least 50 per cent of the region untouched. Down the track, yet more subregions may be created.

Great Southern embraces climates which range from strongly maritime-influenced to moderately continental, and an ever-changing topography: there are the immense eucalypts of the south coast near Denmark and Albany which surround tiny vineyards like Tingle-Wood (taking its name from the Tingle Forest from which it was hewn), the striking round boulders and sweeping vistas of Porongurup, the harder blackboy country of Alkoomi in the Frankland River subregion, and the softer rolling hills of Mount Barker, where habitation seems to have somehow softened the remote savagery of many of the other subregions.

Two of the early prophets of the Great Southern area were Maurice O'Shea and Jack Mann, an unlikely pair in that not only did they never meet each other, but Maurice O'Shea did not even visit the region – his enthusiasm came from an armchair view of its climate. He is said to have expressed the opinion that if he had his time again, it was there that he would establish his vineyards. Jack Mann formed his favourable view of the area as a result of regularly playing cricket in the region between the two world wars.

Almost as unlikely was the first serious consideration given to the region by a wine company. In the early years of the last century, a large area of leasehold land was cleared at Pardelup, just to the west of Mount Barker. Regeneration problems with the scrub saw the land revert to the Crown, and the government sought to interest Penfolds in the project.

When Penfolds declined, the area became the Pardelup prison school. It was left to the distinguished Californian viticulturist Professor Harold Olmo, who was retained by the West Australian Government in 1955 to report on the status of the industry, to recognise the potential of the area for the production of high-quality light table wines.

Even then it took another 10 years for the first vineyard sites to be selected. The choice was prompted by the West Australian Department of Agriculture, which set up a joint venture with the Pearses at Forest Hill. This led to the progressive establishment of vineyards in the region: most were small, and some suffered from isolation (both from markets and from technical expertise). Only one large vineyard was established, by Frankland River Wines, with 100 ha of vines; this was leased by Houghton in 1981 and ultimately purchased by it. The smaller Plantagenet, however, dominated proceedings, making wine not only for itself but for a number of other well-known labels, and only Goundrey ran an operation of any real size in competition with Plantagenet.

**green** is a tasting term applied to a wine (usually young) whose grapes were picked too early, and which has tart, sharp flavours and, in particular, bitter tannins.

**Greenstone Vineyard** (est. 2002) brings together the talents of David Gleave, MW, a high-profile English wine merchant and writer; Alberto Antonini, a graduate of the University of Florence, an Italian flying winemaker with both postgraduate degrees and experience in Bordeaux and California; and Mark Walpole,

a viticulturist managing the 747 ha of Brown Brothers vineyards. In 2002 they purchased an outstanding property on the red soil of the Heathcote region, and planted it to 17 ha of shiraz and 1 ha each of mourvedre, sangiovese and tempranillo. The icing on the cake came with the appointment of Sandro Mosele as contract winemaker; predictably, he makes excellent wines. Exports to the UK, the US and other major markets.

**grenache** is a grape variety which is not, as one might expect, a recipient of the recent surge in national and international interest in Rhône red varietals. Production has remained static since 1997, notwithstanding the huge increase in the overall plantings in Australia since that time. In the admittedly low-yielding 2007 vintage, its 2000 ha produced 15,600 tonnes – compared with its heyday in 1979 of 52,000 tonnes. That level was significantly supported by high-yielding irrigated plantings in the Murray Darling region destined for cheap tawny ports and other fortified wines. The two regions of most importance in the new millennium are the Barossa Valley and McLaren Vale; while there are very old plantings (of about 100 years) in both regions, McLaren Vale seems able to invest the wine with greater colour, flavour and structure than the Barossa Valley can, although any rules such as this are likely to be proved by the exception. In the Barossa grenache the oft-described confection characters come to the fore, which can be useful when blended with mourvedre and shiraz, a common practice.

**gross lees** are the heavy or thick lees formed at the end of the primary fermentation; finer lees are deposited over the ensuing months.

**Grosset, Jeffrey** (and his eponymous winery, established in 1981) has taken on the mantle once worn by John Vickery as the greatest producer of riesling in Australia, crafted from estate plantings in Watervale and Polish Hill (of the Clare Valley). However, that is but one facet of his talents, which also extend to the immaculate Bordeaux blend gaia (Clare Valley), semillon sauvignon blanc (Clare semillon, Adelaide Hills sauvignon blanc) and chardonnay and pinot noir (both Adelaide Hills). He has been the leading force behind the widespread adoption of screwcaps in the Clare Valley, and, thereafter, Australia, stemming from a refusal to accept second best and a fanatical attention to detail. The wines are exported to all major markets.

**Grove Estate Wines** (est. 1989), in the Hilltops region of New South Wales, was established by a partnership of Brian Mullany, John Kirkwood and Mark Flanders. The vineyard is substantial, with 31 ha planted to semillon, chardonnay, merlot, shiraz, cabernet sauvignon, nebbiolo and zinfandel. The majority of the grapes are sold, but 4000 cases of very well made wines (Tim Kirk of Clonakilla is the contract winemaker) are released each year. Exports to the UK.

**Gundagai**, gazetted 25 March 2002, is the unapologetic offspring of a marriage of convenience, its northwestern boundary a straight line stretching between Temora and Junee on the warm to hot plains of New South Wales, thereafter plunging south and east into the heights of the Snowy Mountains around Tumut. (Had that southerly extension not taken place, there would have been a no-man's-land between the southern boundary of Gundagai and the northern boundary of Tumbarumba to the south.)

Prior history of viticulture centred around the warmest parts of the region, notably the first vineyard planted by John James McWilliam (the founder of McWilliam's), who established Mark View near Junee in 1877, before moving to the Riverina in 1912. That Junee vineyard continued in production until the 1950s, the red wines made by Maurice O'Shea at Mount Pleasant providing a fascinating insight into the past at the New South Wales Wine and Food Society lunches in the 1970s.

By far the largest vineyard is the 240 ha planting of Southcorp near the town of Gundagai. Chardonnay, shiraz and cabernet sauvignon account for most of the plantings, which are established on red earth and red podzolics, and on lesser areas of red-brown earths. Tumut is the odd man out in terms of climate, as it has a much lower heat degree day index and significantly higher rainfall than the rest of the region. The remainder has a climate which falls between that of the cooler Hilltops region and the distinctly warmer Griffith area. The climate is strongly continental, with cool nights and warm days, and a conspicuously high mean January temperature sandwiched between much cooler spring and autumn weather.

The wineries are Bidgeebong, Borambola and Paterson's Gundagai Vineyard.

LAT 35°07'S (Junee), 35°17'S (Tumut), 34°38'S (Cootamundra); ALT 210 m (Junee), 267 m (Tumut), 320 m (Cootamundra); HDD 2110 (Junee), 1500 (Tumut), 2050 (Cootamundra); GSR 240 mm (Junee), 420 mm (Tumut), 270 mm (Cootamundra); MJT 24°C (Junee), 21.2°C (Tumut), 23.7°C (Cootamundra); HARV Late February to mid-March (Tumut much later); CHIEF VIT. HAZARD Spring frost

a b c d e f g h i
j k l m n o p q
r s t u v w x y z

**Haan Wines** (est. 1993) was established when Hans and Fransien Haan acquired a 19-ha vineyard near Tanunda (in the Barossa Valley), since extended to 37 ha. The primary focus is on merlot, and in particular the luxury Merlot Prestige, but supported convincingly by viognier, shiraz and the Bordeaux blend released under the Wilhelmus label. Oak plays an obvious role in the shaping of the style, but is immaculately integrated, and does not overwhelm the fruit. Exports to all major markets.

**Hackersley** (est. 1997) is a partnership between the Ovens, Stacey and Hewitt families, friends since their university days, who decided that making their own wine would be cheaper than buying it. They purchased land in the Ferguson Valley district of Geographe and established just under 13 ha of sauvignon blanc, semillon, verdelho, cabernet sauvignon, merlot, shiraz, petit verdot and Western Australia's only planting of mondeuse. Most of the grapes are purchased by Houghton, but enough are retained to make around 1200 cases a year; the quality is reliably good.

**hand-picking** was the only method of harvesting grapes in Australia until 1969, when the first machine harvester arrived after its development in California. A second blow to hand-picking (manual excision of whole bunches from the grape vine) came with the equal pay for women decision by the Arbitration Court, which made employers unwilling to accept part-time work from mothers who dropped their children at school in the morning and collected them in the afternoon. Nonetheless, hand-picking remains the preferred option for makers

of high-quality pinot noir and (to a slightly lesser degree) chardonnay; for small, family-owned vineyards it is common for all varieties, although the increasing sophistication and adaptability of mechanical harvesters operated by independent contractors is steadily reducing it. The two major advantages of machine harvesters, which apply to small and large operations alike, are their ability to work through the night, when temperatures, particularly those of the grapes themselves, are significantly lower than those in the heat of the day, and the speed of picking, which is useful if the weather forecasts are ominous.

**Hanging Rock Winery** (est. 1982) is a tribute to the tenacity of founding owners John and Ann Ellis, who have stood firm in the face of the challenging climate of the Macedon Ranges since establishing the winery, and managed to find ways to fund the business during difficult financial times. The Hanging Rock Macedon sparkling wine and the Heathcote shiraz are the flagbearers, but the 40,000-case production spans every price point, every variety and many Victorian regions, and has proved a recipe for deserved success. Exports to the UK and other major markets.

**hard** is a largely self-explanatory tasting term to describe an unbalanced and unyielding wine suffering from an excess of tannin and/or acid, if red, or acid, if white.

**Hardy, Thomas** (1830–1912) is one of the great names in Australian wine history – in terms of both the man and the wine business he founded. He stepped off the sailing ship *British Empire* at Port Misery on 15 August

1850; a 20-year-old farmer from Devon in England, he had £30 in cash and a few personal possessions in a wooden box. Eight days later he recorded in his diary that he had decided to accept employment as a labourer with another Devon immigrant, John Reynell of Reynella Farm. He wrote, 'Although it was low wages, I thought I had better embrace the opportunity as I have no doubt I shall soon be able to better myself.' After an eventful two years in the Victorian goldfields, he returned to Adelaide in 1853 and purchased a property on the River Torrens, which he called Bankside. In 1857 he made his first wine, matured in a cellar which he had dug by hand at night after working all day in the vineyard. Within another two years he had exported wine to England, and set up a distribution operation for his wines throughout South Australia.

In 1876 the Tintara winery and vineyards, developed by a veritable who's who syndicate of South Australia led by physician and author Dr AC Kelly, went into receivership. The assets included a 283 ha vineyard property and a large number of wine stocks. Thomas Hardy recouped the total purchase price out of the first year's sales of those stocks, and from that point there was no looking back. By 1895 Hardy had overtaken Seppelt as the largest winemaker in Australia, with a vintage of 1.5 million litres. Federation opened further business opportunities, leading to offices and distribution depots in Sydney, Melbourne and Brisbane by 1905.

Thomas Hardy died on 10 January 1912, two days before his 82nd birthday, but the Hardy genes and name are still very evident, management of the business passing through son Robert to Tom Mayfield, thence to Kenneth, then Thomas Walter and Sir James Hardy, before it became a public company. In the first part of the 20th century Hardys extended its operations to Siegersdorf in the Barossa Valley and to Waikerie on the Murray River, expansions which paled in comparision to the move to Padthaway (known then as Keppoch) in 1968, which by the mid-1980s was supplying Hardys with 30 per cent of its annual crush of around 13,000 tonnes. Twenty-five years later, it was busy seeking to reduce its investment in Padthaway.

Shortly thereafter Hardys acquired the England-based Emu Wine Company with its Moffatdale winery and the Houghton Wine Company in Western Australia, plus an astonishing amount of cash at bank. The financial success of the acquisition rivalled that of Thomas Hardy's purchase of Tintara 100 years earlier. It was also around this time, in August 1982, that the wheel turned full circle, when Thomas Hardy & Sons Limited (as it then was) acquired the issued capital of Walter Reynell & Sons Limited, and moved its administration into the Reynella winery.

**Hardys** (est. 1853) in McLaren Vale was long a family-owned winery, its history written by Thomas Hardy. It became a public, stock exchange–listed company as part of the 1992 merger of Thomas Hardy and the Berri Renmano group. It may well have had some of the elements of a forced marriage when it took place, but the merged group prospered mightily over the next 10 years. So successful was it that a further marriage followed in early 2003, with CWA the groom, and BRL Hardy the bride, creating the largest wine group in the world. The Hardys wine brands are many and various, from the lowest price point to the highest, and covering all the major varietals. Exports to all major markets.

**Harewood Estate** (est. 1988) was established in Denmark, Western Australia, and in 2003 James Kellie, a former winemaker with Howard Park, purchased the property with members of his family. A 300-tonne winery was built, catering both for the 5000-case production of Harewood Estate and for contract winemaking services for growers throughout the Great Southern region. The quality of its wines is exemplary. Exports to the UK, Hong Kong and Japan.

**harmony** is for some winemakers and wine writers the most important single indicator of a high-quality wine. It necessarily includes balance, but points to a symbiotic relationship among all the components of quality wine.

**harsh** is a tasting term usually applied to red wine suffering from excess tannins, most often when young.

**hárslevelü** is a white grape from Hungary (see furmint).

**Harvey River Bridge Estate** (est. 2000) is a highly focused business and a division of parent company Harvey Fresh Limited, a fruit juice and dairy product exporter. The estate has 12 contract growers throughout the Geographe region, the 30,000-case production being made in a company-owned winery and juice factory. Exports to the UK, the US, Canada, Malaysia and Singapore.

**Hastings River,** gazetted 25 March 1999, is the sole region in the Northern Rivers Zone, and is home to the only new vineyards to have been established in Australia since 1980 which have not been supplied with irrigation, simply because they have no need of it. The downside is the problems caused by high relative humidity and growing season rainfall in excess of 1000 millimetres.

Viticulture and winemaking in the Hastings River region date back to 1837, when the first vineyard was planted by Henry Fancourt White, a colonial surveyor; by the 1860s there were 33 vineyards in the area. Following Federation and the shift to fortified wine, production declined and ultimately ceased in the Hastings Valley, as it did in many other wine regions, in the early years of the 20th century. In 1980, after 60 years of non-productivity, the French-descended Cassegrain family decided to expand into real estate and associated viticulture and winery interests. As a result they significantly – if improbably – expanded the modern viticultural map of Australia. They pioneered (with considerable help from Dr Richard Smart) new varieties and new ways of managing vineyards to meet the unique climatic challenges of the region, and have indirectly encouraged the development of other vineyards and wineries along the Northern Rivers Zone and adjacent New England region.

The best vintages are those in which the late summer rains are below average, but even in these circumstances the successful outcome of the vintage is dependent on split-second timing of harvest and very careful canopy management. The only assured answer has been the propagation of the French hybrid chambourcin, which is resistant to the mildews that otherwise pose a constant threat. Much the same applies to the other vineyards dotted along the northern New South Wales and southern Queensland coastline.

The gently hilly terrain offers a wide choice of aspect and hence response to (and use of) prevailing winds, which are useful in assisting disease control. The soils vary greatly in fertility, depth and structure, spanning rich alluvial soils and volcanic free-draining soils, and running from sandy through to heavy clay. Some are deep; some overlie gravel; others overlie limestone. The plantings are evenly split between white and red, in descending order of amount grown semillon, chambourcin, shiraz, chardonnay and cabernet sauvignon. Cassegrain towers over the other 13 small wineries in the region, including Bago Vineyards, Inneslake Vineyards and Long Point Vineyard.

LAT 31°27'S; ALT 70 m; HDD 2310; GSR 1080 mm; MJT 22.5°C; HARV Early February to March; CHIEF VIT. HAZARD Vintage rain

**Hay Shed Hill Wines** (est. 1987) is in the Wilyabrup district of Margaret River. Ownership changes and financial constraints had kept its 35,000-case production off centre stage; however, the arrival of former long-term Howard Park winemaker Michael Kerrigan in 2008 (as CEO and co-owner) has changed all that, although the winery had some very good wines in barrel, tank or bottle. This is a label which will become much better known in the second decade of the new millennium.

**header boards** are strong planks of wood cut to fit precisely into the matched fermentation tank (or vat). As the tank is filled with red must, the boards rise to the point where they are held submerged by small protruding lugs on the inside of the tank. This keeps the cap continuously submerged, obviating the need for pigeage or pumping over, although it is common for most of the contents to be removed by a must pump to a temporary tank and then pumped back in. It (rack and return) was a technique favoured by Max Schubert in the development of Grange.

**heat degree days,** often abbreviated to HDD, was devised in 1944 by distinguished US oenologists Maynard Amerine and Albert Winkler. It traces its roots back to 1735, and then to the mid-19th century observation by de Candolle that there is little vegetative growth in the vine at temperatures below 10°C. Amerine and Winkler assumed a seven-month growing season (in Australia October to April) and calculated the number of HDD by taking the difference between 10°C and the mean temperature of the month, multiplying that difference by the number of days in the month, then adding together the resultant figures for each of the seven months. The system has been refined, adapted and criticised, but remains the most widely used and understood system available; Dr John Gladstones has produced the most convincing and detailed adaptation of the system in *Viticulture and Environment* (2002).

The first methodical research in Australia was undertaken by Dr Richard Smart and Dr Peter Dry in 1988, preceding that of Gladstones. They added indices for mean January temperature (in other words, for the warmest month); mean annual range (January minus July temperatures), which indicates the degree of continentality; annual rainfall; rainfall of the seven-month growing season;

aridity (the difference between the vine's need for water and the water provided by rainfall and humidity); relative humidity; and sunshine hours per day. By way of example, the HDD range for Australia has a low of 1020 at Launceston in Northern Tasmania, and a high of 2340 in the Swan Valley of Western Australia.

**heat exchanger** is a tube-in-tube piece of equipment found in the majority of modern wineries, configured in multiple flattened 'S' shapes. The inner tube carries the juice, must or wine which is either to be cooled or warmed, the outer tube carrying the cooling refrigerant or hot water.

**Heathcote,** gazetted 21 August 2002, in the Central Victoria Zone, had a near-death experience when it was excised from the Bendigo region at the last possible moment. Bendigo might well be lamenting its loss, for in the last decade of the 20th century, and into the first decade of the 21st, Heathcote swept to the fore as one of Australia's best shiraz regions.

Heathcote was home to a number of vineyards in the 19th century, all destroyed by phylloxera in the last quarter of that century. All, that is, with the exception of an outlying vineyard planted in 1891 at Majors Creek, south of Graytown, by Baptista Governa. In 1955 that planting was joined by Paul Osicka Wines, a few kilometres to the north, Osicka having the distinction of being the first new venture in central and southern Victoria since the start of the 20th century.

The magic of Heathcote lies in the remarkable strip of soil starting 20 kilometres southeast of the town of Heathcote, continuing until just south of the town, then immediately turning north and running along the Mount Ida Range, and thereafter the Mount Camel Range, for a distance of over 60 kilometres. Viewed from the air, the red soil country is a spectacular scene: square or oblong patterns of vivid red alternate with verdant green rows of vines. On the ground, the slopes of the Mount Camel Range are equally impressive, and it is easy to see why land values have soared. The prized soil is decomposed Cambrian-era igneous intrusion rock known as greenstone, created 500 million years ago and forming the once higher spine of the Mount Camel Range. Progressive weathering caused the spine to move down the side of the range, covering sedimentary layers which now form the subsoil. It has the all-important combination of being well drained while keeping good moisture retention capacity.

As ever, water availability is an issue, and has slowed plantings in those parts which do not have access to the Waranga Western Channel irrigation scheme. Some of the early arrivals, such as Jasper Hill, Red Edge and Mount Ida, were content to persevere with the lengthy establishment phase and have dry-grown vines with sufficiently deep root systems to withstand most droughts, although the very protracted drought which began in the last years of the 20th century has had a major impact on vine health and yields in the vineyards without water.

Substantial vineyards have been developed here by wineries as far afield as Hanging Rock and Tyrrell's; the largest (175 ha) is that of Brown Brothers, with a diverse range of varieties. Most of these vineyards are in the northern end of the region, around Colbinabbin, where the warmer climate and greater water availability make economic sense. Red grapes make up 90 per cent of the plantings, and the vast majority of those are shiraz. Many of the vineyards have a small side bet on other varieties, leading to the planting of cabernet sauvignon, merlot, cabernet franc, sangiovese, grenache, chardonnay, viognier, riesling and marsanne.

There are now 51 wineries, the foremost being Domaines Tatiarra, Greenstone Vineyard, Heathcote Estate, Heathcote II, Heathcote Winery, Jasper Hill, La Pleiade, Mount Camel Ridge Estate, Munari, Occam's Razor, Sherlmerdine Vineyards, Syrahmi, Twofold, Vinea Marson and Wild Duck Creek Estate.

LAT 36°54′S; ALT 160–320 m; HDD 1490; GSR 279 mm; MJT 21°C; HARV Mid-March to early May; CHIEF VIT. HAZARDS Drought; frost

**Heathcote Estate** (est. 1999) is a 40-ha vineyard planted to shiraz (85 per cent) and grenache (15 per cent). It is the venture of Robert and Mem Kirby (of Village Roadshow fame) and is a sister winery to Yabby Lake in the Mornington Peninsula. In 2008 Tom Carson became chief winemaker for the two vineyards, after a long and very successful career at Yering Station. It should not be confused with Heathcote Winery or Heathcote II.

**Heggies Vineyard** (est. 1971), in the Eden Valley, was the second of the high-altitude (570 metres) properties purchased by S Smith & Son in 1971. Plantings on the 120-ha former grazing property began in 1973; the principal varieties are 35 ha of riesling, chardonnay, viognier and merlot. There are then two special

plantings: a 1.1-ha reserve chardonnay block, and 27 ha of various clonal trials. Exports to all major markets.

**Helm** (est. 1973) is the venture of Ken Helm, well known as one of the more stormy petrels of the wine industry and as an energetic promoter of his wines and of the Canberra District generally. His wines have been workmanlike at the least, but recent vintages have lifted the quality bar substantially, with conspicuous show success and critical acclaim for the rieslings. Plantings have steadily increased, and now include riesling, traminer, chardonnay, pinot noir, cabernet sauvignon, merlot, shiraz and cabernet franc. Exports to the UK, Singapore and Macau.

**Henschke** (est. 1868) has to be regarded as the foremost of the not-so-small red wine producers in Australia; Hill of Grace is its flagbearer. Its history, dating from 1842, is encapsulated by its address: Henschke Road, Kyneton SA 5353. Johann Christian Henschke arrived in Australia in 1842, settling at Bethany, but it was left to his son, Paul Henschke, to plant vines in 1868 on the small farm his father had started at Kyneton. Following his death in 1914, his son Paul Alfred extended both the plantings and the cellars, but in the face of fortified wine production, activity stalled until 1949, when 25-year-old Cyril Henschke persuaded his father to renovate and extend the winery.

In 1952 the first Mount Edelstone Single Vineyard Shiraz was made, followed by Hill of Grace in 1958. The generational baton was passed on to Stephen Henschke and viticulturist wife Prue following the death of

Cyril in 1979. While the contribution of so many generations of Henschkes should not be ignored, it is Stephen and Prue who have immeasurably lifted the quality of the wines, and expanded the vineyards throughout the Eden Valley and to the Adelaide Hills. The roll of honour for riesling, gewurztraminer, sauvignon blanc, sauvignon blanc semillon, pinot gris, chardonnay, semillon, cabernet sauvignon and shiraz blends is little short of extraordinary. Exports to all major markets.

**Henty**, gazetted 24 August 2000, is the furthermost Geographic Indication in the Western Victoria Zone, its western boundary part of the border dividing Victoria and South Australia. It is a far-flung region (bigger than either the Grampians or the Pyrenees) but still has relatively few wineries. What it lacks in quantity, however, it makes up for in quality. Previously (unofficially) known as Drumborg or Far Southwest Victoria, the name adopted at the time of Geographic Indications registration honours Edward Henty, the first permanent settler in what was to become the colony of Victoria. He landed at Portland Bay on 19 November 1834, bringing merino sheep and vines from Tasmania. While he presumably planted the vines, they disappeared without a trace, but the sheep flourished. Henty is ideal grazing country, gently undulating, the grass staying green for much of the year in normal seasons.

One hundred and thirty years elapsed before Karl Seppelt identified what was then known as Keppoch (now Padthaway) and Drumborg as promising cool-climate viticulture sites; the first Seppelt vines were planted in 1964. Grazier John Thomson was the next to plant vines (in 1975), seeking to diversify his farming activities, and doing so with great success. While the climate is one of the coolest on the Australian mainland and poses real challenges in cooler vintages, the region can produce wines of quite marvellous intensity, elegance and finesse. When Seppelt planted the first 60 ha of its 100-ha vineyard, knowledge of cool-climate viticulture was minimal. Almost inevitably, wrong varieties and wrong vine-training techniques were employed, and there were times when it seemed possible that Seppelt would sell or abandon the vineyard. Times have changed; given the suitability of the various soils in the region, the generous amounts of high-quality water available and the still-modest land prices, it would not be surprising to see new entrants in the coming decades.

The most important soils stem from volcanic activity, with Drumborg and Hamilton benefiting from moderately fertile, well-drained red kraznozem soils, with equally suited red volcanic soils over a limestone base in the area of Branxholme. The cool climate is neatly summarised by the principal grape varieties, which, in descending order of amount grown, are pinot noir, chardonnay, pinot meunier, riesling, shiraz, cabernet sauvignon, sauvignon blanc and semillon.

While Seppelt does not have a winery in the region, it does release a number of single-vineyard wines from its Henty vineyard. Of the nine wineries in the region, John Thomson's Crawford River leads the way, with Barretts, Bochara and Henty Estate also making high-quality wines.

**LAT** 38°21'S; **ALT** 15–100 m; **HDD** 1204; **GSR** 300 mm; **MJT** 17.7°C; **HARV** Mid-March to mid-May; **CHIEF VIT. HAZARD** Poor fruit set

**hermitage** is a now discontinued name for shiraz, curiously peculiar to the Hunter Valley, Great Western/Grampians and Coonawarra.

**Hewitson** (est. 1996) is the winery of Dean Hewitson, established after he had worked at Petaluma for 10 years, during which time he managed to do three vintages in France and one in Oregon, as well as undertaking his masters degree at the University of California, Davis. It is hardly surprising that his wines are immaculately made from a technical viewpoint, thus maximising the quality of the grapes from the old vineyards he has under contract. He has also managed to source 30-year-old riesling from the Eden Valley and 70-year-old shiraz from McLaren Vale, and makes a Barossa Valley mourvedre from vines planted in 1853 at Rowland Flat (believed, with good reason, to be the oldest in the world) as well as a Barossa Valley shiraz and grenache from 60-year-old vines at Tanunda. Given the provenance and quality of the wines, the prices are modest. Exports to the UK, the US and other major markets.

**Hill of Grace** joins Grange as one of the two most iconic Australian red wines, yet it has achieved this status in a curious, almost accidental, way. The evocative name is a translation from the German 'Gnadenberg', a region in Silesia from where so many of the early German settlers came, and is the name given to the lovely Lutheran church directly across the road from the vineyard. The oldest block of shiraz, called The Grandfather's, was planted by Nicolaus Stanitzki in the 1860s, and is only 0.6 ha. It is highly probable that the cuttings were descended from those

gathered on the Hill of Hermitage in the Rhône Valley by James Busby on Saturday, 10 December 1831. They have always been dry-grown, and are planted on a wide spacing: 3.1 metres between vines and 3.7 metres between rows. The 1-metre-high trellis consists of two wires which carry two to three arched canes with a bud number of around 40 to 50. The foliage is allowed to hang down to form a drooping canopy, which helps reduce shoot vigour. The ancient vines still yield an average 7.5 tonnes to the hectare, attesting to the quality of the soil. The adjacent Post Office Block One (planted in 1910) is 0.3 ha and Post Office Block Two (planted in 1965) is 1 ha. The House Block (1.1 ha) was planted in 1951, the Church Block (0.7 ha) in 1952 and the Windmill Block (0.7 ha) in 1956. The youngest of the group, Post Office Block Young, of 1 ha, was established in 1989.

The original plantings also included riesling, semillon, mourvedre and sercial, the last removed many years ago. Occasionally the mourvedre, grown as bush vines, ripens sufficiently to be included as a small percentage in the Hill of Grace Shiraz.

The land on which the Hill of Grace vineyard is planted was originally sold to Charles Flaxman by a land grant on 31 May 1842 for £1 per acre. It was purchased by George Fife Angas, who resold the land to Nicolaus Stanitzki on 22 April 1873 for £480. Stanitzki had arrived in South Australia in 1844 with his wife Rosalie. After time at Mount Barker, Birdwood and Hahndorf, they settled in a cottage at Parrot Hill, not far from the vineyard. It is believed by the Henschke family that Stanitzki originally had a lease of the property, as was common practice in those days, leading to its purchase in 1873. He died six years later, and his son Carl August Stanitzki inherited the property, ultimately selling it to Paul Gotthard Henschke on 17 December 1891. On 9 January 1951 the property was purchased by Louis Edmund Henschke from Paul Gotthard's widow. Louis was a son of Paul Alfred Henschke, who had worked the vineyard and property for nearly 40 years. Louis married Audrey Margaret Loffler in 1951, and the couple lived on the farm at Parrot Hill throughout their marriage until Louis died on 4 May 1990.

Louis helped his father and brother Cyril Henschke develop the family winery, extending the stone wine cellar at Kyneton and working for a time at Tarac Distillery in Nuriootpa to gain experience in making fortified wines. He was also in advance of his time in having a major interest in the preservation and management of the soil. The vineyard is owned by Audrey Henschke and her children Christopher and Leanne, and is leased to CA Henschke & Company, the legal entity inherited by Stephen and Prue Henschke.

Beginning in 1986 a program of clonal selection (an imprecise term at best) was initiated by Prue Henschke and assistant Ursula 'Uschi' Linssen, with elaborate observation and laboratory analysis designed to identify the performance of the very best vines, and use these as planting material. At the same time Louis Henschke did his own selection, choosing what he thought were good, well-balanced vines based on his long experience as a grower. Cuttings from the selected vines, dubbed Uschi's Selection and Uncle Lou's Selection, were planted in the nursery vineyard at Mount Edelstone to allow for further research. There has thus been a very careful selection of material used to create rootlings for the Hill of Grace vineyard to replace old vines that have expired.

One of the more extraordinary aspects of Hill of Grace is that the first bottling was made in 1958, six years after the first Mount Edelstone red (1952). The various wines from Hill of Grace had until then been sold in bulk to whoever wished to buy them. Indeed, Cyril Henschke (Stephen Henschke's father) was regarded as an early mover among the small- to medium-sized wineries in selling branded wine. Moreover, the wine itself was made in a thoroughly traditional fashion, and saw little or no new oak. Although the striking black label was adopted from the word go, the reputation of the wine grew strictly by word of mouth, much of that within South Australia. Neither Cyril Henschke nor, for that matter, Stephen and Prue Henschke, are particularly outgoing, although Stephen and Prue enjoy enormous respect from all sectors of the wine industry. It is a classic case of the wine doing the talking, not the winemaker. That said, the worldwide fame of Hill of Grace has inevitably led to innumerable requests for presentations of the wines, and vertical tastings have been held from time to time; these have, for obvious reasons, been regarded as major events on the Australian wine calendar.

**Hilltops,** gazetted 9 February 1998, is the northernmost region in the Southern New South Wales Zone, centred around the substantial town of Young. While the climate is unequivocally continental, with substantial diurnal temperature variation during the growing season, the altitude at which most of the vineyards are established ensures a long and even ripening period. Snowfalls in winter are quite common, but pose no threat to viticulture; spring frosts, however, do, and necessitate careful site selection along ridge tops and upper, well air-drained slopes. While substantial rainfall occurs in the growing season, most falls in spring; the dry summer and autumn provide excellent ripening conditions, but make irrigation essential.

Australia may not have been a melting pot to challenge the US in the 19th century, but it was most certainly multicultural, thanks in part to the gold rush decades. Gold brought Nichole Jasprizza from his native Croatia in 1860, but he prospered by selling the gold miners their daily needs – and he planted vines in the area. In 1880 he sponsored three nephews to come to Australia to join the business, and by the early years of the 20th century they had won prizes at the Sydney Wine Show, and extended the vineyards to 240 ha. Grapegrowing and winemaking continued in the area until World War II, when labour shortages curtailed activities; by 1960 the vineyards were so neglected that they were removed and cherries planted in their place.

Only nine years passed before Peter Robertson, together with various members of his family, commenced the establishment of his Barwang Vineyard (in 1969). It was a substantial farming property, with grapegrowing and winemaking minor diversifications from the core grazing activities. When McWilliam's acquired the 400-ha property in 1989, only 13 ha were planted to vines – although even then it was the largest vineyard in the region. McWilliam's has since increased the plantings to over 100 ha, while the Grove Estate vineyard has 55 ha. There are over 400 ha in bearing throughout the region.

The soils are rich and deep, typically dark red granitic clays impregnated with basalt. While capable of holding water at depth, they are free draining and support strong vine growth. These soils persist along the ridge tops and hillsides, which provide the greatest degree of protection against frost. Over 80 per cent of the vines planted are red, and in descending order of amount grown the varieties are shiraz, cabernet sauvignon, chardonnay, merlot and semillon. While the McWilliam's Barwang Vineyard does not have a winery in the region, a range of varietal wines are released under the standalone Barwang label. Chalkers Crossing and Grove Estate are the foremost of the producers with wineries in the region, Freeman Vineyards adding another dimension with its Rondinella Corvina red; in all there are seven wineries in Hilltops.

LAT 34°19'S; ALT 450 m; HDD 1880; GSR 310 mm; MJT 22.5°C; HARV Late March to May; CHIEF VIT. HAZARD Spring frost

hollow is a wine-tasting term describing a wine with foretaste and finish, but with insufficient fruit flavour and/or structure on the mid-palate.

honeyed denotes both the flavour and the mouthfeel of a mature white wine, whether dry (such as aged semillon or chardonnay) or sweet.

Houghton (est. 1836) is Western Australia's foremost winery, its origins going back to the 1830s. On 10 January 1835 a land grant of 3240 ha was made to Revitt Henry Bland;

a few years later he sold the major part of the grant to a syndicate of three British officers serving in India: Houghton, Lowis and Yule. As Colonel Houghton was the senior of the three, the property was named after him, although he never came to Australia, leaving the business under the management of Yule, who subdivided it further.

In 1859 Dr John Ferguson, the colonial surgeon, purchased the home block with its small cottage and vineyard, making 135 litres of wine in that year, some of which was offered for sale. The vineyard and cellars flourished under the control of CW Ferguson, Dr Ferguson's second son, and the property remained in the possession of the family for almost 100 years, finally being sold to the Emu Wine Company in 1950 when it became apparent that no member of the family wished to continue the business. However, prior to this the Mann family had joined forces with the Fergusons as winemakers; in 1920 George Mann left Chateau Tanunda and became winemaker at Houghton. He was joined in 1922 by his son Jack Mann, who became chief winemaker in 1930.

In 1976 Thomas Hardy & Sons acquired the Emu Wine Company, which had in the interim purchased Valencia Vineyards and its substantial Gingin Vineyard, 80 kilometres north of Perth. Under Jack Mann's watch Houghton's White Burgundy, with the diagonal blue stripe across its label, became the largest selling white wine in Australia for a period.

Houghton's viticultural holdings have been extended as far south as the Frankland River (in the Great Southern), and it purchases grapes from all the major regions south of the Swan Valley, most notably Pemberton and Margaret River, to supplement its Frankland River holdings. It has been blessed with a series of skilled winemakers since the departure of Jack Mann, its red wine flagships under the Jack Mann and John Gladstones labels of utterly impeccable quality. It is the Western Australian headquarters of CWA. Exports to all major markets.

**Howard Park** (est. 1986) has two operating wineries in Western Australia, one in the Denmark subregion of Great Southern, the other in the Margaret River region. While some of the Howard Park wines are blends from the two regions, most are single subregion/region wines. The main winemaking facility is the large, state-of-the-art winery in Denmark. The Margaret River property has a capacious cellar door (incorporating Feng Shui principles) and basic processing facilities for the first stage of winemaking.

It is the venture of Jeff and Amy Burch, and has gone from strength to strength since its establishment. Its beautifully made and perfectly balanced riesling, chardonnay, shiraz and cabernet sauvignon, the reds under either the Scotsdale (Great Southern) or Leston (Margaret River) label, are among the best in the state. Exports to all major markets.

**Hunter River riesling** is one of the names once used for semillon, along with Shepherd's riesling, Hunter riesling and even just riesling. Coupled with the outdated use of pinot chardonnay (abbreviated to pinot), this led to Tyrrell's Vat 63 Pinot Riesling (up to 1979) being in fact a blend of chardonnay and semillon.

**Hunter Valley Zone,** and its single region, Hunter (gazetted 18 March 1997), is the most peculiar nomenclature adopted under the Geographic Indications legislation. This should not be taken as pointing the finger of blame at the Geographic Indications Committee, but at the wineries of the Lower Hunter Valley, which stood back and allowed the tail to wag the dog. The only sensible rationale is that some had viticultural interests or long-term contracts with growers in the Upper Hunter Valley as well as in their home bases in the Lower Hunter Valley. To exacerbate the situation, attempts to register various subregions have met with mixed results: Rothbury has failed, Broke Fordwich has been successful, and Mount View and Pokolbin remain in suspense. Even if the three putative subregions are recognised, they will be of little practical relevance.

In 1847 the Hunter Valley Viticultural Society was formed, and during that decade plantings increased from 80 to 200 ha, spread over 50 vineyards. Between 1866 and 1876 the Hunter wine industry grew at a rate as spectacular as the boom which followed almost exactly 100 years later. The number of wine presses increased from 116 to 339; production went from 756,000 litres to 3.75 million litres; and the area under vines rose from 860 ha to 1800 ha. The peak appears to have been 1876, as by 1882 plantings had declined to 1630 ha, although by and large the industry remained fairly prosperous until the economic woes of the 1890s. In the 19th century both Victoria and New South Wales placed prohibitive duties on wines from other states, effectively locking out South Australia; Federation, and Section 92 of the Constitution, changed all

that, and the first 50 years of the 20th century saw the Hunter steadily shrinking in size. This was the era of fortified wine production, for which the Hunter Valley was manifestly unsuited.

In 1956 the valley had only 466 ha of vines in production, but the cycle of boom and bust was far from over. From the end of the 1960s plantings increased at a furious rate, reaching 4137 ha by 1976. The wrong choice of soil and variety, coupled with overproduction, saw the figure fall to 3169 ha in 1983, but from the mid-1990s through the first seven years of the new century the figure rose again, to 4697 ha.

**Huntington Estate** (est. 1969) was the Mudgee venture of Bob and Wendy Roberts, and for a time daughter Susie as winemaker. When the time came to sell in 2006, next-door neighbour Tim Stevens of Abercorn was the logical purchaser. Its 42 ha of mature vineyards, planted principally to shiraz and cabernet sauvignon, and smaller amounts of merlot, semillon and chardonnay, make it one of the more significant wineries in the region.

**hybrid** is a cross between *Vitis vinifera* and another species of *Vitis* (usually American), bred for a number of purposes, principally resistance to the mildews. Chambourcin is the most commonly encountered hybrid in Australia, although (perversely) it is banned in France, notwithstanding the introduction of newer hybrids such as rondo, regent, phoenix and orion.

**hydrogen sulphide,** chiefly found in red wines, results from the reduction of sulphur dioxide or elemental sulphur. It is detectable in tiny quantities, but can be removed from wine in the early stages either by aeration or the addition of small amounts of copper sulphate. If not treated it becomes mercaptan.

a b c d e f g h i
j k l m n o p q
r s t u v w x y z

**indigenous yeast**  see wild yeast.

**intra-cellular fermentation**  see whole bunch.

**irrigation**  can be used for two entirely different purposes. The first is to increase the yield of vines, regardless of the impact on quality. The second is to increase quality, but not quantity, by providing water consistent with the vine's needs at crucial stages of the growing season. In the former scenario, it can be supplied by flood or overhead sprinkler; in the latter, by precisely controlled drip irrigation, allied with moisture-measuring devices buried in the ground.

In Australia, the Riverina, Riverland, Langhorne Creek and parts of Currency Creek have relied on seemingly limitless amounts of water to generate high yields, but the rapidly changing climatic scenario means that whatever water is available in the future will be applied sparsely and precisely. Whether the cost of obtaining water and applying it in this fashion will make grapegrowing in the Riverland and similar areas economic is problematic. In all but a handful of the premium regions of Australia, the need for and use of irrigation will become more acute if, indeed, rainfall decreases and becomes less regular.

**Irvine's white**  is an incorrect name for ondenc, derived from Hans Irvine, who planted 21 ha in 1890 of what he believed was a white champagne grape, but which turned out to be a variety chiefly used for cognac.

a b c d e f g h i
j k l m n o p q
r s t u v w x y z

**Jacob's Creek** (est. 1973) was Australia's first genuinely international brand, starting life as a single shiraz cabernet malbec (the 1973 vintage was the first release in 1976), then extended with a riesling, and as at 2008 encompassing eight single varietals and five blends; seven reserve range wines, and, in the Heritage range, Steingarten Riesling, Reeves Point Chardonnay, St Hugo Cabernet Sauvignon and Centenary Hill Shiraz; and, finally, a single wine at the top, Johann Shiraz Cabernet. In 2007, 8.2 million cases of Jacob's Creek were sold in the domestic and export markets.

**James, Walter** was Australia's first wine writer, between 1949 and the end of the 1950s writing *Barrel and Book, Nuts on Wine, The Gadding Vine, Wine: A Brief Encyclopedia, Antipasto, A Word-Book of Wine, What's What about Wine*, and *Wine in Australia*. His elegant prose is best likened to that of Cyril Ray of England.

**jammy** is a tasting term describing excessively ripe and heavy red-grape flavours, sweet and cloying.

**Jansz Tasmania** (est. 1985) is the specialist sparkling wine arm of the S Smith & Son/ Hill Smith Family Vineyards, although when established it was as a (short-lived) joint venture between Heemskerk and Louis Roederer. Its 15 ha of chardonnay, 12 ha of pinot noir and 3 ha of pinot meunier correspond almost exactly to the blend composition of the Jansz wines. It is the only Tasmanian winery entirely devoted to the production of sparkling wine, which is of high quality. Exports to all major markets.

**Jasper Hill** (est. 1975) was established by Ron and Elva Laughton, and was for a long time the outstanding winery in the Heathcote region, its reputation led by Georgia's Paddock Shiraz and Emily's Paddock Shiraz Cabernet Franc, respectively named in honour of the Laughtons' two daughters. The 25-ha vineyard is dry-grown, and even though the vines are more than 30 years old, prolonged periods of drought make life difficult for man and vine alike. Annual production is 3500 cases. Exports to the UK, the US and other major markets.

**Jim Barry Wines** (est. 1959) is one of the larger family-owned wineries in the Clare Valley, established by the late Jim Barry. Several of his many children, headed by the irrepressible Peter Barry, run the business, which now has a production of around 80,000 cases. The Armagh Shiraz is its undisputed flagbearer, leading a portfolio of high-quality riesling, shiraz and cabernet sauvignon, an offering enriched by the acquisition of a 10.77-ha vineyard in Coonawarra. In the Clare Valley the three major vineyards are The Lodge Hill (59.64 ha), The Florita (36 ha) and the Armagh (26.99 ha), together with miscellaneous smaller vineyards totalling 115.8 ha. Exports to all major markets.

**John Duval** (1951–) is an internationally recognised and much-awarded winemaker who was the custodian of Penfolds Grange for almost 30 years as part of his role as chief red winemaker at Penfolds. He left that role during the unfortunate Rosemount period, but (happily) now has a consulting role with Penfolds, as well as having substantial consultancy businesses in other parts of the world. After leaving Penfolds, he wasted no time in setting up John Duval Wines (est. 2003), taking advantage of his intimate knowledge of the old vineyards of the Barossa Valley. He now has three wines in the portfolio: at the top, Eligo Shiraz; then Entity Shiraz; and on the third tier Plexus Shiraz Grenache Mourvedre. Many winemakers would consider themselves fortunate if they had a wine of the quality of Plexus at the head of their portfolio. Exports to the UK, the US and other major markets.

**Johnson, Hugh** (1939–) is arguably the foremost living wine writer. Born and raised in England, he obtained what he describes as a 'gentleman's degree' from Cambridge in 1960. Like the author, he began his 40-year career in wine simply by being in the right place at the right time, able to gain the attention of people of influence. One was the chairman of Condé Nast and founder of British *Vogue*, Harry Yoxall. It was he who arranged for André Simon, a grand old man of the English wine trade – when Simon was 85, Johnson 23 – to employ Johnson. Simon had founded the Wine and Food Society in 1931, and the idea was that Johnson would in due course become its new editor, looking after Simon as he began to scale back his prodigious literary efforts. From this point on it was just one icon appointment after another for Johnson, becoming the first wine editor of *Vogue*, wine correspondent and travel editor of the *Sunday Times*, wine editor of *Gourmet*, editor of the highly fashionable magazine *Queen*, and so on. He also became a director of Chateau Latour, a wine consultant to British Airways, president of the Sunday

Times Wine Club and of the Circle of Wine Writers (since 1973 and 1977 respectively), and an honorary president of the International Wine and Food Society (since 2002). His international awards are beyond count.

Of his many beautifully written books, the *World Atlas of Wine* (Mitchell Beazley, London, 1971 onwards) stands apart from all others. It demonstrates to perfection Johnson's ability to evoke a large landscape in a dozen or so carefully chosen words. He was, and remains, the most elegant of writers. In this context, the *Art & Science of Wine* (Mitchell Beazley, 1992), which the author and Johnson co-wrote, is of small consequence, but it did mark the fact that we have been friends for over 25 years. The one thing that separates us is that he has never written a formal tasting note and, even less, been tempted to give a wine any form of alpha or numeric score. His most recent book is *Wine: A Life Uncorked* (Weidenfeld & Nicholson, London, 2005).

**Jordan, Dr Tony** (1944–) completed his PhD in physical chemistry at the University of Sydney in 1970, moving to the US (University of Houston) and the UK (University College London) to work for two years as a post-doctoral fellow. Seeking full-time employment he returned to Australia, where he worked as a patent attorney in Sydney. The city life did not appeal, and when he saw an advertisement for a lecturer for physical chemistry and wine science at the nascent Riverina College of Advanced Education (now Charles Sturt University) he applied for and obtained the lectureship; by this time he had already developed a deep interest in the consumption of wine.

When he arrived at Riverina College he joined with Don Lester to create the framework of a course for oenology and viticulture; realising the need for an experienced and qualified winemaker to be the principal lecturer, the college appointed Brian Croser. With Riverina College bedded down, Jordan spent 1977 on sabbatical leave with Dr Helmut Becker at Geisenheim, Germany. Becker guided him through many of the research institutes and best wineries across Europe, adding immeasurably to Jordan's knowledge.

On his return to Australia in 1978 Jordan found that Brian Croser was leaving Riverina College to develop Petaluma, and the two formed a consultancy business called Oenotec. This rapidly gained a large volume of business, as it was the first of its kind in Australia, and continues as at 2009, albeit under different ownership.

In 1986 the author was requested by his legal client Moet Hennessy to find a CEO for its impending Australian sparkling wine venture, and Oenotec was hired to conduct the search. It ended abruptly when Jordan indicated his willingness to accept the position himself – he was clearly the best qualified person. Since that time he has held various roles with the Australian subsidiary of Moet Hennessy, and for a period was its international consultant winemaker for its operations in California, Argentina and Brazil, also becoming responsible for Cape Mentelle, Cloudy Bay (the best known of all New Zealand producers of sauvignon blanc), briefly Mountadam and, of course, Domaine Chandon. In 2008, aged 64, he retired as a full-time employee, but continues to consult for four months of the year to the Moet Hennessy wineries worldwide. He is also developing his SpearGully vineyard at Hoddles Creek, though on a modest, low-key scale, consulting to other wine businesses worldwide. He is on the board of the Australian Wine and Brandy Corporation.

a b c d e f g h i
j k l m n o p q
r s t u v w x y z

**K1 by Geoff Hardy** (est. 1987) is the brand of leading South Australian viticulturist Geoff Hardy, based on his large Kuitpo vineyard in the Adelaide Hills. Much of the annual grape production is sold to leading wineries, but sufficient grapes are kept to produce 3500 cases of high-quality wines each year, made by master contract winemaker Ben Riggs. Pertaringa is a separate, jointly owned McLaren Vale business. Exports to the UK, the US and other major markets.

**Kaesler** (est. 1990) dates back to 1845, when the first members of the Kaesler family settled in the Barossa Valley amid the waves of Silesian immigrants of the time. The Kaesler vineyards date back to 1893, but the Kaesler ownership ended in 1968. After several changes, the present (much-expanded) Kaesler Wines was acquired by a Swiss banking family in conjunction with former flying winemaker Reid Bosward and wife Bindy. Bosward's experience shows in the wines, which now come from 50 ha of estate vineyards, 40 ha adjacent to the winery and 10 ha in the Marananga area. The latter includes shiraz planted in 1899, with both blocks seeing plantings in the 1930s and then in each decade from the 1960s through to the present. The style of the shiraz, in particular, takes no prisoners. Production is a modest 22,000 cases, surplus grapes being sold. Exports to all major markets.

**Kalleske** (est. 1999) is a family-run business that has been growing and selling grapes on a mixed farming property at Greenock in the Barossa Valley for over 100 years. Fifth-generation John and Lorraine Kalleske embarked on a trial vintage for a fraction

of the grapes in 1999. It was an immediate success, and led to the construction of a small winery with son Troy Kalleske as winemaker. The 30 ha of vineyards, with an average age of 50 years, see no chemical fertilisers or pesticides; some blocks are certified organic. The density of the flavour of the shiraz and grenache is awesome; the flagship Johann Georg Old Vine Barossa Valley Shiraz comes from a block planted in 1875. The high quality of the wines has seen production rise to 7000 cases. Exports to all major markets.

**Kangaroo Island**, gazetted 8 December 2000, is the third-largest island off the coast of Australia (nine times larger than Singapore Island, 60 times larger than Hong Kong Island) and offers an extraordinary range of attractions for the tourist, the best known being its native flora and fauna, unpolluted beaches, seals, penguins and coastal scenery. It is also rapidly gaining a reputation for high-quality food products (witness Kangaroo Island chicken, Ligurian bee honey and of course all manner of seafood), with vineyards and wineries now making their contribution. This is an unspoilt and largely undiscovered treasure island for tourists. Daily light plane access (a 25-minute flight from Adelaide airport) and increased sea crossings (for motor vehicles) will result in greater visitation, but hopefully not degrade the island's freshness and beauty.

While the native habitat has been in existence for untold centuries, early attempts to settle on the island proved more difficult than might be imagined today. Likewise, sporadic moves to establish vines in the early 1900s (by the Potts family of Bleasdale), 1951,

1955, and the 1970s all came to nothing. It was not until 1985 that Michael and Rosi Florance succeeded in establishing 1 ha of cabernet sauvignon, merlot and cabernet franc vines, although birds proved a major problem, delaying the first vintage until 1990.

The highest profile development on the island is that of French flying winemaker Jacques Lurton, who has a 300 ha property that is so far planted with 11 ha of sangiovese, cabernet franc, malbec, shiraz, grenache, semillon and viognier. The Islander Estate, as it is known, is the most important single wine venture on Kangaroo Island, with its own onsite winery and a 100 per cent estate-based focus.

The island's slopes are gentle, with the north- and northeast-facing sites being preferred for viticulture. A measure of protection from the prevailing southeasterly winds is the major consideration in site selection. Self-evidently, the climate is wholly maritime-influenced, with the prevailing winds during the growing season (and in particular from December to March) coming directly from the Southern Ocean. Obviously there is no frost risk. The average summer temperature is 25°C, significantly cooler than that of Adelaide, while the winter temperatures are several degrees warmer. The low growing season rainfall makes irrigation desirable, but the quite high relative humidity (75 per cent) renders the vineyards moderately susceptible to the mildews and to botrytis. Overall, the climate is temperate and devoid of extremes, with a particularly even accumulation of heat. Surrounded by the Southern Ocean, it is very well placed to withstand whatever challenges climate change poses through the 21st century.

The soils are chiefly weakly structured, shallow red-brown sands overlying limestone in some sites, and have limited water-holding capacity, which emphasises the need for irrigation. Generally speaking, the soils are similar to those of Padthaway, and can sustain good yields if adequate water is applied. Overall, 80 per cent of the plantings are of red grapes; in descending order of size the varieties are shiraz, cabernet sauvignon, chardonnay, merlot, sangiovese, cabernet franc, riesling and semillon. The leading wineries among the nine in the region are Bay of Shoals, Rookery Wines and The Islander Estate.

LAT 35°50′S; ALT 30–180 m; HDD 1380–1450; GSR 280 mm; MJT 19.4°C; HARV Mid-March to mid-May; CHIEF VIT. HAZARD Birds

**Katnook Estate** (est. 1979), was established by the Yunghanns family but is now 100 per cent owned by Freixenet, the Spanish cava producer. It has 400 ha of organically grown grapes, making Freixenet one of the largest vineyard owners in Coonawarra, thus able to sustain its 125,000-case production, although it also sells grapes to other producers, both inside and outside the region. The historic stone woolshed in which the second vintage in Coonawarra was made (in 1896, during the John Riddoch years), and which has served Katnook since 1980, has been extended and restored. Its range of varietal wines starts below $20 a bottle, and (as at 2008) finishes at $100 a bottle for its flagbearers, Prodigy Shiraz and Odyssey Cabernet Sauvignon. Exports to all major markets.

**Kay Brothers Amery Vineyards** (est. 1890) opened its doors in McLaren Vale, and that same year brothers Herbert and Frederick

Walter Kay built the core of the stone cellars which remain to this day, using a model exhibited at the Chamber of Manufactures. Over the next 100-plus years there have been only three generations of Kays as winemakers: Cuthbert (invariably known as Cud) took over on the death of his father, Herbert, in 1948, and was followed by Colin, a Roseworthy Agricultural College gold medallist. Until 1961, almost all the production was sold in bulk to BP Burgoyne in England. McLaren Vale provided a rich source of wine, at least some of which was put to nefarious purposes by wine merchants in England, chiefly to bolster thin and insipid French wines from indifferent vintages. The 21 ha of estate vineyards centre on shiraz, part over 100 years old, and made into Block 6 Shiraz. The 14,000-case production allows exports to the UK, the US and other major markets.

**Keith Tulloch Wines** (est. 1997) began business in Pokolbin with Keith Tulloch as its owner and winemaker. He is a member of a family which has played a leading role in the Hunter Valley for over a century, and had been a winemaker at Lindemans and thereafter Rothbury Estate before developing his own label. He has the same almost obsessive attention to detail, the same almost ascetic intellectual approach and the same refusal to accept anything but the best as Jeffrey Grosset. He also produces a semillon with a small percentage of barrel fermentation and a few other winemaking tricks, which add a light embroidery to the wine, without impinging on varietal character, or its capacity to age in bottle. All the grapes for the 11,000-case production are contract-grown to exacting

standards. Exports to the UK, the US, Canada, Sweden and Singapore.

**Kilikanoon** (est. 1997) has come a very long way in a short time since its establishment in the Clare Valley. It is owned by a group of investors, led by Nathan Waks (principal cello of the Sydney Symphony Orchestra since 1970, when he was only 19) and Janet Holmes à Court. It has 18 vineyards, of which nine are in the Clare Valley, three in the Barossa Valley, three in the Southern Flinders Ranges and one each in McLaren Vale, Eden Valley and the Adelaide Plains, totalling more than 300 ha. The group sells excess grapes and buys others under long-term contracts from a small group of mainly Clare Valley growers who have supported Kilikanoon from the beginning. Major wine show success has been achieved in both Australia and the UK, the style such that ongoing accolades seem assured for its 40,000-case production. The most significant investment of the Kilikanoon group of owners is Seppeltsfield.

**Kingston Estate** (est. 1979), under the direction of Bill Moularadellis, has the roots of its production of several million cases in the Riverland region, but it has also set up long-term purchase contracts with growers in the Clare Valley, the Adelaide Hills, Coonawarra, Langhorne Creek and Mount Benson. It has spread its net to take in a wide range of varietals, mainstream and exotic, under a number of different brands at various price points. Exports to Europe.

**King Valley,** gazetted 12 October 2007, is one of the five regions in the North East

Victoria Zone, its northern tip at the town of Wangaratta, its southernmost high in the Alpine National Park. The country ranges from basically flat in the north to mountainous in the south. Other than in the plains around Oxley and Milawa (where the country is dead flat), most of the vineyards have been established on relatively gentle slopes, typically north- and northeast-facing. Encompassing the watershed of the King River, this is an important grapegrowing region, albeit one of considerable physical diversity. The King River joins the Ovens River at Wangaratta, and the region runs south through the Oxley Plains for 25 kilometres to Moyhu before entering a number of narrow valleys in the foothills of the Alps, with steep, well-timbered hillsides. At its northern end is the long-established location of Milawa, which is at the region's lowest point (155 metres); at the southern end is the Whitlands Plateau (800 metres), one of the highest viticultural areas in Australia. The plateau unsuccessfully sought to separate itself from the King Valley proper by individual regional registration.

As the statistics show, the climate changes progressively (and significantly) from north to south, from lower northern elevations to higher southern elevations, with an increase in rainfall and decrease in heat summations. Ripening is progressively delayed, the style of wine changes, and at the highest altitude only the earlier ripening white varieties are suited to table wines. However, the climate is ideal for the production of fine sparkling wine base.

King Valley began life as a tobacco-growing region, the rich soils and hard work of the predominantly Italian farmers ensuring highly profitable business. But times change, and as the tobacco leaf market dwindled, other crops had to be found. Graziers, too, were looking to diversify, and with crucial encouragement from Brown Brothers in the early 1970s, viticulture was the route chosen by most. Unsurprisingly, the soil types vary significantly throughout the valley, changing with altitude, slope and site characteristics. However, deep red clay loams abound, at times veering more to grey or brown in colour, but having the same structure. Drainage is good, fertility high, and vigorous growth is encountered in virtually all sites.

The King Valley is capable of producing high yields of good-quality grapes across the full spectrum from chardonnay to cabernet sauvignon, and it supplies grapes to a considerable number of leading wineries across South Australia, Victoria and New South Wales. Progressively more producers now make (or have made) some of their grapes into wine, taking up the excess in times of oversupply.

It is a thriving region, the Italian heritage coming into its own in the last decade of the 20th century as interest in lesser known Italian (plus Russian and Spanish) grape varieties has blossomed, and the wineries have given the King Valley a clearer and more substantial image. In turn, the imaginative use of these alternative varieties in both blends and single varietal offerings has built on that image.

A little over 70 per cent of the plantings are red, led by cabernet sauvignon and merlot in roughly equal quantities; then follow chardonnay, pinot noir, shiraz, sauvignon blanc and riesling.

LAT 36°20'S; ALT 155–860 m; HDD 1350–1580; GSR 640–1410 mm; MJT 20.8°C–22°C; HARV Early March to late April; CHIEF VIT. HAZARD Mildew

**Knappstein** (est. 1969) was established by Tim Knappstein in the same year that Taylors commenced business, also in the Clare Valley. It went through a number of changes of ownership before ending up as part of Lion Nathan. It has 115 ha of mature vineyards in prime locations, which are the source of the grapes both for the Knappstein brand and for other wineries in the Lion Nathan stable, most obviously Petaluma. Its 35,000-case production is exported to all major markets.

**Kominos** (est. 1976), in Queensland's Granite Belt, is owned by the Comino family. Tony Comino is a dedicated viticulturist and winemaker and, with wife Mary, took over ownership of the winery from his parents on its 21st vintage. Comino is proud of the estate-grown, -made and -bottled heritage of the winery and is content to keep a relatively low profile, although the proud show record of the wines might suggest otherwise. This is another Queensland producer to make seriously good wines, capable of holding its own against all comers from the south (as Queenslanders refer to anyone not born in the state). Exports to the US, Taiwan, Hong Kong and Singapore.

**Kooyong** (est. 1996) is one of two wineries in the Mornington Peninsula owned by Giorgio and Dianne Gjergja; the other is Port Phillip Estate. Sandro Mosele makes the wines for both ventures, and is widely regarded as one of the best winemakers on the peninsula, with a few fortunate clients accessing his contract winemaking services. He has both a science degree and a postgraduate winemaking degree from Charles Sturt University. Just as Jeffrey Grosset led the Clare Valley winemakers into the screwcap charge, Sandro Mosele has led the way with the Diam closure, adopted by a majority of the peninsula makers. Kooyong's 5000-case production encompasses a range of outstanding single-vineyard (in fact, single-block) selections of chardonnay and pinot noir. Exports to the UK, the US, Canada, Sweden, Korea, Japan and Singapore.

**Kyeema** was the name of a commercial aircraft that crashed while travelling from Adelaide to Melbourne in 1938. Its passengers included the senior family members of three of Australia's most important wine companies: Hugo Gramp of Gramp's Orlando, Tom Hardy of Hardys and Sidney Hill Smith of Samuel Smith & Sons and Yalumba. Charles Hawker, a federal minister, was also killed when the plane flew into Mount Dandenong in the Yarra Valley, not far short of its planned destination.

a b c d e f g h i
j k l m n o p q
r s t u v w x y z

**labels** on wine bottles in Australia have a number of constraints. The most important is what is commonly called truth-in-labelling, guaranteed by the Label Integrity Program (LIP). This is a control system self-imposed on Australian winemakers, the cost of compliance likewise funded by Australian wineries (by a levy charged on each tonne of grapes crushed). It requires winemakers to keep the most scrupulous and detailed records; this enables an audit to be made at any stage. The records must account for every tonne of grapes processed, whether estate-grown or contract-grown, and track the wine from those grapes, whether it is estate-bottled and -sold, bottled and sold as cleanskins or sold as bulk wine. Each year there is a parallel audit of a given variety within a given region, which charts how much of that variety is made from grapes grown in the region, how much is made from grapes grown elsewhere, and how the wine made from those grapes is disposed of. There are also annual random audits of winemakers large and small, and specific audits where the Australian Wine and Brandy Corporation is put on notice of possible irregularities.

The minimum amount of information required for the label on every bottle of wine sold in Australia is the producer's name and address, the alcohol level, the number of standard drinks the bottle contains, the statement 'Contains sulfites' (unless no $SO_2$ has been added at any time prior to the wine being bottled) and either 'Wine of Australia' or 'Product of Australia'. Additionally, for all wines labelled on or after 20 December 2002 there must be a declaration if any of a number of prescribed allergenic substances have been used during the making of the wine. The relevant substances are milk and casein, egg whites, nuts and isinglass. The legal requirement is that the statement must say either that the substance is in the wine or that it has been used in its manufacture. The most common form of compliance is 'Produced with the aid of milk products and traces may remain', using 'egg', 'fish' or 'milk' as appropriate, these all being fining agents. The hidden catch 22 is that there is no analytical procedure available to prove the negative: that *no* traces whatsoever remain, which may well be the case, particularly if the wine has undergone sterile filtration.

There is no requirement that the vintage, the variety or varieties, or the region or regions be stated. In the vast majority of instances, of course, they are stated, in which case the following principles apply. If a single variety is stated, the wine must contain at least 85 per cent of that variety. If two or more varieties are stated, they must be arranged in descending order of volumetric importance. If only two varieties are shown, the second cannot be less than 5 per cent. (Thus a shiraz viognier with less than 5 per cent viognier has to state shiraz on the front label, but the incorporation of viognier can be disclosed on the back label.)

If the vintage is specified, the wine must be at least 85 per cent of that vintage, and if a single region is specified, the wine must likewise be 85 per cent from that region. If more than one region is displayed, the regions must be shown in descending order of volumetric importance. All of these 'label claims' must be substantiated by records kept at the winery under the LIP.

**lacasse** is an enzyme associated with the formation of botrytis; it can be present in both white and red grapes. It may form before there are obvious signs of botrytis, and is especially damaging to red wine colour, turning it prematurely brown. Flash pasteurisation of the juice or must can be used if the infection is severe, but it is inherently improbable that wine of any quality will result.

**lactic acid** is one of the three forms of acid present in grapes, the other two being malic acid and tartaric acid. It is the mildest of the three acids, and is present in lower concentrations than the other two.

Virtually all red wines undergo a malolactic fermentation, usually spontaneously if the sulphur levels are not too high, but it can be commenced by inoculation. It can proceed in tandem with the primary fermentation or be delayed over winter until the following spring. Aromatic white wines are seldom encouraged or permitted to undergo malolactic fermentation, and it may or may not form part of the making of barrel-fermented wine such as chardonnay. With white wines there is a trade-off between the loss of varietal fruit expression and the gain in both textural and flavour complexity. In the case of red wines, it is wholly beneficial, for malic acid is sharp and harsh, while lactic acid is soft.

**lagrein** is a newly arrived alternative variety of red grape emanating from the Alto Adige region of northern Italy. It produces a deeply coloured and full-flavoured wine, which was first made on a commercial basis in Australia by Nelly and Alan Cooper of Cobaw Ridge in the Macedon Ranges.

**Lake Breeze Wines** (est. 1987) traces its roots back to 1880, when the Follett family arrived in Langhorne Creek to take up a substantial farming property. They began growing grapes in the 1930s, and made the first wine under the Lake Breeze label in 1987. They have 80 ha of vines at Langhorne Creek and a further 13.8 ha on Kangaroo Island. The Langhorne Creek plantings are almost entirely shiraz, cabernet sauvignon, merlot, petit verdot and malbec. Production is 15,000 cases, the major part of the grape production being sold. The style of the wines is typical of that of Langhorne Creek: generous, soft and medium- to full-bodied. The Kangaroo Island grapes are vinified under the False Cape label. Exports to the UK, the US and other major markets.

**Lake's Folly** (est. 1963) has the distinction, which can never be taken away from it, of being the first of well over 1000 Australian wineries to be started by people without any formal winemaking experience or qualifications, operated in tandem with (and usually funded by) the main occupation of the founder. Dr Max Lake (1924–2009) was a hand surgeon who had assembled a large wine cellar and consumed many great wines from around the world before beginning his search for suitable land in the Hunter Valley to plant a vineyard. More importantly, perhaps, in 1960 he had written the first of his many books, *Hunter Wine*, eventually published by Jacaranda Press, as was his second work, *Hunter Winemakers* (1970). He chose well, selecting one of the relatively rare patches of terra rossa in the Hunter Valley, directly opposite the McWilliam's Rosehill Vineyard.

The none-too-subtle scepticism of local winemakers about the prospects for the venture was redoubled when they found he had chosen to plant cabernet sauvignon, and buy new French oak barrels in which to age it. Cabernet sauvignon had disappeared from the valley around the time of World War II, but proof positive of its prior existence was a 1930 vintage blend of 50 per cent each of cabernet sauvignon and petit verdot grown at Dalwood and bottled by Matthew Lang & Company, which Lake drank with Douglas Crittenden in 1960. Lake is said to have regarded it as the finest Australian red he had drunk up to that time, but one has to wonder whether he thought it better than 1953 Grange Cabernet.

Lake was also in front of the field with his decision to have a second label (Folly Red or Cabernet Hermitage) and even a third label (Hunter Valley Estate and Export) for those vintages in which the capricious Hunter Valley climate turned on those trying to ripen and pick grapes in reasonably fine weather. He was also ahead of the game when he planted chardonnay in 1969, although the first vintage was not made until 1974, Tyrrell's and Craigmoor having beaten him by three years.

The first vintage of cabernet sauvignon was a foot-stamped wine from 1966, a great year in the Hunter. Even though Lake regarded the Hunter Valley as his vinous backyard, and had bought and consumed most, if not all, of its great wines, and seen vineyards in 1960 without a single leaf remaining after a violent hailstorm, being there, growing grapes and making wine led him to give the following one- or two-word descriptions for the vintages from 1966 through to 1984: 1966 – dry, hot; '67 – good; '68 – wet vintage; '69 – bushfires; '70 – good; '71 – very wet; '72 – good; '73 – good; '74 – wet; '75 – cyclone loss; '76 – gale loss; '77 – hail; '78 – drought; '79 – dry, good;

'80 – dry, very good; '81 – drought; '82 – top; '83 – excellent; '84 – good rain. (*Plus ça change.*) Over the decades, Lake suffered more than most from cork problems, with many tainted bottles despite having paid the price for what (on appearance) were top-quality corks. Having had the mediocre 1968 vintage wine chosen by the Ritz London for its main restaurant wine list, there was only one way to go, although through the decades there were those who were less than convinced by the quality of the cabernet sauvignon, and said so. On the other hand, the quality of the chardonnays was seldom in doubt, and has often been on a par with, or better than, Tyrrell's Vat 47 Chardonnay.

In 1982 Lake handed the winery over to his son Stephen, who 18 years later sold the business to Perth businessman Peter Fogarty, who had previously established the Millbrook Winery in the Perth Hills. Rodney Kempe has remained the winemaker since 2000 and the quality of the wines has never been better.

The history of Lake's Folly has been given at such length because of its significance in the broader scheme of the Australian industry. And while the late Max Lake may have been understandably bitter when Stephen decided to sell, the fact is that Max's achievements remain undimmed.

**Lamont's Winery** (est. 1978) carries on the tradition of Jack Mann through his daughter Corin Lamont and granddaughter Kate Lamont in this Swan Valley winery (in the Swan District, Western Australia). The once-heroic wine style which was a direct legacy of Mann has been given more elegance without losing what to Mann was a fundamental requirement of any good wine: generosity. This move has been reinforced by Margaret River-grown grapes, which in turn has led to a second cellar door in that region.

**Langhorne Creek,** gazetted 16 October 1998, has been growing grapes since 1860, but is facing challenges unlike any encountered in the intervening 150 years. Its once symbiotic union with the Murray River, the Bremer River and Lake Alexandrina has been shattered by drought, rising salinity and more than 50 years of profligate use of water from the Murray Darling Basin. This has produced a life-threatening situation for its wineries and vineyards; they are responding with salt-mitigation and drought-proofing measures, but with no certainty that they will succeed. It is a situation which will be played out over a period of years, with climate (rainfall, temperatures and wind) in Langhorne Creek and thousands of kilometres to the east and north outside anyone's control. Other relevant factors include government (federal and state) water resource strategies (their effectiveness remains a matter of conjecture), fights with all the eastern capital cities' demands for water, headline-grabbing looming ecological disasters and those with stock seeking more water than is available.

All of this would have seemed like a hybrid horror and science fiction book when Alfred Langhorne left Sydney in 1841 with a mob of cattle and drove them all the way to the flood plain of the Bremer River. He crossed the river, decided far was far enough, and squatted on the fertile ground at what was soon named Langhorne's Crossing. When a bridge was built it was likewise named after him, and the region became known as Langhorne's Creek (the 's' was dropped later).

Frank Potts had arrived in South Australia even earlier (in 1836), and when the government subdivided the area in 1850, he acquired 130 ha, reputedly attracted by the fertile soils and vast red gums. Ten years later he planted a little over 12 ha of shiraz and verdelho on either side of the Bremer River, constructing a unique weir and channel system by which he was able to divert the river during winter, flood irrigating (to a depth of several feet) the vineyard and providing the subsoil with sufficient moisture to last through the entire growing season.

Five generations later the Potts family still presides over Bleasdale, but Langhorne Creek is now a very different place. The enduring link with the past is the Stonyfell Vineyard, established in 1890 by Arthur Formby, but which soon passed into the ownership of Ronald Martin of Stonyfell, and hence into that of Saltram. The striking and individually numbered label of Stonyfell Metala Cabernet Shiraz remains one of the most immediately recognisable of all Australian wine labels.

Lindemans began buying grapes from Langhorne Creek in the 1960s, but it was left to Wolf Blass to put the final seal of approval on the region. He understood better than anyone its ability to provide red wines with abundant flavour and soft mouthfeel at a low price per tonne. The Langhorne Creek component of the wines he made between 1966 and 1990 was critical to their show successes and ready acceptance by the marketplace. Emphatic though the endorsement by Wolf Blass may have been, an even more significant one was made by

Orlando Wyndham, which in the mid-1990s invested $15 million in a purpose-designed state-of-the-art vineyard planted specifically to meet the needs of its world brand, Jacob's Creek. Using GPS and laser-guided planting machinery, vineyards of 300–500 ha were planted in a single season, ultimately lifting the planted area from 1650 ha to over 4400 ha.

The small family-owned wineries of the region (curiously, there is no large company winery in existence) are by and large congregated in its northern part. The underground water on which they traditionally relied (rather than Lake Alexandrina itself) began to show rising salinity in the 1990s, and a number gave up their allocation, replacing it with allocations direct from the Murray River. Those who went entirely down that path now find themselves in an invidious position; those who kept some of their underground entitlements (such as Bremerton Wines) are, for the time being, at least, in a better position. The long-term rainfall of the region was 300 millimetres, but it has been many years since that amount or more has fallen in a 12-month period; praying for rain will become part of standard viticultural practice, it seems.

The problems for the large vineyards will be every bit as great. Here the sheer scale of the investments may make desalination projects theoretically possible, but the cost per megalitre may prove a greater barrier than mastering the technology. The most tangible hope lies in a major pipeline, funded by the South Australian Government and drawing water from upstream (above the last weir) in the Murray River, due to be completed in 2010.

Langhorne Creek is a red wine region first and foremost; cabernet sauvignon and shiraz are by far the most important varieties, accounting for much of the 85 per cent of land under vine devoted to red grapes. Beyond this, most of the mainstream varietals are grown somewhere in the region. The principal wineries or brands solely linked to the region (among 22) are Ben Potts, Bleasdale Vineyards, Bremerton, Brothers in Arms, Casa Freschi, John's Blend, Lake Breeze, Rusticana, Step Road/Beresford, Temple Bruer and Zonte's Footstep.

LAT 35°15'S; ALT 30 m; HDD 1520; GSR 140 mm; MJT 19.9°C; HARV Late February to late April; CHIEF VIT. HAZARD Drought

**Langmeil Winery** (est. 1996) has come a long way since the Lindner family sold its interests in St Hallett and decided to purchase the Paradale winery (built in 1932) and its 5-ha vineyard in the Barossa Valley. This vineyard had 2 ha of shiraz that had been planted in 1843, the oldest surviving planting of the grape in the world. The vines had been planted by Christian Auricht, who had written a family history book titled *Persecution to Freedom*. Richard Lindner, learning of this history, promptly gave the title 'Freedom' to the wine made from this block. Langmeil makes a second shiraz of similar quality from other vines more than 100 years old, and a string of lower priced but high-quality red wines, plus a credible riesling. It is a business in a hurry, with a formidable range of skills available through the various partners, including marketing supremo Zar Brooks. Exports to the UK, the US and other major markets.

**La Pleiade** (est. 1998) is a joint venture between Michel and Corinne Chapoutier (of Rhône Valley fame) and Ron and Elva

Laughton (of Jasper Hill). In the spring of 1998 a vineyard using Australian shiraz clones and imported French clones was planted in Heathcote. It is run biodynamically, and supremely rich and dense wines have been made, possibly shaped in part by the ongoing drought. The single wine each year is made at Jasper Hill, and despite the youth of the vines, it has been of exceptional quality.

**Lark Hill** (est. 1978), in the Canberra District, was established by Dr David Carpenter and wife Sue. It stands high above Canberra at an altitude of 860 metres, level with the observation deck on Black Mountain Tower, and offers splendid views of the Lake George escarpment. The Carpenters have made wines of real quality, style and elegance from the start, but have defied all the odds (and conventional thinking) with the quality of their pinot noirs in favourable vintages. Significant changes have come through son Christopher gaining three degrees, including a double in wine science and viticulture from Charles Sturt University, the progression towards biodynamic certification of the vineyard and the opening of a restaurant in 2007.

**Larry Cherubino Wines** (est. 2005) is the eponymous virtual winery venture of Larry Cherubino, who owns neither vineyards nor winery, instead relying on his numerous contacts in the southern regions of Western Australia, focusing in particular on the Frankland River. Cherubino has a particularly distinguished winemaking career, first at Hardys, then Houghton, and thereafter as consultant/flying winemaker in Australia, New Zealand, South Africa, the US and Italy. The quality of the wines is exemplary. Exports to the UK, the US and Canada

**late harvest** refers to grapes left on the vine until long after the normal harvest date. Late-harvested white grapes are used to make sweet wine (with or without the impact of botrytis), and late-harvested white and red grapes are used to make fortified wines, especially the richer styles.

**layering** is a method of vine replacement that has an ancient history, but is possible only where phylloxera is absent. When a vine dies, a suitable cane from an adjoining vine is pruned only to its maximum length (determined by the spacing between vines along the vine row) and buried in the soil except for its tip, which appears out of the soil at the point where the new vine will eventually grow. The cane will slowly grow its own roots, and the umbilical cord between it and the mother vine can eventually be cut, although it is not uncommon to see it left as a permanent arrangement. If there is no suitable cane, or even where there is, an alternative is to plant a new rootling protected by a plastic cylinder known as a grow-guard, which keeps the young vine safe from attack by rabbits or wallabies, and also promotes a good rate of growth.

**leafroll virus** is present in all countries where grapes are grown, and has a dramatic effect on yield, decreasing it by half, and an equally adverse impact on the colour and flavour of wines made from the grapes. It is believed to have originated in the Near East (rather than the US, the source of all other blights) and has been present since the first grape cuttings came to Europe. In autumn it turns the leaves of red varieties to bright purple red, and those of white varieties to yellow, pleasing the eye but not the palate. Once a vine or vineyard is infected by the virus there is no cure, other than removal of the vines. Its spread became significantly greater in the wake of the grafting which became necessary to combat phylloxera, simply because there were then two sources of possible infection – the rootstock and the scion. Modern methods have been developed to test for the presence of the virus in vines; the virus can be eliminated either by heat treatment or by tissue culture, where new vines are grown in a laboratory from minute pieces of tissue cut from a virus-free vine.

**Leasingham** (est. 1894), in the Clare Valley, was originally known as the Stanley Wine Company, and, in the fullness of time, as Stanley Leasingham. The Stanley Wine Company was formed at the end of 1894 largely to deal with what promised to be a rapidly mounting surplus of grapes from within the district. The founding shareholders were JC Christison, a local brewer; JH Knappstein, one of the largest vineyard owners in the district; Magnus Badger, a local solicitor; and Dr Otto Wein-Smith, the district medical practitioner. The syndicate purchased the Clare Jam Factory and the Stanley Wine Company opened its doors for business in March 1895. Alfred Basedow, a member of one of South Australia's most famous winemaking families, joined as winemaker for that first vintage. Together with one of his brothers, he had completed the winemaking course at Montpellier in France, and had subsequently gained practical experience working as a winemaker in Germany, Spain and Portugal.

Even though the winemaking facilities installed for that first vintage, which amounted to 18,000 litres, were very primitive, the wines took prizes at the Royal Adelaide Wine Show. Production grew in leaps and bounds, and the size of the winery doubled and redoubled. By 1899 the vineyard had reached 162,000 litres, with 450,000 litres of wine in stock. Large quantities had been shipped to England in the previous six months. Basedow was clearly a winemaker in advance of his time. In his post-vintage report for 1900 he said: 'My refrigerator works very well. I have had a blower fixed up to blow a big draft of air onto the pipes, and I reckon I can now cool 1000 gallons [4550 litres] of wine 10° Fahrenheit in a little over an hour with 100 gallons of water.' Another touch of the 1900s was the use of seaweed to insulate the ceiling of the winery.

By 1901 the vintage had reached 360,000 litres and two years later it was 450,000. In that year it was the sixth-largest winery in South Australia, and by the time the 1903 vintage was completed more than 2 million litres of wine were in stock. This rate of expansion, obviously enough, was not sustainable; by 1907 the vintage had fallen to 250,000 litres and 900,000 litres were held in storage.

The frantic pace of the development, and the accumulation of wine stocks up to 1903, had taken its toll on the shareholders. Christison had become involved in a bitter public brawl with BP Burgoyne, the London merchant who had up to that point purchased almost all of Stanley's production. JH Knappstein was forced to return from Perth, where he had a thriving ship's chandlery business, to take control of the situation. He bought the shares of the now thoroughly nervous and disenchanted Magnus Badger and Otto Wein-Smith, and set off to London in 1903 seeking replacement markets for those lost through the argument with Burgoyne. He was sufficiently successful to return to South Australia in 1904 to collect his family, increase his shareholding in the company to 75 per cent, and return to England, where he remained for the next three years. There he worked hard and successfully to build markets for Stanley's wines, principally its export burgundy.

When Christison died in 1911 his widow sold his interest to Knappstein; this was the commencement of a 50-year ownership by the Knappstein family. Like many Australian wine companies up to 1953, the emphasis was on the production of fortified wines, with bulk sales the core of the business. When, thereafter, table wine slowly became more important, the Knappsteins (Mick and Alex) established an all-important relationship with Lindemans; each year, prior to vintage, they would travel to Sydney to ascertain Lindemans' requirements for the coming vintage, and a significant portion of the crush would be made to its requirements. Penfolds, Seppelt, Hardys, Orlando and McWilliam's were also customers.

New vineyards were established, using an innovative share-farming structure with the company's employees. Between 1947 and 1971 over 240 ha of vineyards in the Watervale area were established, riesling dominating the plantings, which increased from 1100 tonnes in 1962 to just under 5000 tonnes by 1970.

It was a time of take-over fever, with many multinationals entering the scene, and, after 10 serious offers were received between 1968 and 1970, the 11th, by HJ Heinz, was too good to refuse. But, like so many other multinational non-wine companies, HJ Heinz found the business much more complicated than it had anticipated, and in 1988 sold the winery to what was then Hardys, an ownership which endured until August 2008, when CWA announced its intention to sell the winery and estate vineyards. Its riesling, shiraz and cabernet sauvignon, released under various labels and price points, are of the highest quality and are exported to all major markets.

**Leconfield** (est. 1974) was established by Sydney Hamilton in Coonawarra, a seemingly unremarkable event. But Syd had retired 20 years earlier, after working with the Hamilton family wine interests in McLaren Vale for 30 years. He had decided to come out of retirement aged 76, and to scour regions as far afield as Tasmania, Canberra and the Victorian foothills of the Alps, the Canberra District interesting him most. Bill Redman was a lifelong friend, and, hearing of Syd's plans, told him that a dairy man with some hectares of red soil in the heart of Coonawarra wished to sell. Hamilton moved decisively, buying the property and erecting the winery in time for the 1975 vintage (made from purchased grapes). With equal speed he planted 8 ha of cabernet sauvignon and 4 ha of riesling, entering vinous folklore a few years later when he explained on the back label of the cabernet sauvignon that the grapes had been hand-picked 'by experienced women'. His aim had been to make a classic Australian wine, and he achieved that aim before (reluctantly) bowing to family pressure: at the age of 84 he sold Leconfield to his nephew, Dr Richard Hamilton, who had established his eponymous McLaren Vale winery in 1972. The quality of the Leconfield wines is beyond reproach, the style elegant and fruit (not oak) driven. They are exported to the US, the UK and other major markets.

**lees** are the deposits formed by dead yeast cells which fall to the bottom of the barrel or tank at the end of primary fermentation. Until the 1980s, New World producers were taught by their universities to separate the lees (first by cold-settling and racking, and, thereafter, by one or other means of filtration) and to dispose of them. Most aromatic and unwooded white wines continue to be made that way, but the situation is very different with chardonnay and pinot noir, where the lees form an integral part of the winemaking process. With both those varieties, the gross lees have a twofold function: they provide a natural barrier to oxidation by absorbing dissolved oxygen in the wine, and they add to the texture and mouthfeel of the wine. While fuller bodied red wines are often racked as soon as the malolactic fermentation has been completed (or, for that matter, before it starts), there is increasing interest in the beneficial role of gross lees. The downside is the extra work involved and the extra space taken by the lees (and hence extra barrels) until the wine is racked off them.

**lees stirring** is practised far more commonly with white wines than with red wines. It involves agitating the lees either by a hand-held implement, used in a low-speed egg-beating action, or by blowing inert gas into the bottom of the barrel. It magnifies the sensory impact of the lees, but (unless it is inert gas) might be seen to compromise the freshness of the wine. It is less frequently used with red wines, particularly where it is not intended that they be filtered.

**Leeuwin Estate** (est. 1974) is, in the view of the author, the foremost producer of chardonnay in Australia. It is now, and was at the time of its establishment in the Margaret River region, owned by the Horgan family, with parents Denis and Tricia at the helm, and son Justin the general manager. Leeuwin Estate has always set the highest standards for the quality of its wines, and has maintained that as the range has widened both in terms of variety and in terms of the second label products.

Cork was an Achilles' heel of the chardonnay; to the relief of Leeuwin's many admirers, it is now bottled under screwcap. Exports to all major markets.

**Len Evans Tutorial** was the last initiative, and, in Evans' view, one of the most important, of his long and creative life. It annually brings together, for five days, 12 of the most promising Australian wine persons (winemakers, sommeliers, retailers, journalists and even simply wine lovers), exposing them to intensive tastings (in various formats) of great wines from all parts of the globe, including (importantly) Australia at one extreme and Domaine de la Romanée-Conti at the other, and five tutors who impart all the knowledge they have at their disposal.

**Leo Buring** is the eponymous brand and business established by Leo Buring; see Buring, Leo.

**Limestone Coast Zone** has as its eastern perimeter the South Australian–Victorian border, which runs only a degree or two off north–south, its northern perimeter a straight line at right angles to the border, and well north of the significant vineyards around Bordertown, its western and southwestern perimeter the Southern Ocean. It has five regions – Coonawarra, Mount Benson, Padthaway, Robe and Wrattonbully – with Mount Gambier going through the process for registration as a Geographic Indication at the time of writing. It is a very important zone as at 2009, and, if the climate were to warm significantly, would become even more important in the years ahead.

**Limousin** is an old French region in which the famous Limoges porcelain is made, but is also home to extensive oak forests which bear its name. The oak is widely used by winemakers, and often grouped with other centre-of-France oaks of Nevers and Troncais.

**Lindemans** (est. 1840) traces its history back to when a royal navy surgeon named Henry John Lindeman resigned his commission to make his way to Australia. He continued on to the Hunter River, and in 1842 purchased a property near the Paterson River which he named Cawarra, an Aboriginal word meaning 'running waters'. In 1843 he planted the first vines, and within a few years had erected a winery and commenced winemaking operations. He thus pre-empted Dr Christopher Rawson Penfold, who arrived at Magill in 1844, believing, as did Lindeman, that wine and health had a symbiotic relationship. Lindeman's winery flourished, and by 1870 he decided it

was necessary to establish a head office and storage and bottling facilities in Sydney. It was first located at the Exchange Cellars in Pitt Street, but subsequently moved to the Queen Victoria Building, where its administration and bottling plant remained until the second half of the 1930s. Lindeman died in 1882, aged 71, and the business was carried on by his three sons, Arthur Henry as winemaker, Charles Frederick as manager, and Herbert having the best of the three jobs, as 'wine-taster'. The coming of Federation in 1901 and the opening-up of the New South Wales market to South Australian wine spelt disaster for many of the smaller wineries which had flourished at the end of the 19th century. But it offered Lindemans, which was, with Penfolds, the best organised company, unparalleled opportunities for expansion.

Over the next 14 years Lindemans acquired the Ben Ean vineyard and winery which had been established by John McDonald in 1870; Coolalta vineyard and winery from the Wilkinsons; Catawba from the Cappers; Warrawee from unknown vendors; and Kirkton from the Kelmans in 1914. It had also previously established a vineyard at Corowa on the Murray River, which provided the grapes for fortified wine. Nonetheless, the acquisition of the Hunter Valley vineyards proved overly ambitious; the Corowa business was important, but did not alter the fact that much of the company's capital was tied up in an area most suited to the production of fine table wine, a style for which there was little or no demand.

In 1923 the Commercial Banking Company of Sydney (which had provided the company with all its loan funds) insisted that its nominee be appointed manager.

That manager was none other than Leo Buring, and he remained in sole command until 1930. Whether through bad luck or poor management, the intervening years saw Lindemans' indebtedness to the bank double. The bank could finally take no more; in 1930 it removed Buring and formally appointed a receiver, a Mr Nelson, who promptly fired two-thirds of the staff, and in a short time had the company operating profitably. However, the after-effects of the Depression, World War II and the size of the accumulated debts combined to make his receivership a lengthy one, and he remained in that role until 1947. For his part, Buring had immediately formed his own company and purchased all his opening stock from the receiver who had so recently replaced him. If that twist were not enough, Lindemans eventually took over Buring's flourishing business, and it became one of the operating divisions of the Lindemans group.

In 1953 the company floated to the public. After a major reconstruction in 1959 it was eventually taken over by Philip Morris Limited in 1971. Up to and including 1970, Lindemans had in fact continued to make limited quantities of superb semillon (variously sold as riesling, white burgundy, hock and chablis) and shiraz (sold either as claret or burgundy). The arrival of Philip Morris put an immediate end to those great wines, as the Sunshine Vineyard (whence the white wines came) was considered uneconomic, and thus abandoned.

In 1965 Lindemans had taken a major and successful strategic step by acquiring Rouge Homme Wines from the Redman family (having unsuccessfully sought to buy Stanley Leasingham). This began the transformation of a New South Wales business to a South Australian/Victorian one. In 1974 Philip Morris provided the funds for the erection of the Karadoc winery, which in due course became the largest winemaking facility (on one site) in Australia.

The great wines of the Hunter Valley quite literally withered on the vine, leaving only the best wines from Coonawarra as flagships, the base of the business becoming fast-moving consumer goods, which HJ Heinz knew only too well. Lindemans Bin 65 Chardonnay was the spearhead for this transformation, which, in economic terms, was highly successful. When Lindemans became part of Southcorp in 1990 the South Australian focus became absolute. The subsequent absorption by Foster's did nothing to change the situation; in February 2009, as part of a far-reaching reorganisation of its business, it announced its intention to sell all its New South Wales vineyards and wineries.

**line** is a tasting term invented by Len Evans. It relates to the impression the wine makes on the palate, and – where it is described as good – signifies a continuity of flavour and texture as the wine progresses from the forepalate through the mid-palate and thence to the finish.

**Lion Nathan** is a New Zealand–based beer business with over 60 per cent of its capital held by Kirin Group of Japan. It has a significant wine presence in Australia by virtue of its ownership of Mitchelton, Petaluma, St Hallett, Smithbrook, Stonier and Tatachilla.

**Lowe Family Wines** (est. 1987) has 22 ha of vines planted in Mudgee, all with organic status, and some moving towards biodynamic certification. As well as its estate plantings of riesling, sauvignon blanc, semillon, chardonnay, verdelho, viognier, pinot noir, cabernet sauvignon, merlot, shiraz, petit verdot, sangiovese, zinfandel and barbera, it buys varieties such as pinot gris and sauvignon blanc from Orange. Exports to the UK, Japan and Denmark.

**Lower Hunter Valley** is the de facto big brother of the Upper Hunter Valley. For ease of reference Lower Hunter Valley in this entry is shortened to Hunter Valley. Its vinous history commenced with James Busby, who in 1825 acquired a property halfway between Branxton and Singleton, which he named 'Kirkton' and where he installed his brother-in-law, William Kelman, as manager. The first vines were planted in 1830, but expanded to 4 ha in 1834, no doubt with the vines Busby had brought from Europe the preceding year. George Wyndham was the next to arrive in the area, and in 1830 planted 600 cuttings supplied by Busby. Most failed to take, but when he tried again the following year the success rate soared. By 1832 there were 10 small vineyards in existence, and the Hunter Valley was on its way.

For those born and bred in Sydney, the Hunter Valley is not only the greatest and the most important wine region in Australia; it is tantamount to the only region. If you come from overseas and have an interest in wine, it is a fair bet it is one of the two wine districts (the Barossa Valley being the other) you will have heard of prior to your arrival and which you propose to visit. For South Australians, it is an object of derision (with a generous dash

of jealousy); for Victorians it is an area which arouses a mixture of curiosity and respect.

To a disinterested observer (if there is such a person) the most obvious characteristic is the peculiarly Australian beauty of the valley. In no small measure this comes from the smoky blue of the Brokenback Range, rising threateningly above the nearest vineyards along Broke Road, and distantly, though clearly, etched as you look back from Allandale and Wilderness Roads – but wherever you are, it is a significant part of the landscape. Apart from the Brokenback Range, the valley has only the most gentle undulations; the vineyards are concentrated on the southern side, and the Barrington Tops, on the northern side, are out of sight.

So there is that feeling of open, endless, timeless space that is so special to Australia. Under the pale blue summer sky, the dark, glistening green of the vines is in stark contrast to the patterns of straw, yellow and golden grass and the more olive tones of the gum trees. Attesting to the modest rainfall, which in any event tends to come in erratic, heavy bursts, the grass is brown through much of the year, tenuously greening in autumn and spring.

The brown landscape hints at what the statistics say loud and clear: the Hunter Valley is an unlikely place in which to grow grapes. But when vineyards were trialled across the state in the 19th century the situation was different. The coastal fringe (around Sydney) was too wet and too humid, and if one moved too far west, spring frosts could pose threats, even though some distinguished wines were made at Rooty Hill and Smithfield until the 1950s and 1960s. More importantly, overall soil fertility on the previously unfarmed

Hunter Valley was adequate, and the modern diseases of downy and powdery mildew were unknown.

So it was that the Hunter Valley came to dominate viticulture in New South Wales extremely rapidly, although once again there are curious historical quirks. All the early vineyards were established well to the northeast of where they are nowadays; it was not until the 1860s that the first vignerons came into the Rothbury and Pokolbin subregions, where many of the Lower Hunter vineyards of today are to be found.

History also reveals that at the Paris Exhibition of 1855 (which led to the 1855 classification of the great Bordeaux wines that stands to this day) James King of Irrawang Vineyard had his sparkling wine – said by the judges to have 'a bouquet, body and flavour equal to the finest champagnes' – served at the table of Napoleon III during the closing ceremony. Another fascinating snippet is that although most of the wines at the exhibition were named by variety and vintage, HJ Lindeman (the founder of Lindemans) produced what one can but guess to be Australia's only Lachryma Christi, far from the slopes of Mount Vesuvius.

The Hunter Valley wine industry of today is inextricably bound up with tourism. The wineries brought the tourists in the first place – starting in the mid-1960s – but today far more dollars are spent on tourism (meals, accommodation and so on) than on wine: the Lower Hunter Valley has no equal in Australia for the abundance of first-class accommodation, restaurants, golf courses and general tourist facilities.

This ready-made market sees the cellar door sales outlets of the wineries full from daybreak to dusk, and provides the cash flow that is so important for the small winery in particular. From the outside looking in, it is an ideal lifestyle (the reality is a little less perfect), and (improbably, some might argue) there will be more, rather than fewer, wineries in the future. So there is a mix of the big and the small, the new and the old, the professional and the amateur; all are geared to make the visitor welcome, and almost all succeed.

For all that, it has to be said that from a viticultural viewpoint the Hunter Valley is a difficult and often capricious place in which to grow grapes. There are larger areas of unsuitable soil (hard, acidic clay) than there are of good soil, and the climate can only be described as perverse. Winter droughts are common, as is the propensity for such rain as there is to fall shortly prior to or during vintage. All things considered, it is truly remarkable that so many excellent wines (notably semillon and shiraz) are produced in the valley with such regularity.

It is one of the warmest and most humid climates in Australia. Of the 750 millimetres of annual rainfall, 530 millimetres occurs between October and April, affecting most vintages. However, the rain, the humidity, the afternoon cloud cover and weak sea breezes all operate to reduce the impact of the heat that would otherwise seriously hamper the production of quality table wine. The soils vary widely, from friable red duplex to deep friable loam (for the shiraz) to sandy alluvial flats (for the semillon).

Overall, 60 per cent of the grapes are white and 40 per cent red. In descending order of importance they are chardonnay, shiraz, semillon, cabernet sauvignon, merlot, verdelho and sauvignon blanc.

There are 155 wineries in the Lower Hunter. Among the most respected are: Audrey Wilkinson Vineyard, Brokenwood, Capercaillie, Chateau Pato, Chatto, De Iuliis, Keith Tulloch, Lake's Folly, McWilliam's Mount Pleasant, Margan Family, Meerea Park, Mistletoe, Oakvale, Pepper Tree, Scarborough Wine Company, Tamburlaine, Thomas, Tower Estate, Tulloch and Tyrrell's.

LAT 32°50'S; ALT 75 m; HDD 2070; GSR 530 mm; MJT 22.7°C; HARV Mid-January to early March; CHIEF VIT. HAZARD Heavy vintage rain

**Lower Murray Zone** is a zone of convenience, a large rectangle aligned north to south, with the Riverland region neatly bisecting it and running east to west. Even before the collapse of the Murray Darling River System, there was little likelihood of other regions being created within the zone, and as at 2009, there seems no likelihood of any regions, or even individual wineries, being established elsewhere in the zone.

a b c d e f g h i
j k l m n o p q s
r s t u v w x y z

**Macedon Ranges**, gazetted 21 August 2002, is the northernmost region of the Port Phillip Zone, which, with its four other regions, describes a circle around Melbourne. The Macedon Ranges is the highest and coolest of the regions, mountains and forests alternating with open, windswept slopes. Burke and Wills passed through in 1860 on their ill-fated journey north, a legacy being the Burke and Wills Track road name used to this day. Small vineyards and wineries sprang up from 1860 onwards, mainly at the southern end of the region around Riddells Creek, but all had disappeared by 1916.

The renaissance began when celebrated Melbourne restaurateur Tom Lazar began to plant his Virgin Hills vineyard in 1968; he was followed by Gordon Knight at Granite Hills in 1970. Two more different personalities cannot be imagined, the mercurial Lazar being worthy of a biography in his own right. Gordon Cope-Williams came next in 1977, then John Ellis at Hanging Rock in 1982. Many others have followed since, but none has found viticultural life particularly easy – the scale of most vineyards is very small.

Site selection (altitude, protection from wind and spring frosts, and maximum sun interception from north- and northeast-facing slopes), the careful matching of site and grape variety, razor-sharp canopy management and relatively low yields are all prerequisites for success. Even then success will not come every year; there have to be those extra few degrees of heat, and those extra hours of sunshine in the warmer Melbourne summers, to get the best results. This is the coolest wine region on the Australian mainland.

It is the type of region which would benefit from increased warmth, spreading the options for many of the wineries. Whether the two pinot noir and chardonnay superstars of the region, Bindi Wine Growers and Curly Flat, would agree is another question; they have managed to meet all the challenges of the climate so far. Likewise, the sparkling wine specialists of Hanging Rock and Cope-Williams might also take leave to disagree.

In 1984, 70 ha of vines from 25 growers supplied the four wineries then in operation. Now there are 50, with Bindi Wine Growers and Curly Flat the top two, closely followed by Domaine Epis, Granite Hills and Hanging Rock (in alphabetical order), then MorganField, Mount William and Paramoor.

LAT 37°25'S; ALT 300–700 m; HDD 970–1050; GSR 290–370 mm; MJT 17.2°–18.5°C; HARV Mid-March to early June; CHIEF VIT. HAZARD Cool season; frost

**maceration** lies at the heart of rosé and red wine making, but has limited relevance for white wine vinification. It takes place while the juice of the grape remains in contact with the skins, seeds and stems (in the latter case, where retained) of the grapes (the must), and spans the period before the onset of fermentation, the fermentation proper and post-fermentation contact. In a conventional red wine fermentation (one without whole bunches) it will be coextensive with a period of time required for all the sugar to be converted to alcohol (strictly speaking, ethanol). It leads to the extraction of the tannins, anthocyanins (including flavour precursors) and non-glycosylated flavour compounds from grape skins, flesh, seeds and stems. Once fermentation starts, and there is limited or no temperature control, fermentation will be completed in around three days. While this may be perfectly acceptable for large-volume, low-cost commercial wines, makers of fine wines have found many ways to increase the maceration period, and, indeed, to fundamentally alter the way it impacts on the eventual wine.

The first is pre-fermentation maceration, commonly called cold soak, which, in the context of cold cellars and cool to cold ambient temperatures, and no use of cultured yeast, may span many days. In the New World the must will be chilled to 10°C or below; in the Old World, high levels of sulphur dioxide may be used to delay the onset of fermentation.

At least up to the end of the 19th century, when cultured yeasts were unknown, and heat exchangers non-existent, a period of pre-fermentation maceration must have occurred in the majority of instances. The type of extraction achieved in an aqueous solution is considered by some winemakers to be superior to that which follows, and, in particular, to that of post-fermentation maceration. The role of sulphur dioxide, and in particular the level used, is a matter of debate. It was a technique developed by Lebanese oenologist and consultant Guy Accad in Burgundy in the 1970s and 1980s, as he endeavoured to duplicate the depth and strength of the burgundies made in the 19th and early 20th centuries.

The cooler the primary fermentation, the longer it will take. It is here that makers of pinot noir in particular are caught. Most believe it is desirable to reach 33°C (one or two noted Burgundian makers aspire to 40°C, which will kill all but acclimatised yeast strains), but with a dramatic shortening of the main maceration period. For other red varieties, lower temperatures are sought (anywhere between 20°C and 30°C) and post-fermentation

maceration is very common. It is generally seen as a necessary step to soften the otherwise harsh tannins of red wines (other than pinot noir), and is achieved by polymerisation of those tannins. It is, in essence, a controlled form of oxidation, and it requires considerable experience to determine whether 7 days, 14 days or longer is the appropriate time.

*Carbonic maceration*
Carbonic maceration involves the enzyme (rather than yeast) triggered conversion of sugar to alcohol within undamaged berries either connected to whole bunches or carefully destemmed. The process will continue until the alcohol in the berry reaches 2.5% alc/vol, whereafter it will quickly stop, as the alcohol effectively kills the enzymes. Continued fermentation will depend on yeast penetrating the berry.

**McGuigan Wines** (est. 1992) is the most prominent face of the group which until 2008 was called McGuigan Simeon, but was renamed Australian Vintage Limited in that year. It is Australia's fifth-largest producer and fifth-largest exporter. Its headline wines come from the Hunter Valley, the Barossa Valley, Coonawarra, Adelaide Hills, the Eden Valley and the Limestone Coast Zone. The volume base of the business has been sourced from the Riverland and the Riverina; how much it needs to refocus its business remains to be seen. Exports to all major markets.

**McHenry Hohnen Vintners** (est. 2004) brings together the David Hohnen and Murray McHenry families, which established this Margaret River producer. As founder of Cape Mentelle, David Hohnen has a long and deep knowledge of Margaret River, while Murray McHenry has had similar experience in wholesale and retail wine distribution. The 6500-case production is of high quality, but also includes some left-field blends from the 16 varieties on the 120-ha vineyard, including a marsanne chardonnay roussanne blend, a shiraz grenache mataro (common enough in the Barossa Valley but unique to McHenry Hohnen in the Margaret River) and tempranillo petit verdot cabernet sauvignon. Exports to the UK, Canada and NZ.

**machine-harvesting** began with the arrival of the first machine harvester from California in 1969. In the 40 years since, the design of machine harvesters has been continually improved; in the early decades the removal of the bunches was violent, resulting in high percentages of mog (material other than grapes) finding its way into the bins positioned on either side of the tractor to receive the grapes. Significant physical damage of the vines was commonplace, especially with inexperienced drivers. Forty years later it is difficult, if not impossible, to tell whether a machine harvester has passed down the row without closely inspecting the vine to verify that the grapes have been removed. The advantages of machine-harvesting are its significantly lower cost than hand-picking; the speed of harvesting, especially if adverse weather is approaching; and the ability to pick in the hours between midnight and early morning, when the grapes are coolest. While precise figures are not available, it is widely accepted that over 90 per cent of Australia's annual grape production is machine-harvested.

**McLaren Vale**, gazetted 2 September 1997, lagged behind the Barossa and Clare valleys in the development of the South Australian wine industry in the 19th century. Although John Reynell laid the foundations for Reynella in 1838, and was followed by Thomas Hardy in 1853, viticulture and winemaking in the McLaren Vale region remained largely within the province of those two enterprises until the late 1880s. The district was first settled and intensively farmed in the early 1850s, with the establishment of extensive wheat fields. Development continued through that decade and the 1860s, and numerous flour mills were constructed. Just as in the Clare Valley (and the country beyond) 20 years later, unscientific and extravagant farming methods soon depleted the soil. Again, just as in the Clare Valley, numerous wheat farmers had small vineyard holdings to provide wine as part of the wages for their labourers. When the wheat fields disappeared, so the small vineyards were abandoned as the population moved out of the district. By the mid-1870s the township of McLaren Vale was very nearly deserted.

Thus it was that the major vineyards were maintained by John Reynell and Thomas Hardy; in 1876 Thomas Hardy was able to purchase the third largest vineyard in the area, Tintara, which had been established by Dr AC Kelly over 15 years earlier. There were some other vineyards and wineries, notably George Manning's Hope Farm, which was planted in 1850 and known as Seaview. But it was not until 1888 that viticulture began to assume the importance it has today. From this point on what was described as vine mania swept over the whole of South Australia, with all the major winegrowing regions reflecting its impact.

In 1887 and 1888 JG Kelly established the Tatachilla Vineyard, planting 50 ha in just two years. In 1890 the Kay Brothers founded Amery; in 1891 the Johnston family followed suit with Pirramimma, and in the same year WH Craven purchased Hope Farm and substantially extended the cellars. In 1895 Frank Wilkinson made the first wine at Ryecroft and in 1896 HV Pridmore built temporary cellars known as The Wattles, soon to become a major and more permanent base. Katunga commenced business in the same year, and in 1900 Pirramimma and Wirra Wirra made their first vintages.

In 1903 over 3 million litres of wine were made by the 19 wineries in the district. In order of importance they were Thomas Hardy & Sons Limited (which alone produced 765,000 litres), followed by W Reynell, Horndale, Vale Royal, Tatachilla, The Wattles, Amery, Clarendon Vineyard, Kanmantoo, Pirramimma, Wirra Wirra, Mount Hurtle, F Potts, Hope Vineyard, Mrs Douglas, Ryecroft, Katunga, Formby and E Potts. The major part of the production was of full-bodied red wine, and the major market was the UK. Long after exports from other regions of Australia had declined, or had altered to sweet fortified wines, McLaren Vale continued to supply Britain with substantial quantities of dark-coloured, high-alcohol 'red burgundy'. This trade continued on a large scale until well into the 1950s; its subsequent decline was as much due to the desire of the wineries to establish their own identity and labels as to any falling-off in demand.

McLaren Vale was ideally placed to supply the burgeoning interest in red table wine in Australia in the early 1960s. Throughout the rest of that decade, and for the first part of the 1970s, the district was a prosperous one. But with the almost overnight appearance of the cool-climate culture, the vignerons of the McLaren Vale area were confronted with a wine market that had changed beyond all recognition in less than 10 years.

After a period of uncertainty, McLaren Vale rose to the challenge, and for a while was home to more small wineries than any other region in Australia. To this day it is dominated by small- to medium-sized producers, the one very obvious exception being Hardys (CWA). All the wineries other than Hardys Reynella and Geoff Merrill Wines are on the southern side of the Onkaparinga National Park and River, the hills of which create a spiny backbone running diagonally across the top one-third of the region. Suburban pressure guarantees that all future development will take place south of the Onkaparinga River, which is more a river in name than in fact. Indeed, it is chronic water shortage which had slowed the development even before the collapse of the Murray Darling River System, and will significantly inhibit future plantings. This will mean that more grapes and wine grown and made in McLaren Vale will remain there, and be labelled as such, rather than being siphoned up to the Barossa Valley by large (and some small) wineries.

There is a wide variety of soil types, even though red-brown loamy sands dominate. The structurally similar grey-brown loamy sand with yellow clay subsoils interspersed with limey deposits, and a slightly more sandy version of the same, are common. This tendency to a more sandy character reaches a peak around the Blewitt Springs region. Finally, there are patches of black or red friable loams of the Coonawarra terra rossa.

There is a substantial mesoclimatic variation throughout McLaren Vale, due to varying exposure to the cooling influence of the Gulf of St Vincent, which marks the long western border of the region. There are also significant changes in altitude as the region merges with Adelaide Hills. Summer rainfall is low, and irrigation is considered essential for young vines. Site selection, and site/variety marriage, are all-important.

There is no doubt that McLaren Vale's greatest wines are shiraz; always rich and velvety, they typically have an edge of bitter chocolate. Rising alcohol levels are an issue for the region, but no more than that of the Barossa or Clare Valley. Its other weapon is grenache; here it reaches levels of distinction unequalled by all but a handful of such wines from the Barossa Valley. It has better colour, more vinosity and more structure than that of the Barossa Valley, the confection nuances of that region nowhere to be seen.

It is not surprising that 80 per cent of the plantings are red, and that shiraz dominates that 80 per cent. Thereafter (in descending order) all the following varieties have a significant place in one or other winery's portfolio: cabernet sauvignon, chardonnay, grenache, merlot, semillon, sauvignon blanc, riesling, pinot noir, cabernet franc, chenin blanc and petit verdot.

There are 123 wineries; the most highly regarded are d'Arenberg, Geoff Merrill, Hardys, Mitolo, Mr Riggs Wine Company, Primo Estate, SC Pannell and Wirra Wirra. There are another 20 wineries producing wines of similar quality in a majority of vintages.

LAT 34°14'S; ALT 50–200 m; HDD 1910; GSR 180 mm; MJT 21.7°C; HARV Mid-February to late April; CHIEF VIT. HAZARD Drought

macroclimate is regional climate.

McWilliam's (est. 1877) was founded by Samuel McWilliam when he planted vines at Corowa, on the Murray River. The family then extended its operations to Junee and established a substantial winery there around the turn of the 20th century. It is little known that the Junee vineyard (though not the winery) continued in production until the 1950s. The grapes were taken to McWilliam's Mount Pleasant in the Hunter Valley and the wine was made there by Maurice O'Shea, the last vintage (1952) producing a wine which 20 years later was still full of character.

It was Samuel's son, John James McWilliam, who moved decisively to the Riverina: the first water was supplied for irrigation on 13 July 1912, and within a month or so he had taken up a lease at Hanwood and planted 35,000 cuttings. By 1917 he had erected a winery at Hanwood, followed by another at Yenda in 1920. As the Murrumbidgee Irrigation Area (as it was then known) prospered, so did the McWilliams: it was the start of a long association which was to make the family company one of the wealthiest in Australia before changes to the Income Tax Assessment Act effectively denied private companies the ability to reinvest part of their earnings.

That was far in the future when McWilliam's acquired a fully operational winery at Beelbangera in 1944; the fourth winery, just across the Murrumbidgee River at Robinvale, was designed by Glen McWilliam in 1961. In a sign of the times, the only winery to survive is Hanwood.

The McWilliam clan is a large one, and it

was not until the 1990s that any facet of the senior management of the company passed out of family hands. Two members in particular made lasting contributions to the company: long-term CEO Don McWilliam (since retired), and Glen McWilliam, a brilliant engineer who designed both wineries and winemaking equipment that broke new ground. As matters stand, it was exceedingly fortunate that JJ McWilliam moved to the Murrumbidgee region rather than the Murray. The family has also had the long-term services of gifted winemakers, none more gifted than Maurice O'Shea at McWilliam's Mount Pleasant.

The first CEO from outside the family to succeed was Kevin McLintock, a marketing genius who structured a deal with Gallo which has underwritten the export expansion of the McWilliam's wines. The company has also moved to diversify its vineyard holdings, buying the Barwang Vineyard in the Hilltops region of New South Wales (and significantly expanding its size) and Lillydale Estate in the Yarra Valley; very importantly, progressively acquiring Brand's Laira in Coonawarra, and vastly extending its vineyards; and, finally, acquiring the Evans & Tate brand (Margaret River) following the meltdown of that company.

The continuing feature of the McWilliam's group wines is that, without exception, they over-deliver at their price points, which range from $7 to $75. Exports to all major markets.

**McWilliam's Mount Pleasant** (est. 1880) dates from when Charles King planted what is now known as the Old Hill vineyard on some of the best red soil in the Hunter Valley. Early in the following century it was purchased by the O'Sheas; O'Shea senior was Irish and his wife French. It was her influence which led to their son Maurice O'Shea being sent to Montpellier in France to study viticulture and oenology. He returned to Australia in 1921 and took over as winemaker in 1925. He renamed the vineyard Mount Pleasant and the winery L'Hermitage, and proceeded to expand the vineyards.

It has been suggested that he was not a good business manager, and that it was this which led him to sell a 50 per cent interest to McWilliam's in 1932, marking the company's entry into the Hunter Valley. He may indeed have lacked business acumen, but it is hard to imagine a more difficult time in which to build a business. The market of the day was dominated by fortified wine, which O'Shea had no interest in making, and the Great Depression respected no one. The remaining share was purchased by McWilliam's in 1941.

Whatever be the truth, there has never been any doubt about O'Shea's genius as a winemaker. Over the 40 years he was winemaker at Mount Pleasant, a constant stream of magnificent white and red wines was produced. It has been said more than once that these were all made in small quantities (often there would be only one 2275-litre cask of a given wine, producing 250 dozen); that these wines represented the pick of the vintage, and that much more wine of lesser quality was made; and that many of his greatest wines were not vinified by O'Shea, but were purchased shortly after vintage and taken to Mount Pleasant for maturation and bottling.

That is all true, but it serves only to underline his brilliance. His ability to recognise a great wine immediately after the end of its primary fermentation, coupled with his skill in getting the wine into bottle at the right moment, can be properly understood only with the wisdom of hindsight that we now have. Those privileged few who at any time in the last decades of the 20th century have drunk O'Shea wines made in the 1930s and '40s, will be only too glad to join in praising one of the four greatest winemakers of the 20th century. One of the greatest wines was the 1937 Mountain A Dry Red, still superb after 40 years.

In 1956 Maurice O'Shea died, and Brian Walsh took over as winemaker, a position he held for more than 20 years. He in turn was succeeded by Phillip Ryan, still chief winemaker in 2009; thus in 80 years Mount Pleasant has had only three winemakers. Since the death of Maurice O'Shea the great strength of McWilliam's has been its large-volume but exceedingly good Elizabeth Semillon and the much smaller volume of the Single Vineyard Lovedale Semillon, the latter not produced every year. These wines develop magnificently over 30 years if the cork continues to do its job – which, unfortunately, has not always been the case with McWilliam's (or any other user of cork for Hunter semillon). (McWilliam's now uses screwcaps for its semillons.) The red wines wandered in the wilderness, with intermittent releases such as the 1959 Rosehill, but since the start of the 1990s some superb examples of Hunter Valley shiraz have been released under the OP & OH (Old Paddock and Old Hill) label and under the Maurice O'Shea label, which is often based on the 100-year-old shiraz plantings.

The story of Maurice O'Shea's life has been brilliantly told by Campbell Mattinson under the title *Wine Hunter: The Man Who Changed Australian Wine* (Hachette Australia, Sydney, 2006).

**maderised** was a once commonly used term to describe oxidative changes in white table wines.

**Main Ridge Estate** (est. 1975) was the first to build a winery on the Mornington Peninsula, four years before Elgee Park. Elgee Park had planted the first grapes in 1972, three years before Main Ridge, where the first grapes were harvested in 1975 and vinified – on a trial basis, with consultancy help, in a small shed. Nat and Rosie White produce around 1200 cases of immaculately crafted wine each year from grapes grown on their equally meticulously tended estate plantings. Having initially put their eggs in a cabernet sauvignon basket, and having conspicuous, albeit brief, show success with that variety, they moved to focus on chardonnay and pinot noir, which occupy most of their 3-ha vineyard. Exports to Singapore.

**Majella** (est. 1969) was established by 'Prof' Brian Lynn, who began the planting of 60 ha of riesling, cabernet sauvignon, merlot and shiraz. He was content to sell the grapes to other wineries in the Coonawarra district, notably Wynns, but as the years passed became increasingly aware of the high quality of the grapes. This ultimately led to the decision in 1991 to erect a winery and turn part of the production into wine for sale under the Majella label. It is first and foremost a red wine producer, the Musician Coonawarra Cabernet Shiraz one of the best value blends of its kind in Australia. The Malleea, a similar blend, at the opposite end of the price spectrum, is also made from a blend of cabernet sauvignon and shiraz. In between are single varietal wines of merlot, cabernet sauvignon and shiraz, all unfailingly good. Exports to the UK, the US and other major markets.

**malbec** was an important red grape in Bordeaux prior to the arrival of phylloxera, and was displaced by cabernet sauvignon in the plantings that followed; it is now to Argentina what shiraz is to Australia. Here its irregular set, and tendency to produce slightly jammy fruit flavours, have always kept it on the periphery. There are, however, one or two distinguished malbecs, most notably that of Ferngrove Vineyards in the Frankland River subregion, by Woodlands in the Margaret River, by The Islander Estate on Kangaroo Island, and by Wendouree in the Clare Valley. The region to produce the largest tonnage of malbec is, or has been, Langhorne Creek, with Ben Potts, Bleasdale and Bremerton to the fore. As at 2008 there were 362 ha planted; this is 28 ha less than in the prior year. The Clare Valley has long produced high-quality cabernet malbec blends, the greatest from Wendouree, but Leasingham was also able to coax something special from the blend.

**malic acid** is one of the two principal acids in grapes (and present in nearly all fruits and berries). In all red wines and some white wines it will be deliberately converted into the much softer lactic acid.

**malolactic fermentation** see fermentation.

**Manjimup** and Pemberton (both gazetted 14 February 2006), in the South West Australia Zone, waged a long, drawn-out battle over the name of a proposed single region: some parties wished to call it the Warren Valley. The ultimate decision was to split the two competing camps, and, as a pragmatic solution, to create Manjimup and Pemberton as different regions; moreover, it is true that Manjimup is slightly warmer on most (but not all) indicators. It is a very youthful region, with no vineyard plantings prior to 1988, and now with only 10 wineries. There was also a dispute over the varieties which would be best suited to the regions; Dr John Gladstones was, as usual, correct in identifying the similarities between the climate of Manjimup and Bordeaux, writing, 'The wines produced from the appropriate grape varieties should be very much in the mainstream of Bordeaux style.'

The best soils of the region belong to the Kennan-Queenup series of sandy, gravelly loams created over millions of years by the erosive effects of the Warren River and its tributaries. An ironstone laterite gravel layer several metres below the original horizon has been eroded so that the gravel has been mixed with red soil formed from the underlying granite to produce a red, gravelly loam.

The principal grape varieties are two-thirds red, one-third white, and in descending order of importance are chardonnay, cabernet sauvignon, merlot, shiraz, pinot noir, sauvignon blanc, viognier and verdelho. The most successful wineries are Chestnut Grove, Peos Estate and Sinclair.

LAT 34°26'S; ALT 200–300 m; HDD 1422; GSR 288 mm; MJT 19.9°C; HARV Mid-March to mid-April; CHIEF VIT. HAZARD Late season rain

**Mann, Jack, MBE** (1906–89) came to the Swan Valley, in the Swan District, when (in 1910) his father, George, was appointed winemaker by the founder and owner of Houghton, CW Ferguson. In 1922, aged 16, he was made apprentice and worked the first of his 51 consecutive vintages at Houghton. In 1930 he succeeded his father as chief winemaker and began one of the most exceptional careers in winemaking from what was an isolated outpost far from the eastern states. In a country which was preoccupied with making fortified wines, sherry leading the way, he managed to win the Champion Trophy for his oloroso sherry 13 years in succession. (The so-called Championship Wine Show rotated around the capital cities.) He used a butcher's mincer to crush the grapes for both fortified and table wine, which is unthinkable in the 21st century. But he also wanted to make table wine. The turning point came when the first Seitz filter machine was imported into Australia, allowing sterile filtration. In 1937 he made a big, full-flavoured white wine from chenin blanc which won first prize at the Melbourne Wine Show. When one of the most famous judges likened it to the great white burgundies of France, Houghton White Burgundy was born. The wine, with its distinctive blue diagonal stripe across the label, was the largest selling dry white wine in Australia for decades.

A giant of a man in every way, he coined more memorable one-liners than any other Australian winemaker before or since. His three Cs were 'Cricket, Christianity and Chablis'; 'Wines have to be glowing with life, blessed with refinement and adorned with flavour'; 'No wine is worthy of the name unless it can be diluted with 50 per cent water and retain its flavour'; 'Cricket is the only game played in heaven'; 'Wine is born when the miracle of fermentation converts nature's leaden metal into liquid gold'; (surprisingly) 'In my opinion, the greatest grape is the noble cabernet. Cabernet sauvignon is the only variety that would be tolerated in heaven' (there was almost no cabernet sauvignon in Western Australia); and he despised cold fermentation, describing it as 'cold castration of wine'. In his retirement he would visit the winery, and if he found an empty stainless steel fermentation tank (tested by tapping it) he would exclaim to the chief winemaker, Peter Dawson, 'No bad wine in there, my boy!'

**marc** is the residue of grape skins and seeds after the pressing process has been completed, and can be distilled into a spirit bearing the same name. There are also opportunities to extract resveratrol from the marc: resveratrol is one of the components of grapes identified as important in the prevention of coronary heart disease.

**Margaret River**, gazetted 30 October 1996, is one of the most immediately recognised regions of Australia by both domestic and international audiences. It is the foremost Geographic Indication in the South West Australia Zone, with 138 wineries as at 2008. It has seen spectacular growth since 1985: plantings having increased from 500 ha in 1985 to 5500 ha as at 2008. By pure chance one of the central figures in the limited amount of viticulture and winemaking in the 19th century was Ephraim Clarke, grandfather of the late Dr Kevin Cullen, who, with wife Diana, established Cullen in 1971. Clarke planted his vineyard at Bunbury in 1890, and continued to make wine until his death in 1921; it was inherited by his son, but the vineyard subsequently disappeared into the suburban sprawl of Bunbury. The cellars in Clarke Street remained intact through the 1980s, before falling into disuse.

The climate of Margaret River is more strongly maritime-influenced than any other major Australian region. It has the lowest mean annual temperature range, of only 7.6°C, and for good measure has the most marked Mediterranean climate in terms of rainfall, with only 200 millimetres of the annual 1160 millimetres falling between October and April. The low diurnal and seasonal temperature range means an unusually even accumulation of warmth. Overall the climate is similar (in terms of warmth) to that of Bordeaux in a dry vintage.

The landscape constantly varies, given character by the abundance of small creeks and gentle valleys, as well as by the profusion of native trees, shrubs and flowers. In physical terms a degree of protection from sea wind is the most important factor. The principal soil type is that of the ridge which runs from Cape Naturaliste to Cape Leeuwin: it is predominantly gravelly or gritty sandy loam formed directly from the underlying granite and gneissic rock. The soils are highly permeable when moist, but quickly shed moisture from sloping sites, and overall water-holding capacities are low.

The principal grape varieties are fairly evenly split between red and white; in descending order of importance they are cabernet sauvignon, chardonnay, sauvignon blanc, semillon, shiraz, merlot, chenin blanc and verdelho. The plantings more or less precisely reflect the styles which Margaret River is most famous for and suited to. That said, cabernet merlot blends are important, as are blends of sauvignon blanc and semillon. These two blends are those of Bordeaux, and it's no accident that the wines are as good as they are. The best wineries (in alphabetical order) are Ashbrook Estate, Brookland Valley, Cape Mentelle, Cullen, Devil's Lair, Howard Park, Leeuwin Estate, Moss Wood, Stella Bella, Vasse Felix, Voyager Estate, Woodlands and Woodside Valley Estate, followed by Amberley Estate, Chalice Bridge Estate, Chapman Grove, Clairault, Driftwood Estate, Evans & Tate, Gralyn Estate, Hay Shed Hill, Lenton Brae, McHenry Hohnen Vintners, Pierro, Redgate, Rockfield Estate, Sandalford, Thompson Estate and Wise Wine; this is a roll of honour greater than that of any other region.

LAT 33°57'S; ALT 40 m; HDD 1690; GSR 200 mm; MJT 20.4°C; HARV End February to mid-April; CHIEF VIT. HAZARD Silvereye birds

maritime climates have a small temperature range between the average mean temperature of the hottest month and that of the coldest month, and a commensurately low day–night (diurnal) range. This type of climate is due to the proximity of oceans or other large water bodies, notably lakes. The risk of frost in such regions is low.

marsanne is grown in relatively small quantities in the northern Rhône Valley of France and in Switzerland. This white grape variety was almost certainly brought to the Yarra Valley by the Swiss retinue of Charles Latrobe's wife, Latrobe being the first governor of Victoria. It was grown at Yeringberg and Chateau Yering, and it was these vineyards that supplied Tahbilk with the cuttings which eventually led to Tahbilk's holding of 35 ha (replanted after phylloxera in 1927). Until a resurgence of the variety in France, this was the largest single planting in the world. Tahbilk is the major practitioner, and vertical tastings back to 1953 suggest that it follows a similar path to Hunter semillon. Up to five years is the development phase; 6–10 years is the period of maximum manifestation of varietal character; and beyond 10 years there is the potential for maximum complexity (or death). The arrival of screwcaps may well lead to these periods being significantly lengthened. Curiously, and despite its apparent popularity in restaurants, national plantings have declined since 2004, amounting to only 213 ha in 2008.

**marzemino** is a red grape variety sparingly grown in northern Italy. Unsurprisingly, its Australian roots have been set down in the King and Alpine valleys, with three producers making it: Chrismont, Dal Zotto and Michelini Wines.

**Maurice O'Shea Award** was created by McWilliam's Wines to honour the memory of its greatest winemaker, Maurice O'Shea. It is awarded to an individual, institute or corporation who has made a historically significant and outstanding contribution to the Australian wine industry. It was introduced in 1990, and up to 1998 was awarded annually; thereafter it has been awarded every second year. Its recipients have been Max Schubert, AM (1990), Len Evans, OBE, AO (1991), Ron Potter (1992), David Wynn, AO (1993), the Jacob's Creek brand (1994), the author (1995), Hazel Murphy, AM (1996), Brian Croser, AO (1997), Dr Bryce Rankine, AM (1998),

Dr Wolf Blass, AM (2000), The Australian Wine Research Institute (2002), Guenter Prass, AM (2004), Dr Ray Beckwith, OAM (2006) and Dr John Gladstones (2008).

**Mayfield Vineyard** (est. 1998) in Orange is a property – including the house in which owners Richard and Kathy Thomas now live, and its surrounding arboretum – with a rich history as a leading Suffolk sheep stud, founded upon the vast fortune accumulated by the Crawford family via its biscuit business in the UK. The Thomases planted the 37-ha vineyard in 1998, with merlot (15.3 ha) leading the way, followed (in descending order) by cabernet sauvignon, sauvignon blanc, chardonnay, pinot noir, riesling and sangiovese. The wines are marketed under the Mayfield Vineyard and Icely Road brands. Exports to the UK, the US and Sweden.

**Meadowbank Estate** (est. 1974) in Southern Tasmania is an important part of the Ellis family business on what was once a large grazing property on the banks of the Derwent. Increased plantings are under contract to Hardys, and a splendid winery has been built to handle the increased production. The winery has expansive entertainment and function facilities, capable of handling up to 1000 people, and offering an arts and music program, plus a large restaurant. Exports to Germany, Sweden, the Netherlands and Hong Kong.

**Medieval Warm Period** was first chronicled by Emmanual Le Roy Ladurie in *Times of Feast, Times of Famine: A History of Climate since the Year 1000* (first published in French in 1967, and by Doubleday & Company in 1971 – the first English version). By studying the advance and retreat of the glaciers, the starting dates of vintages recorded in the monasteries of France, and the ring growth of California redwoods, Ladurie traced the changes in climate over a period of 1000 years. He chronicled in detail what has become known as the Medieval Warm Period, which, in its broadest gambit, lasted from 750 to 1230 AD, with a peak period of 1080 to 1180 AD. During this period the temperature was 1°C warmer than the average of the 20th century. Vineyards flourished all over England, the monks in the English monasteries becoming vignerons for the first time. Anecdotal stories tell of the Rhine River in Germany ceasing to flow, and being able to be crossed by foot at various points, and wine being cheaper than water.

**Meerea Park** (est. 1991) at Pokolbin in the heart of the Lower Hunter Valley is the brainchild of Rhys Eather, a great-grandson of Alexander Munro, a leading vigneron of the mid-19th century; he makes the wine at the former Little's Winery at Palmers Lane in Pokolbin, which was purchased in 2007 and is now named Meerea Park. All the wines are produced from grapes purchased from growers, primarily in the Pokolbin area, but also from the Upper Hunter, and as far afield as Young. Exports to the UK, the Netherlands, Germany, Canada and Singapore.

**mercaptans** are thiol compounds, formed from hydrogen sulphide and caused by yeast reacting with sulphur in the lees after the end of fermentation. If the hydrogen sulphide is not quickly removed from the newly fermented wine (by aeration achieved through racking,

or by the addition of copper sulphate, both of which are simple tasks) it becomes bound, forming mercaptans, and is difficult to remove. It manifests itself in a range of unpleasant odours extending from burnt rubber to garlic, onion, gamey meat, stale cabbage and asparagus, all building on the original sulphide aroma of rotten eggs. Once quite common in Australian wines, it is now far less frequently encountered.

**merlot** was seemingly unstoppable over the 25 years from 1980 to 2005/06: in 1980, 68 tonnes were crushed, in 1990 it was 2300 tonnes, in 2001, 80,000 tonnes, and from 2004 through to 2008 it stabilised as 125,000 tonnes. It is difficult to imagine that future plantings of this red grape will increase, although there may be a shift in the regions where it is grown. Merlot flourishes in Bordeaux, which has a climate similar (for example) to Coonawarra and the slightly warmer Margaret River. By 2005 it was promiscuously planted through virtually every region in Australia, many of them far too warm for merlot to display varietal character; it instead ended up either thin and dilute or soupy and fat. There is also a feeling shared by many experienced winemakers that the clones available are distinctly inferior to those of Bordeaux.

The most important issue of all straddles the vineyard and the winery: what are the desirable and what are the undesirable characteristics of merlot? What should its structure be, and what should its taste be? Or, more shortly, what is the style the maker should aim for? It is clear that there is little agreement in Australia or California on these questions, and that, even in France, on the right bank of the Gironde, with the Robert Parker Jnr influence (now aided with the arrival of concentration equipment), the guidelines are changing.

Traditionally, it was lighter in colour, lower in acid and, most importantly, in extract and tannin, than cabernet sauvignon. While it had an essential core of sweet fruit, it also had aromatic and flavour nuances of herb (herbaceousness) and olive. In other words, it was clearly different from cabernet sauvignon not only in structure (lighter in body and less tannic), but also in flavour. Château Petrus, of course, has always been an exception, making wine with many of the characteristics of the cabernet-dominant Haut Medoc, but the trend is definitely to riper, more luscious, more concentrated wines which increasingly blur the lines between merlot and cabernet sauvignon. Australia, with its range of climate from cool to warm to hot, is readily able to produce merlot in the Parker style. One particular example is Tatachilla in McLaren Vale, which has won many gold medals and trophies with wines which might unkindly be classed as 'wannabe cabernets'.

So the decisions for the winemaker are: how ripe merlot should be before it is picked; whether or not it should be given extended post-fermentation maceration to boost its body and tannins; and the amount of new oak, French and/or American, it should be given. While these are real choices, with significant consequences, the rest of the winemaking is largely standard practice.

**mesoclimate** is site climate, often confused with microclimate.

**metallic** is the taste of metal, sometimes encountered in red wines which have been treated with copper sulphate to remove mercaptans, or as a result of *Bretannomyces* remaining after attempts to remove it with sulphur dioxide.

**méthode champenoise** is the technique of making sparkling wine (as employed in Champagne) in which the all-important second fermentation takes place in the bottle in which the wine is ultimately sold.

**microclimate** is the climate within a grape vine canopy, and is much misused and/or misunderstood.

**micro-oxygenation** was developed in France in the 1990s by research scientists Patrick Ducournau and Thierry Lemaire. It involves the use of oxygen in red wine in tank or barrel to soften the tannins and increase complexity. The technique improves the mouthfeel, enhances the colour stability and intensity (and thus the oxidative stability) and decreases reductive characters and vegetative aromas.

A precisely measured and controlled stream of micro-sized bubbles is fed into wine in tank through a ceramic diffuser at the bottom. By the time one might have expected bubbles to appear on the surface, there are in fact none, because all the oxygen has been absorbed by the wine. The chemistry involved is extremely complex, but the changes induced by micro-oxygenation are easily observed by tasting.

In the first phase (micro-oxygenation is carried out progressively over a period of one to six months), the tannins increase in aggressiveness and intensity on the palate, and the varietal aromatics' intensity and complexity decrease. This is called the structuring phase.

The harmonisation phase then follows, the optimum end-point reached when the wine exhibits the maximum complexity, tannin, softness and suppleness, and has its aromatic qualities returned and enhanced. Excessive oxygenation leads to irreversible loss of freshness and varietal character, and bitter, dry tannins. Skilled use of the equipment, and careful sensory evaluation, are prerequisites if this is to be avoided. Indeed, when it became apparent that international sales of the equipment were lagging in the face of belief that the process did not work, each sale was linked to a real-life demonstration of the equipment in the purchaser's winery at no extra cost. It is now used in all the leading winemaking countries of the world, spanning every level of quality; Michel Rolland (the leading French wine consultant) is an unabashed supporter of its use. In Australia a patent has been granted for a similar system with a different mode of oxygen diffusion.

**Millamolong Estate** (est. 2000) in Orange has been the centrepiece of Australian polo for over 80 years. For an even longer period, generations of James Ashtons (differentiated by their middle name) have been at the forefront of a dynasty to make *Rawhide* or *McLeod's Daughters* (rural family soap operas) seem tame. In the context of this, 28 ha of chardonnay, riesling, cabernet sauvignon, shiraz and merlot may seem incidental, but it happens to add to the luxury accommodation at the main homestead, which caters for up to 18 guests.

**Millbrook Winery** (est. 1996) is the leading producer in the Perth Hills region of Western Australia. The strikingly situated winery is owned by Perth-based entrepreneur Peter Fogarty and wife Lee, who also own Lake's Folly in the Hunter Valley and Deep Woods Estate in Margaret River. It has 7.5 ha of estate plantings, supplemented by contract-grown grapes, notably in the Geographe region. Shiraz viognier is the outstanding estate-grown wine. Exports to the UK, Belgium, Germany, Denmark, Russia, Malaysia, Hong Kong and Japan.

**Miller's burgundy** was an incorrect name for pinot meunier used at Great Western and elsewhere, the name coming from the fine white hairs on the underside of the leaves.

**Minchinbury** was a once-famous brand of sparkling wine made by Penfolds, but it was also a significant part of the viticultural scene in the greater Sydney area between 1821 and 1977. When Captain William Minchin retired from the New South Wales army in 1819, he was granted 4000 ha of land near Rooty Hill. After his death in 1821 his daughter inherited the property, shortly afterwards selling it to a Dr McKay. He planted the first grapes at what was by then known as Minchinbury, and used convict labour to work the land and build the winery of dressed stone with walls that were 8 feet thick in places. The original cellars remained in use for the next 150 years.

Towards the end of the 19th century James Angus bought the winery and vineyards, and extended both. In the late 1890s he began making sparkling wine under the direction of Leo Buring; during this period phylloxera attacked the vineyard, necessitating its complete replanting with grafted vines. Nonetheless, Frank Penfold Hyland was sufficiently impressed with the Minchinbury wines to purchase the vineyards and cellars in 1912. For the next six years the property was managed by Leo Buring and, when he left, he was replaced by Ivan Combet, who remained as winemaker until his retirement at the end of the 1960s. In 1949 over 100 ha of vineyard were in production, but encroaching urban development made the land so valuable that pieces were progressively sold off; by 1973 a little under 14 ha remained, gewurztraminer accounting for half, along with riesling, trebbiano and some chasselas. It was the traminer and riesling which made the Penfolds famed Trameah, first sold in 1920. The author tasted bottles of the wine made in the 1960s and '70s, and it is no surprise that this wine, along with occasional 100 per cent gewurztraminers (nine, incidentally, just as traminers), had significant show success.

The land value was such that in 1977 the remaining hectares were sold.

**Miramar** (est. 1977) is owned by veteran winemaker Ian MacRae, and has 35 ha of mature riesling, sauvignon blanc, semillon, chardonnay, cabernet sauvignon, merlot and shiraz in Mudgee. MacRae has been able to fashion excellent white wines in a region more suited to red wines, having had success in the Mudgee Wine Show over many decades. Part of the grape production is sold to others, the remainder vinified to make around 6000 cases a year.

**Mistletoe Wines** (est. 1989), in the Lower Hunter Valley, has had a strangely chequered history given the exceptional quality of the wines made since Nick Patterson became winemaker. It is owned by Ken and Gwen Sloan, and can trace its history back to 1909, when a substantial vineyard was planted on what was then called Mistletoe Farm. The Mistletoe Farm brand made a brief appearance in the late 1970s, but the Mistletoe of today was not founded until 1989. The 5000-case production features outstanding shiraz and semillon.

**Mitchell** (est. 1975) was established by Andrew and Jane Mitchell in an old stone apple-packing shed built into the side of the slope beneath the hill in the Clare Valley on which Andrew Mitchell's parents' house was situated, with its surrounding apple orchard. Andrew and Jane now live in the house, and the apples are no more, 8 ha of vines having taken their place. They also have two much larger vineyards, one of 53 ha at Watervale, the other 48 ha at Auburn. Riesling, shiraz and cabernet sauvignon are the principal wines, with the McNicol label for top-of-the-range riesling and shiraz, which are held back three or four years after the standard varietal wines are sold. Exports to all major markets.

**Mitchelton** (est. 1969) commenced the planting of its vineyard in 1969, having retained the services (in 1967) of Colin Preece to help plan and lay out what was essentially a vast market garden of experimental varieties. Preece believed that the sandy alluvial soils on the banks of the Goulburn River would not allow phylloxera to attack the vines, but his faith was quickly shown to have no foundation. That said, after the grapes from the 1972 vintage were sold to Brown Brothers, 1973 was made in a partially completed winery, with tanks used exactly where they had been offloaded from trucks, and 1974 was the wettest vintage in the Goulburn Valley region for 50 years. Thus the need to evaluate the most appropriate varieties and to replant on grafted rootstock was not a matter of urgency. It was nonetheless a baptism of fire for young winemaker Don Lewis (he eventually retired in 2004), who arrived with Colin Preece in 1974 by boat, the underground cellars having been completely flooded. In 1975 the long-term vineyard plan was agreed, and by 1977 winery equipment and procedures had been significantly upgraded.

All of this happened while members of the Shelmerdine family and receivers appointed by lenders became involved in bitter legal disputes. The immediate cause of the problems was the over-capitalisation of the site, with an expensive but basically useless observation tower and a large restaurant complex built to handle the hordes of tourists from Melbourne who never in fact arrived. The litigation was finally resolved in 1980, when the Valmorbida family purchased Mitchelton. They in turn sold the winery (and vineyards) to Petaluma in 1994, and thus it is all now part of the Lion Nathan Group. The 220,000-case production has always had riesling, marsanne, shiraz and cabernet sauvignon as mainstays, but the willingness of Mitchelton to buy grapes from other regions across the length and breadth of Australia has underwritten the diversification of the portfolio. Exports to all major markets.

**Mitolo Wines** (est. 1999) has had a meteoric rise since Frank Mitolo decided to turn a winemaking hobby into a business; even then, his hobby winemaking dated back only

to 1995. If this were not enough, Mitolo is a virtual winery, owning neither vineyards nor its own winery. It is a reflection of the outstanding winemaking skills of contract winemaker Ben Glaetzer, and the quality of the shiraz from McLaren Vale (predominantly) and Barossa Valley which is bought for the label; cabernet sauvignon and sangiovese are also in the mix. The 20,000-case production has retail distribution in Australia, and exports to all major markets.

**mondeuse** originated from the Savoie region of France, and was brought to Australia in the early years of the 20th century in the wake of phylloxera by François de Castella, and planted at the Rutherglen Research Station. For many years Brown Brothers was the only maker of wines from this red grape variety, using it in a blend with shiraz and cabernet sauvignon. Small amounts have since been planted in the Hunter Valley and Granite Belt, with Bullers Calliope following the lead of Brown Brothers.

**mondeuse blanche**, a white grape variety, is one of the two parents of shiraz, but is not commercially produced in Australia.

**Montalto Vineyards** (est. 1998) is owned by John Mitchell and family, which acquired an existing vineyard in the Mornington Peninsula planted in 1986, and extended it to 11 ha, half being pinot noir, the other principal varieties chardonnay and pinot gris. The wines, contract-made by Robin Brockett at Scotchmans Hill, have been of a consistently high standard, the second label Pennon Hill offering excellent value. The 4500-case production focuses on chardonnay and pinot noir.

**montils**  is a minor white grape variety of the Cognac area of France, although in decline. Plantings in Australia were made in the Hunter Valley, where it was usually known as aucerot; Maurice O'Shea was the chief exponent of the variety. While the occasional bottle may be found, the vines have been removed. Its naturally low pH suggests it may come back into favour in the hotter parts of Australia.

**Moondah Brook**  (est. 1968) in the Swan Valley is part of CWA, but has its own special character, as it draws part of its fruit from the large Gingin vineyard, 70 kilometres north of the Swan Valley, and part from the Margaret River and Great Southern. From time to time it has excelled even its own reputation for reliability with some quite lovely wines, in particular honeyed, aged chenin blanc, generous shiraz and finely structured cabernet sauvignon. Exports to the UK and other major markets.

**Moorilla Estate**  (est. 1958) is the second-oldest winery in Tasmania, established by the Alcorso family. As well as the original home designed by Sir Roy Grounds, it incorporates what will be the most highly rated art museum in the southern hemisphere – built at a cost of over $70 million – on its completion in 2009, a surgically clean micro-brewery, an entirely new winery, a high-quality restaurant and five self-contained chalets. All this a mere 15 to 20 minutes' drive from Hobart. It has a full range of table wines, and exports to the US and Singapore.

**Moorooduc Estate**  (est. 1983) is one of the jewels of the Mornington Peninsula, with owner/winemaker Dr Richard McIntyre making outstanding chardonnay and pinot noir with wild yeast fermentation, wife Jill presiding over a high-quality restaurant. Exports to Hong Kong and Singapore.

**Mornington Peninsula**,  gazetted 18 March 1997, holds many secrets within in its maze of twisting hills and valleys. It is easy to become lost in the Adelaide Hills, and it is equally easy to find yourself heading in the wrong direction on the wrong road in the central and southern end of the peninsula. One of its secrets is the absence of any sign of viticulture and winemaking in the 19th century, which has often led to the assertion that none existed. It did (chiefly in the Hastings area), but on a small scale, and it disappeared in the early years of the 20th century. Vines first reappeared in 1948, when a member of the Seppelt family planted riesling on a 68-ha property on Harrisons Road, Dromana. Shortly thereafter, that property was acquired by the Broadhurst family, close relatives of famous Melbourne retailer and wine judge the late Doug Seabrook, who maintained the vineyard and made the wine until the vines perished in a bushfire in 1967. Four years later a chance lunchtime conversation between David Wynn and Baillieu Myer at Myer's property reignited the flame, this time permanently. Wynn expressed regret that the Seabrook experiment had ended, leading Myer to establish Elgee Park in 1972.

In common with other cool-climate regions, the initial growth was slow, and it was not until the late 1980s that the number of new wineries began to increase more rapidly. It is tempting, and may indeed be true, to characterise the peninsula as the holiday playground for the wealthy citizens of Melbourne and its surrounds. It is equally true to say that there are countless and ever-changing vistas, many taking in the surrounding Bass Strait ocean and the bays of Port Phillip and Westernport. The relatively small size of the majority of properties (but not all) and high values per hectare meant that the cost of entry was high; in most cases, these start-up ventures also had sufficient resources to either use contract/consulting winemaking services or employ a full-time winemaker. This in turn meant that even though the vines were by definition young, and much had to be learnt about the interaction of site climate, soil and variety, quality wines were the rule rather than the exception.

There was nonetheless a perception in the minds of many observers that production would remain small, with cellar doors providing the major outlet for the wines. In fact, as the vines have matured, knowledge has been gained and the number of wineries has mushroomed, the peninsula has become ever more confident. Its wines are now found on the majority of the best wine lists in Melbourne restaurants, and have more than adequate representation in Sydney.

The climate is profoundly maritime-influenced. The wind is either blowing from the north and west across Port Phillip, or from the south and east across Bass Strait – and usually, in this part of the world, it is blowing from somewhere. That the climate is cool is not in dispute; exactly how cool is strongly dependent on site and aspect, for weather stations provide heat summations ranging from about 1080 near Main Ridge to 1240 at Dromana, and higher again at Moorooduc. Certain it is that whatever heat is measured will have been evenly accumulated, for frosts are as rare as prolonged hot, dry winds. Relative humidity is high, stress is low, sunshine hours are abundant, and rainfall plentiful during winter and spring. If warmer vintages persist past 2009, its competitive edge over other Port Phillip Zone regions (except for the Bellarine Peninsula of Geelong) will increase.

There are three main soil types. Yellowish brown and brown soils over friable, well-drained clay are the first of the principal soil types; around Red Hill and Main Ridge deep and fertile red soils of volcanic origin dominate; much sandier soils are in evidence at Moorooduc.

Pinot noir and chardonnay remain its principal wines, albeit with some high-quality shiraz grown, quality cabernet and merlot being the rare exceptions to prove the rule. The best wineries include Allies, Darling Park, Dromana Estate, Eldridge Estate of Red Hill, Hurley Vineyard, Kooyong, Main Ridge Estate, Merricks Creek, Montalto Vineyards, Moorooduc Estate, Paringa Estate, Port Phillip Estate, Prancing Horse Estate, Red Hill Estate, Scorpo, Stonier, Ten Minutes by Tractor, The Cups Estate, Tuck's Ridge, Willow Creek Vineyard and Yabby Lake Vineyard.

LAT 38°20'S; ALT 25–250 m; HDD 1080–1570; GSR 320–386 mm; MJT 18.8°C–20°C; HARV End March to early June; CHIEF VIT. HAZARDS Autumn rain; birds

Morris (est. 1859) is the greatest name in the panoply of fortified wines from northeast Victoria; Chambers Rosewood should be a challenger, but elects to keep a low profile, however sublime the best wines in the cellar may be. The Morris family has stood proud over the Rutherglen region since its establishment, albeit with fluctuating fortunes, phylloxera sounding the death knell for the glorious two-storey Fairfield mansion, built in the early 1880s, and boasting the largest cellars in the southern hemisphere, capable of holding the equivalent of three vintages of 1 million litres each. GF Morris, who had built Fairfield, died in 1910 and the family name survived thanks to the decision of his 28-year-old son, CH (Charles) Morris, to buy his own land at Mia Mia in 1897. In 1928, third-generation CH (Mick) Morris was born, sent to Scotch College in Melbourne and thereafter to Ormond College (within Melbourne University), where he successfully studied for his bachelor of science degree before gaining his diploma in oenology from Roseworthy Agricultural College. He obtained practical experience in other wineries, mainly in the Barossa Valley, before coming back to the business in 1953. In 1970 the family decided to accept an offer from Reckitt and Colman, which acquired Orlando the following year, making Morris effectively an Orlando subsidiary. It remains in Orlando Wyndham ownership (and ultimately Pernod Ricard, owner of Orlando) after an abortive attempt to sell it in 2007. The octogenarian Mick Morris is still involved in the making and, in particular, the blending of the wines, the day-to-day responsibility falling on son David Morris. The greatest wines are the Rare Muscat and Topaque, with only 1000 bottles released each year to preserve the integrity of the complex solera system. A small amount of 1928 muscat (single vintages being extremely rare) tasted in 2008 had the explosive intensity and richness of the Seppelt 100 Year Para Liqueur.

**Moss Wood** (est. 1969) was established by one of the three medical founding fathers of the

Margaret River region: Doctors Tom Cullity, Kevin Cullen and Bill Pannell. Bill Pannell prowled the region digging holes in the ground before selecting his site 8 kilometres north of Cullen and Vasse Felix, on Metricup Road. This area is known as the Wilyabrup subregion, and it and the Wallcliffe subregion, adjoining it on its southern boundary, are home to the leading wineries of the region. The original plantings were of cabernet sauvignon, and through the 1970s this was the only wine released. It remains the cornerstone of Moss Wood, and demand continues to substantially exceed supply. The demands of commuting from Perth led to the appointment of Roseworthy graduate Keith Mugford, first as assistant winemaker, then as chief winemaker, and finally becoming (with wife Clare) the owner of the winery. In 2000 Moss Wood acquired Ribbon Vale Estate, and now releases the wines from that vineyard under the Moss Wood banner, but vineyard-designated. Moss Wood also makes highly regarded semillon and chardonnay, and a pinot noir which polarises opinions.

**mouldy characters** in wine can derive from grapes significantly affected by powdery mildew, but more commonly they are from inadequately cleaned barrels, and – most frequently – from corks affected by trichloranisole.
**Mountadam** (est. 1972) remains a conundrum. It was established by visionary wine marketer David Wynn for the benefit of his winemaker son Adam, high on the windswept hills of the upper Eden Valley, complete with what was then a state-of-the-art winery. Wine quality was at best variable, perhaps due in part to the vagaries of vintage, and in part to winery practices. The one wine

to largely surmount these issues was and is the chardonnay. Somewhat surprisingly, it was purchased by Cape Mentelle (at the behest of Moet Hennessy Wine Estates) in 2000 and, less surprisingly, it was on-sold in 2005 to Adelaide businessman David Brown, who also owns Padthaway Estate. Since that time, and the arrival of former Petaluma winemaker Con Moshos, determined efforts have been made to lift the quality and consistency of the wines. Exports to the UK, the US, Poland and Japan.

**Mount Barker,** gazetted 15 August 1997, is generally regarded as the senior and most important subregion of the Great Southern. It is situated fairly and squarely in the centre of the Great Southern, and has in its scope Forest Hill Vineyard, established in 1966, and Plantagenet, established in 1974 and long the mother-winery providing contract winemaking services to many of the smaller producers in the subregion. The Albany Highway runs north–south, the Muirs Highway east–west, the two intersecting at Mount Barker and acting as magnets for the majority of the wineries in the subregion – the notable exceptions being Poacher's Ridge Vineyard and Xabregas in the southwestern quadrant.

Situated as it is in the very heart of the Great Southern, the continental aspects of the climate make this quintessential country for riesling and shiraz. While, as with the rest of the region, rainfall is winter–spring dominant, late vintage rains can create problems. Mount Barker's continentality also means greater diurnal temperature fluctuations and the occasional spring frost. The Plantagenet Plateau, with Mount Barker its centre point, is marked by its relatively poor marri soils,

lateritic gravelly/sandy loams coming directly from granite rock protrusions. Yields are generally low, in places very low.

The principal grape varieties in descending order of importance are riesling, shiraz, cabernet sauvignon, chardonnay, sauvignon blanc, merlot and cabernet franc. The most important wineries in the subregion are Chatsfield, Forest Hill Vineyard, Garlands, Gilberts, Goundrey (albeit with an uncertain future) and Plantagenet.

LAT 34°36'S; ALT 180–250 m; HDD 1488; GSR 287 mm; MJT 19°C; HARV Early March to mid-April; CHIEF VIT. HAZARDS Spring frosts; late vintage rain

**Mount Benson** was officially recognised as a Geographic Indication on 18 March 1997. For reasons which are now of academic interest, it did not take in the more recent Robe GI, which sits immediately to its south. There was no history of viticulture prior to 1989, when the first vines were planted by Peter and Leah Wehl, who began the progressive establishment of what is now a 24-ha vineyard, planted two-thirds to shiraz and one-third to cabernet sauvignon. This property is now the third-largest in area, after the 38-ha biodynamic vineyard established by the Rhône Valley firm of M Chapoutier & Company (heading a joint venture) and, most obviously, the 160-ha Norfolk Rise Vineyard and attendant 2000-tonne winery, which was established in 2000.

The climate is unequivocally cool, strongly maritime-influenced by the nearby ocean on one side and (at Robe) the lakes on the other. The winters are cold and wet; the growing season is long, cool and dry. The winds are predominantly from the south, southeast and southwest, and are particularly strong during the spring and early summer. Overall, summer temperatures are 3°C lower than at Coonawarra; budburst occurs two weeks earlier, yet harvest is much the same time.

The principal soil type is generally described as terra rossa, a red-brown soil that varies from sandy to loamy and which is typically associated with limestone. The limestone may outcrop or occur 10–50 centimetres below the surface. The terrain on which the vineyards have been planted is gently undulating, the surrounding natural bushland scrubby, and giving little clue to the potential of the area from a viticultural viewpoint.

LAT 31°09'S; ALT 50–150 m; HDD 1226; GSR 217 mm; MJT 22.7°C; HARV Late March to late April; CHIEF VIT. HAZARDS Spring frost; poor fruit set

**Mt Billy**  (est. 2000) was established by Victor Harbor dentist John Edwards, turning a lifelong hobby into a business, when he purchased the 3.75-ha Southern Fleurieu property on the hills behind the town, planting 1.2 ha each of chardonnay and pinot meunier, used as the base for sparkling wine. In 1999 grenache and shiraz were purchased from the Barossa Valley, and it is in this direction that the business has since been directed, Antiquity Shiraz (from ancient vines) and Circe Shiraz Viognier being contract-made by two of the best younger winemakers in the Barossa Valley, Dan Standish and Peter Schell.

**Mount Gambier**  is situated in the southernmost portion of the Limestone Coast Zone, 25 kilometres to the east of the Victorian border, and with a climate similar to that of Henty in Victoria. Few plantings existed before the mid-1990s, but plantings have grown substantially since. Chardonnay,

pinot noir and sauvignon blanc dominate, the first two varieties being used for both sparkling and table wine production. By far the greater part of grape production is sold to major wine companies which, on present indications, will not establish vineyards of their own, no matter how desirable the grapes are. As at 2009 it had not sought registration as a Geographic Indication.

**Mount Horrocks**  (est. 1982) celebrated its 25th birthday in 2007, driven from the word go by the steel will of Clare Valley winemaker/owner Stephanie Toole, the life partner of Jeffrey Grosset. Mount Horrocks and Grosset share a winery, but have different vineyards (Mount Horrocks has a 3.5-ha vineyard at Auburn, and a 9-ha vineyard in Watervale) and separate cellar doors. The wine styles too have their own identity, the Mount Horrocks portfolio comprising shiraz, semillon, cabernet sauvignon, riesling and the cordon cut sweet white wine. Exports to the UK, the US and other major markets.

**Mount Langi Ghiran Vineyards**  was established in 1969, 1970 or 1971 (various accounts give one of those three years) in the Grampians by Don, Gino and Sergio Fratin with the planting of 15 ha of shiraz, cabernet sauvignon and riesling. While the vineyard was well chosen, winemaking was rustic. It began to turn the corner in the early 1980s when Trevor Mast started to assist as a consultant; he purchased the property later that decade. Wine quality improved thereafter to the point where the shiraz was widely regarded as one of the best cool-climate examples in Australia, and the vineyards began expanding to their present 80 ha, with a substantial portion of the oldest plantings covered by permanent, clear span netting providing protection against hail and birds. In 2002 the winery was acquired by the Rathbone Family Group (owner of Yering Station, Parker Coonawarra Estate and Xanadu Wines), which subsequently took production to 60,000 cases, including a range of vineyard-designated shiraz, and striking rieslings in different styles. Overall wine quality is outstanding. Exports to all major markets.

**Mount Lofty Ranges Zone** takes in the Clare Valley, Adelaide Plains and Adelaide Hills regions, a union of convenience if ever there was one, the terroir, climate, topography and wine style of each region being dramatically different from that of the other two.

**Mount Mary** (est. 1971) was established in the Yarra Valley by the late Dr John Middleton, one of the great, and truly original, figures in the Australian wine industry. He liked nothing more than to tilt at windmills, his annual newsletter growing longer as each year passed, although the paper size did not. The only change was the reduction in font size, and ultimately very strong light or a magnifying glass (or both) was needed to fully appreciate the barbed wit and incisive mind of this great character. The family (with David Middleton at the helm) is continuing to maintain the winery and the estate vineyards which produce all of its grapes. Production expanded in the wake of new plantings in 2000. Chardonnay, pinot noir, Quintet (the five red Bordeaux varieties) and Triolet (the three white Bordeaux varieties) are all made in the ultra-refined style which has always marked the vineyard.

**Mount Trio Vineyard** (est. 1989) was established in the Porongurup subregion by Gavin Berry and Gill Graham, initially as a sideline while Gavin Berry was winemaker at Plantagenet. They have slowly built up the Mount Trio business, increasing the estate plantings from 2.5 ha to 8 ha of riesling, sauvignon blanc, chardonnay, pinot noir, cabernet sauvignon, merlot and shiraz, which provide the bulk of the 7000-case production. Exports to the UK, Denmark and Singapore.

**mourvedre**, still widely called mataro in the Barossa Valley and previously esparte in the Grampians, was one of the James Busby collection, and was an important red grape variety in the Barossa Valley, Clare Valley and McLaren Vale until dwarfed by the explosion in plantings of cabernet sauvignon and shiraz. It has always been used in the making of fortified wines in tawny port style, there often blended with shiraz and grenache, and it is this blend which accounts for much of its current use in making table wine. Its most distinguished use as a straight varietal is the Hewitson Old Garden Mourvedre from vines planted in 1853 at Rowland Flat in the Barossa Valley. (The Silesian settlers in the Barossa called their vineyards gardens, and the 'Old Garden' name had already been bestowed on the block by the end of the 19th century.) This is believed to be the oldest planting of mourvedre in the world. As at 2008, 785 ha were under vine, significantly (and surprisingly) down from a peak of 1238 ha in 2002.

**mousy** (pronounced with a hard 's', thus 'mouzee') is a red wine fault associated with (but not the same as) Bretannomyces, usually occurring when red wines have been inadequately protected by sulphur dioxide before bottling. It is an unusual taint in that it is normally detected 10 or 20 seconds after a wine has been tasted, and also in that sensitivity to the taste varies widely between experts, apparently due to subtle differences in the pH of the tasters' saliva. A common method of confirming its presence is to wipe the wine across the base of the forefinger and thumb of the hand, and then smell the result.

**mouthfeel**  is a tasting term emcompassing all the textural components of wine, most obviously alcohol, acid and tannins, but also extending to the interaction of those components with varietal flavour.

**Mr Riggs Wine Company**  (est. 2001) is the very successful McLaren Vale venture of Ben Riggs, who established it after 14 years as winemaker at Wirra Wirra. Numerous northern hemisphere vintages, and experience at other Australian wineries, have all added to his skills, and he runs a very active and highly regarded contract winemaking service for a number of well-known South Australian wineries, offering a 'grape-to-plate' service. While riesling and viognier are part of his portfolio, he is first and foremost a red wine maker, with shiraz and shiraz viognier usually leading the way; however, his European experience has come to the fore with some of the best tempranillos in Australia. Exports to the UK, the US and other major markets.

**Mudgee**,  gazetted 24 August 2000, was first settled in 1822 by George and Henry Cox, the year after James Blackman and William

Lawson first entered the district. The village of Mudgee was gazetted on 12 January 1838, and is the second-oldest settlement west of the Great Dividing Range. Many of its National Trust–classified buildings date back to the second half of the 19th century, the oldest to 1852.

Vines were first planted in 1858 by Adam Roth, one of a number of German 'vine-dressers' who had been brought to Australia some years earlier as the result of the exhortations of William Macarthur, who needed skilled labour for his substantial vineyard at Camden. The German influence was as important in Mudgee as it was in the Barossa Valley, with the Roth and Kurtz families sustaining viticulture for a century or more; and others, such as Frederick Buchholz, making a major contribution in the last century. Having served his time with Macarthur, Roth was given a 37-ha grant on the banks of Pipeclay Creek in 1858 and immediately planted part of it to vines. In 1872 gold was discovered at the quaintly named nearby settlement of Home Rule; the diggings quickly spread to within a kilometre of Roth's property, which he had named Rothview. Once again gold and vines proved a symbiotic pairing, and once again the astute realised there was a more assured income to be made from feeding the miners than from chasing the elusive pot of gold.

Grapes, wine and vegetables brought premium prices; by 1880 there were 13 wineries in the district, five of them owned and operated by Adam Roth's sons, while the sixth and youngest remained at Rothview to help his father. Andreas Kurtz was a German immigrant from Württemberg who followed closely on the heels of Adam Roth, planting grapes in the 1860s, and establishing one of the other wineries. The largest of all was that of Frederick Buccholz, who established his 80-ha vineyard and Fredericksburg Winery adjacent to Rothview. In 1888 he was a successful exhibitor at the Centennial Exhibition in Melbourne, but the bank crash and the depression of the 1890s badly hurt his business, and the property was sold in 1899.

Anti-German feeling in Mudgee during World War I also paralleled that of the Barossa Valley, and Fredericksburg was renamed Westcourt. Either at that time or before, perhaps even in 1899, it had passed to the Roth family, and was owned for many years by Bill Roth. In 1930 Colin Laraghy, winemaker at the then-famous Smithfield Winery on the outskirts of Sydney, came to Mudgee to arrange long-term contracts with the few local growers who were persisting with wine grapes. One such was Bill Roth at Westcourt, and Laraghy supplied him with cuttings to increase his range, including a white grape.

When Jack Roth married, and inherited his father's winery (by then renamed Craigmoor), he decided to expand the winery and its production, and purchased Rothview from his brother Bill. The white vines from the Laraghy cuttings had prospered, but Jack Roth never vinified them separately. All his white grapes went together to make a dry white, released in an old-style riesling bottle with a label in the shape of a grape leaf, and bearing neither vintage nor variety.

But the Laraghy-originated vines caught the attention (and respect) of Alf Kurtz, who worked on Craigmoor as well as tending to his own small family vineyard some distance down the road. When in the mid-1960s he decided to establish Mudgee Wines, he obtained cuttings from the Craigmoor plantings and established them at his own vineyard. It was here that they were discovered and identified as including chardonnay by a visiting French ampelographer, Dr Denis Boubals, brought to Australia on a six-month study tour by the CSIRO. Boubals in turn told Mildara's Bob Hollick of his discovery, adding that the clone was virus-free and one of the best he had seen anywhere in the world. The small planting was to become the source block for much of Australia's chardonnay; it was almost certainly a James Busby selection. It may not have come as any great surprise to Alf Kurtz, because he had labelled the wine made from it as white pinneau, and had shared a bottle with Boubals and Dr Peter May on the day they had visited his winery.

Back at the turn of the 19th century winemaking (and grapegrowing) was on the wane in Mudgee as it was in so many other regions of Australia. One of Australia's most enterprising wine-medicos, Florentine-born Dr Thomas Henry Fiaschi, had gone against the trend and established a vineyard and winery at Buberra, 3 kilometres from Craigmoor, in the early part of the 20th century. He died, aged 74, in 1927, at which time only his winery and that of Craigmoor remained in operation. It, too, passed into disuse, so that when Alf Kurtz established Mudgee Wines in 1964, his was only the second winery in the district.

In more recent times, Mudgee has had a turbulent existence. In 1974 two Italian-born engineers who had become wealthy courtesy of a large-scale construction business in Australia built Montrose, which dwarfed all the other wineries in the region. Partly due to a financial dispute between the owners, it passed into the ownership of Orlando Wyndham in the 1980s, and became the base for Orlando's New South Wales operations when it closed its Hunter Valley winery in 1997. In the aftermath of Orlando deciding to move all its winemaking operations back to South Australia, it was acquired by the Oatley family in 2007, who spent $10 million upgrading it (as well as acquiring seven vineyards totalling 465 ha spread across the region) and renaming it Robert Oatley Vineyards. For good measure, the family also acquired the Craigmoor cellar door and restaurant.

Even larger (or more expensive) was the erection of the $20 million Simon Gilbert Winery in 1993; although funded by a listed company on the stock exchange, it quickly fell prey to financial pressures which, as at 2009, showed no sign of abating.

Mudgee is a red wine district first and foremost, with shiraz and cabernet sauvignon constituting nigh on 75 per cent of the total plantings; 30-year-old sangiovese, barbera and nebbiolo, established by Montrose and its then-Italian winemaker, the late and much-loved Carlo Corino, are obtaining a new lease of life under the energetic Oatley ownership and marketing. Chardonnay dominates the white plantings, with semillon in second place.

Situated as it is on the western slopes of the Great Dividing Range, Mudgee has a very different climate from its neighbour on the other (coastal) side, the Hunter Valley. Spring frosts and cold nights delay budburst; rainfall and humidity are lower; sunshine hours are greater; and irrigation is essential on all but the most favoured sites. The summer and autumn days are very warm; while harvest is four weeks

behind the Hunter Valley, this is by no means a cool region.

The most common soils are similar or identical to those found in many – indeed, the majority of – Australian wine districts: slightly acidic loam or sandy loam topsoils over neutral clay subsoils. These brownish-coloured soils are quite friable and moderately fertile, and both surface and subsoils are relatively well drained.

There are 42 wineries in the region; among the more important are Abercorn, di Lusso, Frog Rock, Huntington Estate, Lowe Family, Miramar, Robert Oatley Vineyards, Prince Hill and Thistle Hill.

LAT 32°36'S; ALT 450–600 m; HDD 2050; GSR 360 mm; MJT 22.9°C; HARV Late February to late March; CHIEF VIT. HAZARD Drought

**Murdock** (est. 1998) has a little over 14 ha of vines in Coonawarra, and 10 ha in the Barossa Valley. The Coonawarra cabernet sauvignon, made at Balnaves, has been of the highest quality since the first vintage, but the Barossa shiraz and a Coonawarra cabernet Barossa shiraz blend (The Merger) stand alongside the cabernet sauvignon. The wines have a polish which is typical of the wines created by Balnaves winemaker Pete Bissell.

**Murphy, Hazel, AM** (1948–) began her involvement with the Australian wine industry as an employee of Austrade in London, where she forged a reputation as energetic, innovative and committed to the cause of Australian wine. She left Austrade to become head of the Australian Wine Bureau in London for more than 10 years, commencing in 1986 when Australia's exports to the UK were still very small. With a limited budget, and a marketing campaign revolving around the simple idea of putting glasses of Australian wine in as many hands as possible, she played an enormously important role in the increase of UK imports from 765,000 litres per annum in 1986 to around 73 million litres a year in 1996/97, when she left to become a marketing consultant to several major Australian companies. She was the recipient of the Maurice O'Shea Award in 1996.

**Murray Darling**, gazetted 16 June 1997, has increasingly occupied centre stage in 2007 and 2008, albeit for all the wrong reasons. By far the most important aqueous artery for eastern Australia, it has been brought to its knees by a combination of generations of excessive and irresponsible use of irrigation water, a prolonged drought and (more contentiously) the impact of climate change. What is little understood is that, despite the higher end value of every gigalitre of water used by the wine industry than that of any other user, grapes account for less than 10 per cent of the water drawn from the Murray (and Murrumbidgee) River: in 2005/06 (before water shortages distorted the figures), it amounted to 407 gigalitres out of the total usage of 4666 gigalitres.

The Murray Darling has a history worthy of a television epic, with a heady mix of political intrigue and duplicity, a wild west frontier backdrop, the canvas an endless stretch of red sandy desert growing little more than saltbush, tumbleweed and spinifex, and business ventures which blossomed and failed in the space of a few years, only to rise again from the ashes. The central players were George and William Chaffey, irrigation engineers who were at the forefront of creating the orange groves of California using irrigation water in the 1880s, and the vision of future prime minister Alfred Deakin, who, having seen the work of the Chaffey brothers, lured them to what was to become Mildura on the Victorian section of the Murray River. Part of the knowhow they brought with them was the necessity of obtaining permanent land and water rights, to ensure the ongoing viability of the nascent Mildura. Bureaucratic delays so frustrated them that in 1887 they moved to Renmark, with the unconditional support of the South Australian Government.

With formidable energy they quickly laid out plans for that town, including the side streets and parklands which remain a feature of Renmark to this day. Stung by jealousy and having unsuccessfully sought tenders from others, the Victorian Government then invited the Chaffeys to return, on the precise terms they had failed to obtain the first time around. The return of the Chaffeys saw the town of Mildura's population rise from a handful to 3000 people by 1890, many taking up 4-ha lots already supplied with water. The town was laid out in much the same way as Renmark, with substantial parklands and public places held in perpetual trust.

In 1892 the Chaffeys built Chateau Mildura, but they were brought down by events outside their control: the great bank crash of 1893 which affected every state, and a prolonged drought which halted all river traffic on the Murray. There was simply no way for the varied produce of the region to get to the Melbourne (or any other) market, and in 1897 William Chaffey was declared bankrupt. The railway finally arrived in 1903, and the region slowly rebuilt its economic fortunes. In the meantime, most of the vineyards had been grafted from wine to table or drying grapes, and the unsold wine at Chateau Mildura had been distilled into brandy, leading to the closure of the winery in 1908. In the ensuing years there were two further bankruptcies and two reconstructions, all with the Mildura name and all with the continued involvement of the exceptionally resilient William Chaffey, who died in 1925. Renmark, the principal town on the South Australian section of the Murray, had a less tempestuous history, as did the towns downstream, ending with Waikerie.

The climate is hot, with high evaporation rates and low rainfall, making irrigation essential, both to succour the vines and to prevent the ascent of salinity through the soil. The climate is also continental, resulting in long sunny days and noticeably cooler nights. Modern viticultural and winemaking techniques mean that this climate can be seen as one of the region's strengths. Long sunshine hours ensure fruit ripeness, while a strongly winter-dominant rainfall results in low incidence of disease and (water availability assumed) allows the viticulturists the choice of how much moisture the vine receives during the growing season. In lieu of the flood irrigation, overhead sprays and generally unrestricted use of water in bygone decades, micro-management of water has to become the main strategy for survival. Underground drip lines allied with tensiometers or gypsum blocks (devices for precisely measuring the soil moisture content at various depths) will become crucial, and a body of knowledge will emerge through research and real-life practice which will guide viticulturists in determining

the precise times during the growing cycle when water will be most beneficial.

The most important producers on the South Australian section of the river are Angove's, Banrock Station, Kingston Estate and Oxford Landing; on the Victorian side are Deakin Estate, Lindemans Karadoc, Robinvale (the first certified biodynamic winery in Australia), Trentham Estate and Zilzie.

The soil is unique to the Murray River system, but spreads along its entire length. It is technically known as calcareous earth, ranging from brown to red-brown loamy sand, sandy loam or loam. The surface soils are permeable, but parched watertables (partly due to soil properties and topography, partly due to management practices associated with salinity build-up) can create problems in some areas, and lead to increased need for irrigation.

LAT 34°10′S; ALT 55–70 m; HDD 2150–2240; GSR 130–150 mm; MJT 23.7°C; HARV Early February to mid-March; CHIEF VIT. HAZARD Drought

**Murray Darling River System** has three rivers: the Darling River (2740 kilometres), the Murrumbidgee River (1575 kilometres) and the River Murray (various authorities giving different lengths between 2530 and 2756 kilometres). The Murray is the third-longest navigable river in the world, after the Amazon and Nile. These three rivers constitute the Murray Darling Basin, which covers one-seventh of the total area of Australia. It contains 40 per cent of all Australian farms, producing wool, cotton, wheat, sheep, cattle, dairy produce, rice, vegetable oil, seed, grapes (wine and table), fruit and vegetables. In all, this represents one-third of Australia's food supply and supports over a third of Australia's total gross value of agricultural production.

The socioeconomic consequences of ongoing damage to the system would be little short of catastrophic.

Fruit, grapes and vegetables use the least amount of water, in aggregate only slightly more than that used for cotton, and a quarter of that used for livestock, pasture, grains (other than rice) and others. However, the three have the highest return per megalitre: $1900 for vegetables, $1500 for fruit and $900 for grapes. The added value for grapes (a multiplier of 12 times, made up of winemaking, bottles, corks/screwcaps, cartons, labels, freight, distributor wholesale margin and retailer margin, plus salaries) takes the effective return for grape-growing way beyond that of either fruit or vegetables, where the added value is very low.

**muscadelle** is of diminishing importance (having, in any event, started with a small base) in the making of table wine around the world. Its best known international role was as the third white grape component in the great sweet wines of Sauternes, Bordeaux, but it is fast losing popularity in the face of sauvignon blanc and semillon. It is also rapidly declining in Australia: 4347 tonnes were crushed in 1987; 2597 tonnes were crushed in 1997; and by 2007 the crush had fallen to 889 tonnes. This fall from grace stems from its prior use as a blend component in low-priced bulk and cask wine. What remain are the plantings in northeast Victoria where muscadelle is the variety used to make topaque (formerly tokay), one of Australia's greatest fortified wines. Indeed, given the choice between tokay and muscat of similar age and quality, most winemakers will choose tokay. No other country in the world uses muscadelle for this

purpose, or at least not to produce single varietal fortified wine, which automatically limits its export potential. Protracted discussions with the EU, complicated at the last moment by the admission of new member state Hungary, have resulted in an agreement to phase out the use of the name tokay and replace it with topaque over a 10-year period.

**muscat** is an imprecise and short name for two very different varieties, each of which has multiple synonyms. The first is muscat à petits grains, and the second is muscat gordo blanco, Australian usage for muscat of alexandria.

**muscat à petits grains** is one of the great chameleons, grown with enthusiasm in 13 countries, each of which has three or four synonyms for the variety. In all but a couple of instances altered spellings do not entirely obscure the name: for example, muskuti in Greece; zutimuscat in Serbia and Montenegro, weisse muskettraube in Germany, and so on. The French ampelographer Dr Pierre Galet believes it to be the world's 12th most planted variety, but it has the added complication that its skin colour varies from yellow (that is, white) to orange, to gold, to pink, to red, to brown and to black. In Australia its synonyms are white frontignan, frontignac, orange muscat and brown muscat.

Unlike muscadelle, it has held its own in plantings, although its 263 ha in 2008 (which includes 28 ha still coming into full bearing) producing plus/minus 3100 tonnes (the figure is surprisingly variable) puts it in the minnow league of varieties in Australia. It is used to make dry or off-dry table wines, with an intensely fragrant and flowery bouquet, and a flavour which can only be described as grapey, variously labelled frontignac, orange muscat or simply muscat.

However, as with muscadelle, its greatest manifestation is in the fortified wine of northeast Victoria which is just called muscat (and will continue to be forever). While winemakers might prefer topaque of similar age and complexity to a given muscat, the latter achieves heights which topaque can't match. Like Narcissus drowning in his reflection, one can lose oneself in the aroma of a great old muscat. All this, and one has not yet felt the necessity of actually tasting the wine. The moment destroys the calm which preceded it: an old muscat has an explosive intensity of luscious flavour, combined with high acid and a twist of wood-derived volatility, which strips the saliva from the sides of the taster's mouth, leaving the flavour in undiminished magnificence for minutes after the last millilitre has been swallowed.

Muscat thus walks side by side with Australian topaque, red-brown in its youth and simply smelling and tasting of a grape and raisin mix, the colour progressively deepening and turning to olive-brown as it ages, the swirl of aromas (and rancio) intensifying as it ages. While its development ends when it is bottled, it can then be kept in bottle for months or years, although the makers can tell how long the wine has been 'imprisoned' in the bottle, away from the air which has been part and parcel of its development in the barrel.

The makers of Rutherglen muscat initiated the four-tier classification system which has since, with their agreement, been extended to topaque and tawny. The region may be specified, as it is in the official classification which is reproduced verbatim below, but if it isn't, the word 'Australian' should be substituted. The absence of any guide to average age is deliberate, but the higher the classification, the greater the average age will in fact be.

*Rutherglen Muscat* is the foundation of the style; displaying the fresh raisin aromas, rich fruit, clean spirit and great length of flavour on the palate which are the marks of all the muscats of Rutherglen.

*Classic Rutherglen Muscat* displays a greater level of richness and complexity, produced through the blending of selected parcels of wine, often matured in various sizes of oak cask to impart the distinctive dry rancio characters produced from maturation in seasoned wood.

*Grand Rutherglen Muscat* takes the flavour of Rutherglen muscat to a still higher plane of development, displaying a new level of intensity, depth and concentration of flavour, mature rancio characters, and a complexity which imparts layers of texture and flavour.

*Rare Rutherglen Muscat* is rare by name and by nature. These are the pinnacle Rutherglen muscats, fully developed and displaying the extraordinary qualities that result from the blending of selected parcels of only the very richest, and most complete wines in the cellar. Rare Rutherglen Muscats are only bottled in tiny quantities each year, but for those privileged to taste them, these are wines of breathtaking complexity, texture and depth of flavour.

**muscat gordo blanco,** or more correctly muscat of alexandria, was once a cornerstone variety for white wine production in Australia, its very high yield – around 20 tonnes per hectare on average – putting it in third place after chardonnay (which towers over all other white varieties, accounting for 50 per cent of white wine production) and semillon. Like muscat à petits grains, it is an ancient variety, believed to have originated in Egypt, and propagated around the world. In the Southern Rhône it is used to produce muscat vin doux naturel, which is in fact entirely unnatural, as it is lightly fortified to leave sweet, grapey flavours from the unfermented portion of the wine. Brown Brothers adds to the many faces of muscat of alexandria by labelling it lexia, yet another synonym. Its principal use is to add juicy/grapey flavours to otherwise flat and featureless bulk/cask wine blended from colombard, trebbiano and Riverland-grown semillon.

**must** is the mixture of red grape juice, skins and seeds after the grapes have been destemmed or (if whole bunches) wholly or partly crushed, before fermentation. During fermentation it is known as fermenting must.

a b c d e f g h i
j k l m n o p q
r s t u v w x y z

**Nagambie Lakes,** gazetted 9 April 2001, has a rich history, centring almost entirely around Tahbilk (which has dropped the 'Chateau' from its name after over 100 years of use). For once gold did not play a direct role in the arrival of the first settlers, who were following in the tracks of Major Thomas Mitchell. He crossed the Goulburn River on 9 October 1836, noting the fertile soils, abundant water and easy terrain of the region.

Phylloxera spelt the end for the other smaller vineyards and wineries in the district, and when the Purbrick family purchased Chateau Tahbilk in 1925, it was the only operating winery. Indeed, the only other significant winery (in commercial terms) to be established in the Goulburn Valley has been Mitchelton (in 1969), and even it had a prolonged struggle before becoming successful. The history of these two wineries is taken up in their respective entries.

The two wineries more than compensate for the lack of numbers: the National Trust-classified Tahbilk retains more of its 19th century atmosphere than any other winery in Australia. New buildings have been added with the utmost care and sensitivity, and are barely noticed. Tahbilk is surrounded by the billabongs and backwaters of the Goulburn River (and by the river itself on one side), a setting it shares with Mitchelton. The special qualities of this part of the Goulburn Valley have resulted in the creation of the Nagambie Lakes subregion. It is within this slightly cooler area that most of the best performing wineries in the greater Goulburn Valley region are to be found.

The essentially flat countryside is never boring: white-trunked eucalypts (frequently massive), a profusion of bird life and the wandering watercourses create a unique atmosphere. In the height of summer, when the temperatures soar and the canopy of the vines starts to wilt under the heat, a cool and shady spot is never far away. A striking café has been opened by Tahbilk above and over the river; it doubles up as a cellar for Dalfarras, the personal venture of Alister and Rosa Purbrick.

There are three principal soil types: red and brown sandy clay loams; similar hard duplex soils, but yellow-brown in colour; and gritty/gravelly quartzose sands laid down by the prehistoric wanderings of the Goulburn River. The sandy soils held phylloxera at bay, and it is for this reason that Tahbilk has shiraz vines in production that date back to the 1860s.

Thanks in no small measure to the success of Tahbilk, Mitchelton and McPherson Wines, white varieties account for a somewhat unexpected 44 per cent share of total plantings in what might otherwise be regarded as red wine country. In descending order the varieties are shiraz, chardonnay, cabernet sauvignon, sauvignon blanc, marsanne and merlot. The foremost wineries in the region are Dalfarras, McPherson, Mitchelton and Tahbilk.

**LAT** 36°42'S; **ALT** 130–350 m; **HDD** 1694; **GSR** 250 mm; **MJT** 21.2°C; **HARV** Early March to early May; **CHIEF VIT. HAZARD** Spring frost

**Narkoojee** (est. 1981) was established on a dairy farm in Gippsland owned by the Friend family. It is within easy reach of the old gold mining town of Walhalla and looks out over the Strzelecki Ranges. The wines are produced from a little over 10 ha of estate vineyards, with chardonnay accounting for half the total. Former lecturer in civil engineering and extremely successful amateur winemaker

Harry Friend changed horses in 1994 to take joint control, with son Axel, of the family vineyard and winery, and hasn't missed a beat since; their skills show through with all the wines, none more so than the chardonnay. Exports to Canada, Ireland and Asia.

**National Association for Sustainable Agriculture Australia (NASAA)** see organic viticulture.

**native yeast** is most commonly called wild yeast.

**nebbiolo** is accepted as the most noble of the many hundreds of Italian red grape varieties. Its nobility is consistent with its reluctance to perform well outside its kingdom in Piedmont, and also with the autocratic and unbending nature of its greatest wine, barolo.

With many years of age, it is possible to see stylistic links with pinot noir, another reluctant traveller. But however fussy pinot noir may be, it does not approach the reluctance of nebbiolo to perform in Australia. Nebbiolo has been grown in the King Valley, McLaren Vale, Adelaide Hills, Mornington Peninsula, Heathcote, Mudgee and Murray Darling, and in none of these regions has it yet produced wines of unambiguous class. It may be that the combination of better clonal selection and greater vine age will produce worthwhile results in 10 or 20 years' time, but it will take a brave and financially secure vigneron to prove the point.

**nematodes** are microscopic roundworms which take various forms. Some are part of the normal vineyard ecosystem, feeding on bacteria or fungi, but others feed on grape vine roots, thus debilitating the vine and producing symptoms of stress. More vineyards in Australia are planted on rootstock resistant to nematodes than are grafted to withstand phylloxera; some rootstocks are resistant to both parasites.

**New England Australia**, gazetted 23 January 2008, was the name given to the region (without the word 'Australia') by the first graziers to arrive and settle there. The summer rainfall ensures that the gently rolling hills of the main tableland section are lush and green, interspersed with creeks and rivers.

John Oxley had passed through in 1818 as he explored northern New South Wales, and with the promulgation of the Settler's Act in the late 1830s (permitting occupation of unsettled land for a nominal fee) the first graziers arrived in 1839.

In that year George Wyndham, already established at Dalwood in the Hunter Valley, successfully applied for a 12,000-ha holding at Bukkulla, and a 40,000-ha run near Inverell (named Nullamanna), which was then the outermost settled land in New South Wales. Wyndham may be best known for his winemaking, but he was also instrumental in establishing Hereford cattle in the state, and his dairy at Wyndham Estate shows he was a renaissance man when it came to attempting to grow crops, plants and fruit-bearing trees of every description.

In 1841 he set off to Bukkulla with a herd of cattle, but records show that he also took vine cuttings from Wyndham Estate, dipping them in creeks along the way, and duly established a vineyard which produced substantial quantities of wine for blending with the lighter wines of Dalwood. While blending was the major use of Bukkulla's wines, an order recorded in the Wyndham books of account in the 1860s shows that nine dozen Bukkulla Red were purchased for 60 shillings a dozen, 36 dozen Dalwood Red for a mere 26 shillings a dozen, while even Fine Dalwood Red brought only 32 shillings per dozen. Bukkulla's wines were also exported direct (in barrel) to England.

The 1851 discovery of gold at Rocky River, near Armidale, resulted in a veritable flood of miners, reaching 5000 within a few years; further goldfields were established near Glen Innes, and later on tin, bismuth, molybdenite, manganese, sapphires and diamonds were also mined there. As was the case in Victoria, miners had a voracious thirst and, if lucky, the money to slake that thirst.

In 1852 George Wyndham's sons took over management of the two properties, that at Bukkulla also becoming a horse stud. Vineyards proliferated, and on 24 June 1882, the *Sydney Mail* described Inverell as 'one of the foremost wine producing neighbourhoods in the colony'. There were 30 vineyards in production, the three largest being Bukkulla, Beaulieu and Roslyn. Producers' names on medals included Bukkulla, Nullamanna, Afu Ila, Rosenstein, Roslyn and Rob Roy. These medals came from as far afield as Bordeaux, Paris, London, Calcutta and Amsterdam.

The *Sydney Mail* description does not seem so far-fetched when JB Keene of HM Customs in England, with an encyclopedic knowledge of wines, wrote:

The whole of them [samples from Bukkulla and Dalwood] are fine, strong, full-bodied, well-flavoured and sound, and have a character and quality above the average of most wine-producing countries. The lowest quality is better than a large proportion of the ordinary wines of Europe, while the best would not suffer in comparison with the finest known growths.

In an all too familiar story, the wineries progressively went out of production in the first half of the 20th century as the removal of tariffs in the wake of Federation, and the outbreak of World War I, hit hard. The Australia-wide swing from table to fortified wine also had an impact here, and in other parts of New South Wales. Fire, frost and very high transport costs all added to the difficulties, and the last winery ceased operating in World War II.

In 1968 local medical practitioner Dr Keith Whish decided to plant a vineyard, and brought the cycle to a full turn by obtaining his cuttings from Penfolds' Dalwood Vineyard. He named the vineyard Gilgai (a nearby town), eventually expanding it to 6 ha, but was a lone soldier until the 1990s. His son, Charles Whish, is a senior winemaker with Foster's, but opted not to follow in his father's footsteps, presumably realising that McLaren Vale is a more hospitable environment than the challenging New England region. (Gilgai has since been sold.) As at 2007, there were over 40 vineyards, ranging in size from a few vines to over 50 ha. Cassegrain (at Port Macquarie) is the largest purchaser of grapes from New England.

A final word: the correct, officially gazetted, name of Australia's newest wine region is New England Australia, notwithstanding usage of the term 'New England' as the regional name having spanned three centuries. It seems international recognition of regional names could have led to objections from New England in the US, though not from 'Old' England.

The New England climate can, without hyperbole, be described as unique. It lies in the zone of transition from the dominantly summer maximum rainfall areas of northern Australia to the dominantly maximum rainfall areas of the southern part of the continent. Nonetheless, December and January are the wettest months, but the rain abates in March, when vintage typically begins, with April the driest month. Moreover, as Dr John Gladstones, in his book *Viticulture and Environment*, points out, the highest temperatures during the growing season are remarkably moderate, favouring medium-bodied wines.

The soils are in four main groups; the most common is granitic, well drained and not particularly fertile – happily, this is the best vineyard soil. There is also some planting on alluvial river soils suited to white grapes. The varied topography gives rise to the elevation, mostly over 600 metres, and similar to that of the adjoining Granite Belt, which delays harvest and thus avoids major problems with vintage rain. The New England Highway, which runs through the centre of the region, largely follows the spine of the Great Dividing Range.

The principal grape varieties, in descending order, are shiraz, cabernet sauvignon, chardonnay, merlot, riesling, pinot noir, verdelho and tempranillo. The leading wineries are Blickling Estate, Deetswood, New England Estate, Richfield Estate and Whyworry.

LAT 29°14′S (Glen Innes); ALT 300–1400 m; HDD 1413–2126; GSR 539–604 mm; MJT 19.2°–22.8°C; HARV Early March to early April; CHIEF VIT. HAZARD Spring frost

New World is a loose but widely used expression encompassing all southern hemisphere wine regions/countries, and also North America. Before too long, it will include China, India et al.

noble rot is a common name for what is correctly called botrytis.

Norfolk Rise Vineyard (est. 2000) is by far the largest and most important development in the Mount Benson region. It is owned by a privately held Belgian company, G & C Kreglinger, established in 1797. In early 2002 Kreglinger acquired Pipers Brook Vineyard; it will maintain the separate brands of the two ventures. The Mount Benson development commenced in 2000, with a 160-ha vineyard and a 2000-tonne winery, primarily aimed at the overseas markets. Exports to the UK, the US and other major markets.

North East Victoria Zone encompasses the regions of Rutherglen, King Valley, Alpine Valleys, Beechworth and Glenrowan, with the usual mix of climate, soil and topography, ranging from very warm to cool.

Northern Rivers Zone stretches from Newcastle to the Queensland border; its eastern boundary is defined by the Pacific Ocean, its western by the top of the Great Dividing Range. It has one small region centred on Port Macquarie and the Hasting River, which gives that region its name.

Northern Slopes Zone runs parallel with the Northern Rivers Zone, but is on the inland side of the Great Dividing Range, and extends towards the massive Western Plains Zone. It includes the New England Australia region, which occupies a substantial part of the zone.

**Northern Tasmania**  is not an official region, as the island of Tasmania constitutes a de facto zone, and has – quite sensibly – declined the opportunity to seek to register such of the regions as qualify under the 500-tonne/five-vineyard requirements of the Geographic Indications legislation. For the history of the region before 1956, see Tasmania.

Between 1956 and 1960 Frenchman Jean Miguet was working on a civil engineering project in Tasmania and establishing his 1-ha vineyard at Lalla, north of Launceston and just to the east of the Tamar River. He called his vineyard La Provence to remind him of his southern French heritage; it was close-planted on a 1.2 × 1 metre spacing on clay soil on a north-facing hillside, and although he returned to France in 1974, dying not long thereafter, the vineyard remained, and is the oldest planting in Tasmania. It passed into the ownership of the Bryce family in 1980, but another decade was to pass before French authorities became aware of the name of the vineyard, and forced a name change, to Providence Vineyards.

Dr Andrew Pirie obtained (uniquely) his doctorate at the University of Sydney with his study of homoclimes for France and Australia, which led him to the Pipers River region in the correct belief that the climate was similar to that of Burgundy. What was not similar was the deep red, rich soils of Pipers Brook. In the meantime, Launceston identity Graham Wiltshire had wended a circuitous route leading to a 1.2 ha vineyard at Legana, and the establishment of a small winery in the early 1970s, the first commercial winery in Northern Tasmania. An even more complicated chain of events led to the forming of a consortium in 1975 to acquire a substantial property at Pipers Brook, directly facing that which Andrew Pirie had purchased the year before. Until 1980 all the commercially released Heemskerk Wines came from the Legana Vineyard, but thereafter they have come from the rapidly expanding Pipers Brook Vineyard. Prior to the 1984 vintage a sizeable winery was erected, and a series of vivacious, minty cabernet sauvignons were made which were excitingly different and had considerable success in wine shows. (Today they would be considered green, weedy and unripe.) In April 1985 Heemskerk announced a joint venture with Louis Roederer, and Jean-Baptiste Lecaillon was put in charge. He remained in Tasmania for some years, but the joint venture was ultimately terminated without public release of any of the wines, and Lecaillon returned to Roederer to be appointed chief winemaker.

By 1984 the Pipers Brook area had six vineyards, the Tamar Valley had 11 and the east coast three (out of a state total of 31). The entire state produced 240 tonnes of wine grapes that year; within another 20 years, the crush had risen to just under 6400 tonnes from about 100 wineries. Two of the three major wineries in the north, Pipers Brook and Tamar Ridge, have 185 and 378 ha of vines respectively; the third, Bay of Fires (owned by CWA) has only 27 ha of estate vineyards, but buys substantial amounts of contract-grown grapes.

The north of Tasmania has a range of terroir and climate as diverse as the southern half of Victoria, the east side of the Tamar

River, the Pipers River area and the northwest coast having distinctly different soils and macroclimates, able to ripen every variety from chardonnay and pinot noir to shiraz and cabernet sauvignon.

No one the least bit familiar with Tasmania will be surprised by the ever-changing but always beautiful landscape; those vineyards facing the Tamar River offer breathtaking vistas.

The atmosphere of the Pipers River area is very different, much being undulating and forested, the undergrowth lush and the roadside grass remaining green for most of the year. It was indeed Andrew Pirie's observation of the last feature which was one of the factors that led him to establish Pipers Brook Vineyards here. The green of bush and vineyards (in summer) then provides a compelling contrast with the vivid red basalt-derived soils.

The climate of the Pipers River area is comparable to that of Champagne and the Rhine Valley; 40 per cent of the annual rainfall is recorded in the growing season, and the relatively high humidity also ameliorates stress, promoting vigorous growth. Take in the soils, and the reasons for the varietal choice (of white grapes and pinot noir) become even more evident. Spring frosts are a serious problem, necessitating wind machines or overhead sprinklers in many sites. The figures for the Tamar Valley are superficially similar, but this area achieves physiological ripeness far earlier than Pipers River, and allows late-ripening varieties to do relatively well.

Almost all vineyards are on slopes facing north, northeast and east. The vivid red soils of the Pipers River area are very deep, free-draining, friable and fertile; those of the Tamar Valley are gravelly basalt on a clay and ironstone base.

The leading wineries (out of a total of 52) include Barringwood Park, Bay of Fires, Clover Hill, Dalrymple, Jansz Tasmania, Pipers Brook, Pirie Estate, Providence Vineyards, Stoney Rise, Tamar Ridge and Waterton Vineyards.

LAT 41°27′S; ALT 80–210 m; HDD 1020; GSR 310 mm; MJT 17.2°C; HARV Early April to late May; CHIEF VIT. HAZARD Spring frost

**North West Victoria Zone** encompasses the Murray Darling and Swan Hill regions, the former stretching for several hundred kilometres along the Murray River, and a major contributor to the annual crush, the latter a much smaller region, still on the Murray River, but running southeast from the Murray Darling.

**nose** is an all-encompassing term embracing both aroma and bouquet.

**nutty** has traditionally been used to describe the characteristic pungent flavour and aroma of sherry, due in part to wood age and to the presence of acetaldehyde, but also quite commonly used to encompass one aspect of oak-induced characters in white table wine.

a b c d e f g h i
j k l m n o p q
r s t u v w x y z

**oak** has been an integral part of winemaking for at least 1000 years, although its particular applications have changed. Its versatility stems from the fact that it is one of the strongest hardwoods, yet is also physically easy to work, and relatively light in weight. There are three key species of oak: *Quercus alba*, or white oak, grown in the US and accounting for 40 per cent of the world's supply, and two European oaks, *Q. petraea* and *Q. robur*, which account for the remaining 60 per cent. The major wild cards hidden behind these figures are the vast oak forests in the various countries that were once part of the Soviet Union. Not only are there no figures readily available, but it is believed that many of the forests have been poorly managed and may not be able to supply oak suitable for use in the wine industry.

In Australia (and elsewhere) oak is principally used for fermentation vats, and as storage and maturation vessels. Oak vats are upright (the planks arranged vertically, usually in a circular format, but sometimes oval) and contain 5000 litres and upwards. The widespread advent of stainless steel seemed to sound the death knell for oak vats, as stainless steel is easier to clean, and far easier to install temperature control systems in. However, since the early 1990s there has been renewed interest in oak vats, not simply because of the oak flavour they impart when new, but for subtle differences in the structure and texture of red wines in particular.

In the 19th century the most common form of maturation storage was large ovals built and stored horizontally, with the face of the oval including a hatch which, when the cask was emptied, allowed a small-framed adult (or a child) to enter and clean the inside of the cask, chiefly by scraping away tartaric acid deposits. These casks have a virtually indefinite life, and are still used in many older wineries. Here, too, there has been some revival of interest.

The maturation of table wine in oak (always remembering that many white wines, and some low-priced red wines, receive no oak maturation at all) involves three types of barrel: barrique (with a capacity of 225 litres), hogshead (300 litres) and puncheon (500 litres). While hogsheads and puncheons have been widely used since the birth of the Australian wine industry, since 1950 there has been a major and continuing change in the choice and use of barrels. In the wake of World War II, all imported goods had to receive a licence prior to arrival in the country. In 1948 the annual report of the Australian Wine Board lamented the lack of suitable oak for the manufacture of hogsheads and vats, noting that a very small amount of American oak had been imported, and further commenting that investigations were being made into the quality and availability of French oak. Two years later the board commented that 'Oak from France has unfortunately proved that the quality of this timber as received in Australia is quite unsuitable' and went on to press for greater import volumes of American white oak staves and vat timber 'to meet the urgent requirement of the industry for storage and maturation vessels'. Not surprisingly, American oak dominated the market once import licences were removed, and remained the oak of choice for shiraz (and other red wines) up to the 1990s. The move to French oak for white wines (such as chardonnay and, to a lesser degree, semillon) gained pace in the second half of the 1980s, although American, German and Hungarian oak are still in use for lesser quality white wines.

Running alongside these changes was a growing realisation that the flavour imparted by the various forests of France (Allier, Nevers, Troncais, Vosges and Limousin) was altogether different from the flavour of American oak, the latter imparting far more vanilla flavours. Next came examination of the tightness of the grain, the period during which the oak had been matured after being cut into planks (two or three years), the conditions of storage, and equally, if not more importantly, the way the barrels were made. Increasing attention was also given to the barrel-making process, which (traditionally) involved heating the staves over a small fire of oak chips which softened the wood and allowed the staves to be bent into the shape necessary for the barrel; thus the toast could be specified by the winery as light, medium or heavy, with an even more recent specification for the heads (the face of the barrel) to be toasted or not. Led by barrel maker Dargaud & Jaegle, the alternative of softening the staves by immersion in boiling water has proved very successful in moderating the impact of new oak.

**oak chips** provide a significantly cheaper way of imparting oak flavour into wine. Here, too, there has been rapid progress in the degree of sophistication of both the type of chips (forest of origin, toast, size and so forth) and their use in the winery (the best results coming when the chips are placed in small netted bags in the fermenting juice or must).

**Oakridge** (est. 1978) has undergone a move from one side of the Yarra Valley to the other,

and a series of ownership changes, since its establishment. Through a protracted period of financial instability, from which it emerged in 2008, winemaker (and now part-owner) David Bicknell continued to produce outstanding wines, headed by the small-volume, left-field but brilliantly successful 864 series, with several tiers underneath at price points carefully selected to cover all sectors of the market. The 864 Chardonnay is at the very top of the Australian chardonnay tree. Exports to the UK and Asia.

**oak staves**, or inner staves, are small planks of new oak which can be inserted in fermenters or maturation vessels. They perform much the same function as oak chips. Here, too, there is a wide choice available.

**oeillade** was the incorrect name once used for cinsaut, particularly when grown in Langhorne Creek.

**oidium** is the term used in France for powdery mildew.

**oily** is a white wine descriptor for wines which have excessive extract or (with some varieties) excessive alcohol.

**Old Kent River** (est. 1985), in the Frankland River subregion of Great Southern, was established by Mark and Debbie Noack, who have earnt much respect from their neighbours and from the other producers to whom they sell more than half the production from the 16.5-ha vineyard on their sheep property. The quality of their wines has gone from strength to strength, Mark having worked particularly hard with his pinot noir. Exports of the 3000-case production go to the UK, the US and Asia.

**O'Leary Walker Wines**  (est. 2001) was established when David O'Leary and Nick Walker decided to leave the shelter of the large wineries for which they had worked for many years and set up their own brand, with additional income from contract winemaking. Supported by 36 ha of vines at Watervale in the Clare Valley and 14 ha in the Adelaide Hills, they have a flourishing business, regularly producing wines of impeccable quality. Exports to the UK, Ireland and Singapore.

**oloroso**  was a Spanish name applied to old, rich, full-bodied apera, usually sweet but not necessarily so. Its use in Australia is no longer permitted; instead medium sweet or sweet will be used.

**ondenc**  is a once important but now virtually extinct white grape variety from southwest France. It was imported by Hans Irvine (the owner of what is now Seppelt Great Western between 1887 and 1922) in the latter part of the 19th century in the mistaken belief that it was one of the Champagne varieties, and was called Irvine's white. It was correctly identified as ondenc by French ampelographer Paul Truel in 1976, and has appeared as such in sparkling wines made by Seppelt since that time. It is still grown by Montara in the Grampians, and has found its way across to the Barossa Valley (where it was called sercial, a madeira variety, until correctly identified by Truel).

**Options Game, The**  was invented by Len Evans in 1968. The rules were honed and fined by a group which met every Monday lunchtime at Len Evans' restaurant, Bulletin Place, in Sydney. Three of the regular attendees (including the author) were lawyers, so, in its purest form, there was an exceedingly strict protocol. Each person brings a bottle of wine, which is decanted out of sight of the other tasters, into a bottle simply bearing a number or initials. Thus the bottles brought to the table give no clue as to the origin of the wine, but the person presenting the wine knows which is his/hers. Each person takes it in turn to ask five multiple-choice questions of the other players about his/her wine. In all except two instances (four major communes of Bordeaux, and the communes of Haut Medoc) only three choices may be offered. One of those choices has to be correct. When answers to a question have been offered by all players, the person whose wine it is, and who asked the question, will say which answer is correct. (Answers are given on a rotating basis: person B, then C, then D, then E for the first question, then person C, then D, then E, then B for the next, and so on.) Thus as the questions progress, players know more and more about the wine. A maximum of two questions can be asked about the vintage of the wine, but there is no restriction on the number of questions about variety, region or maker. A well-constructed series of five questions will leave the exact identity of the wine able to be determined by the last question.

**Orange,**  gazetted 31 October 1997, is a rapidly developing region in the Central Ranges Zone, one of two regions (the other being Adelaide Hills) to have its boundaries dictated by altitude, most dramatically so on its eastern side. It was an important orchard area producing apples, pears and cherries for both local and domestic markets, but in common with so many other places of its ilk in Australia, the export market for fruit has diminished, and vines have taken the place of orchards in various locations. The vineyards all huddle in the northern half of the region, chiefly spread either side of the town of Orange. Although an experimental viticulture station was established at Molong (a few kilometres outside the northeastern boundary) in the 1940s, nothing came of that until Bloodwood Estate planted the first commercial vineyard in 1980.

Its unquestioned cool climate comes about through its altitude, which ranges between 600 and 900 metres; snow decorates the vineyards in winter, but it seldom lasts long. All but one of its 42 wineries are family-owned and -run, and all are relatively small. The hilly, indeed mountainous, nature of the region (dominated by Mount Canobolas) affords often spectacular panoramic views, and the number of exotic trees planted throughout affords a blaze of orange and gold colours in autumn. The one corporate vineyard is Cumulus.

Within 60 kilometres of the town of Orange, one can find viticultural climates varying from distinctly warm to the cold 1200 HDD on the upper slopes of Mount Canobolas (which rises to 1396 metres). Overall, mild to warm midsummer temperatures, seldom rising above 32°C, are offset by cool to very cool nights during the growing season. The high ultra-violet light levels at low temperatures are also highly beneficial for ripening and flavour development. Wind is both friend and foe, helping to reduce the major climatic threat of spring frosts, but interfering with fruit set on sensitive varieties such as merlot.

The lovely, undulating hilly country is of fundamental importance in determining site selection. Reflecting the different geological ages of the parent rocks, the soils fall into three main groups: well-drained, friable, deep red-brown clays (derived from basalt) found on Mount Canobolas; deep red-brown/yellow-brown clay loams over a medium clay and shale base interspersed with gravel; and, finally, at lower elevation, patches of terra rossa associated with visible limestone.

The leading wineries (from a total of 42) are Belgravia, Bloodwood, Borrodell on the Mt, Brangayne of Orange, Canobolas-Smith, Cumulus, Mayfield Vineyard, Millamolong Estate, Patina, Phillip Shaw and Printhie.

LAT 33°15'S; **ALT** 600–900 m; **HDD** 1200–1309; **GSR** 440 mm; **MJT** 19.9°C; **HARV** Mid-March to early May; **CHIEF VIT. HAZARDS** Spring frosts; birds

**orange muscat** see muscat à petits grains.

**organic viticulture** is practised to a greater or lesser degree in all the major wine-producing regions of the world. While the legislative control of methodology differs from country to country, the basic principles do not: the list of permitted compounds approved for use in vineyards is small. Broadly speaking, natural elements or compounds which have not been treated or processed to alter their state can be used (most notably elemental sulphur and copper sulphate, the components of Bordeaux mixture), but manufactured or synthesised compounds for use as fertilisers, fungicides and/or pesticides are prohibited, as is any organism which has been genetically modified. The distinction can also be expressed as that between products which act by virtue of their presence on the exterior of leaves and grapes, and those which penetrate the vine, its leaves or grapes, and which are known as systemics. The regime requires constant monitoring of the vineyard throughout the growing season, which takes more man hours than are required for conventionally run vineyards. In turn, cooler, more humid growing conditions will create greater challenges than dry, warm regions. Behind this short list of sprays that are approved on the one hand and banned on the other lies a broader and deeper strategy, aimed at improving the structure of, and beneficial bacteria, fungi and other similar organisms in, the soil. Thus cover crops are commonly grown and then ploughed in, while naturally occurring grasses and weeds may perform similar functions. Composts of various kinds are used to both create extra nutrient and enhance the water-holding capacity of the soil.

Some vignerons practise organic viticulture without making specific reference to it on the labels or supporting literature for their wines. This choice allows the vigneron to fall back on systemic sprays to control downy mildew, powdery mildew or botrytis which has reached the point where it cannot be controlled by organic methods. Others simply wish to avoid the three-year conversion process and the associated paperwork and inspection regimes.

Those who desire certification have to apply to the National Association for Sustainable Agriculture Australia (NASAA) and embark on the certification process and enter into an agreement to operate according to NASAA's standards. Following an initial vineyard inspection, there will be a pre-certification period of one year, designed to demonstrate the vigneron's ability to manage the vineyard organically, prior to gaining 'in-conversion' status. No mention of NASAA organic certification can be made in this period. Inspection will be arranged towards the end of the initial 12 months to ascertain the degree to which the standard requirements have been met. Certification as 'in-conversion' may be achieved at this point, followed by a second review by NASAA and the signing of a licence agreement. This second phase generally takes two years, and during this time vignerons may sell their products as certified organic in-conversion. After three years of consecutive organic management, full certification may be granted, and the NASAA certified organic logo applied.

Australia and the US distinguish between wine made from organically grown grapes and organic wine, which is wine made using organically grown grapes and without the addition of any sulphur dioxide during the winemaking process. The advent of screwcaps has made sulphur-free wine less prone to bacterial spoilage or oxidation, and correspondingly lengthened its shelf life.

**Orlando** is one of the three pillars (the fourth disappeared when Foster's acquired Southcorp) of the industry, similar to the four pillars of banking. Its roots go back to 1847, when Johann Gramp moved to the diminutive Jacob's Creek and established the first vineyard in the Barossa Valley, albeit of modest size. The original stone cellars and house still stand by the creek. In 1887 Johann Gramp's son Gustav took control, establishing a larger winery at Rowland Flat where (much expanded) it stands today, adjacent to the Jacob's Creek Visitor Centre.

Growth was steady but hardly spectacular. The 1903 vintage produced 34,000 litres, compared with 112,000 litres at Basedow, 810,000 at Yalumba and 1,980,000 at Seppeltsfield. The rate of development increased thereafter. In 1912 the business was incorporated as a limited company, and in 1920 Gustav's son Hugo became managing director (he was killed in the Kyeema air crash of 1938). By the end of World War II Gramps' Orlando was firmly established as an important producer of table and fortified wine.

In 1953 Orlando triggered a technical innovation which was to revolutionise the Australian white wine industry. Both Colin Gramp (Hugo's son), who was by then managing director, and the Hill Smiths of Yalumba had been anxious to import newly designed German stainless steel pressure fermentation tanks. These had been developed in Germany not so much for fermentation of wine as for the preservation of unfermented grape juice. With the after-effects of World War II still being felt by the Australian economy, only one import licence was immediately available. Orlando was the first recipient. In August 1952 the tanks arrived, and the first vintage was made in 1953; that of Yalumba arrived a year later.

The style of the riesling which resulted was so radically different from anything that had preceded it that it was inevitably misunderstood (and rejected) by many in the industry. But the senior judges, headed by George Fairbrother, understood it well enough to award it first prize in both the Adelaide and Melbourne shows, and Orlando's Barossa Special Riesling was born. This wine has better claim than any other single wine to be the ancestor of modern-day aromatic white wines.

Orlando continued to evolve and grow through to the end of the 1960s, but in 1971 fell prey to Reckitt & Colman of the UK, as had Morris wines of Rutherglen the previous year. The making of Orlando as a major force came with the development of the Jacob's Creek brand, the first vintage of which was made in 1973. On the domestic front the successful development of the cask in 1974 provided Orlando with a golden opportunity, which it was quick to take with its Coolabah brand, one of the reasons why in the next 10 years Australia's per capita wine consumption doubled.

Despite its success, Reckitt & Colman decided to divest itself of its wine interests, and a senior team of Orlando executives completed a management buy-out in 1988, at a price believed to be in the region of $75 million. History does not officially relate how much they received (and hence how much money they made) when Pernod Ricard bought 80 per cent of the company from the team in 1989. Between 1985 and 1990 there was a series of acquisitions reminiscent of the tale of the old lady who swallowed a fly. In 1985 Wyndham Estate (which 10 years earlier had acquired Hollydene Vineyards) acquired the Saxonvale winery and vineyards; and in 1988 it acquired the Montrose and Craigmoor wineries and vineyards and Amberton Wines, all in Mudgee. Following the 1989 Pernod Ricard acquisition of 80 per cent of Orlando, it acquired Wyndham Estate (and its various subsidiaries) from what was then BRL Hardy. Thus not only could it claim to have in its ancestral roots the oldest winery in the Barossa Valley, but, courtesy of Wyndham Estate, the oldest winery in Australia (Wyndham having been established in 1824).

**O'Shea, Maurice** (1897–1956) was the son of a Parisian mother, Leontine (Beaucher), and Irishman John Augustus O'Shea. He was the first of their six children, and was left to head the family in 1912, when his father died at the age of 42. John O'Shea's business had been (and for the family continued to be) the New South Wales Wine and Spirit Company. Undismayed by her husband's early death, Leontine O'Shea sent Maurice to France in 1913 to finish his schooling at Montpellier. He then spent two years at the Institut National Agronomique, Paris-Grignon, an agricultural college near Paris regarded as having the best wine courses in Europe. He then went back to Montpellier University to obtain a degree in viticultural science, emerging with qualifications in mathematics, botany, history and chemistry, and was promptly enrolled as a lecturer in analytical wine chemistry, interspersed with trips through the fine regions of France.

After seven years, aged 23, he somewhat reluctantly returned to Australia, and soon thereafter to the small Hunter Valley vineyard and winery built by Charles King in the 1880s, named Mount Pleasant. He was to become one of the great winemakers of the 20th century, standing alongside Colin Preece of Seppelt Great Western, Max Schubert of Penfolds and Roger Warren of Hardys – the last because he

shared with O'Shea a remarkable talent for recognising the quality of wines barely through ferment, and how they might be synergistically blended with others. The Great Depression and the minuscule market for fine table wine led to McWilliam's buying a 50 per cent share in the business in 1932, a strangely quixotic decision by the thrifty Scottish McWilliam clan. In 1944 McWilliam's purchased the remaining half of Mount Pleasant from O'Shea, but O'Shea remained in sole charge of the winery and continued to make an extraordinary array of often enigmatically named wines (the reds were shiraz, some with a percentage of pinot noir, the whites semillon) until his death in 1956. Some of the wines were from the estate plantings, but many more were wines purchased from Tulloch's, Tyrrell's and Elliott's when just through fermentation, then to be matured (and possibly blended) at Mount Pleasant. Names appearing on bottles included Mountain A, Mountain C, Henry I, II and III, TY and Richard (usually Tyrrell wines), HT (Tulloch) and Charles (Elliott). Others were simply labelled Light-Bodied Dry Red, Dry Red (occasionally with Hermitage Pinot or Hermitage as a subtext) and even Full-Bodied Dry Red. There have always been suggestions that some of these wines included blend components from Baileys of Glenrowan, Hardys and Tahbilk, but the winery records disappeared shortly after O'Shea's death.

The 1937 Mountain A Dry Red was one of the greatest, but wines made through the 1940s (particularly 1944, 1945 and 1947) were still utterly remarkable 60 years later where the cork either had not failed or had been replaced along the way. Needless to say, as the years went by, the issues of ullage, oxidation and cork taint became steadily more apparent. Campbell Mattinson's *Wine Hunter* (Hachette Australia, Sydney, 2006) is a superbly written biography of Maurice O'Shea.

**oxidation**  occurs when oxygen is absorbed by wine in sufficient quantities to cause and/or accelerate certain chemical changes in its composition. In broad terms, these changes result in browning of the colour and loss of freshness and fruit expression on the bouquet and palate. The rate and degree of change is determined by the volume of the wine and the amount of oxygen present. Thus it can occur in tank or barrel prior to bottling, in the bottle, and in the glass after pouring. The rate of change in the first instance is measured in weeks or months; in the second instance in months or years; and in the third instance in minutes or hours. Louis Pasteur wrote, 'Oxygen is the enemy of wine', underlining the fact that the beneficial processes of ageing are anaerobic, and thus not dependent on oxygen.

The opposite of oxidation is reduction, which gives rise to some very complex chemistry, and the measurement of the redox potential of a wine. In lay terms, this means the likelihood of the wine moving from its point of balance and becoming reduced or oxidised. Prior to being bottled, it may be appropriate to introduce small quantities of oxygen to eliminate sulphur-derived compounds in red wine, though seldom (if ever) with white wine. For further discussion see random oxidation.

Oxidation of fortified wine aged in barrels for decades is an entirely different process, and is desirable when properly controlled. For further discussion see rancio.

**oxidised**  see random oxidation.

abcdefghi
jklmnopq
rstuvwxyz

Padthaway, gazetted 29 November 1999, runs in a thin strip north by northwest of Naracoorte in South Australia, the second region to be established in the Limestone Coast Zone (the first was Coonawarra). Padthaway is almost eerily cigar-shaped, the southern portion dropping off at a slight angle like the ash on a cigar. Less than 5 kilometres at its widest, it is 60 kilometres long, the Riddoch Highway running more or less centrally through the region from start to finish. If you can pass through Coonawarra without noticing very much, you can pass through Padthaway without noticing anything at all, for there are no towns in any meaningful sense, just a few groups of houses at Keppoch (in the south) and Padthaway (in the north).

The region's potential was pinpointed by a Seppelt committee appointed in the early 1960s to select suitable vineyard sites for large-scale planting of early-ripening grape varieties. The requirements were ready availability of land (at a modest price), a cool climate and plentiful water for irrigation. The committee's research turned up a 1944 CSIRO report which had focused on a 3200-ha strip of country north of Naracoorte – about 300 kilometres southeast of Adelaide, near the South Australia–Victoria border – and which concluded: 'The soil type is variable in depth and there are usually some stony portions on each of the small patches in which it occurs. It is a terra rossa soil … the deeper sites of the terra rossa soils should make first-class garden soils.'

Only then did the Seppelt viticulturists visit the region. They duly identified a strip which ran for 16 kilometres along the Naracoorte to Padthaway road, and which fell within the narrow 550-millimetre rainfall zone – but had unlimited underground water. One of the nearby principal farming and grazing properties was Keppoch Park, and Seppelt gave the name Keppoch to the region, a choice initially adopted by Thomas Hardy when it purchased its first land in 1968. Lindemans arrived the same year, but selected land further north, at Padthaway, and used that name. Wynns, the other big company landholder, has never made a regional wine (all of its production is blended, some into sparkling wine) so did not enter the tug-of-war over the name.

After a decade or more of confusion, all agreed on Padthaway, which went some way to giving the region a sense of identity. However, it was not until 1998 that any of the major players installed more than field crushing stations. In that year Stonehaven, an $18 million, 10,000-tonne winery on land south of the Padthaway township, was built by Hardys, but in 2008 it was offered for sale by CWA, the parent company of Hardys. How quickly it will be sold is not clear; the other major companies are also divesting themselves of assets, so the most obvious candidate would be the family-owned Browns of Padthaway, which could then possibly establish a syndicate with the other local growers which have created brands but no winery of their own.

To add historical insult to injury, Seppelt initially decided to concentrate on red wines (relying on Drumborg in far southwest Victoria to produce the white wines), while Lindemans envisaged the region as a producer of medium-quality white and red wine to go into its lower to mid-priced bottle range (casks were then but a bright idea for the future, with numerous technical problems unsolved).

Padthaway falls within a buffer zone between Victoria and South Australia which imposes strict controls on water usage. No further irrigation rights are being granted, and this has restricted (and will in the future restrict) the spread of viticulture. The first major independent grower (the Brown family) supplies Orlando, which acquired 165 ha of land and established a vineyard of its own in the latter part of the 1980s. Local farmers and graziers, the Longbottom and Bryson families, followed suit in the mid-1990s, both with large vineyards, selling most of the grapes, but having part contract-made for their brands, Henry's Drive and Morambro Creek respectively. To this day the one great tourist drawcard is Padthaway Estate.

What is more, it is only since the mid-1990s that Padthaway has been given a chance to show what it can really do with wine quality. Prior to that, flood irrigation (leading, incidentally, to ever-increasing salinity), minimal pruning and management practices designed solely to maximise yield per hectare were the rule rather than the exception, and these continue to be practised in some lesser vineyard blocks.

As one would expect, given its proximity to Coonawarra, and given the absence of any significant mountains, the climate of Padthaway is similar to that of Coonawarra, but warmer. It was no doubt the climatic statistics which led to its founders' realising that it would ultimately succeed better as a red wine area.

The landscape avoids the dead-flat monotony of Coonawarra, but the slopes are gentle. The principal 'garden soil' identified by the CSIRO in 1944 is in fact the same soil which dominates the Barossa Valley, Clare Valley, Watervale and McLaren Vale: red-brown loamy sand soils. There are also patches of surface soil identical to the bright red soil of Coonawarra. The three most widely planted varieties are shiraz, chardonnay and cabernet sauvignon.

LAT 36˚37'S; ALT 50 m; HDD 1610; GSR 180 mm; MJT 20.4˚C; HARV Early March to early May; CHIEF VIT. HAZARD Spring frost

**Padthaway Estate** (est. 1980) is the name of both a producer of sparkling wine made in a 19th-century stone woolshed bordering on National Trust status and the luxury accommodation of the Padthaway Homestead provided in a handsome two-storey stone home on the property.

**palate** is the third leg of the colour, bouquet, palate trilogy used to assess the quality of wine, and encompasses the flavour (or taste), structure and texture (or mouthfeel) of the wine once it is taken into the mouth, and after it is swallowed or expectorated (the latter forming part of the finish or aftertaste).

**palomino** is the Spanish white grape used in the making of sherry in Spain; it has a similar function in Australia, especially for lighter, dry styles. Virtually all the plantings are on the Riverland in South Australia, but they are shrinking fast as the overall popularity of the category declines, falling to 50 ha in 2008.

**Paringa Estate** (est. 1985) is Mornington Peninsula's foremost winery if show success is any guide. It is true that relatively few of the peninsula's wineries enter shows outside Victoria, but even if they were to do so, it is hard to believe they would have the success achieved by Lindsay McCall, the former school teacher and now founder/owner/winemaker of Paringa Estate. With near-monotonous regularity, he produces outstanding pinot noir and shiraz at three levels and chardonnay at two levels, together with an exceptionally good pinot gris and a riesling which can rise above the limitations of a maritime climate. Total production is little more than 12,000 cases, which allows the meticulous attention to detail which lies behind these outstanding wines. Exports to the UK, Denmark, Korea, Singapore and Hong Kong.

**Parker Jnr, Robert** (1947–) is the most influential wine critic in the world, manipulating consumer choices from China to Switzerland and every place in between, including Australia. He is the publisher of the *Wine Advocate*, a monthly magazine with over 50,000 subscribers, and has written more than 14 books. He has received France's highest honour, appointed a Chevalier dans l'Ordre de la Légion d'Honneur in 1999, and Italy's highest honour in 2002 when he was made a Commendatore (Commander) in Italy's National Order of Merit. He did more than anyone else to make the 100-point scoring system the most widely used. His liking for full-bodied red wines is well known, and he is especially fond of limited-production, high-alcohol shiraz made in the Barossa Valley and McLaren Vale. It is not the least bit surprising that he polarises views and that he has been the subject of defamation proceedings and some highly critical books. That said, most fair-minded people would accept that he is a person of integrity, even if they strongly disagree with his views.

**Parker Coonawarra Estate** (est. 1985) was established by John Parker and family. It is situated at the southern end of Coonawarra, on classic terra rossa soil over limestone. Cabernet sauvignon is the most important variety, with 17.45 ha under vine, coupled with minor plantings of merlot and petit verdot. In 2004, some years after John Parker's death, the property was acquired by the Rathbone family, thus joining Yering Station, Mount Langi Ghiran and Xanadu. Winemaking continues under the direction of Peter Bissell at Balnaves of Coonawarra; the flagship red is Terra Rossa First Growth (predominantly cabernet sauvignon) then Terra Rossa Cabernet Sauvignon and Terra Rossa Merlot. Exports to all major markets.

**Patina** (est. 1999) was established by Gerald and Angie Naef, whose family home in Woodbridge in the Central Valley of California was surrounded by the vast vineyard and winery operations of Gallo and Robert Mondavi. It would be hard to imagine a more different environment than that provided by Orange. The Naefs left California in 1981, initially establishing an irrigation farm in the northwest of New South Wales, but 20 years later moved to Orange, and by 2006 Gerald Naef was a final-year mature-age student of wine science at Charles Sturt University. He set up a micro-winery at the Orange Cool Stores, and his first wine was a 2003 chardonnay, made from vines planted by him in 1999. At its first show entry, in 2006, it won the trophy for Best White Wine of Show at the Orange Wine Show.

**Paulett** (est. 1983) was established by Neil and Alison Paulett in the Polish Hill

River subregion of the Clare Valley; the old homestead and surrounding trees were razed almost immediately by bushfires – before there had been a chance to plant any vines. Son Matthew is responsible for the 25 ha of estate vineyards. Riesling and shiraz are the principal wines, with a flagship version of each (Antonina Riesling and Andreas Shiraz) introduced in the 2000s. Exports to the UK, NZ and Hong Kong.

**Paxton** (est. 1979) is the eponymous brand of David Paxton, one of Australia's best known viticulturists and consultants. He founded Paxton Vineyards in McLaren Vale with his family, and has since been involved in various capacities in the establishment and management of vineyards in several leading regions across the country. Former flying winemaker son Michael (with 14 years' experience in Spain, South America, France and Australia) is responsible for making the wines.

There are five vineyards in the 67.87 ha McLaren Vale family holdings: the Thomas Block, the Jones Block, Quandong Farm and Landcross Farm Settlement and Homestead. Here an underground barrel store has been completed and a cellar door opened in the original shearing shed. Paxton has become the first member of '1% for the Planet' (www. onepercentfortheplanet.org). By 2006 all of the five vineyards were being managed using full biodynamic principles. Both before and after becoming biodynamic, the shiraz and shiraz grenache releases have been of very high quality, and the chardonnay better than most. Exports to the UK, the US, Canada, Denmark and Sweden.

**pedro ximinez** is the second Spanish white grape variety traditionally used in the making of sweeter, heavier styles of sherry, but perhaps better known for the luscious, almost black, fortified wine grown in the region of Malaga. Colloquially called PX, its once extensive plantings in the Riverland and in the Riverina have significantly decreased with the ongoing reduction in the sales of fortified wines, to the point where its plantings are less than those of palomino.

**Peel**, gazetted 4 September 2001, is an oddly shaped region born of convenience rather than viticultural or even economic logic. Its western extremity is bordered by the Indian Ocean, and it seems nigh on certain that when the boundaries of the zones were created, and in particular that of the Greater Perth Zone, it was assumed that the western boundary would be more or less defined by the Darling Range. Ultimately, the district was shaped like an axe, the handle represented by the north–south coastal section, the blade a straight-sided oblong reaching far into the Central Western Australia Zone and (untidily) a small section falling in the South West Australia Zone. Nowhere else in Australia do the boundaries of regions and zones so overlap, and the inland portion (with only one winery, Wandering Brook Estate, near the one-horse town of Wandering) sits within the Central Western zone. Thus the discussion of Peel has to relate to the portion to the west of the Darling Range, in particular to the portion north of Mandurah, by far the largest settlement in the region.

The European settlement of Peel dates back to 1829 when visionary Thomas Peel brought three ships of migrants from England for the Peel Settlement Scheme. He was apparently totally unprepared for both the climate and the work required to put the country into shape for farming, and quickly retired to the beach to drink gin and tonic (or its equivalent) under the protection of umbrellas. The British Government was understandably unimpressed and three-quarters of his grant was revoked. Nonetheless, Thomas Peel was left with 101,215 ha; this founded what became known as the Peel Estate, from which the vineyard takes its name.

In 1846 the first mine (lead, silver and zinc) in Western Australia was opened; while short-lived, it presaged the large-scale mineral sands, gold and bauxite mining and processing operations that commenced in the 1970s. A vineyard was established near Pinjarra in 1857, and remained in production for over 40 years, winning a gold medal at the 1878 Melbourne Centenary Exhibition, before being uprooted by the owner's widow in 1898.

The coastal region has a Mediterranean climate with cool, wet winters and dry summers, the afternoon sea breezes reliably fresh; inland and at higher altitudes land breezes are stronger, rainfall higher and temperatures slightly lower. The eastern extension of the Peel region, incorporating the Darling Plateau around Boddington/ Wandering/Mount Saddleback, takes in very old granitic, gravel soils totally different from the limestone sands and fluvial sediments of the coastal area, which have significant groundwater reserves 3–15 metres below the surface.

The vineyards are planted to chenin blanc, chardonnay and verdelho (in that order, and in total making up 60 per cent); the remaining 40 per cent is planted to shiraz and cabernet sauvignon. The one winery of any significance is Peel Estate.

Peel Estate (est. 1974) was established by Will Nairn on the classic sandy soils of the coastal part of the region, which are best navigated after rain, not before. He has always been proud of his wood-matured whites, and in particular chenin blanc, but the signature wine of the estate is shiraz; every year Peel Estate holds a Great Shiraz Tasting for six-year-old Australian shiraz, and puts Peel Estate in a blind tasting (attended by 100 or so people) against Australia's best. It is never disgraced. Exports to the UK, the US, Malaysia, Japan and Singapore.

Pemberton, gazetted 14 February 2006, is senior to and more important than its neighbour Manjimup, the two regions having fought a fierce battle for a prolonged period over the choice of name (the Warren River was suggested to cover both) and whether they should be separate regions. Manjimup would undoubtedly protest over its relegation, but its southern neighbour holds the winery cards to establish the legitimacy of its claim.

The history of viticulture at Pemberton is recent, the first vines being planted by the Western Australian Department of Agriculture in 1977 on an experimental block midway between the towns of Pemberton and Manjimup. Given the prolonged standoff on regional boundaries and names, the choice of site was ironically felicitous.

The region has a slightly cooler and wetter climate than Manjimup, although site climates can always move outside the norm. It has a larger aggregation of wineries than Manjimup, and has achieved more in winemaking terms. It shares with Manjimup an at times disconcerting lushness and richness to its forests, fields and waterways, particularly in red soil country. With both the Warren and Donnelly rivers flowing through the region, the valleys and slopes, plus the lakes and streams, and the often vivid red soils, all make this a region of great beauty.

Pemberton also has fewer sunshine hours, more rainfall (except in January and February) and greater relative humidity than Manjimup – although temperature variability remains about the same. The high annual rainfall means that a number of vineyards do not use irrigation, but the very pronounced winter/ spring dominance can lead to stress late in the growing season if subsoil moisture diminishes.

Most (85 per cent) of the Pemberton region remains under native vegetation, with magnificent marri forests in the northern half, moving to karri in the south. There are two major soil types. The first is lateritic gravelly sand and gravelly loam overlying medium clay of moderate water-holding capacity. These moderately fertile soils are found on many of the higher slopes around Pemberton. The second soil is the more fertile karri loam, formed directly from the gneissic country rock, and – together with the abundant winter and spring rainfall – leading to vigorous growth.

The split between white and red grapes is roughly equal; the battle still rages over the suitability or otherwise of the region for pinot noir, but with the passing of the years it has become apparent that pinot noir is not the variety best suited to the climate and soil.

The leading wineries (from a total of 23) are Bellarmine, Fonty's Pool Vineyards, Picardy, Salitage and Smithbrook.

LAT 34°27'S; ALT 170 m; HDD 1394; GSR 361 mm; MJT 19.2°C; HARV Early March to mid-April; CHIEF VIT. HAZARD Silvereye birds

**Penfolds** (est. 1844) of the Barossa Valley is recognised throughout the wine world as a great producer of red wine, thanks in no small measure to Grange, the brand value of which is far in excess of any other Australian contender, and in the same class as the greatest names of Bordeaux, Burgundy and the Napa Valley. The fact that its ultimate ownership has changed on a number of occasions since its acquisition by the Tooth Brewery in 1976 has not dimmed its lustre, notwithstanding the notorious discounting of 1971 and 1972 Grange by Tooth's after it acquired the company.

The beginning of the Penfolds story is the arrival of an English physician, Dr Christopher Rawson Penfold, and his wife, Mary Penfold, in Adelaide in 1844. Before he left England Penfold had purchased a land grant at Magill, on the outskirts of Adelaide and at the foot of the Mount Lofty Ranges. It was here that he planted the vine cuttings he had brought with him from England, their ends dipped in sealing wax to prevent them from drying out on the journey. The cuttings took; Penfold's aim was to produce wine for his patients, particularly those suffering from anaemia. 'A little wine for thy health's sake' is an age-old prescription, and one which Penfold frequently handed out. Before long winemaking had ceased to be an incidental adjunct to medical practice, the great soil of Magill working the same magic then as it does over 150 years later. The Penfolds had built the low stone cottage which still stands at the Magill Vineyard and which they called The Grange, and Penfold lived there until his death, at the age of 59, in 1870.

Mary Penfold outlived her husband by 25 years; together with her daughter and son-in-law, she ran and expanded the business, acquiring the neighbouring vineyards and cellars of Joseph Gillard in 1881. She installed Gillard as manager of The Grange, a position he held until 1905. In that year Leslie Penfold Hyland (Mary's grandson, who, with his brother Frank, had changed his name by deed poll in honour of his grandfather) took over management of the South Australian operations. Frank Penfold Hyland had opened the Sydney office one year earlier; he had entered the business in 1892, spending three years in France studying winemaking.

By 1903 Penfolds was by far the largest of the numerous wineries surrounding the Adelaide metropolitan area. In that year it produced 450,000 litres of wine, and was poised on the threshold of a program of expansion which continued for 70 years. In 1904 Frank Penfold Hyland bought the historic Dalwood Vineyards near Branxton; in 1910 the McLaren Vale Cellars were purchased; and in 1912 the Minchinbury vineyards and cellars at Rooty Hill near Sydney were acquired, with Leo Buring installed as manager. In the middle of this, the most significant expansion of all occurred. In 1911 Penfolds commenced operations at Nuriootpa, building a new winery to process a guaranteed 1000 tonnes of grapes to be provided by local growers, at a minimum price of £4 per tonne. The cellars were expanded in 1913, and the largest pot-still in Australia was

installed to produce grape spirit. The same year Penfolds began construction of a large winery at Griffith, although the first vintage was not made until some years later. In 1920 yet another winery and distillery were built, this time in the Eden Valley, east of Nuriootpa. For some time the wine was made at Eden Valley and taken to Nuriootpa for maturing; as road transport improved the roles were reversed, with Eden Valley being converted into maturation cellars for sherry.

For two decades Penfolds consolidated its position, and in 1942 it commenced another round of acquisitions. In that year it acquired the vineyards of the old Hunter Valley Distillery; the HVD Vineyards, as they came to be known, were retained until 1982, when they were sold to Tyrrell's, marking the end of an 80-year Penfolds involvement in the Hunter Valley. In the following year, 1943, Penfolds acquired the historic Auldana Vineyards and cellars near Magill. These had been established 101 years earlier, when Patrick Auld purchased 93 ha of land which he subsequently planted. Auldana became famous as the home of St Henri, made by Jack Davoren.

The 1943 acquisition of Auldana was of great importance at the time, but the purchase of the 160-ha Kalimna Vineyard in 1945 was to prove even more important. Kalimna had always been a major vineyard and winery, producing over 400,000 litres of wine at the turn of the century, when it was run by William Salter. From that time on it was owned by D & J Fowler Limited, and virtually all the production was exported to the UK. World War II had interrupted that trade, and Fowler was a willing vendor. The principal varieties at Kalimna were cabernet sauvignon (including Block 42 Cabernet Sauvignon, planted in the 1880s, believed to be the oldest planting in the world) and shiraz, with mataro and cinsaut since progressively replaced by cabernet sauvignon and shiraz. The source block for the early vintages of Bin 28 Dry Red and Bin 389, Kalimna has always been of enormous importance in the Penfolds scheme of things.

In 1948 the already immense Nuriootpa cellars were extended further following the acquisition of an additional hectare of land adjacent to the main winery. The winery size increased to 3 ha, with a storage capacity of over 30 million litres.

The Penfold Hyland family could not have imagined in their wildest dreams that the sending of their senior Magill winemaker, the 35-year-old Max Schubert, to Jerez in Spain to study sherry making would be the direct cause of Penfolds' subsequent rise to world fame. He was the first person outside the Penfold family to be sent on such a trip, and was directed to go first to London to check on the condition of Penfolds' wine stocks held in warehouses at the London Docks; the wine was stored in paraffin-waxed Australian casuarina wood hogsheads. He spent three weeks in London, and Penfolds' London agent obtained an extension for his trip, which would allow him to follow the vintage around Europe, starting in Spain and Portugal, then working through France (Bordeaux, Paris, Champagne) and finishing in Germany. It was in Spain that he observed the extraordinary effect which could be achieved by fermenting grape juice in new small oak barrels: an intensity and complexity of aroma and flavour were achieved which he had never previously experienced. While he

did not believe it was of any use for Australian sherry making, he wondered what effect it might have on dry red or dry white wine. When he reached Bordeaux, the unusually large 1950 vintage was well in train, and he observed newly fermenting wine being taken direct to barrel at Chateau Rausan Segla and Pontet Canet, both chateaux being under the ownership of the Cruse family, headed by Christian Cruse.

In 1960 Penfolds made its ill-fated move from Wybong to the Upper Hunter. It marked one of the few obvious mistakes the company made in a swashbuckling corporate career of more than 100 years. By the time Wybong Estate was sold to Rosemount in 1977, hundreds of thousands of dollars had been written off. The move to South Australia's Riverland in 1973 was far more successful, although even here life has not always been easy. The property is at Morgan and has 520 ha of vineyards. It is a remote place, with unbelievably inhospitable saltbush plains on either side. It is only the Murray River which gives life to the vineyard, and even here there are mixed blessings, and drought-induced challenges.

The 1976 acquisition of Penfolds by Tooth & Company heralded a prolonged period of rationalisation. Minchinbury and Wybong Estate were sold in 1977; the following year the Griffith winery was closed down; in 1980 Auldana was disposed of; in 1982 the HVD Vineyard was sold to Tyrrell's; and in 1983, amid great public controversy, almost all of the estate vineyards around Magill were sold.

In the meantime, Tooth & Company had been acquired by the Adelaide Steamship Company, which in turn acquired the very large

Kaiser Stuhl Cooperative, thus privatising it. In 1985 Tulloch, Seaview and Wynns became part of the group; Tollana and Loxton followed in 1987; then, in 1990, a grand alliance which became known as Southcorp was put in place with the addition of Lindemans, Leo Buring, Rouge Homme, Mathew Lang, Seppelt, Queen Adelaide and Hungerford Hill. Throughout the corporate card shuffling and merry-go-round, Penfolds' winemaking team, successively under the direction of Max Schubert, then Don Ditter and then John Duval (who in turn headed up winemaking teams including the long-serving John Bird), built a veritable empire of red wines sitting below Grange, roughly divided into three groups. The first group is the Special Bin wines, each produced on a one-off basis, the most famous being 1962 Bin 60A Coonawarra Cabernet Sauvignon Kalimna Shiraz, which in fact towers over any Grange made in the 1960s (or thereafter). It was to be another 42 years before Bin 60A reappeared (in 2004), but other notable so-called Bin wines based on a similar philosophy appeared in 1966 (Bin 620 Coonawarra Cabernet Sauvignon Shiraz), 1967 (Bin 7 Coonawarra Cabernet Sauvignon Kalimna Shiraz), 1980 (Bin 80A) and 1990 (Bin 98) (both the same blend as Bin 60A and Bin 7), interspersed with 1982 (Bin 820 Coonawarra Cabernet Sauvignon Shiraz) and 1990 (Bin 920 Coonawarra Cabernet Sauvignon Shiraz). Block 42 Kalimna Cabernet Sauvignon was made in 1996 and 2004.

In commercial terms, the most important wines were the Bin wines, starting with Bin 28 Kalimna Shiraz in 1959, then Bin 389 Cabernet Shiraz in 1960, Bin 128 Coonawarra Shiraz in 1962, Bin 707 Cabernet Sauvignon in 1964, and, much later, Bin 407 Cabernet

Sauvignon in 1990 and Bin 138 Grenache Shiraz Mourvedre in 1992. All of these wines have been made, and continue to be made, in significant quantities, far in excess of the 500 or so cases of the Special Bin wines in bygone years. Even here, however, the inventory is not complete. In 1953 Schubert made an experimental Cabernet Sauvignon Grange which was and is a glorious wine, but which was discontinued because of the lack of supply of cabernet; it came solely from Block 42 in the Kalimna Vineyard from vines planted in the 1880s. The first St Henri was made in 1953 as an experimental wine; the first commercial vintage followed in 1957. Later came Magill Estate Shiraz, in 1983, and RWT Barossa Shiraz, in 1997.

In the early 1990s, then CEO Ross Wilson threw down the challenge to the winemaking team to find and make a white wine to sit alongside Grange. This ultimately gave birth to Bin 144 Yattarna Chardonnay, first made in 1995, and to a range of supporting chardonnays, the white portfolio subsequently extended to rieslings. The big-volume wines have been Rawson's Retreat at the base level, then Koonunga Hill and then the Thomas Hyland range. The one thing which separates Penfolds from every other red wine maker in the world is the depth and breadth of the portfolio, with wines at every price point from (in 2008 terms) $15 to $500 a bottle.

The final twist of the knife came in 2001 with the ill-fated merger with Rosemount Estate. The transaction was dependent on management control being ceded to Rosemount, with CEO Keith Lambert taking over the reins of Southcorp. The economic disaster which followed made headlines in the press, ultimately leading to his departure, and to the takeover of Southcorp by Foster's in 2005.

**Peninsulas Zone** has but one relatively small region, the Southern Eyre Peninsula.

**Penley Estate** (est. 1988) is owned by winemaker Kym Tolley, who describes himself as a fifth-generation winemaker, the family tree involving both the Penfolds and the Tolleys. He worked for 17 years in the industry before establishing Penley Estate in Coonawarra, and has made every post a winner since, producing a succession of rich, complex, full-bodied red wines and stylish chardonnays. The production of 40,000 cases a year comes from 111 precious hectares of estate plantings, with substantial quantities of grapes surplus to Penley's requirements being sold each year. Exports to all major markets.

**Pepper Tree Wines** (est. 1993) in the Lower Hunter Valley is a substantial venture by any standards. It has 35 ha of vines at its Tallavera Grove vineyards at Mount View, 12 ha in Coonawarra, 35 ha in Orange and 100 ha in Wrattonbully. Its appointment in 2007 of Jim Chatto as winemaker has secured the services of one of the best young winemakers in Australia. Exports to the US, Canada, Switzerland, Indonesia, Singapore, China and NZ.

**Perricoota**, gazetted 25 March 1999, one of only two regions in the Big Rivers Zone (the other being the Riverina), gets its name from Perricoota Station, established in the 1850s and purchased in 1911 by the Watson brothers, whose descendants still own and farm the property. At first blush, one might assume that the region was created to fill in the gap between the Murray River and the Riverina. In fact it is but a pinhead in size compared with the Riverina, and there is still a large gap between the two regions, doubtless without available water. So it is that the Murray River constitutes the southern boundary of Perricoota, thus dividing the twin towns of Moama (on the New South Wales side) and Echuca (on the Victorian side).

While viticulture has long been a significant part of the agricultural scene on the southern side of the Murray River, it was not until 1995 that vineyards were planted on the northern side, and two years later the first commercial vintage was harvested in the Perricoota region. (Sporadic attempts had been made in the middle of the 19th century, but were unsuccessful.)

In 1999 the 500-tonne production level required for registration as a region under the Geographic Indications legislation was achieved. The same uncertainties exist for the vineyards in the region as for others along the Murray River. The three wineries in the region are Morrisons Riverview, St Anne's Vineyards and Stevens Brook Estate. Chardonnay, shiraz and cabernet sauvignon are their principal wines.

LAT 36°5'S; ALT 100 m; HDD 2100; GSR 224 mm; MJT 22.8°C; HARV Early February to mid-March; CHIEF VIT. HAZARD Spring frost

**Perth Hills**, gazetted 25 March 1999, is a thoroughly logical region, sitting as it does on the western escarpment of the Darling Range in the Greater Perth Zone. It is a pretty place, with constantly changing vistas. The exotic native vegetation grows in rich profusion:

Western Australia was given far more than its fair share by nature, and this is shown to full advantage in the Perth Hills, with patches of introduced exotics from Europe and elsewhere adding an unexpected contrast near streams and in home gardens. Moreover, it is only 22 kilometres from Perth, making it easily accessible to daytrippers.

Viticulture has been practised intermittently in the Perth Hills for over a century, but generally on a tiny scale. The first known winery was built in the 1880s, and continued production until it was burnt down in 1945. Thus while Despeissis was able to report in 1902 that grapes grown in the Mundaringa-Chidlow subregion ripened two to three weeks later than in the Swan Valley, the longest established of the present-day wineries (Hainault) dates back to only 1980, and until the latter part of the 1990s none of the wineries crushed more than 50 tonnes a year. That has changed with the arrival of first Millbrook and even more emphatically with the opening of Western Range.

The tempering influences which reduce the heat summation and delay ripening for 10–21 days (compared with the Swan Valley) are: first, the altitude; second, the free air drainage; and third, exposure to afternoon sea breezes. Warm evenings, however, mean continuous ripening, and frosts pose no threat at any time of year. Overall, Dr John Gladstones likens its climate to that of the Douro Valley in Portugal.

Rivulets and (often dry) creek beds, ridges, hills and valleys criss-cross the region in every direction, offering an almost unlimited choice of aspect and slope, but those sites cut off from the sea breeze influence tend to be warmer rather than cooler. The valley slopes

have ironstone and gravel sandy loams and gravelly loams which overlie clay, similar in type to many parts of Western Australia, and once covered with marri. They are well suited to viticulture, being of moderate fertility, producing moderate yields.

The five most important varieties, in descending order, are shiraz, chardonnay, cabernet sauvignon, merlot and pinot noir. The two wineries to consistently produce good quality wines are Millbrook and Western Range, with Hartley Estate not far behind.

LAT 31°59'S; ALT 150–400 m; HDD 1770; GSR 220–250 mm; MJT 23.3°C; HARV Late February to mid-March; CHIEF VIT. HAZARD Birds

**Petaluma Wines** (est. 1976) was established by Brian Croser, although it was several years before he began the planting of its vineyards in the Piccadilly Valley of the Adelaide Hills, and built the winery. It grew on the foundation of three wines. The first was an estate-grown red from Coonawarra, simply labelled thus, the first vintage in 1979 being a cabernet sauvignon shiraz blend, but subsequently made without the assistance of shiraz (which, in any event, came from the Clare Valley). Next in importance was the Clare Valley riesling from the estate-owned Hanlin Hill Vineyard. The third leg, chardonnay, went through many regional permutations, starting as 100 per cent Cowra, then a blend with Clare Valley chardonnay, progressively seeing the inclusion of Piccadilly Valley material until finally becoming a 100 per cent Piccadilly wine, part estate-grown, part from purchased fruit. It was the trailblazer for winemaking in the central, and highest altitude, portion of the Adelaide Hills. In the early 1990s Petaluma became a public company listed on the stock exchange, and in 1994 it acquired Mitchelton, then progressively added first Knappstein and later Stonier and Smithbrook, thus covering the Mornington Peninsula, Clare Valley, Goulburn Valley, Coonawarra and Pemberton. It was a lure which proved irresistible to Lion Nathan, which mounted a takeover offer in 2001; this succeeded after a prolonged defence. Brian Croser remained as CEO for some years, then continued as a consultant before finally severing his ties with Petaluma. However, the Tiers Vineyard which separated his house from the winery remained in Croser family ownership, and in 2008 the winery (though not the brand) was repurchased as part of the Tapanappa structure. Lion Nathan is building a replacement winery, which would appear to signify that it has no intention of selling the Petaluma brand back to the Croser interests. Exports to all major markets.

**Peter Lehmann Wines** (est. 1979) had a turbulent history from the crucible of its formation through to its acquisition by the California-based Hess Group in 2003. Its formation is intertwined with the life and career of Peter Lehmann, who can aptly be described as the personification of the Barossa Valley. He has devoted his life to its people and its wines, and he has been a staunch and often outspoken defender of both. His credentials for this role were impeccable. He was born at Angaston in 1930, the son of a Lutheran pastor, and is a fifth-generation descendant of German forebears who had moved to the Barossa Valley almost a century earlier. He worked first at Yalumba, where he spent 13 years, then moved to Saltram in 1960; he remained there until 1979.

In that year the then largest wine agglomerate in the world, Seagram, acquired Saltram from Dalgety. It was a time of particular problems in the Barossa Valley, with a large grape surplus and the probability of that surplus increasing. Lehmann keenly felt the plight of the numerous Barossa growers with whom he had dealt over the years, and was only too aware that if he stayed at Saltram he would have little or no power to help them. He also believed that the grapes produced by the growers were of worthwhile quality, and if turned into wine by a skilled winemaker using modern equipment would produce a premium product with a ready market. So Masterson Barossa Vignerons Proprietary Limited was formed, inspired by Damon Runyon's great character Sky Masterson. It was indeed something of a gamble, but Lehmann took care to reduce the odds against the venture succeeding by enrolling as shareholders Cerebos (Australia) Limited and the Anders family company, Andvin Proprietary Limited. While each of the partners had considerable resources, they were an odd couple, and Peter Lehmann operated in an often difficult financial environment, as investors came and went, until its successful listing on the stock exchange in 1994.

A fiercely contested takeover in 2003 ultimately resulted in ownership being vested in the Hess Group, an outcome for which Peter Lehmann and wife Margaret had equally fiercely fought. Given the success of the company (as at 2007 it was the eighth-largest exporter of branded wine by value, and the 11th-largest producer by volume of branded wine, with a significantly lower ranking in terms of total crush, all pointing to the value of the brand), the result was well worth the effort put into the fight.

This brand value has come about through the development of a portfolio that begins with high-volume varietal wines chiefly sourced from the Barossa Zone (Barossa Valley and Eden Valley), selling at prices which afford appropriate margins (the most spectacular example being its 100,000-case production of semillon, greater than McWilliam's or any other semillon producer in Australia) and finishes, at the other end, with high-quality, small-volume wines which are held back for up to five years before release. Foremost among these are the Reserve Riesling, Reserve Semillon and Stonewell Shiraz, all with exceptional wine show records. Exports to all major markets.

**petite sirah**  is, or should be, the same red grape variety as durif; it is a name used in California for a number of varieties other than durif, but the majority are one and the same as durif.

**petit meslier**  was a once significant white variety in the Aube region of Champagne which has all but disappeared owing to its sensitivity to downy mildew and botrytis; poor set was an additional nail in its coffin. The only grower in Australia is James Irvine, who incorporates it in the Irvine sparkling wine.

**petit verdot**  was a more prevalent red grape variety in Bordeaux before phylloxera than after, but slid even further in the 1960s and 1970s as earlier ripening merlot and cabernet franc replaced it. It is, indeed, the latest ripening of all the red Bordeaux varieties, and,

like cabernet sauvignon, is deeply coloured – but it is even more tannic than cabernet sauvignon. With better clonal selection and better management of vineyard diseases, petit verdot has made a small comeback; Chateau Latour, for example, has been increasing the amount of petit verdot planted in its vineyards. Late ripening is not a problem for California and, while plantings there are not significant in area terms (not much more than 100 ha), the grape is spread thinly across Bordeaux (or Meritage) blends, consumers being fascinated by the idea of 2 or 3 per cent in a blend.

In Australia the variety has come from nowhere in a relatively short time. Mount Mary in the Yarra Valley has been growing it since its inception in 1971, as a small part of a Bordeaux-based blend (Mount Mary calls its wine Cabernets Quintet), but an increasing number of winemakers are releasing single variety petit verdots. Pirramimma has had outstanding success, and makes by far the best version; the Riverland and Murray Darling exponents are perhaps simply content with its ability to produce both colour and tannin irrespective of the yield. It is here that plantings have soared at breakneck speed since 1999, when the variety first merited separate mention in the official statistics. By 2008 plantings had risen to 1354 ha. There are signs that the increase in plantings may have peaked.

**Pewsey Vale**  is a single-vineyard Eden Valley brand with a history dating back to 1847, when the first vines were planted by Joseph Gilbert. The vineyard and winery were visited by Ebenezer Ward in 1862, and a very detailed account appears in his collected articles in *The Vineyards and Orchards of South Australia*, first published in the *Adelaide Advertiser*. The initial plantings were (using the spelling of the time) verdeilho, gouais, riesling, shiraz and carbonet. Gilbert soon realised that verdelho, riesling, shiraz and cabernet sauvignon gave the best results, and so increased their plantings every year. He recounts a tasting in Adelaide when the 1854 riesling was compared with 'some choice Hock, considered to be the best wine of its class ever imported to this colony. The decision was in favour of the colonial product.' In 1862 Gilbert was still busily extending the already large cellars, likewise the vineyard. But like cool-climate vineyards across the length and breadth of Australia, Pewsey Vale faded away at the end of the 19th century. When Yalumba moved back in to the property in 1961, in partnership with Geoffrey Angus Parsons, the proprietor of Pewsey Vale Station, only the history books recorded its prior use as a vineyard. Yalumba correctly foresaw that riesling would be the best suited variety, and progressively lifted the plantings to 40 ha; various other varieties, including cabernet sauvignon and semillon, were trialled, but in the final outcome the riesling is now accompanied by 2 ha each of gewurztraminer and pinot gris. Yalumba also made history in 1977 when it bottled the riesling of that year under screwcap. Trials before 1977, and history since the late 1990s, fully justified the choice of the closure from a quality (and longevity) viewpoint. However, retailers and consumers rejected the screwcap because it connoted cheapness, and after a few years (including a bizarre time when corks were inserted underneath the screwcap) the experiment was abandoned. Yalumba did not waver in its faith, though, and in the second half of the 1990s quietly put stocks of the Pewsey Vale Contours Riesling (under screwcap) into a maturation reserve scheme, releasing each vintage when five years old, and sweeping all before it in the show circuit. In 2007, after much experimentation, it also released a 9.5% alc/vol wine modelled on the Mosel (Germany) kabinett. Exports to all major markets.

**pH** is technically described as the negative logarithm of hydrogen ion activity or concentration in wine (or any other liquid). It is the single most important marker for soils, grapes and wine, in the latter case having much to do with the potential longevity. A measurement of 7 is effectively neutral, and is typically that of drinking water. Grapes, must and wine are acidic, with pH values generally between 3 and 4, sometimes less than 3 for sparkling wines, and over 4 for fortified wines. Because the scale is logarithmic, wine with a pH value of 3 has 10 times as much hydrogen ion activity as one with a pH of 4. Limestone soils have a high pH, of up to 9, whereas the degraded sandstone soils found in various parts of eastern Australia can be less than 5, requiring adjustment before planting.

Traditionally, quality wines' pH values ranged between 3.2 and 3.6 (at the bottom end for white wines, towards the top end for red wines); wines in this range have refreshing acidity and brighter and clearer colour, and are more resistant to bacteria (with or without the support of sulphur dioxide). The lower the pH value, the more effective a given quantity of sulphur dioxide will be. One of the trends observed between 1985 and 2005 in many parts of the world was the rise in alcohol levels, with a concomitant rise in pH. The prime method of reducing pH is by adding acid (tartaric and citric are the principal additives), with newer techniques involving hydrogen ion exchange or, increasingly commonly, reverse osmosis. The addition of sulphuric acid is highly effective, but it is an illegal additive in all the major wine-producing countries.

**phenolics** are highly reactive chemical compounds found in substantial quantities in the stems, seeds and skins of grapes; they also occur in juice and pulp. They include the anthocyanins of red grapes, the natural vegetable tannins of grapes, and many flavour compounds. The most important group are flavonoids, which include anthocyanins, catechins and flavonols which contribute to the colour, astringency, bitterness and texture of wine; 90 per cent of the phenolic content in red wine is made up of flavonoids. The proportion in white wines is lower because of less extraction from skins, stems and seeds, but the tannin polymers present in white wines, formed without anthocyanins, taste bitter or astringent. In moderation these are positive attributes, but when present in excess they give rise to the tasting term 'phenolic', normally restricted to white wines which lack precision and purity. One of the many hundreds of specific phenols to have caught attention since 1995 is resveratrol, the antioxidant found in red wine which is believed to be one of the drivers of the cardiovascular protection afforded by wine.

**PHI** (est. 2005) is a joint venture between two very influential wine families: De Bortoli and Shelmerdine. The key executives are Stephen Shelmerdine and Steve Webber (and their respective wives). It has a sole viticultural base: the Lusatia Park vineyard (in the Yarra Valley) of the Shelmerdine family. Unusually, however, PHI owns only specific rows of vines, not even blocks, although the rows are continuous. They are pruned and managed quite differently from those on the rest of the block, with the deliberate aim of strictly controlled yields. While the joint venture was only entered into in 2005, De Bortoli had been buying grapes from the vineyard since 2002, and so has had the opportunity to test the limits of the grapes. The outcome has been wines of the highest quality, and a joint venture that will last for many years. The name, incidentally, is derived from the 21st letter of the ancient Greek alphabet, which symbolises perfect balance and harmony. It has put courageous pricing – for a new kid on the block – on its wines, but this reflects the confidence the families have in their wines. The wines produced are sauvignon blanc, chardonnay and pinot noir. Exports to the UK.

**Philip Shaw** (est. 1989) was established by Philip Shaw, former chief winemaker of Rosemount Estate and then Southcorp wines, who first became interested in the Orange region in 1985. In 1988 he purchased the Koomooloo Vineyard, and began the planting of 43 ha of sauvignon blanc, chardonnay, shiraz, merlot, cabernet franc and cabernet sauvignon. Exports to the UK, the US and other major markets.

**Phillip Island Vineyard** (est. 1993), in Gippsland, was established by the Lance family as an extension of their Yarra Valley–based Diamond Valley Vineyards, the rationale being a super cellar door for both the Phillip Island wines and the Diamond Valley wines, capturing the very large tourist trade the island enjoys, largely thanks to its penguins. Development was slow, and it eventually proved necessary to permanently net the 2-ha vineyard to protect it from wind and birds. To the extent that the strategy was flawed, it was simply because the quality of the wines (and their cost of production) was beyond the needs of the tourist market. That said, the quality of the chardonnay, pinot noir and sauvignon blanc has never been in doubt. Exports to Indonesia.

**phylloxera,** like powdery mildew and downy mildew, was a deadly gift to Europe from the US. While sprays were ultimately developed to control the mildews, effective and acceptable chemical treatment to control phylloxera has never been developed, and it remains the most devastating of all vine diseases. It was brought to Europe on American vines which are resistant to it. These in fact provided the long-term answer: grafting vinifera scions onto American rootstocks. It is a microscopic, yellow, root-feeding aphid which has an extraordinarily complex life cycle which may or may not involve a winged form; may or may not involve sexual reproduction; may or may not involve living above the earth; but which multiplies at a devastating rate, with four to seven generations in any year. The end result is the progressive death of the vine over a period of two or three years, during which time it becomes steadily less fruitful. George Ordish's *The Great Wine Blight* (2nd edition, Pan Macmillan, London, 1987) and Christy Campbell's *Phylloxera – How Wine Was Saved for the World* (HarperCollins, London,

2004) are two excellent references for wine consumers, each incorporating the fascinating history of its spread through France and around the world.

Phylloxera made its way to Australia in 1877, first appearing at Geelong, and leading to the compulsory destruction of all but a handful of vineyards in that region through an Act of the Victorian Parliament. There is considerable evidence to suggest that northeast Victoria, in particular, played a role in what was a purely political decision, because grafting onto American rootstocks had been accepted as one of the two effective solutions (the other was the injection of highly toxic carbon disulphide into the soil, which caused almost as much damage to those who applied it as to the phylloxera). Whether or not the decision did reflect a desire by northeast Victoria to rid itself of what was then a major competing wine region, phylloxera wound its way north, sparing the Yarra Valley, the Grampians and the Pyrenees, but devastating Bendigo and the Goulburn Valley. It was spread by humans, either on vines, on agricultural equipment or simply in earth adhering to a vehicle or even boots.

In the latter part of the 20th century phylloxera appeared first in the Strathbogie Ranges, and thereafter in the King Valley, despite strict protocols which had been developed for cleaning agricultural equipment moving from one region to another, and even stricter controls on planting material. In 2006 one vineyard in the Yarra Valley was found to have phylloxera. The vines were promptly destroyed, and a Phylloxera Infected Zone (PIZ) with a 5-kilometre radius from the site was declared. In 2008 a nearby vineyard was found to be infected; it is a certainty that it will slowly spread throughout the valley. While the cost of replanting vineyards will be great, it will take place over many years, if not decades.

**Picardy** (est. 1993) is owned by Dr Bill Pannell, wife Sandra and son Daniel; Bill and Sandra founded Moss Wood winery in the Margaret River in 1969. Picardy initially reflected Bill Pannell's view that the Pemberton area was one of the best regions in Australia for pinot noir and chardonnay, but it is now clear that Pemberton has as much Rhône and Bordeaux as Burgundy in its veins. Exports to the UK, the US and other major markets.

**Pierro** dates back to 1979, when Dr Michael Peterkin, with degrees in medicine and oenology, began the establishment of this Margaret River winery. The 10,000-case production all comes from estate-grown grapes, and the three wines, semillon sauvignon blanc, chardonnay and cabernet sauvignon merlot (the last in both varietal and reserve forms), are among the best in the Margaret River. Exports to the UK, the US, Japan and Indonesia.

**pigeage**, strictly speaking, is the treading of red must by foot. However, it now extends to manual plunging using a plate affixed to the plunger, and to hydraulic versions which do away with the countless hours of physical exertion otherwise required. See also punch-down.

**Pikes** (est. 1984) is the Clare Valley venture of viticulturist Andrew Pike, for many years the senior viticulturist with Southcorp, and

winemaker brother Neil. They have patiently built the business since its establishment, and now have 26 ha of riesling and 13.5 ha of shiraz out of a total of over 65 ha. The most recent addition has been 1.24 ha of albarino. The 35,000-case production is spread across a wide mix of varietals and blends – riesling, shiraz and cabernet sauvignon merlot on the conventional front and an exceptional Luccio Sangiovese Merlot Cabernet Sauvignon blend – the prices as pleasing as the palate. Exports to the UK, the US and other major markets.

**pinot gris** is a white mutation of pinot noir, and every bit as unstable as its parent. The story of its spread across the old Austro-Hungarian Empire would have pleased Agatha Christie, as would the absolute plethora of names under which it travels. Moreover, that plethora is mirrored in the finished wine style. Tokay d'Alsace in a warm vintage is typically the most powerful of all the Alsace wines, which is saying something. Hugely floral, with an almost viscous palate of overripe fruit flavours, and high alcohol, it demands food as trenchantly as any Italian red. Pinot grigio from Italy's north and northeast, made in traditional Italian fashion, and which has been responsible for the flood of pinot grigio into the US, is water white, devoid of aroma and has barely any taste. It is the perfect example of what a New Zealand winemaker had in mind when he said, 'Making pinot gris is like painting a picture with white paint.'

Yet another manifestation is the Hungarian szurkebarat, which takes up where the *vendange tardive* of Alsace leaves off. In a country which produces the most exotic late-harvest wine in the world (Hungary's tokaji, which has absolutely nothing to do with tokay, despite its name), szurkebarat stands tall as a wine with enormous extract.

Thanks to its naturally low acidity, the variety has to be grown in a cool climate if it is to provide convincing wine. Thus its meteoric rise in New Zealand is not surprising: prior to 1997 the production was so insignificant it was not separately recorded, but by 2008 it had reached 26,156 tonnes. Its plantings in Australia have grown many times more rapidly than those of any other recent arrivals. Its plantings (including those still coming into bearing for each of the years in question) were 329 ha in 2004, 708 in 2005, 1352 in 2006 and 2835 in 2008. Production has grown commensurately, and it has become a refuge of choice in cafés and brasseries for the members of the ABC (Anything But Chardonnay) Club. The fact that if labelled 'pinot grigio' (simply the Italian version of the name, rather than French) sales are even more brisk underlines the fact that presentation is every bit as important as substance. Only thus can its indiscriminate plantings across warm, irrigated regions as well as cool regions be explained. Viewed across the regions, it does not have any single, recurrent varietal flavour or aroma. Apple, pear, honeysuckle, mineral and citrus are the most commonly used descriptors and can be found to a lesser or greater degree in most of the wines, but reality would suggest 'lesser' is the operative word.

**pinot meunier** is best known as the third grape in Champagne, developing more quickly than chardonnay and pinot noir, and thus helping non-vintage blends. As in France, the principal use of this red grape variety in Australia is in sparkling wines, although even here it is a relatively new arrival on the scene. The exception (as with many lesser known varieties) is Best's at Great Western, which has pinot meunier that is well over 100 years old, and which it uses to make a red table wine, sometimes blended with pinot noir, and sometimes released as a straight varietal. Those who use it to make a table wine (other than Best's) are not always certain what they should do with it: use it to make a rosé, blend it with pinot noir or release it as a straight varietal? Best's, because of its magnificent storehouse of old vines, certainly leads the field. Its production is too small to merit separate recording in the Australian Bureau of Statistics' records.

**pinot noir**, a red grape variety, makes its appearance in European historical records earlier than any other variety; whether this is because of, or in spite of, its tendency to mutate into other closely related varieties (pinot gris, pinot meunier and pinot blanc) is not clear. This tendency to mutate is also reflected in the plethora of clones (there are 46 recognised in France alone), the choice of which has a profound influence on the quality and style of the wine. Unsurprisingly, early names varied significantly, and in modern times it travels under all sorts of synonyms in the many countries in which it grows. It seems to have been cultivated in Europe for at least 2000 years, and to have been called morrillon pinot in the 4th century BC.

Its battle for supremacy with gamay in Burgundy dates back well before the adoption of the name 'pinot noir' in the 14th century. In 1395 Phillip the Bold issued a decree ordering the uprooting of 'the bastard Gamay', a decree honoured more in the breach than the observance in the southern parts of Burgundy. Its arrival in the Champagne region – along with chardonnay and pinot meunier – predated the development of champagne (the wine) as we know it today, following the doubtless apocryphal cry of Dom Perignon: 'Come quickly, Brothers, there are stars in the wine.'

One is left to speculate whether the earliest wines made in the Champagne region benefited from the Medieval Warm Period, and whether chardonnay and pinot noir may have ripened sufficiently to make wholly satisfying table wine. Certainly, it is extremely sensitive to all aspects of climate, requiring a narrow band of total heat during the growing season, neither too hot nor too cool. Its extreme sensitivity to place is paralleled by the importance of clonal selection, a process given special attention in the last 30 years of the 20th century and extending into the 21st century.

Clones 113, 114 and 115, identified by Professor Raymond Bernard at the University of Dijon, were soon replaced in favour of the lower yielding, smaller berried clones 677 and 777 (114 had proved the best of the initial three in most, but not all, regions). While conventional wisdom pointed to a mix of these 'new' clones, many of the most famous estates preferred the 'clonal massif' field selection of their own vines, a largely arbitrary selection.

The inherent allure of great pinot noir and the reputation (and fortune) to be gained by successfully growing and making it led both the Old World outside France and the New World to plant it. The early efforts in California and Australia were equally disastrous: areas far too warm were selected,

with the result that in the 1970s, Californian pinot noir grapes sold for less per tonne than Thompson's Seedless.

Pinot noir came to Australia courtesy of James Busby's collection from Clos Vougeot in 1831, and was grown in the Hunter Valley with (by the standards of the time) some success; Maurice O'Shea used a percentage of pinot noir (normally small) in many of his best wines. These to one side, it became progressively apparent that there are a limited number of regions in which pinot noir can be cajoled into making fine table wine. Its use in sparkling wine is an entirely different question until one reaches the zenith of this style. Statistics are not available to precisely quantify the amount, but more than half of all pinot noir grown in Australia is used for sparkling wine. Tasmania is rapidly asserting itself as the best region for pinot noir grapes, held back only by the small size of all but two of the makers. The southern Victorian regions to have unequivocally proved their worth are Geelong, Gippsland, Henty, Macedon Ranges, Mornington Peninsula and the Yarra Valley. The ability of the Adelaide Hills to grow quality pinot noir is site specific, as it is in the Porongurup and Albany subregions of Great Southern in Western Australia. There is no question that consumption of pinot noir has increased over the first decade of the 21st century, but plantings have remained virtually unchanged, at around 4500 ha. The explanation lies at least partly in imports from New Zealand and Burgundy.

Pipers Brook Vineyard (est. 1974) is the best known of all Tasmania's wineries. It was founded by Andrew Pirie, but he has long since severed his ties with it. It is now owned by Kreglinger SA, a Belgium-based sheepskin business, which also owns the Norfolk Rise Vineyard and winery at Mount Benson in South Australia. Pipers Brook has over 185 ha of vineyards, supporting both the Pipers Brook and Ninth Island labels, the latter providing Pipers Brook with much of its 90,000-case annual sales. Exemplary packaging and a strong export network keeps Pipers Brook on the front foot.

**Pirie Estate** (est. 2004) is the eponymous brand of Andrew Pirie. He manages 30-ha of vineyards in the Tamar Valley area of Tasmania (riesling, sauvignon blanc, gewurztraminer, chardonnay, pinot gris and pinot noir), but only part of the production is vinified for sale under the various Pirie labels. Moreover, his main responsibility is that of his role as CEO of Tamar Ridge, where he is in overall charge of winemaking. Wines are released under the Pirie (varietal and Reserve) and South labels.

**Pirramimma** (est. 1892) remains very much in the Johnston family control. It has 192 ha of vineyards in McLaren Vale, and was one of the early movers with petit verdot. It thereafter put its toe into the water with tannat, but these two varieties apart, the varietal choice is as disciplined as are the family members. Exports to all major markets.

**Plantagenet** (est. 1974) was the first winery, and operated the first commercial vineyard, in the Great Southern region. (The Forest Hill Vineyard had been planted previously, but was a Department of Agriculture trial.) Tony Smith headed the syndicate which set

Plantagenet on its path from the beginning; until the 1990s it played a key role as a contract winemaker for others in the region, as well as developing its own wines, spearheaded by riesling, shiraz and cabernet sauvignon, each of which took it in turns to outshine the others. Its 132 ha of vineyards are spread across Wyjup, Bouverie, Rocky Horror I, Rocky Horror II and Rosetta. The 90,000-case production is exported to all major markets.

**planting density** of vines has varied enormously over the millennia in Europe; the difference in Australia is of lesser magnitude, but still substantial. It has often been observed that the configuration of vines has been determined by cultivation methods. Before the arrival of phylloxera in Europe, planting density was as high as 40,000 vines per hectare; the practice of layering was used without regard to vine rows simply because in many vineyards there were no rows, and weeding was done by hand. From this chaotic beginning came the idea of arranging the vines in rows, the spacing between the rows set at the width of a small horse-drawn plough. In Europe a typical spacing was 10,000 vines per hectare, with vines planted 1 metre apart along the rows, and a row width of 1 metre. The first tractors that appeared were similar to the insect-like, over-the-row tractors of today, with the wheels straddling the vines and thus running between adjacent rows.

Tractors in Australia, by contrast, were originally multipurpose vehicles, needing a row width of up to 3.7 metres, complemented by a spacing of 2.5 metres between the vines along the row, resulting in a planting density of 1080 vines per hectare. With the advent of cool-climate vineyards in particular, coupled with purpose-designed four-wheel-drive tractors, much narrower row spacing became possible, typically 2–2.2 metres between the rows, and 1.5–2 metres between vines, with a resulting density of over 2000 vines per hectare. Higher density plantings do exist, a few with the 1 metre by 1 metre classic configuration, with the aim (though not always the consequence) of naturally reducing the crop on each vine through inter-vine competition.

**Plunkett Fowles** (est. 1968) is the new face for two families committed to building a prominent international wine business in the Strathbogie Ranges. The co-managers, Sam Plunkett and Matt Fowles, are in their late 30s and late 20s, with both winemaking and business skills. They say they are committed to a strategy of selling wine that exceeds the expectations for any given price point, and see shiraz as one of the key varietals for this strategy; alternative varieties are also part of the strategy. Exports to the UK, the US and other major markets.

**Polleters** (est. 1994) was established by Pauline and Peter Bicknell, who purchased the 60-ha property in the Pyrenees on which their vineyard now stands in 1993, at which time it was part of a larger grazing property. The first vines were planted in 1994, and there are now 6 ha in total, planted to shiraz, cabernet sauvignon, cabernet franc and merlot. In the first few years the grapes were sold, but since 2001 part of the production has been used to make their own impressively rich and powerful wines. The grapes are hand-picked, fermented

in open vats with hand-plunging, and matured for 18 months in American oak.

**polymerisation** is a process which, in base terms, involves smaller molecules combining to form larger molecules, and is common in all living material. As wine ages, smaller phenolic molecules (tannins) combine to form larger tannin polymers and pigmented tannins, which eventually grow so large that they fall from the solution as sediment. This process of polymerisation also leads to substantial changes in mouthfeel, the tannins becoming progressively rounder and softer, ultimately leaving a minimal textural imprint.

**Pondalowie Vineyards** (est. 1997), in Bendigo, is the venture of Dominic and Krystina Morris, who have established 5.5 ha of shiraz, 2 ha each of tempranillo and cabernet sauvignon, and a little viognier and malbec. With winemaking experience in Australia, Portugal and France, they have produced a series of ever-interesting wines of high quality. Exports to the UK, Singapore and Japan.

**Poole's Rock** (est. 1988) (and its associated label, Cockfighter's Ghost) is the substantial Hunter Valley wine business patiently put together by former Macquarie Bank chairman David Clarke since 1988, albeit with its roots going further back in time. The 23-ha Poole's Rock vineyard at Broke was the starting point, but the acquisition of the 74-ha Glen Elgin Estate at Pokolbin (with 11 ha of vines) and a 2500-tonne winery (previously the Tulloch winery) has taken the business to another level. As well as semillon, chardonnay and shiraz grown in the Hunter Valley, the operation reaches out as far as Tasmania (for pinot noir) and Coonawarra (for cabernet sauvignon). Exports to all major markets.

**Pooley Wines** (est. 1985) has involved three generations of the Pooley family in the development of the business in Southern Tasmania. John Pooley is responsible for the two vineyards, one of 8 ha at Campania, and the other of 2.4 ha on a heritage property at Richmond, with an 1830s Georgian home. Son Matthew Pooley oversees the contract winemaking at Hood Wines winery.

**Porongurup** is the fifth of the subregions of Great Southern, somewhat untidily locking into Mount Barker on its western boundary. There the similarity with Mount Barker ends, because all but a handful of the 13 wineries are situated on the Porongurups Range, a very different physical feature from the Mount Barker Plateau. Great stands of towering eucalypt forest and a massive series of rounded granite knobs and boulders give way to sweeping views out over the Stirlings in one part, and towards Esperance in another.

A feature of the climate is a night-time thermal zone, created by a layer of warm air which rises above the denser cold air sliding down the hillsides of the subregion and settling on the lower valley floor. It is on these slopes that most of the vineyards are planted. The excellent air drainage further diminishes the risk of frost. Throughout the region, soil types are often named after the dominant eucalypt species of the location. Thus the soils are deep karri loams derived from weathered granite (as opposed to the marri soils of Mount Barker, which nonetheless have a similar parent source).

The principal grape varieties in descending order of importance are riesling, shiraz, cabernet sauvignon, chardonnay, merlot, cabernet franc, verdelho and pinot noir. The leading wineries are Abbey Creek Vineyard, Castle Rock Estate, Duke's Vineyard, Gibraltar Rock and Mount Trio Vineyard.

LAT 34°10'S; ALT 250–300 m; HDD 1441; GSR 310 mm; MJT 19°C; HARV Mid-March to early May; CHIEF VIT. HAZARD Birds

**port** was the name used for fortified red wine, a usage no long allowed by the EU Wine Agreement. However, the terms 'vintage' (for what was previously called vintage-style port), 'ruby' (rarely used, but a vintage style given an extra period in barrel), and 'tawny' (for tawny-style port) are permitted. Vintage is typically bottled within six months after harvest (and fortification) and will mature in bottle in a similar fashion to red table wine. Tawny remains in large oak vats or barrels for a few years or many decades, and is usually a blend of wine of varying ages; the older the average age, the higher the quality (and, of course, price).

**Port Phillip Estate** (est. 1987) was purchased by Giorgio and Dianne Gjergja in 2000 from its founder, leading Melbourne Senior Counsel Jeffrey Sher. In 2007 construction began on a futuristic, multimillion-dollar restaurant, cellar door and winery complex, which, together with the expansive vistas, will make this the focal point of the Mornington Peninsula. The quality of the pinot noir and chardonnay (at several price points) is outstanding, that of the syrah and sauvignon blanc very good; a quirky barbera and arneis round out the range. Exports to the UK, Canada and Singapore.

**Port Phillip Zone** encompasses the five regions encircling Melbourne: clockwise from the southwest they are Geelong, Sunbury, the Macedon Ranges, the Yarra Valley and the Mornington Peninsula. They share a fundamentally similar climate: cool Mediterranean, meaning the rainfall is winter–spring dominant, and without the extremes of day–night, and winter–summer, temperatures. These extremes are to be found in continental (or inland) climates. All five regions can be reached by car from Melbourne's CBD within an hour plus (Mornington Peninsula) or minus (Sunbury, Macedon Ranges). With the qualified exception of parts of Sunbury and Geelong, they offer spectacular scenery; the Mornington Peninsula (especially) and Yarra Valley cater for every wish of the day tourist. However close and compact the regions may be, there are some parts of the zone not included in those regions, leaving wineries in some surprising locations metaphorically marooned.

**post-fermentation maceration** describes the deliberate decision to leave the fermented wine in contact with the skins and pips for periods varying from a few days to a month or more. The effect is to fully extract all available colour, but, more crucially, to soften the tannins by a process known as long chain polymerisation.

**Potter fermenters** were designed by then youthful engineer and stainless steel fabricator Ron Potter. They are erected on appropriate scaffolding so that the cone-shaped bottom of the tank can be opened directly into a waiting press (the juice having previously been run off by gravity). They also include dimple-plate cooling jackets on the exterior of the tank, allowing precise temperature control. The design has been licensed to many major wine-producing countries.

**Potter, Ron** founded the largest manufacturer of stainless steel winemaking equipment in Australia in the late 1950s. In 1962 he designed and sold the first Potter fermenters, which became the standard design for red wine fermenters, sold in their thousands both in Australia and in many other parts of the world. Ron Potter was the recipient of the Maurice O'Shea Award in 1992.

**powdery mildew**, called oidium in France, is a worldwide scourge of vineyards. It is native to the US, and has little or no effect on native American vines. It reached France in 1854, devastating the vines and resulting in the smallest vintage since 1788. It attacks all the growing parts of the vine, spreading a powder-like white mould on leaves, stalks and grapes. If not checked it renders the grapes unfit for winemaking. It develops in warm weather, and does not require rainfall or high humidity, either of which can be the trigger for downy mildew. In Australia (and elsewhere) preventive sprays of sulphur, lime and water have to be regularly applied through the growing season.

**Prass, Guenter, AM** was one of the pioneers of controlled fermentation of white wine in the 1950s, beginning in 1953 with the first pressure fermentation stainless steel tank imported from Germany. Then and throughout his life, he worked for Orlando. He ultimately became managing director, and was a key part of the team which had groundbreaking success with the perfection of the wine cask and the establishment of the Jacob's Creek brand. It is no accident that Jacob's Creek won the Maurice O'Shea Award in 1994, a decade before Prass was the recipient of the same award.

**Preece, Colin** (1903–79) was born in Adelaide and attended Unley High School before enrolling at Roseworthy Agricultural College, taking the optional subject of oenology, and graduating as dux in 1923. He had intended to take on the management of the family's flour mill, but his interest in oenology led to his employment with Seppelt & Sons Limited at the Seppeltsfield winery. When Reginald Mowatt resigned as winemaker/manager of Seppelt's Great Western winery, Colin Preece was appointed to take his place. There he remained for over 30 years, making a series of wines of sublime quality. While the most admired of those wines were red, he also made some very good white wines from riesling and chasselas. He used an alpha and numeric designation for each of the wines that is almost as Delphic as the system used by Maurice O'Shea at Mount Pleasant. The commercial wines made in larger quantities included Arawatta Riesling, Rhymney Chablis, Moyston Claret and Chalambar Burgundy. The wines were given a letter corresponding to the vintage (thus G was for 1950, H for 1951, J for 1953 and so forth). These wines, often made in quantities of as little as 250 cases, could be extraordinarily complex in terms of their composition. Thus a 1951 Type H 66-68 Great Western Claret included 1820 litres of 1947 red pressings, 2366 litres of 1946 red pressings,

1365 litres of an otherwise unspecified Claret Special Blend and 819 litres of Scaletti's Dry Red (these figures and details are taken from the blend books at the winery). Preece worked on the principle that the vintage given would be the youngest component, rather than the more common opposite case. The greatest of the innumerable wines is generally reckoned to be 1953 Type J 34 Great Western Claret, which was a prolific show prize winner between 1953 and 1961, and a bottle opened in 1993 was still vibrantly youthful. The author has to admit to acute embarrassment at a disparaging tasting note from the early 1980s of 1962 Bin CH 20 (a special labelling of 1962 Chalambar); perhaps it was a bad bottle, for every other bottle opened between then and the early years of this century has been of the highest possible quality.

Preece's red wine making techniques (again, taken from the winery records) were somewhat unorthodox: most notably, he delayed picking until the grapes reached 15 degree baumé or thereabouts, and then added water to the must to bring the ultimate alcohol back to around 13% alc/vol. His blends, even of small production runs, could be of different vintages, different regions and different varieties. In this respect he had a similar talent to that of Roger Warren of Hardys. He retired in 1963, but his memory lives on in the few remaining bottles of his greatest wines.

**pre-fermentation maceration** is the term used to describe red wine must which, either by reducing the temperature or by adding significant amounts of sulphur dioxide, has been inhibited from commencing fermentation. Over the centuries, cool cellars in France and elsewhere in Europe would necessarily have ambient temperatures keeping the must below 15°C, the turning point for the onset of fermentation. Moreover, indigenous yeasts were relied on, and, because the population density of these yeasts was naturally low, the onset of fermentation would be a leisurely process. In the New World, and in particular in Australia, late summer and autumn temperatures are most likely to result in the must having temperature well in excess of 15°C, and heat exchangers are used to reduce the temperature to around 10°C. See also Accad, Guy.

**press**, or wine press, falls into three basic groups. First is the horizontal continuous press, which is continuously loaded with the must and simultaneously discharges the pressed marc. This is used for low-quality, high-volume wines. The second type, the basket press, has a vertical slatted circular basket, and compresses the grapes with a circular plate that fits precisely within the confines of the basket and is moved downwards. This type of press was once headed for obscurity but is now enjoying a renaissance in smaller wineries for pressing red grapes. While limited in size and involving extra manual handling, it often results in a soft extraction of wine at the end of fermentation. The third type is the bag (or bladder) press, which occurs in various configurations. It is arranged horizontally, the pressing resulting from the inflation of the bag inside a circular steel drum. The drum may have no external openings once loaded (the tank press) or it may have permanently open drainage points (the more common universal press). Bag presses are extremely precise, and can extract as little or as much juice or wine as the winemaker wishes, but in all instances with a relatively thin layer of grapes or must spread around the exterior of the bag.

**pressings** are of particular relevance with red wines, and come from the final stages of the press cycle, with greater tannins (though curiously no greater colour) than the free-run wine. They may or may not be ultimately blended into the main portion of the wine, depending on their quality and the style of wine sought.

**primitivo** is a synonym for zinfandel; it was thought these were two different red grape varieties until DNA profiling proved otherwise.

**Primo Estate** (est. 1979) is the venture of one-time Roseworthy Agricultural College dux Joe Grilli, and was originally established in the Adelaide Plains, but is now situated with a new winery and cellar door complex in McLaren Vale. The top-of-the-range red wines are made and released under the Joseph banner. The cabernet sauvignon merlot, once called Moda Amarone but with the 'Amarone' now dropped in deference to EU concerns, continues to use a portion of semi-dried grapes. Grilli's Italian heritage is increasingly obvious with the shiraz sangiovese and nebbiolo wines (the latter one of the best examples in Australia), albeit with shiraz and the cabernet merlot leading the way with the red wines, and a colombard sauvignon blanc (the sauvignon blanc a recent addition to the colombard) and the biennial release of the Joseph Sparkling Red of the highest quality. The 37.5 ha of estate vineyards are now split between the original Adelaide Plains plantings, McLaren Vale and Clarendon, the last near the Adelaide Hills border.

**Prince Hill Wines** (est. 1993) has become the new name and identity for Simon Gilbert Wines, following several years of financial travail. The business plan for the very large, well-designed winery was to make wines from grapes grown on the various regions along the western side of the Great Dividing Range of New South Wales; while logical, the expected volume of business did not and has not eventuated.

**Printhie Wines** (est. 1996) is the venture of Jim and Ruth Swift, who planted 33 ha of shiraz, cabernet sauvignon, merlot, pinot gris and viognier, and built the largest winery in the Orange region, with sons Dave and Ed subsequently assuming much of the business responsibility. Notwithstanding its substantial estate vineyards, Printhie also purchases grapes from other growers in the region. The wines are modestly priced given their high quality, and will gain further weight as the vines age. Printhie can fairly claim to be the premier winery in Orange. Exports to the US and Denmark.

**Providence Vineyards** (est. 1956) of Northern Tasmania incorporates the pioneer vineyard of Frenchman Jean Miguet, which the Bryce family purchased in 1980. The original 1.3-ha vineyard has been expanded to a little over 3 ha, and grenache and cabernet sauvignon (left from the original plantings, and unsuitable for the area) have been grafted over to chardonnay, pinot noir and semillon. Miguet

called the vineyard 'La Provence', reminding him of the part of France he came from, but after 40 years the French authorities forced a name change.

**pruning** in Australia takes many forms. At one extreme is the traditional cane pruning, with two canes (or rods) wrapped in opposite directions along the cordon or fruiting wire (the lowest in the trellis). At the other extreme is minimal pruning, which dispenses with any form of winter pruning, allowing the vine to grow indiscriminately, but then skirts (trims the underneath of the canopy) in summer to allow air passage under the vines and carries out a certain amount of leaf trimming on the sides of the vines. This was a low-cost approach which was for some time used in some major Coonawarra vineyards, but is now (happily) out of favour. For further discussion of the various forms of pruning, see canopy management.

**punch-down** is the Australian (and Californian) term for the French term pigeage. It is used for manual or mechanical immersion of the upper layer (or cap) of red grape berries and bunches where there has been some crushing or destemming, and for the gradual crushing of whole bunches in the fermenter without prior destemming.

**Pyramid Hill** (est. 2002), in the Upper Hunter Valley, is a partnership between the Adler and Hilder families; Richard Hilder is a veteran viticulturist who oversaw the establishment of many of the Rosemount vineyards. Nicholas Adler and Caroline Sherwood made their mark in the international film industry before moving to

Pyramid Hill in 1997. There are 71.5 ha of chardonnay, semillon, verdelho, shiraz, merlot, cabernet sauvignon and ruby cabernet, with a computer-controlled irrigation system backed up by a network of radio-linked weather and soil moisture sensors, which constantly relay data detailing the amount of available moisture at different soil depths to a central computer, thus avoiding excess irrigation and preventing stress. Most of the grapes are sold, but some are retained for the estate label. Exports to the UK, Canada, Japan and Singapore.

**Pyramids Road** (est. 1999) was born when Warren Smith and partner Sue moved to the Granite Belt region in 1999. With encouragement and assistance from the team at Ballandean Estate, the first vines were planted in 1999, the first vintage following in 2002. The current vineyard area (2009) is just 2 ha (shiraz, cabernet sauvignon, merlot, mourvedre and muscat); further plantings are planned but the total will not exceed 4 ha. All wines are made on site; the production area can be viewed from the cellar door.

**Pyrenees**, gazetted 29 June 2000, in the Western Victoria Zone, dates its viticultural history back to 1887, when Edwin Horatio Mackereth planted the first vines; as the number of his children grew, so did the size of his vineyard and winery. On his death the winery passed to his sons, Edwin, John, Charles and Alfred; Alfred, at the age of 91, wrote to Dr WS Benwell in 1962, recalling the history of the vineyard, which met with great success in its heyday. An important red grape was 'pinneau', which was used to make both red table wine and port. Whether this was

pinot noir or pinot meunier is not certain: both were available and fairly widely propagated at Geelong, which would have been one possible source (the other being the commercial nurseries, such as Cole's, in the Melbourne metropolitan area).

The winery won numerous prizes: the certificates were sufficiently numerous 'to paper a good-sized room', wrote Alfred Mackereth. Much of the wine was exported: 'Local people used to drink it too, but few Australians were wine drinkers.' The operation was sufficiently profitable for Edwin to leave the Victorian police force and join his brother Charles in the day-to-day management of the vineyard. Following the death of Charles in 1908, at the age of 28, John – a music and drawing teacher – reluctantly assumed the role of vigneron. With considerable acumen, Alfred remained a bank manager, looking at the winery with increasingly jaundiced eyes as the market for its output progressively declined.

Towards the end of World War I Edwin began negotiations to sell the winery and vineyards to Seppelt. At the time it was still a substantial operation, with a storage capacity in excess of 90,000 litres and three wine shops in Avoca. The sale fell through at the last moment. Apparently Edwin wished to retain some of the winemaking equipment; Seppelt, suspicious that he might set up in competition, insisted on all or nothing.

Seppelt bought Hans Irvine's winery at Great Western instead, and Avoca's grip on oenological life slipped away. Seppelt returned to eye the district with some care and interest in the 1960s, but was unable to secure options over sufficiently large parcels of land to make the venture commercially viable, so it withdrew once again. In 1929 Mackereth finally sold the property to a Methodist minister named Dawson, who promptly closed the winery, smashed the cellars and pulled out the last 20 ha of vines.

At Moonambel, northeast of Avoca, a Mr Adams established the first vineyards; these subsequently passed to J Kofoed and became known as Kofoed's Mountain Creek. In 1941 François de Castella wrote that 'the vineyard still flourishes', but it went out of production in 1945.

There was then a hiatus until 1963, when Remy Martin (of France) formed a joint venture with Melbourne wine merchant Nathan and Wyeth to establish a brandy-making business named Chateau Remy, planting trebbiano and doradillo. When the local brandy market collapsed in the wake of the imposition of excise duty, Remy Martin (for various periods the owner of Krug, Charles Heidsieck and Piper Heidsieck) decided to switch to sparkling wine making, yet another bizarre twist, for if the Pyrenees is suited to anything, it is to the production of full-throated red wines.

Chateau Remy is now Blue Pyrenees Estate, which, having finally rid itself of the trebbiano and doradillo, produces pleasant but not remarkable sparkling wines from chardonnay and pinot noir (and table wines). The subsequent growth of vineyards and wineries, Mount Avoca following next in 1970, was leisurely, and it was not until the late 1990s that the large Glenlofty Vineyard of Southcorp (now Foster's Wine Estates) and the even larger adjacent Glen Kara Vineyard (investor-funded) brought the Pyrenees up to speed.

It is a quintessential Australian wine region, the vineyards appearing sporadically between the ever-present eucalypts. The wineries cluster in two groups: the larger between the towns of Moonambel and Redbank, the smaller around the rather larger town of Avoca. For tourists, there is one outstanding destination: the Warrenmang Resort, with a top-flight restaurant and much cabin-style accommodation along a hillside overlooking the vineyard. It is only if you approach the region from the south or west that the name Pyrenees makes sense: the range rears out of flat countryside, the skyline marked with ever-changing and angular faces.

The inland location (and to a certain degree the altitude of 220–375 metres) gives rise to low midsummer relative humidity and substantial diurnal temperature ranges in spring and early summer. Late summer daytime temperatures are moderate, lowering the overall heat summation. The major limitations on viticulture are low growing season rainfall and the absence of underground water. This is true, also, of the new areas on the southern side of the Pyrenees Range, which are significantly cooler; the requirement of water (and danger of spring frosts) is still substantial.

There is a mixture of grey-brown sandy and brown loamy sand soils. All have a relatively hard and acidic subsoil, improved by liberal applications of gypsum. Coupled with the climate, they result in moderate rather than vigorous growth. Three-quarters of the vineyards are planted to shiraz, cabernet sauvignon and smaller amounts of merlot and pinot noir; chardonnay and sauvignon blanc are the white varieties.

The leading winery is Dalwhinnie, but Amherst, Berrys Bridge, DogRock, Horvat Estate, Jardine, Polleters, Pyren Vineyard, Pyrenees Ridge, Summerfield, Taltarni and Warrenmang all make high-quality shiraz.

LAT 37°09'S; ALT 220–375 m; HDD 1530; GSR 220 mm; MJT 20.9°C; HARV Late February to late April; CHIEF VIT. HAZARDS Drought; cockatoos

a b c d e f g h i
j k l m n o p q
r s t u v w x y z

**Queensland Coastal** is an unofficial name drawn in part from a Queensland Government strategy document released in December 2004 by the minister for wine (yes, there was such a person). It takes in the Gold Coast and Hinterland district, the Brisbane and Scenic Rim district, and the Sunshine Coast and Hinterland district, which between them then had no less than 40 wineries-cum-cellar doors, the most important by far being Sirromet.

**Queensland Zone** takes in the two officially recognised regions – Granite Belt and South Burnett – as well as a number of regions spread along the coast north of Brisbane, with one major intrusion into the Darling Downs, centred on Toowoomba.

a b c d e f g h i
j k l m n o p q
r s t u v w x y z

**rack and return**  is the process of siphoning or pumping the juice from an active red fermentation, leaving the skins in place, and then returning the juice, sprinkling it over the skins. It both cools and aerates the must, also helping to increase the extraction of colour and tannins. In modern wineries, the juice may be passed through a heat exchanger to either cool it (usually) or warm it (less commonly).

**racked, racking**  is an important part of the winemaking process for white and red wines alike. With red wines, the procedure will take place a number of times (typically two or three); with white wines, perhaps only once. In each case it involves the careful transfer of clear wine from the sediment collected in the bottom of the vessel, typically a barrel if red, chardonnay or other barrel-fermented white wine, or a tank in the case of aromatic and other non-wooded white wines. The first racking will normally take place shortly after conclusion of the primary and secondary malolactic fermentation. With small-volume, high-quality wines it is more than likely that the wine will have been taken to barrel prior to fermentation (if white) or shortly after primary fermentation (if red). In these instances, the first racking will result in a substantial quantity of thick, almost muddy, sediment. Later in the process the residue will become progressively finer. The French term sur lie (typically in muscadet) refers to a wine which has been taken direct from contact with lees to the bottle. Makers of small-volume chardonnay will seek to achieve a similar process, but with the likelihood of a final (brief) intermediate stage involving settling in tank at low temperatures. The more skilful the

racking, the less need there will be for fining or filtration to clarify the wine.

**rancio**  denotes a distinctive developed character of an old dessert wine stemming from a degree of aldehydic oxidation, and is achieved when the wine is saturated with oxygen without being spoilt. Despite the description, it is a highly important character of fortified wines which have spent a long time in barrel.

**random oxidation**  is more correctly called sporadic oxidation; if it were truly random, no cause could be found. 'Sporadic' allows for a cause, but without any particular pattern or frequency. It is at best a fine semantic point, and the more familiar term, 'random oxidation', is used in this encyclopedia.

The nature and causes of random oxidation first came under the scientific microscope in May 1999, when the Australian Wine Research Institute began an ongoing trial with a young unwooded semillon sealed with 14 different closures. These included the two most commonly used grades of one-piece natural cork (called Reference 2 and Reference 3 by the Portuguese suppliers); the Amorim Twin Top cork, with a body of granulated cork and discs of natural cork at either end (an adaptation, if you like, of the sparkling wine cork); a closure made from cork ground to the consistency of flour and subjected to highly technical treatment before being reformed and glued, known as Diam; various synthetic (plastic) corks; and a screwcap under the proprietary Auscap brand name.

The wines were opened, tasted and analysed at six-month intervals over the next eight years. At each point the screwcap wine had retained more free sulphur dioxide, had better colour and a brighter, fresher fruit than all others. The Diam closure came second, then the Twin Top, next the two natural corks, and last the synthetic closures. Over the period of the trial, the difference in the performance of the various closures became steadily more obvious.

Part of the scientific analysis measured the oxygen permeability of each of the closures. Screwcaps allowed between 0.0002 and 0.0008 millilitres per day of oxygen permeation, with a mean of 0.0005; Diam 0.0007 to 0.0013, with a mean of 0.0010; and Reference 2 cork 0.0001 to 0.1227, with a mean of 0.0179. In other words, if the screwcap has a range of 4, in terms of permeability, cork has a range of over 1200. The permeability of cork has been disputed by researchers elsewhere in Australia and Europe, but all concede that the oxygen-barrier performance of cork does vary substantially, the variability increasing markedly with age. It is a natural product, and the variability should not come as a surprise.

In Australia, Penfolds, in conjunction with others, monitored the development of a high-quality red wine (1996 Bin 389 Cabernet Shiraz) from the time of bottling in 1997. Four closures were used: screwcap, Reference 2 cork (44 × 24 millimetres) and two commercially available synthetic closures. Three bottles of each closure were analysed and tasted (using rigorous tasting procedures) in 2000 and then biennially. The results from 2004 were released to the public.

The wine sealed with synthetic closures lost its sulphur dioxide at a consistent rate (as between bottles) far in excess of that sealed with a screwcap (which was likewise at a consistent rate). The bottles sealed with cork lost sulphur dioxide at variable rates: on each occasion between 2000 and 2004, the amount retained varied by 50 per cent, the highest retention similar to that of the screwcap, the lowest similar to that of the synthetics. Colour development followed a similar pattern.

The sensory analysis rated the screwcap- and cork-closed wines as having significantly higher levels of fruit intensity than the wines under synthetic closures. Conversely, the wines sealed with synthetic closures were rated as significantly more developed than those with screwcap or cork closures. Overall, there was relatively little difference between the screwcap bottle development and that of the bottles with the best corks. As at the end of 2008, over 90 per cent of all Australian white table wines were sealed with screwcaps, compared with 68 per cent of all red table wines (excluding sparkling and fortified wines). The higher percentage of white wines has several causes. First, oxidation can be immediately recognised by accelerated colour development. To the untrained eye, or where there are no other wines of the same age and variety to afford comparisons, the signs may not be obvious. To the expert taster, they are sure signs of a major problem. The other reason is that white wines do not have anthocyanins, which in themselves can provide some protection against oxidation. Moreover, because of the greater flavour and textural impact of red wines, low levels of oxidation are less obvious than they are in white wines. Finally, $SO_2$ additions have traditionally been somewhat higher to red wines than to white wines.

The greatest French wine scientists had also been united in their view (for well over 100 years) that wine does not require continuous access to oxygen to develop. The first was Louis Pasteur, who went further still, declaring oxygen the public enemy of wine. Then, in 1898, Emile Duclaux, a French researcher wrote: 'In bottles, so long as the cork is sound … the protection of the wine in relation to oxygen is absolute or near-absolute. New absorptions of oxygen are impossible.' In 1947, Jean Ribéreau-Gayon compared bottles with good corks with glass flasks sealed with airtight glass stoppers. There was no difference. In 2000, Pascal Ribéreau-Gayon was emphatic: 'Reactions that take place in bottled wine do not require oxygen.' Yet the belief persists that, if closed with a screwcap and deprived of oxygen, wine will somehow suffer retarded development.

Southcorp researchers (Allen Hart and Andrew Kleinig) concluded:

> We have been able to demonstrate that red wine will continue to mature and develop both with and without additional oxygen being available to the wine. However, increased availability of oxygen greatly increases the rate at which a red wine will mature, and hence shortens the drinking life of the wine. In an anaerobic environment such as a bottle of red wine sealed with a screwcap or crown seal, some wines may develop reductive characteristics. In contrast, bottled red wine stored in a more aerobic environment such as with a synthetic closure, will prematurely develop oxidised characters.

**Rankine, Dr Bryce, AM**  was born in South Australia and educated at the universities of Adelaide (BSc 1945, MSc 1953), California and Stellenbosch (DSc 1971). On the basis of his bachelor of science degree, he spent four years as a bacteriologist with FH Faulding & Company Ltd in Adelaide. In 1950 he joined the CSIRO wine research group, which was part of the Waite Precinct. For the next 17 years he carried out research and extension work and study for the Australian wine industry. In 1978 he joined the Roseworthy Agricultural College as head of the School of Viticulture and Oenology; he was later appointed dean of the Faculty of Oenology. He retired in 1986, and thereafter carried on an active career as a consultant. He is the author of more than 200 scientific and technical papers and several books, including *Wines and Wineries of the Barossa Valley* (Jacaranda, Brisbane, 1971), *Making Good Wine* (Sun Books, Melbourne, 1989) and *Evolution of the Modern Australian Wine Industry* (Ryan Publications, Adelaide, 1996). He was the recipient of the Maurice O'Shea Award in 1998.

**recorking**,  reduced to its most basic, is the replacement of an old cork with a new one. The makers of classed growth (the 1855 classification set out five tiers or growths: first, second, and so on; see riesling) Bordeaux reds which kept substantial reserve stocks of good vintage (less of poorer vintages) would examine the bottles in their cellar after 30 or 40 years. They would then make a decision as to whether they would recork all the bottles, topping up any ullage with the same wine, or only recork and top up those wines which had in fact developed ullage. The former practice would guarantee that (in the absence of TCA) all bottles would be similar, but not the same; the latter would, over the years, result in substantial variation from one bottle to the next. Some chateaux would decide not to recork any of the wines, fearing oxidation or the possibility of TCA contamination with the second cork. Whatever the choice, the old British wine trade axiom 'There are no great old wines, only great old bottles' would become ever more true as the wine aged.

In Australia, Penfolds has run a highly successful recorking clinic, in association with auctioneers Langton's, since 1991. These clinics are only for Penfolds red table wines, 15 years or older, with low levels, leaking corks or poor cellaring history. The protocol is that the expert team running the clinic will taste a tiny sample of the wine. If it is still sound, it will be topped up (with a younger but otherwise similar wine) and recorked, and a certificate will be glued to the back of the bottle specifying the date it passed through the clinic. If the wine is unsound, it will simply be recorked, with no added wine, and without any certificate. The clinic was developed primarily as a service to collectors of Grange, but it is also used on other top-end red wines in the Penfolds portfolio. It tours the capital cities once every two years, and is always booked out. It is periodically staged in New York and London, when demand requires it. It hardly need be said that the wear and tear on cork-sealed bottles in the Australian climate, and the number of occasions on which they are likely to be moved during their life (new house purchases, divorces, auctions and so forth), places far greater demands on the cork than are likely on bottles which have come direct from the bottling line down to a cellar with a constant temperature of around 12°C and then remain there.

**Redman** (est. 1966) is the greatest family dynasty in Coonawarra. Founded by Bill Redman, in March 2008 the Redman family celebrated 100 years of winemaking in Coonawarra. The 2008 vintage also marked the arrival of Daniel as the fourth-generation Redman winemaker. Daniel gained winemaking experience in Central Victoria, the Barossa Valley and the US before taking up his new position.

**reduction** is the polar opposite to, but linked to, oxidation. In winemaking texts the link is often discussed as the 'redox' potential of a wine. The problems are: first, it is a constantly changing relationship as the see-saw of oxidation and reduction swings one way or the other; second, the chemistry is dauntingly complex; and third, for example, the sweaty aromas encountered with sauvignon blanc (akin to reduction) may be nothing more than varietal character. Reducing conditions are desirable (especially for white wines) during the period between the completion of fermentation and bottling, simply because oxidation will thus not be taking place. With red wines the problem can easily be dealt with by racking, particularly if the wine is deliberately splashed into a tank or other vessel before being returned to the barrel. If persistent, it can be removed by the addition of small amounts of copper sulphate. Once the wine is bottled, the situation changes, as the hydrogen sulphide, mercaptans and thiols, which form under reducing conditions, will likely be denied the oxygen which might cure the problem.

The issue of reduction has become more important since the introduction of screwcaps. Opponents of the use of screwcaps suggest their use causes reduction. This is strongly disputed by those who use screwcaps, on the basis that it is a case of shooting the messenger. They believe that wine which does not carry with it hydrogen sulphide, mercaptans or thiols will not develop reduced characters under screwcap. They point out that reduction is not unique to wines bottled with screwcaps, partly because the gas impermeability of a very good cork is for a variable period the equivalent to that of a screwcap.

**regions** see Geographic Indications.

**residual sugar** (in winemaking circles often abbreviated to RS) is the measure of glucose and fructose which, either accidentally or deliberately, remains unconverted to alcohol during the course of fermentation. It is normally expressed as grams of sugar per litre of wine, and can vary between 1 gram per litre and over 500 grams per litre. White and red wines described as dry may contain 2 grams per litre, the sweetness completely obscured by the countervailing acidity and other extracted compounds or flavours in the wine. Indeed, it is rare to find a wine with less than 1 gram per litre of residual sugar, simply because yeasts cannot metabolise trace quantities of other sugars (such as pentoses); nor can these trace quantities be tasted – that is, these wines will appear to be totally dry.

Aromatic wines such as riesling grown in cool climates may contain as much as 25 grams

per litre of sugar yet taste fruity but dry, particularly where the pH is below 3 and the acid in excess of 8 grams per litre. The juice from grapes picked at 13 baumé will contain 233 grams per litre of residual sugar, and, if fermented dry, will end up with an alcohol of 13.9% alc/vol. If, on the other hand, fermentation is arrested when the alcohol reaches 11% alc/vol, the juice will contain 50 grams per litre of sugar. If the fermentation is arrested so that the wine has 8% alc/vol, there may be up to 100 grams per litre of residual sugar. Even at this level, the sweetness may be interpreted more as juicy fruit flavours, and be most apparent on the mid-palate; the finish and aftertaste may be fresh and juicy rather than sweet.

Once one gets into the upper end of Hungary's tokaji essencias, the wine must have a minimum residual sugar of 250 grams per litre, but can attain twice this amount. The same is true of exceptional trockenbeerenauslese from Germany. At this level of sweetness the wine is stable, and may take years to ferment part of the sugar: Jancis Robinson, in *The Oxford Companion to Wine* (3rd edition, 2006, p. 567), records a German wine harvested at Nussdorf in the Pfalz in 1971 which was picked with about 870 grams per litre of sugar, and had reached only 4.5% alc/vol after fermenting for 20 years, producing a wine with about 480 grams per litre of residual sugar.

In Australia between 1955 and 1975, what were called spätlese rieslings were far from uncommon, and the best (particularly Leo Buring) were exceptionally fine wines at 30 years of age in the relatively rare instances where the corks had not given way (the sugar in sweet wines acts as a lubricant, allowing ready penetration of wine along the sides of the cork). The style then disappeared until the start of the 21st century, when winemakers in Tasmania, Pemberton and other cool regions began experimenting with earlier picking and leaving unfermented sugar. The first Tasmanian version was labelled FGR riesling, which might have stood for many things, but in fact meant 'Forty Grams Residual' (sugar). These wines are loosely based on the Mosel kabinett style.

Again, in Australia a clear distinction has to be made between commercial or commodity wines with relatively low prices selling in volume through supermarkets in Australia and abroad. Here residual sugar of 4–10 grams per litre is routinely used in both white wines and red wines, as it has been demonstrated on countless occasions that consumers may talk dry, but drink sweet. Most people buying wine of this description are in fact unaware that part of the flavour comes from residual sugar. Quality barrel-fermented white wines (notably chardonnay) and all quality red wines are (or should be) dry.

**resveratrol** is a phytoalexin, a class of antibiotic compounds produced as a part of a plant's defence system against disease. While present in other plants, resveratrol's most abundant natural sources are in *Vitis vinifera* grapes, and the highest concentration is in the skin of the grape. The resveratrol content of wine is related to the length of time the grape skins are present during the fermentation process, and hence is found in far higher levels in red wine than in white wine. Up to this point, there is no doubt or disagreement. What is yet to be proved is that resveratrol has special cardiovascular

protective effects. There is only one study, the Copenhagen City Heart Study (2000), which suggests that red wine has a greater protective effect than other forms of alcohol, including white wine and beer. Other studies have contradicted the Copenhagen study, or at least not supported it. Moreover, the Mayo Clinic in the US points out that resveratrol is not the only substance in red wine that has a cardiovascular effect. The antioxidants quercetin and epicatechin are also found in red wine, and are more effective antioxidants than resveratrol.

**reverse osmosis** has come into increasingly widespread use around the world (including Australia) since the mid-1990s. It relies on cross-flow filtration, a technique which sees the liquid (juice or wine) flowing parallel to the filter membrane under pressure, which causes water, some salts and alcohol to pass through the membrane filter. It is most often currently used for two very different purposes: alcohol reduction and must concentration, the latter ultimately leading to an increase in alcohol. Where it is used for alcohol reduction (its most common use in Australia), the colourless liquid which passes through the membrane is composed almost entirely of water and alcohol, the remaining wine passing back to the tank. The alcohol is then removed from the permeated liquid by distillation, and the water returned to the wine, so to produce a wine of reduced alcohol content. Because the water came from the grapes in the first instance, its return to the wine is not caught by laws preventing the addition of water. A sub-variant is low sugar juice (LSJ, removal of sugar from the must), where all the water removed is added back to, say, 50 per cent of the original juice.

When used for must concentration, the water removed is simply discarded; this is a particularly useful practice in a wet, rainy year. Somewhat controversially, the process has been more widely used even in good vintages to increase the alcohol and overall flavour of wines, as this appeals to the US market.

In Australia the main use of reverse osmosis is on finished wines, where the selective removal of water and alcohol concentrates all other components. Interestingly, if one starts with a wine with, say, 15% alc/vol, as the alcohol is progressively reduced down to, say, 12.5% alc/vol, there may be three points, or sweet spots, along the way where the mouthfeel and flavour are in sensory balance. Thus rather than simply calibrate the equipment so that a 15% alc/vol wine ends up as a 13% alc/vol wine, a decision will be made along the way to terminate the process somewhere between 13% alc/vol and 15% alc/vol.

Less common usages are to reduce volatile acidity, to remove *Bretannomyces* and (the winemakers hope) to reduce smoke taint (from bushfires).

**Richfield Estate** (est. 1997) is the New England venture of Singapore resident Bernard Forey, who is the majority share-holder in the owning syndicate. The 500 ha property, at an altitude of 720 metres, was selected after an intensive survey by soil specialists. Just under 30 ha of shiraz, cabernet sauvignon, merlot, semillon, chardonnay and verdelho were planted, the first vintage coming in 2000.

Winemaker John Cassegrain is also a shareholder in the venture, and much of the wine is exported to Thailand and Malaysia.

**riesling**, says Jancis Robinson (*The Oxford Companion to Wine*, 3rd edition, 2006, p. 577), 'could claim to be the finest white grape variety in the world on the basis of the longevity of its wines and their ability to transmit the characteristics of a vineyard without losing riesling's own inimitable style'.

The ancestral homes of riesling are today's Austria, Germany and Alsace. As with all the major *vinifera* varieties, the early records of riesling are open to question (and to interpretation) because of variations in spelling. The first use of the term 'riesling' was in 1552, but it seems that the quality of the variety (under various spellings) was well known by the late Middle Ages, and it had become widely planted in the Rhine and Mosel valleys by the mid-16th century. It made its appearance in Alsace even earlier, being recognised in 1477 as one of the foremost varieties by the Duke of Lorraine; the wine itself was first described in 1628. It is highly probable that it was established in Austria's Wachau region on the Danube around the same time.

Its status grew steadily over the 17th and 18th centuries, reaching its high point in the 19th century. When the 1855 classification of Bordeaux divided its 61 greatest producers into five growths (or classes), mature German riesling brought higher prices than first growth Bordeaux. 'Mature' in this context meant up to 50 years, or even more. It was quite usual for the wine to be kept in old wooden vats, the interior coated with layers of tartaric acid, which prevented any semblance of oak flavour from appearing in the wine and also made the vat impervious to the entry of oxygen through its walls. One of its greatest protagonists was Queen Victoria, who allowed a producer in

Hochheim to rename its vineyard Konigin Victoriaberg, the distinctly ornate label including the British royal coat of arms.

Riesling was an early arrival in Australia. One of the first specific references to it can be found in Ebenezer Ward's *The Vineyards and Orchards of South Australia*; here he records that Mr Joseph Gilbert of Pewsey Vale had riesling wine from both the 1852 and 1854 vintages, and that the latter had been tasted by experts in Adelaide who pronounced it to be very good. It quickly became entrenched in the Barossa Valley, recognised and enthusiastically adopted by German settlers from Lutheran Silesia.

Before long, however, its name was adopted by other varieties. In the Hunter Valley, a local nurseryman by the name of Shepherd supplied vines which were called Shepherd's riesling in the 1850s; in due course the name was changed to Hunter River riesling, and thereafter shortened simply to riesling. No problem, except that the variety was in fact semillon, and only McWilliam's had a small planting of true riesling. To confuse matters further, this semillon-called-riesling was sold in a riesling bottle, and listed by restaurants under the header of riesling.

In the Clare Valley – destined, ironically, to become the foremost region of the variety in Australia – the altogether inferior variety crouchen was called Clare Valley riesling. But worse was to come: in the midst of all this confusion, riesling was used to denote a (very loosely defined) style, and 'Rhine' was tacked onto the front to denote a wine made from true riesling.

Nowhere was this better demonstrated than in the Hunter Valley, where Lindemans waved their magic wand over semillon to produce riesling, hock, chablis and white burgundy, the difference lying in slightly different picking dates, vineyard plots and/or alcohol.

Nonetheless, in the white wine boom of the late 1960s and 1970s, riesling became Australia's leading white variety, its tonnage rising from 1900 in 1966 to an all-time high of 44,000 in 1986. It was not until 1992 that chardonnay overtook it, and thereafter the two varieties went in opposite directions, riesling in decline until 2001, chardonnay soaring upwards. (As at 2008, riesling produced 39,305 tonnes, chardonnay 428,082 tonnes.)

In 1994, a group of very determined Clare Valley vignerons, led by Jeffrey Grosset, began a campaign to have the use of the generic name 'riesling' abolished, and for the simultaneous dropping of the technically incorrect 'Rhine', thus limiting the name to the true variety. It was opposed by the big companies, in particular those who were heavily involved in the cask market, where generic terms (riesling, chablis, claret, burgundy and so on) were used, and varietal names were not. (The casks were typically made from an unholy blend of lesser varieties, with trebbiano, sultana and others in the white wines.)

The campaign finally succeeded in 2000, partly because of the near-finalisation of the Australia–EU Wine Agreement, but more to get those pestilential Clare Valley makers off corporate backs. In the same year that same group decided to abandon the use of corks, and move en masse to Stelvin screwcaps. A tsunami followed: by 2008 over 90 per cent of Australian white wines on the domestic market, and close to 100 per cent of all rieslings, were sealed with screwcaps.

The Australian techniques for making riesling have been fine-tuned but not fundamentally changed since the 1960s, and encourage (or allow) less variation than any other varietal wine style. The grapes are whole-bunch pressed (that is, without crushing – this is the one change facilitated by the development of tank presses with an inflatable inner bag and the exclusion of oxygen), and the resultant juice is either cold-settled at very low temperatures, centrifuged or cross-flow filtered. The objective in each case is to have star-bright juice with absolutely no phenolics.

The juice will then be inoculated with a neutral cultured yeast and fermented at a low temperature (12–15°C). Once fermentation is finished, the wine will be racked off its lees, sterile filtered, and taken to bottle as quickly as possible, usually within three or four months of vintage.

It will never regain the position it had in 1980, when more bottles of riesling were sold than all other white varieties combined. That said, there has been a distinct revival of interest in riesling since the mid-1990s. Part of this has been sparked by imports of German riesling (particularly from the Mosel Valley), but the largest factor has been the advent of screwcaps protecting the aroma and flavour of riesling whether it be young, semi-mature or mature.

In 1993 its 3600 ha had it in second place behind chardonnay, with 6100 ha. In 1997 chardonnay plantings had reached 13,700 ha, semillon had moved into second place with 4800 ha, and riesling was third with 3400 ha. Thereafter it benefited from the great planting boom between that year and 2005, its area rising to 4400 ha, but it had by then been pushed into fourth place (among the classic varieties) by the 5500 ha of sauvignon blanc. Behind the numbers there has, however, been another positive change: the variety has been removed from warm areas (such as the Riverland) and planted in Tasmania, the Great Southern and the Clare and Eden valleys, all ideally suited to the variety.

**Riverina**, gazetted 12 November 1998, was brought to reality by the crippling Federation drought at the end of the 19th century and into the 20th. A feasibility study had been carried out by Sir Samuel McCaughey, which led to a Bill presented to the New South Wales Government in 1904. A change of government delayed consideration of the Bill, but it was only a question of time before the scheme was implemented. The question was referred to the Parliamentary Standing Committee on Public Works in 1906, and in evidence before that committee McCaughey observed:

> In my opinion the waters of the rivers of the Commonwealth, if placed on the surface of the ground so that they could be utilised for irrigation, together with a supply for stock and household purposes, would be of more value to Australia than the discovery of gold; for gold will eventually become exhausted while water will continue as long as the world lasts.

McCaughey's words were both prophetic and ironic, as the very same water issues reappeared 100 years later. Nonetheless it was not surprising that on 31 October 1906 the committee approved the scheme, and shortly after the Burrinjuck and Murrumbidgee Canals Construction Act was passed.

Despite the immensity of the scheme – it involved the building of the Burrinjuck Dam 390 kilometres upstream and a number of intermediate weirs – it became operational in less than six years. The first water was supplied for irrigation on 13 July 1912, and within a month or so JJ McWilliam had taken up a lease at Hanwood and planted 35,000 cuttings.

At that time McWilliam's main winemaking operations were based at Junee, where there were extensive vineyards, and the first Hanwood vintage was crushed there. By 1917, however, they had erected a winery at Hanwood, followed by another at Yenda in 1920. As the Murrumbidgee Irrigation Area (MIA) prospered, so did the McWilliams: it was the start of a long association which was to make the family company one of the wealthiest in Australia. It is hard to say which has benefited the most from that association, so great has been the contribution of the McWilliam family to winemaking in the district (and indeed to Australia).

In 1913 control of the venture was passed to the specially created Water Conservation and Irrigation Commission, and by April 1914 over 600 farms covering 9700 ha were in operation. (It was not until 1924 that it became possible to purchase land freehold; all the early farmers received perpetual leases, and the size of each holding was severely limited.) World War I interrupted progress, but its cessation and the flow of returned servicemen seemed to present an ideal opportunity to give the scheme new impetus.

The theory was fine, but the reality less so. Many of the servicemen had no previous experience on the land (and certainly none

of viticulture); the blocks were too small for economic operation; and those who decided to embark on grapegrowing often selected inferior grape types and inappropriate viticultural methods. On the other side of the ledger, the commission started a vine nursery in the early 1920s, and the first wave of Italian immigrants arrived around the same time. Many of these came from winemaking areas around Treviso in the north and Calabria in the south, and almost all had viticulture in their blood.

Drought threatened the area again during World War II, and by the 1950s major problems were being encountered. One of the principal problems already confronting the areas along the Murray River was salinity, a problem for which there is no long-term solution. The Riverina had been lucky, as there was very low salinity in the surface water. But extensive rice farming in particular started to raise the underlying watertable (which was very salty), and by the early 1950s salinity and waterlogging had become major threats. A system of subsoil tile drainage was developed; this has since been installed on a massive scale, and the threats have been partially averted.

For the first 40 years of its existence the MIA produced virtually no table wine. The vast bulk of its production was of fortified wine (and between 1926 and 1938 much of this was exported), reflecting two things. First, and most importantly, it met the demands of the market. Second, it was assumed that this was all, indeed, the district was suited to.

The end of beer rationing in 1953 changed all that. Up until that time the Australian population, largely denied its natural drink and desperate for alcohol in any form to help remind it that the horror of the war was indeed over, had accepted cheap fortified wine as an alternative. Once beer became readily available, these markets dried up overnight. Glen McWilliam, McWilliam's technical and production director and one of the unsung heroes of the Australian wine industry, determined that he would show that the area could certainly produce table wine of quality.

He tackled the problem both in the winery and in the vineyard. In conjunction with the Viticultural Research Station and the CSIRO, many new varieties and clones were imported and trialled; it was a slow process, and it was not until the end of the 1950s that the first trickle of new varieties of wine became available, and not until 1963 that the first 'new' wine (a cabernet sauvignon) was made. Meanwhile, in the winery he had embraced the technology pioneered by Orlando and Yalumba in the mid-1950s for the handling of white grapes, adapting it to the particular requirements of the region.

With an extraordinarily intuitive flair for design and a deep understanding of what can be done with stainless steel, he developed the peculiar elongated steel fermentation tanks which double as white wine drainers (of juice from the crushed grapes) and which were so much the mark of McWilliam's. Coupled with the increasing use of refrigeration and must-chilling, and later with the advent of mechanical harvesting at night, McWilliam's paved the way for the MIA to take a major share of the growth in table wine consumption from less than 2 litres per capita to 29.2 litres per capita per annum (as of 2007).

De Bortoli, too, has been a major and successful innovator, growing to become another one of Australia's large, family-owned wineries. It led the way in developing botrytis semillon in this most unlikely climate, picking the grapes as late as June, four months after normal maturity for table wine. The quality of the modestly priced De Bortoli table wines is exemplary. De Bortoli was established in 1928, and Casella is a relative newcomer, dating back only to 1969. It is the phenomenal success of the [yellow tail] brand which has pushed Casella into third place after Foster's and CWA in export sales of branded wine, with De Bortoli in sixth place. McWilliam's, De Bortoli and Casella are in a significantly stronger position than the producers relying on the Murray Darling River System. Water security and availability on the Murrumbidgee River, fed by the Burrinjuck Dam, are of a much higher order than on the Murray Darling. How long this will continue to be the case is not certain.

Another face of the Riverina is the home for what started life as the Riverina College of Advanced Education and is now Charles Sturt University, Wagga Wagga Campus, the next most important wine school in Australia after the University of Adelaide. It is here that A&G Industries was founded by Ron Potter, inventor of the eponymous fermenter; the company is now the largest stainless steel wine fabricator in the southern hemisphere.

The Riverina is a scenically barren area, which may have something to do with the region's penchant for efficiency and mega-sized businesses: the vineyards are laser flat, the wineries functional and the cellar door sales areas a rococo blend of Australian–Italian do-it-yourself architecture. As a final deterrent to visitors, Griffith is a long way from anywhere.

The climate is hot and dry, although

slightly cooler than South Australia's Riverland and Victoria's Sunraysia. All forms of perennial agriculture here depend on irrigation from the Murrumbidgee River. Grapegrowing is reliable and yields are high with a minimal disease load. With a low requirement for sprays, growers have adopted low-impact vineyard management systems. Autumn rainfall, which usually commences in April, is essential for the development of botrytis in semillon.

The soils are generally sandy loam overlying a sandy clay loam or clay subsoil; however, as they were deposited by ancient streams, they are highly variable. They range from red sandy earths through to red and brown massive earths. While free-draining near the surface, subsoil waterlogging has continued to be a problem, particularly with associated salinity build-up.

There are roughly equal quantities of shiraz, semillon, chardonnay and cabernet sauvignon planted. The major wineries are Beelgara Estate, Casella, De Bortoli, Lillypilly Estate, McWilliam's, Nugan Estate, Riverina Estate and Westend Estate.

LAT 34°00′S; ALT 140 m; HDD 2201; GSR 200 mm; MJT 23.8°C; HARV Early February to early March; CHIEF VIT. HAZARD Drought

**Riverina College of Advanced Education** (often abbreviated to Rivcol, or similar) was the forerunner to Charles Sturt University, which took over the Rivcol campus.

**Riverland**, gazetted 10 December 1998, the only region in the Lower Murray Zone, was conceived in 1887, when the South Australian Government quickly stepped in to capitalise on the problems George Chaffey

and brother William had encountered as a result of bureaucratic bungling by the Victorian Government. With unconditional government support the Chaffeys selected Renmark, on the west bank of the Murray, as the site for the commencement of irrigation in South Australia. With formidable energy, the brothers quickly laid out the site of the town, with the wide streets and parklands which remain a feature to this day.

It was not long, however, before the Chaffeys were back in Victoria, developing Mildura for what was by then a chastened government. In 1893 the Renmark Irrigation trust took over responsibility for the area, and for maintaining the irrigation channels which had already started to fall into disrepair. The trust has since been responsible both for the town of Renmark and for 4800 ha of orchards and vineyards in the district; it is in turn effectively run by local landholders.

It is ironic that when the Chaffey brothers returned to Victoria, the severe and prolonged Federation drought resulted in the Murray River becoming a series of waterholes, with dire financial consequences for all involved in the irrigation schemes, not least the Chaffeys. Both then and now the raison d'être for all the regions feeding from the Murray River was the combination of a hot, dry climate with little or no disease pressure, and seemingly unlimited irrigation water supplied at a nominal price. So long as the water was available, the red sand desert became an oasis, stretching many hundreds of kilometres along the banks of the Murray.

Yields of 10–15 tonnes per acre (150–240 hectolitres per hectare) of chardonnay could be easily achieved from mechanically pruned and mechanically harvested grapes. Even at $300 a tonne it was profitable business for the grapegrower, and enabled the big wine companies to secure market dominance in the UK in short order, and thereafter in the US. (At the height of the boom in the 1990s chardonnay achieved prices of over $1000 a tonne.)

As the 21st century arrived, opportunities and challenges came in quick succession. Exports were still increasing rapidly, demand for the Riverland grapes likewise. Then came the three large vintages of 2004, 2005 and 2006, resulting in significant surpluses, which forced prices down. At the same time, the drought intensified as inflows into the Murray Darling reached an all-time low, and strict controls were placed on the amount of water which could be used for irrigation. Almost overnight, growers found themselves confronted by a dilemma with no obvious answer. The crucial questions were how much water would be available over the next five years, and how much it would cost. If the water supply was sharply reduced, and its cost increased, could the grapegrowers expect to receive a high enough price per tonne to produce a profit?

In January 2009 Oxford Landing Estate announced that it was commencing a five-year experiment designed to establish whether vines could be sustained and a commercial crop obtained from those vines with only 10 per cent of the normal water application. While the outcome will be of considerable interest, it will not necessarily apply to all vineyards in the Riverland. The soils and subsoils are not totally uniform, and nor is the level of salinity.

Accepting that water availability (rather than cost) will be the key, the signs point

to the survival of the fittest – those with large holdings and strong balance sheets. The majority of smaller growers may have to abandon their vineyards and sell their water rights in a turbulent market, simply because there is no likelihood that the rights will deliver more than a token percentage of the theoretical water entitlement they confer on the holder.

Even the fittest, however, will be faced with diminished yields (no bad thing in itself) and the need to persuade buyers to pay higher prices per tonne. Here the pendulum swings of demand and supply for cabernet sauvignon and chardonnay will be as important as they will also be difficult to predict, making long-term planning especially hazardous.

The climate is hot, with high evaporation rates and low rainfall making irrigation essential; it is also continental, resulting in long sunny days and noticeably cooler nights. Modern viticultural and winemaking techniques mean that this climate can be seen as one of the region's strengths. Long sunshine hours ensure fruit ripeness, while a strongly winter-dominant rainfall results in low disease incidence and allows viticulturists the choice of how much moisture the vine receives during the growing season. The soils are red-brown sandy loams often overlying a limestone substrate. Fertility rates are moderate. As with the entire Murray Darling Basin, salinity is an increasingly important issue and will affect all aspects of land use in future generations.

The principal grape varieties in descending order are cabernet sauvignon, chardonnay, muscat gordo blanco, grenache, merlot, colombard and petit verdot. The leading wineries in the region are Angove Family

Winemakers and Kingston Estate, as are the large vineyards of Banrock Station and Oxford Landing Estate, with brand names recognised around the world.

LAT 34°17'S; ALT 70 m; HDD 2084; GSR 139 mm; MJT 23°C; HARV Mid-February to early April; CHIEF VIT. HAZARD Occasional spring frost

**Robe** joined the list of registered regions on 15 August 2006, but might equally have been included as part of Mount Benson (both are in the Limestone Coast Zone). Robe takes its name from the eponymous historic and beautiful town, with many limestone houses built in the 19th century, and a boat harbour for the lobster-fishing vessels which work day and night in the lobster season. The largest vineyard is that established by Southcorp in 1994, which produces some very elegant chardonnay and shiraz; only the chardonnay has been bottled separately (and then only once). There are those who think these wines deserve a better fate than to be anonymously blended away.

The climate is unequivocally cool, strongly maritime-influenced by the nearby ocean on one side and the lakes on the other. The winters are cold and wet, the growing season is long, cool and dry. The wines are predominantly from the south, southeast and southwest, and are particularly strong during the spring and early summer. Overall, summer temperatures are 3°C lower than Coonawarra; budburst, though, occurs two weeks earlier, yet harvest is at much the same time.

The principal soil type is generally described as terra rossa, a red-brown soil that varies from sandy to loamy and which is typically associated with limestone. The limestone may outcrop or occur 10–50 centimetres below the surface. The terrain on which the vineyards have been planted is gently undulating, the surrounding natural bushland scrubby, and giving little clue of the potential of the area from a viticultural viewpoint.

The main wineries are Governor Robe Selection and Karatta.

LAT 37°09'S; ALT 50–150 m; HDD 1226; GSR 217 mm; MJT 22.7°C; HARV Late March to late April; CHIEF VIT. HAZARDS Spring frost; poor fruit set

**Robert Channon Wines** (est. 1998) was founded when Robert Channon, a corporate lawyer born and trained in England, decided to quit a prominent Australian law firm and (together with wife Peggy) establish, in the Granite Belt region, 8 ha of chardonnay, verdelho, shiraz, merlot and cabernet sauvignon under permanent bird protection netting. The initial cost of installing permanent netting is high, but in the long term it is well worth it: it excludes birds and protects the grapes against hail damage. Also, there is no pressure to pick the grapes before they are fully ripe. The winery has established a particular reputation for its verdelho.

**Robert Oatley Vineyards** (est. 2006) is the latest venture of the Oatley family, previously best known as the owners of Rosemount Estate until it was sold to Southcorp. The founder of both businesses is chairman Bob Oatley, and the new venture is run by son Sandy, with considerable hitting power added by deputy executive chairman Chris Hancock. A succession of yachts called *Wild Oats* have had outstanding success in the annual Sydney to Hobart Yacht Race. The family has long owned vineyards in Mudgee, but the new business has been rapidly expanded by the acquisition of the Montrose winery, the Craigmoor cellar door and restaurant, and seven vineyards (totalling 465 ha) spread across the Mudgee region. The Montrose winery had a $10 million upgrade in the wake of its acquisition by the Oatley family.

**Robinson, Jancis, OBE, MW** (1950–) is, in the opinion of the author, the foremost author and wine writer in the world, her monumental *The Oxford Companion to Wine* not only the best book ever written on the subject, but a book which will never be bettered. For good measure, the second-best wine book ever written, *The World Atlas of Wine*, is now under the joint authorship of herself and Hugh Johnson, the original author. This all came from an almost accidental start. She had studied mathematics and philosophy at the University of Oxford, England, and then worked for a travel company for a time. She started her wine writing career on 1 December 1975 when she became assistant editor for the trade magazine *Wine and Spirit*. Within nine years she had become the first person outside the wine trade to become a Master of Wine; she was made an OBE in 2003. She has become an accomplished television presenter, anchoring a 10-episode wine course on BBC2 television in 1995, since reissued on DVD. She has won innumerable major awards for her writing.

**Robinvale** (est. 1976), in the Murray Darling, was one of the first Australian wineries to be fully accredited by the Biodynamic Agricultural Association of Australia. Most, but not all, of the wines are produced from biodynamically grown grapes, with some made preservative-free. Production has grown dramatically, no doubt reflecting the interest in organic and biodynamic viticulture and winemaking. Exports to the UK, the US, Canada, Belgium, Korea, Vietnam and NZ.

**rootstock** is the part of a vine which provides the root system, onto which the scion is grafted. The technique was adopted in Europe in the 1880s as the only fully effective defence against phylloxera. The rootstock will be one of the 13 American *Vitis* species, all of which became resistant to phylloxera over the millennia of coexistence in the US. The only species of vine in European and Middle Eastern regions is *V. vinifera*, and there are three species in Asia (which are not used for grafting). The scion is the variety of *V. vinifera* which will provide the annual growth of wood, canes, leaves and – of course – grapes. Other than the Sydney Basin, Victoria is the only state with areas of active phylloxera (and hence grafted vines), but other areas both within and without Victoria do have populations of grafted vines to deal with issues such as nematodes, acidity or heavy soils. The vigour of the rootstocks will determine choice; many are invigorating but only a few are devigorationg, and it is the latter which are of particular interest in Australia.

**rosé** wines have been made for centuries; the first wines from Bordeaux were made from white and red grapes picked and fermented together, the wine called 'clairet', which ultimately gave rise to the term 'claret' to describe the red wines of Bordeaux of modern times. There are five ways to make rosés, the most common in Australia utilising crushed or destemmed red grapes which are chilled and allowed to macerate for between 12 and 48 hours before all or part of the juice is drawn off (by static draining or pumping, rather than by pressing) and then cold-fermented in the same way as a white wine. With broken or barely crushed grapes, this is known as the 'bleeding' or saignée, the must producing a more concentrated wine. In other words, there will be two fermentations of two entirely different musts, one for the rosé, the other for red table wine.

The other methods (largely restricted to the Old World) are: the blending of white and red wines; the light pressing of whole bunches of red grapes, with the resulting juice run off and fermented without any skin contact; the crushed grapes and juice being fermented together for one to three days before the juice is run off; and, finally, the heavy fining of red wine to remove tannins, followed by colour-stripping by treatment with active carbon. Here the resulting quality is very low.

**Rosemount Estate** (est. 1969), in the Upper Hunter Valley, achieved a miraculous balancing act, maintaining wine quality while presiding over an ever-expanding empire and dramatically increasing production through the 1990s. The wines were consistently of excellent value; all had real character and individuality, and more than a few were startlingly good. The outcome was the merger with Southcorp in 2001. Unfortunately, what seemed to be a powerful and synergistic union turned out to be little short of a disaster. Southcorp lost more than half of its market capitalisation and more than half of its most effective and talented employees, and is now part of Foster's. Exports to all major markets.

**Roseworthy Agricultural College** was established in 1883, and virtually from the outset viticulture was a compulsory subject and oenology an optional one in its diploma of agriculture course. Viticulture and oenology received particular attention following the appointment of Professor AJ Perkins in 1892. In 1936, under the guidance of Alan Hickinbotham, the college established a diploma in oenology, the first students graduating in 1938. In 1978 the course was upgraded to a degree (bachelor of applied science in oenology, which included viticulture). In 1974 a new two-year wine marketing course was introduced, which later offered the alternative of a correspondence course. In 1991 it became a campus of the University of Adelaide; all courses (with the exception of the wine marketing course) were transferred to the Waite Precinct, with the winemaking course becoming part of the degree course in agricultural science. The teaching winery which Roseworthy had set up decades before was closed, but the research facilities of the Waite Institute have taken its place.

**Rothbury Estate** (est. 1970) in the Hunter Valley was the brainchild of Len Evans. Only he could have mobilised the capital necessary to bring to completion the striking winery building; to plant the extensive vineyards, some of which – with the wisdom of hindsight – should not have been planted because the soil was not appropriate; to have special bottles made in a mould which precisely replicated the bottle used by the Domaine de la Romanée-Conti (and created many problems with its weight and neck size); and to have a front label which stated the vintage and vineyard, but not the variety. The variety was irrelevant because it was, self-evidently from the colour, either semillon or shiraz. For good measure, a Fred Williams (noted Australian artist) painting was used, but reproduced in miniature in black and white. The vision splendid, as it was once called, gradually dimmed as the often inhospitable climate of the Hunter Valley struck, as white and red booms came and went, as the range of wines was progressively extended well beyond the first two varieties and the boundaries of the Hunter Valley became increasingly irrelevant, and as one financial backer replaced another before Mildara Blass made a takeover offer which was bitterly, but unsuccessfully, defended by Len Evans. Once in Mildara Blass ownership, the brand continued to disintegrate at an even more rapid rate, until the winery and vineyards were sold to Hope Estate, leaving Rothbury Estate as no more than a name on a label.

**roussanne** is the white grape blood brother of marsanne, its place of origin the northern Rhône Valley, and its use is to balance marsanne with more spine, perfume and acidity. Like viognier, were it not for its unpredictable yield, its presence might well be greater. The most distinguished marsanne roussanne blend in Australia is made by Yeringberg, with a varietal wine made by St Huberts, both in the Yarra Valley. There was a slow but steady increase in plantings from 2005 to 2008, with 69 ha now under vine.

**ruby cabernet**, a red grape variety, was bred by Professor Harold Olmo at the University of California, Davis, in 1949, by crossing carignan with cabernet sauvignon. The object was a high-yielding vine with grapes that had strong colour while retaining some cabernet characteristics. It was also expected that the variety would perform well in hot regions. As in California, Australian plantings expanded rapidly, only to decrease with similar rapidity. In 1966 there were 644 ha; it reached a peak of 2530 ha in 2004, before falling to 1142 ha in 2008, and there is every likelihood that the decline will continue. The reality is that the wine is of mediocre quality at best.

**Rutherglen**, gazetted 2 September 1997, was briefly an exception to the rule of wine following in the wake of the discovery of gold. Gold was to set the northeast aflame, but the vines came first. Major Thomas Mitchell, who crossed the Goulburn River at what became the site of Tahbilk, performed the same service at Gooramadda, near Rutherglen, in 1836 when he crossed the Murray River. The Gooramadda run, as it came to be known, was taken up by Lindsey Brown in 1839. Three of his farm workers were from Germany, and when they moved to nearby Albury they established vines. In 1851 they persuaded Brown that he should start a vineyard at Gooramadda. The vines flourished and Brown became an instant disciple; Charles Hubert de Castella records that '[Brown] was in the habit of settling miners' discussions as to the depth of which sinking [digging shafts] should be carried. "To get gold," he would say, "you need sink only about 18 inches [45 centimetres] and plant vines."'

Others listened and soon followed. John Graham planted vines at Netherby in 1859, and in 1862 brought the first steam-plough into the district for the enormous cost of £1200. He faded from the scene, as did Roderick Kilborn (1863), Camille Reau at the Tuilleries, Joseph Webster (1864), Alexander Caughey at Mount Prior (1868), then Anthony Ruche, Hugh Fraser, Joseph Pearce, James Prentice and William Cullen. While these names are represented no more, the Tuilleries and Mount Prior homesteads are still magnificent reminders of the opulence of 19th-century Victorian living.

However, there were yet other vignerons whose families have carried on: Campbell, Chambers, Gehrig, Morris and Sutherland Smith. Of these, George Frederick Morris had the greatest impact. He was an English bank clerk who unsuccessfully prospected for gold on the Ovens River, but who made sufficient money as a wholesale trader at Beechworth to move to Rutherglen in 1859 and buy a 100-ha property. He planted 4 ha as an experiment; as he was pleased with the results, another 12 ha followed soon after. But while the vines grew and the winemaking was accomplished without undue difficulty, the market was not there. So for a while Morris concentrated on other crops. Nonetheless, by 1869 Rutherglen was the largest winegrowing area in the state, with 2407 ha producing just under 800,000 litres of wine.

But the 1870s marked a low period in the northeast. Gold had been discovered in 1860 on what became the Main Street of Rutherglen, but by 1870 the surface gold had been largely worked out. There was a lull until 1886, when means were devised to work the deep alluvial leads, and prosperity returned. In the intervening 15 years the miners had largely drifted away and a mini-recession occurred. Some turned to viticulture, adding to the problems of finding a market.

Ironically, one man who made literally no attempt at all to dispose of his wine seems to have provided the spark which led to the major period of growth in the district. Hubert de Castella, in *Notes of an Australian Vine Grower*, first published in 1882, tells the story of Anthony Ruche, who, 20 years earlier, had established a 1 ha vineyard. In 1880 he was persuaded to sell his entire stock to an enterprising Melbourne wine merchant. Hubert de Castella takes up the tale:

Ruche, the wine grower, until then had clung to his casks like a hen to her chickens, and had never sold until his back was to the wall, in a few cases only because he was forced by the few creditors who supplied his humble needs. It was his mania. Selling his wine was a heartbreak for him. Consequently when one of his barrels was put up for sale it used to fetch a good price, even when other vine growers could not sell theirs. Besides, the man was an expert, and if he was so keen on keeping his wine it was because he rightly had a very good opinion of it.

Having cost the merchant 4 shillings and 9 pence a gallon (4.5 litres), the wine brought between 6 shillings and 21 shillings per gallon at auction. To what extent the ensuing publicity was responsible we will never know, but in the following six years plantings in the Shire of Rutherglen trebled, rising from 2770 ha in 1880 to 7410 ha in 1886. George Frederick Morris had jumped the gun, it seems; he had expanded his plantings to 250 ha during the 1870s, and in the early 1880s he built the beautiful two-storey Fairfield homestead. At the same time he constructed the largest wine cellars in the southern hemisphere, which held the equivalent of three vintages of 1 million litres each.

By far the greatest part of Fairfield's production was exported to London. In the latter part of the 19th century a very large trade in Australian wine was built up, with BP Burgoyne taking the lion's share. It was no doubt his success with the immensely rich and alcoholic burgundies, much appreciated in Victorian England, which led him to acquire Mount Ophir, and to the long-term connection that company had with the London trade. Fairfield won 425 first prizes in a 20-year show career spanning exhibitions held in London, Amsterdam, Paris, Calcutta, New Zealand, South Africa, Perth, Melbourne and Sydney.

In 1883 the Murray District Vinegrowers' Association was formed, with George Sutherland Smith as its first president. A powerful lobby group which represented a large source of income for the state, it was instrumental in securing the passage of legislation providing for a bounty of £2 for every acre of grapes planted. One does not have to be especially cynical, either, to believe it was behind the government decree ordering the destruction of the Bendigo vineyards when phylloxera was discovered there in 1893. Even if the vain hope of arresting the spread of the pest came to naught, the destruction would remove a source of competition in the same way as the removal of the Geelong vineyards had 10 years earlier.

The government bounty caused indiscriminate planting in several areas, not the least being the northeast. In 1895 there were 4340 ha of vines in Rutherglen, and of these 613 were still to come into bearing, attesting to the rate of planting. But troubled times lay ahead. In 1899 phylloxera was positively identified in the region. With nothing left to protect, the government finally adopted the action it should have taken in Bendigo (and, arguably, Geelong): it encouraged growers to replant with phylloxera-resistant rootstocks supplied by the government at a subsidised price.

Between 1890 and 1910 virtually every vineyard in the northeast was destroyed; a considerable number were replanted, but many were not. Those that were not replanted by the outbreak of World War I disappeared from the scene permanently. Up to 1914, and in the period from 1918 to 1925, much of the local production was exported to the UK. Local sales were largely effected through Melbourne merchants, with WJ Seabrook and John Connell & Company being regular buyers. Wine was sold at cellar door through a 2-gallon (9-litre) licence, but little or none of it was bottled or labelled. You brought your own container and the vigneron filled it direct from cask. Prices ranged from 3 shillings per gallon for table wine through to 6 shillings per gallon for sweet fortified wine. WH Chambers at Rosewood had one of the rare single-bottle licences; here prices were 6 pence per bottle for table wine and 1 shilling per bottle for fortified wine. Nonetheless, the same rule applied: you brought your own bottles.

The collapse of the export market in the late 1920s, and the onset of the Depression, brought even harder times to the northeast. Wine prices slumped to below the cost of production, the only comfort being that all the other Australian regions suffered similarly.

World War II destroyed the once-buoyant export market, and precipitated a further major decline in the fortunes of the district. The three largest vineyards, Mount Ophir (280 ha), Fairfield (250 ha) and Grahams (250 ha), pulled out their vines in the second half of the 1950s as the export market to the UK continued to decline. Others, such as Morris, quickly turned to red wine production. But it was basically due to the superb quality of its fortified wines, wines that have no peer, that the northeast survived first phylloxera, then the Depression and finally the 1951 excise on fortified wine and the after-effects of the removal of beer rationing.

The present-day great fortified wine-makers of the region are spread along a narrow band of soil which tracks the progress of the Murray Valley Highway, which runs east–west in a more or less straight line in the northern third of the region. The second group of wineries track the meandering of the Murray River, and are better known for table wines than for fortifieds, with the exception of All Saints Estate, which has a foot in each camp. This leaves the southern two-thirds of the region virtually bereft of wineries, with only two micro-sized ventures, Lilliput and Watchbox.

The fortified wines are fashioned by the strongly continental climate, with very hot summer days and cold nights. The growing season can be threatened at one end by spring frosts (exacerbated by cold air draining down from the mountains to the south) and at the other end by the abrupt arrival of autumn rain. But when conditions are favourable, the high sugar levels needed for the fortified wines (and which power the full-bodied red table wines) are attained. Equally important, perhaps, are the soil and topography, or, if you wish, the terroir. There are consistent patterns of soil throughout the district: a poor quartz gravel on the gentle hilltops, then a band of red loam on the lower slopes of the hills and, finally, grey sandy loam on the flats. The gravelly hilltops have now largely been abandoned as uneconomic, although capable of producing very good wine; and the great fortified wines come from the red loam which snakes its way through and around Rutherglen, which is home to Buller, Stanton & Killeen, Campbells, Chambers Rosewood and, at its easternmost point, Morris.

The leading wineries are All Saints Estate, Buller, Campbells, Chambers Rosewood, Cofield, Morris, Pfeiffer, St Leonards Vineyard, Stanton & Killeen and Warrabilla.

LAT 36°10′S; ALT 170 m; HDD 1770; GSR 297 mm; MJT 22.3°C; HARV End February to early May; CHIEF VIT. HAZARD Spring frost

a b c d e f g h i
j k l m n o p q
r s t u v w x y z

**saignée** is the French word for 'bleed', and refers to the drawn-off juice from red must which is fermented to make rosé.

**St Hallett** has several versions of its genesis, one dating from 1912 when Carl Richard Lindner purchased a property on St Hallett Road in the Barossa Valley and planted a vineyard, a small winery following in 1918. The other date is 1944, when a new winery was erected on St Hallett Road. Through the 1970s and until 1983, Robert O'Callaghan was winemaker, before moving on to establish Rockford in 1984. By then the winery had attracted attention for its Old Block Shiraz, and in 1988 the brilliant marketing supremo Bob McLean joined the business as managing director and shareholder. Rapid growth followed, Old Block becoming known both nationally and internationally, and in 1988 St Hallett merged with Tatachilla to form Banksia Wines, listed on the stock exchange. Within a relatively few years, Banksia was acquired by Lion Nathan, and the 100,000-case St Hallett is now part of the substantial Lion Nathan empire. Shiraz in various forms and at different price levels (headed by Old Block, then Blackwell) remains the core of the business, but its Eden Valley Riesling can excel. The Poacher's Blend, Barossa Semillon and Gamekeeper's Reserve Barossa Shiraz Grenache provide the volume. Exports to all major markets.

**St Huberts** (est. 1862) was established when Charles Hubert de Castella purchased a portion of Yering Station from his brother Paul de Castella. Hubert had lived in the Yarra Valley between 1854 and 1857, and returned to his native Switzerland in 1856, only to find the lure of Australia too strong. He had intended to establish a sheep station, but on returning in 1862 found that sheep were too expensive and that his brother's wine made at Yering was in great demand. So it was to vines that he turned, quickly establishing 40 ha and increasing total plantings to 80 ha by 1875. Massive cellars were built, with the capacity to hold two or three vintages. But the establishment expenses were understandably very large, and sales lagged in the face of the poor reputation which 'colonial' wine had at the time. This poor reputation was brought about by large quantities of wine being made by numerous small vignerons, many of which had little or no idea about the basics of winemaking.

In 1875 the St Huberts Vineyard Company was formed to take over the enterprise, with Hubert de Castella retaining a major interest. The injection of new capital did little to alleviate the problems, and further reconstruction took place in 1879 when Hubert, in partnership with Andrew Rowan, repurchased St Huberts from the company. A period of prosperity followed: Rowan was an energetic and effective marketer.

François de Castella, put in charge of St Huberts between 1886 and 1890, recalled the 1880s in a paper delivered to the Victorian Historical Society in 1942. It is a remarkable near-contemporary record of the Yarra Valley, in which he observed:

> Rowan did much to put St Huberts on the map, and its wine on every restaurant's list. With the de Castella and Rowan regime, dawned an era of prosperity for St Huberts. The vineyard of 250 acres [101 ha], then

in its prime, produced several vintages of over 70,000 gallons [318,500 litres] each. Relieved of the worry of wine sales, my father could give all his attention to vineyard and cellars. Wines of exceptional quality resulted, most notable vintages being 1875, 1879, 1883 and 1887. Every four years was a vintage year, though several others were nearly as good.

In 1890 Andrew Rowan acquired Hubert de Castella's share in St Huberts. He planned to revive the vineyard but, like many, was crippled by the 1893 bank crash and Depression. The only solution was for more attention to be given to dairying, cattle and pigs, activities that (unlike wine) paid their way. Another blow came when the manager/winemaker, David Dickson, slipped on grapes during the 1897 vintage, fell down an elevator shaft and subsequently died from his injuries. By 1902 St Huberts was in the hands of builder and contractor David Mitchell, who already owned 25 ha of vineyards. He thus became the vigneron with the largest vineyard holding in the district. When he died in 1916, St Huberts rapidly declined, then went out of production. The cellars remained deserted for decades and were finally destroyed by fire in the 1950s.

The vineyard was replanted in 1968 by the Cester family, whose major income came from growing chickens and game birds. The 19th-century grandeur of St Huberts was nowhere to be seen as the winery was set up in the chicken sheds, and remained there until acquired by Rothbury Estate, which in turn fell prey to Mildara Blass. Its wines are now made at Coldstream Hills from 100 per cent estate-grown grapes.

**St Leonards Vineyard** (est. 1860) is an old favourite, relaunched in late 1997 with a range of premium wines cleverly marketed through a singularly attractive cellar door and bistro at the historic winery on the banks of the Murray. All Saints Estate and St Leonards are wholly owned by the Brown family members Eliza, Angela and Nicholas, all of whom are involved in the business under the leadership of Eliza.

**Salitage** (est. 1989) is one of the showpieces of Pemberton. The 25-ha vineyard and winery is owned by John Horgan and family, brother to Denis Horgan of Leeuwin Estate. Its principal wines (with both a first label and a second label) are sauvignon blanc, chardonnay and pinot noir. Exports to the UK, the US and other major markets.

**Salomon Estate** (est. 1997) is the Currency Creek venture of Bert Salomon, an Austrian winemaker with a long-established family winery in the Kremstal region, not far from Vienna. He became acquainted with Australia during his time with import company Schlumberger in Vienna; he was the first to import Australian wines (Penfolds) into Austria, in the mid-1980s, and later became head of the Austrian Wine Bureau. He was so taken by Adelaide that he moved his family there for the first few months of each year, sending his young children to school and setting in place an Australian red wine making venture. He retired from the bureau, and now is a full-time travelling winemaker, running the family winery in the northern hemisphere vintage, and overseeing the making of the Salomon Estate wines at Boar's Rock in the first half of the year.

**Saltram** (est. 1859) was founded by William Salter and his son Edward – the business was established under the name of W Salter & Son. William Salter had arrived in South Australia from England 20 years earlier, and had turned his hand with great success to many activities (mostly in the Barossa Valley) in the meantime. A religious man, he had named the property he bought and developed near Angaston 'Mamre Brook', after a verse in Genesis describing some of Abraham's land.

The first vintage, in 1862, was made in a cave-like cellar excavated in the side of the hill up which one still drives to reach the present-day Saltram winery. Production was of red wine, usually fortified, and between 1859 and 1882 markets were gradually established, first in South Australia, then Melbourne and ultimately New Zealand. The latter market was opened by Alfred Percy Birks, who subsequently founded AP Birks' Wendouree Cellars in the Clare Valley. In 1882 Saltram entered into a marketing arrangement with Thomas Hardy & Sons, who undertook to purchase and then market all of Saltram's production. This led to the establishment of Saltram in the English trade.

By 1891 the vintage had reached 180,000 litres, and by 1903 it had risen to 290,000 litres. Incredibly, until 1891 all the grapes were crushed in special treading boxes, with the workers wearing knee-boots made by a local bootmaker. In that year a hydraulic press and pump driven by a 4-horse-power steam-engine was purchased. To be more accurate, two were purchased; the first was too big to fit between the vats, and was resold to AP Birks at Wendouree.

The winery passed through several generations until Leslie Salter was appointed manager in 1902. He became close friends with Ronald Martin at Stonyfell, and when Saltram was converted to a company in 1920, Stonyfell took a one-third interest, with Ronald Martin as chairman and Leslie Salter as managing director. Following Leslie Salter's retirement in 1937, Saltram was managed by Stonyfell, and in 1941 became a subsidiary of that company. There was a close working relationship between the two companies: the winemaking was carried out at Saltram, and the maturation and bottling at Stonyfell.

In 1972 Dalgety Australia Limited made its ill-fated venture into the wine industry. In that year it acquired Saltram, Stonyfell, Krondorf and Loxton Estate. As they did to Reed International and Gilbeys, winemaking and the wine industry remained closed books to Dalgety. Bruised and defeated, Dalgety sold Saltram to Seagram in 1979. Seagram was at that time the world's largest wine and spirits company, and after some years seemed to forget it had an Australian outpost. In the early 1990s Rothbury Estate acquired Saltram with a substantial share issue in lieu of cash; in 1996 both Rothbury and Saltram became part of the Mildara Blass group (now part of Foster's) after a very determined but unsuccessful effort by Rothbury founder, Len Evans, to fight off the takeover. Its winemaking operations are now consolidated in the massive Foster's winery complex. While its 150,000-case production covers all the major varieties with brands at three price points, its various shiraz labels lead the way.

**Sandalford** dates back to 1840, when a Crown grant of a little over 500 ha on the banks of the Swan River was given to John

Septimus Roe, the colony's first surveyor general, in recognition of his services. He planted a mix of table grapes and multipurpose muscat. In 1862 the property was leased to former convict Malachi Reidy Meagher, who successfully sought a licence to acquire 630 litres of spirit to fortify the 19,400 litres of wine he had made. Thereafter the vineyard was largely neglected, and it was left to John Frederick (Fred) Roe to redevelop it in the early decades of the 20th century, primarily as a grower and exporter of table grapes. There was in fact no house on the property; the family home was in Perth. Commuting by train and a 5-kilometre walk on weekends, he dug wells and increased the plantings. Retiring from the Bank of New South Wales, he moved full-time to the property, initially in a simple iron shelter. Soon there were two dwellings, one for himself and one for a married couple who helped with the work.

In the post–World War II years his sons John and David Roe decided to start commercial winemaking, with John the viticulturist and David the winemaker. However, David Roe died unexpectedly in 1969. A private company was then formed and it acquired the Sandalford wine interests in 1971. John Roe and a West Australian merchant bank became the principal shareholders, and funds for development resulted in the acquisition of a large property in the Margaret River in 1972. A substantial vineyard was established, and in the late 1970s the Inchcape group of London purchased the investors' shares, leaving John Roe with his 30 per cent. In 1991 Inchcape added the last 30 per cent, but within 12 months Perth businessmen Peter Prendiville and

Paul Norton had acquired the company from Inchcape, and the Prendiville family subsequently became the sole owner.

Sandalford has 22 ha of vines in the Swan Valley, and 96 ha in Margaret River, the latter responsible for the majority of the high-quality table wines spanning sauvignon blanc semillon, chardonnay, verdelho and, notably, shiraz and cabernet sauvignon. The 100,000-case production is exported to all major markets.

**sangiovese** is the dominant red grape variety in Tuscany, Italy, with over 100,000 ha of vineyard, thus the cornerstone of all chianti. The prosperous and vibrant Tuscany of today bears no resemblance to the directionless, debilitated region of the 1960s and '70s. Much work has been done on improved clones, and while part of the recovery was due to the development of super Tuscan reds incorporating various percentages of cabernet sauvignon and merlot, 100 per cent varietal sangiovese has also made a major impression on both Italian and international markets. While some of this work has come to benefit Australian plantings, sangiovese is struggling to hold its own here, plantings becalmed at 510 ha (2008), after a peak of a little over 600 ha in 2001.

**saperavi** is a Russian red grape variety (the word in fact means 'dyer' in Russian) which has exceptional colour, partly derived from its skin, but also from its deep, pink flesh. It also holds its acidity well, ripening later in the season. First commercially propagated by Symphonia Wines in the King Valley, as at 2008 it was grown in a total of only eight vineyards.

**sappy** is a somewhat ambiguous tasting term denoting a touch of herbaceous or stalky character often found in young wines, particularly pinot noir, and which may be a sign of potential quality.

**sauvignon blanc,** a white grape variety, was identified in 1997 as one of the two parents of cabernet sauvignon, cabernet franc being the other. Anyone who has tasted partially ripe cabernet sauvignon will know it offers a mix of crushed herbs, grass and asparagus, with a minerally acid framework, eerily similar to its parent. Sauvignon blanc needs a genuinely cool climate, and the lessons of Europe (where it was planted in places unsuited to it as well as the wholly suited Loire Valley) have had to be relearnt across the New World. The moment the climate becomes a little bit too warm, the variety loses focus, and the wines become bland at best, degenerating into oily coarseness at worst. South Africa, Chile and – conspicuously – New Zealand have become major players, the Marlborough region of New Zealand now being one of the best, and certainly the largest, regions in the world. The ease of vine management in the generally laser-flat terrain of Marlborough, together with the economies of scale, also make it the most efficient producer; the last blunted only by the very high cost of planted or unplanted land.

It has in one sense been surprising that Australia has been able to develop its own sauvignon blanc resources, even if supported by large volumes of sauvignon blanc/semillon blends. As of 2008 its 6404 ha put it in third place after chardonnay and semillon. The Adelaide Hills and Margaret River are the key regions for unblended sauvignon blanc, Margaret River clearly leading the way with semillon/sauvignon blends, with an interesting, albeit smaller, union of Hunter Valley semillon and Orange sauvignon blanc.

**savagnin blanc,** a white grape variety, was inadvertently established in 20 commercial vineyards in Australia in the belief it was albarino.

**Schubert, Max, AM** (1915–94) was born on 9 February 1915 at Moculta in the Barossa Valley, the son of Adolf Karl Schubert (Karl) and Emilie Clara Schubert (Clara) née Linke. Clara's father and uncle were partners in a business manufacturing farm machinery sold throughout Australia. Karl worked at the Linke factory for about 10 years prior to 1918, and after his marriage lived with Clara in one of the several factory cottages on the Linke property. Like the others, it was partially made of mud and thatched with straw, with an earth floor. Max, together with his three surviving brothers and a sister, learnt German because all church services were conducted in German, and Karl and Clara were deeply religious. Every night after dinner Karl would read to the family from the bible for at least half an hour; they prayed before all meals; and the children went to Saturday school at the church. Clara's English was poor, and she spoke to the children in German, but was answered in English. Indeed, it was not uncommon in those days for first- and second-generation émigrés to speak no English.

The family moved to Nuriootpa in 1920, when Max was five, and within a few years he was earning small amounts from a variety of jobs in local businesses, including the butcher and thereafter the greengrocer. By the time he was a teenager, with the Great Depression still a fact of life, he had enough casual employment to pay his school fees. His first (and only) permanent employer was Penfolds; Schubert got the job because he told them he was 16 (the minimum legal age), when in fact his birthday was some months away. He started in the lowest position in the company, as an odd job man, feeding the horses, cleaning out the stables, polishing the floors of the small offices, fetching the mail and running messages. When Penfolds employed its first chemist, an Austrian named John Farsch, Max became his assistant, learning how to culture flor yeast for dry sherry, and how to seed it into barrels. At that time bacterial spoilage was endemic in the cellars, and Max was responsible for regularly checking every hogshead to make sure it was not contaminated.

It was not long thereafter that he came to the notice of Leslie Penfold Hyland, who was based at Magill. He told Schubert he was to come and work at Magill, which necessitated a move to board and lodgings on the outskirts of Adelaide. Schubert had no sooner arrived than Leslie Penfold Hyland instructed him to enrol in the Adelaide School of Mines, to learn chemistry, and to work with Farsch, the chemist. The massive problem confronting all South Australia's winemakers was a high percentage of wines which were mousy. Winemakers would fine mousy wines, but within months, the mouse (as it was called) would reappear. The only answer was to bottle the wines immediately after fining. However, in 1935 and 1936 Ray Beckwith (by then Penfolds' research chemist at Nuriootpa) and John Fornachon were to solve the problem with the aid of the first pH meters used in the wine industry in Australia.

Schubert's career was put on hold when he volunteered as a soldier during World War II; it has been said he did so remembering the stress and anxiety of his mother during World War I, when so many Barossans were suspected of support for the Germans. This was the best way he could prove their suspicions wrong, although he made no secret of the fact that he did not enjoy the life of a soldier.

He returned from the war to take up employment with Penfolds once again, and in 1948 was appointed production manager at Magill Winery. The story of his trip to Europe and the development of Grange Hermitage (now known as Penfolds Grange) has been told elsewhere. In 1960 he was appointed national production supervisor (effectively chief winemaker), and in the same year the production of Grange was officially resumed. He remained chief winemaker until 1973, when he retired, the position passing to Don Ditter. In 1984 he was awarded the Order of Australia (AM), further recognition coming in 1988 when *Decanter* magazine named him its Man of the Year, and in 1990 when he won the inaugural Maurice O'Shea Award. Thus the recognition he was due came many years after his retirement, but – happily – before his death, aged 79, in 1994.

Endeavouring to compare Max Schubert's contribution to winemaking with that of Maurice O'Shea, Colin Preece, Roger Warren, David Wynn, Ray Beckwith and John Fornachon is an apples and oranges comparison at best. If, however, you link Schubert, Fornachon and Beckwith, their joint contribution exceeds that of any other individual.

**scion** is the upper part of the vine grafted onto rootstock. The scion is almost invariably of the *Vitis vinifera* family, and will be any one of that family's innumerable varieties. The scion will be identical in both leaf growth and shape, and the grape bunches and individual berries will be identical, to those of the same variety planted on their own roots.

**Scotchmans Hill** (est. 1982) is the largest winery in Geelong, with a 70,000-case production, and significant contract winemaking on top of that. It was established by the Browne family, and thanks to long-serving (and only) senior winemaker Robin Brockett, consistently produces high-quality chardonnay, pinot noir, shiraz and cabernet sauvignon, at three price points (pinot gris and sauvignon blanc also part of the portfolio). Exports to all major markets.

**Scott Henry** is a vine training/canopy management system devised in the early 1980s by the Oregon vigneron whose name it takes. It is particularly useful where soil and rainfall promote vigour which is otherwise difficult to control. Properly managed, it allows higher yields without loss of quality, and is used to good effect in Australia.

**SC Pannell** (est. 2004) sprang to life when Stephen (Steve) Pannell (and wife Fiona) finally jumped ship from CWA to establish their own winemaking and consulting business. It came as no surprise that he should immediately make and release sauvignon blanc, shiraz, grenache and shiraz grenache blends of the highest quality, his greatest satisfaction coming from grenache and shiraz grenache blends, all

sourced from McLaren Vale. (The sauvignon blanc comes from the Adelaide Hills.)

**screwcaps** were invented in 1856 to seal glass jars, and in 1889 a screwcap was patented in the UK by one Dan Rylands. In 1926 they were introduced on whiskey bottles, and in the 1930s the University of California, Davis, conducted trials on bottled wine, including a 1936 colombard which was opened over 60 years later and found to be in very good condition. In the 1950s a number of companies developed versions of the screwcap, led by Le Bouchage Méchanique (LBM), which trademarked Stelcap. In 1959 systematic research began, in particular comparing the performance of Stelcaps with one-piece corks. In 1965, improved sealing wads demonstrated no difference between the performance of premium corks and Stelcaps; trials in Alsace in 1966 confirmed the results. In 1968 official approval was given in France for use of the closure as a seal for wine, and the following year Chateau Haut Brion commenced commercial trials. In 1970 Australian Consolidated Industries (ACI) obtained the licence to manufacture Stelcap closures in Australia, and Yalumba trialled Stelcaps over previously inserted corks. In 1970 and 1971 screwcaps were evaluated in Switzerland with white wines made from chasselas, and in 1972 the first commercial bottling of wine with screwcaps was carried out in Switzerland.

In 1973 a trial began in Australia under the direction of ACI and the Australian Wine Research Institute in conjunction with seven wine companies, and from 1975 to 1976 Saltram, McWilliam's, Yalumba, Hungerford Hill and others released red and white wines with screwcaps. It was in the latter year that the results of three-way blind tastings conducted over the prior three years confirmed the success of the screwcap manufactured by ACI and called Stelvin. In that year Yalumba carried out the first commercial bottling of riesling under Stelvin, Montana in New Zealand following suit. In 1979 Chateau Haut Brion abandoned the hitherto successful trial after the caps had failed due to defective liner materials. Notwithstanding the absence of any technical problems in Australia, Yalumba and the other companies ceased the use of screwcaps because of market resistance. At the same time the use of screwcaps in Switzerland was growing rapidly, reaching 10 million screwcaps per year in 1990 and exceeding 60 million by 1995. Californian producer Sutter Home had gone down the same track, and in 1995 sealed more than 10 million bottles with screwcaps. In 2000 Australian winemakers in the Clare Valley banded together to launch their rieslings under screwcap, quickly followed by New Zealand, and by 2003 worldwide shortages of screwcaps led to five-month production lead times.

In 2004 the large Burgundian negociant business of Jean-Claude Boisset was presented with bottles of a 1966 Mercurey, a pinot noir from the Chalonnaise region of Burgundy, and reported, 'It turned out that the wine had absolute freshness, great body and was in superb condition.' This led to Boisset commercially releasing bottles of red burgundy up to grand cru level wine under screwcap. Boisset had, however, been pre-empted by the release of grand cru chablis under screwcap by Michel Laroche. Continuing trials by the AWRI through the first decade of the 21st century repeatedly confirmed the superiority of screwcap over all other closures in terms of freedom from taint, and, more importantly, freedom from random oxidation.

In 2004, 25 per cent of all Australian wines were bottled under screwcap. By 2009, 78.2 per cent of Australian wines were so closed; 12.1 per cent used one-piece (conventional) corks, 4.8 per cent used Diam, and the remainder was spread across the membrane-covered ProCork, Twin Top, the glass-button Vin-o-lok, the curious plastic Zork and various synthetic corks.

It is asserted by some that screwcaps cause reduction, but the vast majority of researchers and scientists do not agree, postulating that wine bottled with the potential to show reduction will do so regardless of the closure, and will in fact do so, in particular, with cork closures. (Some synthetic materials are capable of absorbing thiols and other precursors.) This apart, the argument that screwcaps inhibit the proper ageing of red wine is rejected by most (but not all) researchers. They point out that the changes of age are anaerobic, and that the amount of oxygen in solution in the wine when it is bottled, and any oxygen introduced into the headspace between the bottom of the closure and the top of the wine, will be consumed within one month of bottling. Thereafter the changes will be anaerobic unless the cork fails to prevent the ingress of oxygen, which leads to random oxidation.

semillon, a white grape variety, was one of the more than 600 varieties collected by James Busby during an extraordinary wine odyssey through Europe, starting in Spain and finishing in Champagne. Unfortunately, not all survived the trip to Australia. He collected 52 of the classic varieties on his trip but, having bypassed Bordeaux, procured the Bordeaux varieties from the nursery of the Luxembourg Garden at Paris. Vines propagated from the six cuttings procured from the Luxembourg nursery provided the basis for the semillon which went almost immediately to the Hunter Valley, planted at his brother-in-law James Kelman's vineyard, then finding its way to a local nurseryman called Shepherd. Correct nomenclature in those days was a hit-and-miss affair, and the grape (and wine) soon became known as Shepherd's riesling and in time changed to Hunter River riesling, usage which survived on some wine labels until the 1980s.

Whether or not anyone raised elsewhere than Sydney has any empathy with (young) Hunter Valley semillon is beside the point: the greatest semillons are made in the Hunter Valley by treading a very narrow path. The grapes will be picked with a potential alcohol of 10–10.5% alc/vol; they will (usually) be whole bunch pressed, and the juice cold-settled, or centrifuged to total clarity. A carefully selected, neutral cultured yeast will be used for the fermentation, which will take place at low temperatures (about 15–18°C) in stainless steel tanks. As soon as the fermentation is finished, the wine will be racked off its lees, sterile filtered and bottled as soon as possible, usually mid-year. If the wine is to be held in bottle for around five years prior to release, the level of free sulphur dioxide and of $CO_2$ at bottling will be somewhat higher than it will be for a wine destined for release in the year of its vintage.

At the opposite end of the spectrum is (or was: mercifully it is in fast retreat) the Barossa Valley approach of crushing the grapes and giving the must extended skin contact prior to pressing, then barrel fermenting the wine in German or American oak. The fat, oily, coarse, rapidly ageing wine which resulted was, to say the least, unfortunate, and did nothing to raise the reputation of the variety. The most miraculous transformation has been that wrought by Peter Lehmann under the direction of chief winemaker Andrew Wigan. The winemaking team simply took a near-identical approach in the winery to that of the Hunter Valley, the only difference being slightly higher alcohol (11–11.5% alc/vol). Two wines are made, one released in the year of vintage, the other five years later. Both are under screwcap, and the late release (Margaret Semillon) is from the best vineyard blocks in the Eden Valley.

However, in various parts of Australia (notably the Adelaide Hills and the Margaret River), semillon picked at the same potential alcohol as the Barossa Valley (around 13% alc/vol), whole bunch pressed and then partially barrel-fermented in French oak, and often blended with sauvignon blanc in the manner of white Bordeaux, makes an excellent wine.

Australia briefly flirted with semillon chardonnay blends, but not for any noble purpose. On the contrary, in the 1970s and '80s, when chardonnay was in desperately short supply, the 'sem-chard' (a name as nauseating as 'cab sav', and invented in California) was a marriage of convenience, sanctified – if that's the right word – for the sole purpose of making the chardonnay stretch further. The acceptance of the blend in the US has resulted in a revival of its fortunes, but has done little for its quality: the wine sells on price point (low) and shelf position. Finally there is botrytis semillon, every bit as luscious as (French) sauternes, and made in a similar fashion, barrel-fermented and aged for up to 12 months in French oak.

The plantings of semillon remained largely unchanged between 2005 and 2008, but both plantings and tonnage are likely to retreat from their 2008 levels of around 6700 ha and 100,000 tonnes as production from the Murray Darling, and perhaps the Riverina further down the track, decreases.

**Seppelt** (est. 1868) is but a shadow of its former self, with the separation of the Seppeltsfield brand, winery and fortified wine stocks. The upside of this is that Seppelt has become a wholly Victorian operation, its winery with its unique underground cellars (or drives) created in the wake of the petering-out of the gold mines in 1870. Joseph Best, who founded what is today Seppelt, made the princely amount of 170 litres of wine in his first vintage, in 1868. But the business grew rapidly, and former goldminers excavated what was to all intents and purposes a large underground winery. By the time of Joseph Best's sudden death in 1887 at the age of 57, his wines had won numerous gold and silver medals at international exhibitions in London, Philadelphia, Bordeaux and Amsterdam, not to mention the 1875 Melbourne Intercolonial Exhibition, where he took first prize. A bachelor who died intestate, his estate was offered for sale and purchased by Hans Irvine, a Ballarat businessman. It comprised 22 ha of vines, 182 ha of grazing land and the cellars with a stock of around 318,500 litres of wine. The purchase price was £12,000.

Irvine embarked on a major expansion program, immediately planting another 16 ha

of grapes in the area surrounding the winery, and between 1880 and 1890 acquiring an additional 60 ha of vineyard 4 kilometres to the south in a locality known as Arawatta. In 1890 he planted 21 ha of a variety which he called white pinot, and which for many years was called Irvine's white; it was finally identified as ondenc, a variety grown in the south of France. There can be little doubt Irvine thought he was planting chardonnay, and one can only imagine what might have happened had he procured the correct variety, for these plantings were established with one thing in mind: to produce bottle-fermented sparkling wine according to the méthode champenoise. In the same year he employed a French-trained champagne maker who was born near Rheims in France and who had worked at Pommery. Charles Pierlot was joined shortly after by another Frenchman, Julian Grellet, who was in charge of the vineyards.

In 1892 new red-brick cellars were erected at a cost of £2000: 110 feet long and 60 feet wide (33.5 x 18 metres), the cellars had a capacity of 300,000 gallons (1.365 million litres) of wine. Specialised machinery was imported from France for the making of the sparkling wine, and Hans Irvine was in business. Pierlot left after an argument in 1896, but apparently returned two years later. Certainly the 'champagne' making flourished, and by 1907 over 1.6 kilometres of drives had been excavated; these provided storage both for the bottles of sparkling wine and for the 300-gallon (1365-litre) oak vats of table wine.

Although he was married, Hans Irvine had no children. In his capacity as president of the Victorian Viticultural Society he had become close friends with Benno Seppelt of

Seppeltsfield, as a consequence of which Benno Seppelt was given a right of first refusal to acquire the property if Irvine ever decided to sell. This occurred in 1918; Hans Irvine died four years later while on a visit to London, at the age of 66.

The first manager/winemaker appointed by Seppelt was Reginald Mowatt, a Roseworthy Agricultural College graduate, who remained at Great Western until 1932. Between 1918 and 1923 an additional 50 ha of vineyard were established, followed by 4.5 ha in 1928. In 1932 Mowatt resigned, and was replaced by another Roseworthy graduate, Colin Preece, who had worked at Seppeltsfield since his graduation in 1923. It was the start of a glorious era for Great Western, for Preece turned out to be a most talented winemaker, and had a rare understanding of the rather particular style of Great Western fruit.

It is similar grapes (Great Western is now known as the Grampians) which are the basis for the present-day intake, which takes in the shiraz planted in 1928 adjacent to the winery, the wholly owned Glenlofty vineyard in the Pyrenees, the Mount Ida vineyard in Bendigo and the Drumborg vineyard in Henty, all supplemented by a substantial amount of grapes from prime vineyards across the central and southern Victorian regions.

**Seppelt 100 Year Para Liqueur** see Seppeltsfield.

**Seppeltsfield** (est. 1852) remained in the ownership of the Seppelt family for over 100 years, and was managed by the Seppelt family after it was listed on the stock exchange in 1970. The story begins with Joseph Seppelt, who arrived in South Australia with his wife, Johanna, and two sons, Oscar and Hugo. The son of a wealthy factory owner, he brought with him adequate capital, and in February 1852 he purchased a number of blocks of land in the Tanunda district. The family business in Germany had involved the manufacture of tobacco snuff and liquor products; however, after finding that the district was unsuited to tobacco growing, Joseph Seppelt turned his attention to corn, wheat and grapes. He also persuaded his neighbours to plant grapes, and the first vintage was made in the family dairy.

In 1867 the nucleus of the present-day vast complex of stone buildings which constitutes Seppeltsfield was built. From this point on the business grew at a quite remarkable rate: by 1875 the estate was 225 ha, and the 1867 winery had been doubled in size. Three years later a massive building program quadrupled the capacity of the 1875 building, and in 1885 yet another winery was commenced. The 1887 vintage was 900,000 litres, with a very large portion of production being exported to England. Growth continued unabated: 2 million litres of wine were produced in 1903; approximately one-third of this came from the Seppelt vineyards, which by this time had grown to 600 ha.

While the Seppelt business proliferated significantly over the next 70 years, little of it has relevance to the Seppeltsfield of today. What is paramount is the quite exceptional array of fortified wines which date back to 1878. The pinnacle is the 100 Year Para Liqueur. The first barrels were laid down in 1878 by Benno Seppelt, and barrels have been laid down each year ever since. As they age, and the volume shrinks, they are gradually combined into one 500-litre puncheon, and when wine is finally drawn off for bottling, only part is taken, the remainder being transferred to a smaller barrel, and so on. Benno Seppelt specified that the wine was not to be bottled until it was 100 years old, and subsequent generations obeyed that command, so the first release was in 1978, and there has been and will continue to be an annual release.

Through a series of corporate takeovers, Seppeltsfield became part of Foster's, and in 2007 was sold to a syndicate of investors headed by Nathan Waks and Janet Holmes à Court (see Kilikanoon).

**Setanta Wines** (est. 1997) is a family-owned operation in the Adelaide Hills involving Sheilagh Sullivan, her husband, Tony, and brother, Bernard; the latter is the viticulturist, while Tony and Sheilagh manage marketing, administration and so forth. Of Irish parentage (they are first-generation Australians), they chose Setanta, Ireland's most famous mythological hero, as the brand name. The beautiful and striking labels tell the individual stories which gave rise to the names of the impeccably made wines. Exports to Ireland, of course; also to the UK, Dubai, Singapore, Hong Kong and Japan.

**Sevenhill Cellars** (est. 1851) was born of the promise of religious freedom, which brought many races and creeds to South Australia in the 1840s. The success of the German Lutherans in settling in the Barossa Valley became well known in Europe, and in 1848 a wealthy Silesian farmer, Franz Weikert, determined to gather a band of his countrymen to emigrate to South Australia.

Silesia, now part of Poland but then one of the provinces of Prussia, was predominantly Catholic, and Weikert applied to the Superior of the Jesuits of the Austro-Hungarian province for two chaplains. The Jesuits had themselves received an expulsion order from Emperor Leopold two weeks earlier, so the request was well timed.

Two priests volunteered. One returned to Europe through ill health shortly after his arrival; the other, a Tyrolean who had been ordained for only six weeks, was Father Kranewitter. The group landed in Port Adelaide on 8 December 1848. Dissension had broken out on the trip, so it was a relatively small party that accompanied Weikert to Clare, where he had decided to settle. Kranewitter accompanied Weikert, and settled nearby at Neagles Rock, southwest of the township of Clare. In April 1849 he was joined by Brothers George Sadler SJ and John Schreiner SJ. They worked day and night, walking overnight to Burra to sell butter to the miners until the purchase of a horse increased both their mobility and their earnings.

In January 1851 Father Kranewitter was able to buy the first parcel of land, part of a property known as Open Ranges, for the sum of £2 an acre, payable by instalments over 20 years. He renamed the property Sevenhill (without an 's') because it was hoped it would become a centre of Catholicism in the north, a little Rome with its seven hills. With the marvellous sense of humour which continued in the person of Brother John May, they named the tiny stream which (sometimes) flows through the property the Tiber. Their grand plans called for a college, a college-church, colonnaded walks around a paved quadrangle, and a village with broad streets – Industry Road, Commercial Street, College Street and so on.

Later in that same year the priests obtained cuttings from the Hawker brothers' farming property, Bungaree, for the purpose of establishing a vineyard to make sacramental wine. (These vines, to the west of the winery, are still in production.) Wine purchased in Europe for this purpose was not only expensive, but frequently arrived diseased and out of condition. The vineyards flourished, and Brother Schreiner (who, like Kranewitter, was an Austrian) is credited with having brought tokay and crouchen (or Clare riesling, as it was then called) to the district. The first wine press was built by Brothers Schreiner and Schneider in 1863, and was capable of processing four buckets of grapes at a time – hardly large-scale winemaking. Rough cellars had been excavated in 1851 and were covered by a lean-to. The magnificent underground arched stone cellars, still very much in use, were built in the early 1860s, and Mintaro slate fermentation tanks were installed; these remained in use until the 1970s.

While it has been suggested from time to time that Sevenhill made only sacramental wine until the 1950s, this is simply not so. Even as early as 1858 it seems they were not averse to selling a little brandy, while records from the 1890s show that the 'best claret' was sold for 6 shillings a gallon (4.5 litres), 'the keg to be returned as soon as possible'.

In 1863 the decision was taken to build the splendid church which now dominates Sevenhill. The foundation stone was laid on 15 August 1864, and building operations commenced the following month. A year later, with the stonework only partially completed

(and filled with wood), building operations were halted owing to lack of funds. The Brothers had shown an all-too-temporal failure to control expenditure, and for several years Sevenhill battled to survive. This it did; building operations were resumed in 1870 and the church was completed in 1874.

Throughout this time Brother John Schreiner remained in charge of winemaking; indeed, since 1851 there have been only seven winemakers at Sevenhill: 1851–84, Brother John Schreiner; 1884–89, Brother Francis Lenz; 1889–1916, Brother Patrick Storey; 1917–24, Brother Peter Boehmer; 1925–52, Brother George Downey; 1952–72, Brother John Hanlon; 1972–2002, Brother John May; and from 2005, Liz Heidenreich.

In 1925 Brother George Downey took up his position as winemaker, and immediately produced a wine which was remembered with awe and affection by wine lovers such as the late Max Lake, who was privileged to drink it. The cellar book gives little hint of what was to come: after recording that all of the shiraz, tokay, grenache, pedro and frontignac were fortified with 'fifteen proof gallons [68 litres] of spirit to every 100 gallons [450 litres] of wine' (and that only the mataro, doradillo and riesling were made as dry wine), it goes on: 'There was three and a half press full's [sic] (little square press) of skins to 400 gallons [1820 litres] of liquid shiraz, a little bit too light in colour, for a good-coloured port.' Evidently the pressings had done their work well, because the words 'a little bit too light in colour' had been crossed out later and the concluding words 'for a good-coloured port' written in with the same hand (Downey's) but with a different pen. This became the 1925 Sevenhill Port, recognised as one of the greatest wines of its style ever produced in Australia, and on a par with the 1945 Stonyfell.

In 1952 Brother John Hanlon became winemaker, and for the first time Sevenhill bottled red wine became available through retail outlets. Brother John May records that: 'During Brother John Hanlon's time the last horse was sold for 35 pounds, and two tractors were purchased to begin the era of mechanised vineyard farming at Sevenhill. He installed concrete Hume pipe fermentation tanks, a continuous press and numerous pumps to facilitate winemaking.'

The arrival of Brother John May in 1972 heralded a significant increase in and restoration of the estate vineyards, by now 72 ha, and the erection of a modern processing and fermentation winery with all the equipment considered essential in the 21st century. He ceased to be physically involved in winemaking in 2002, whereafter lay winemakers were employed. As at 2009 Liz Heidenreich was winemaker, the first woman to hold this position. The rosy-cheeked John May goes to work five days a week, involved in an advisory capacity, and conducts tours, collects the mail and does the banking and so forth. He says, 'For me, retirement is only a word,' adding, 'I have never had an argument over pay,' an oblique way of saying he received no wages as a winemaker.

**Shadowfax** (est. 2000) is one of the leading wineries of Geelong, established in the Werribee Park development, little more than 20 minutes' drive from Melbourne. The home on the property was built in the 1880s by the Chirnside family, and known as The Mansion. It was then the centrepiece of a 40,000-ha pastoral empire, and the appropriately magnificent gardens were part of the reason why the property was acquired by Parks Victoria in the early 1970s. The Mansion is now The Mansion Hotel, with 92 rooms and suites, and a highly rated restaurant. The striking winery has given birth to a consistently outstanding range of wines, part estate-grown, part from Geelong, and part from regions such as Adelaide Hills, Heathcote and the Macedon Ranges. Different styles of chardonnay and shiraz are the main focus. Exports to the UK, Japan, NZ and Singapore.

**Shaw & Smith** (est. 1989) was begun when Martin Shaw, a highly intelligent and skilled flying winemaker and Petaluma winemaker, joined forces with cousin Michael Hill Smith, the first Australian to receive a Master of Wine, and who was responsible for the MW program being expanded to take in other countries. (Previously any aspirant had to live and work in England as a prerequisite to sitting the exams.) Their business has developed from a virtual winery, with contract-grown grapes and shared-space winemaking at Petaluma, to an Adelaide Hills estate-based 51-ha vineyard at Balhannah and a winery, administration and cellar door complex which is at once very beautiful and highly functional. Its 35,000-case production, and its financial driver, has been and is its sauvignon blanc, but since 2000 its M3 Chardonnay and its shiraz have leapt to the very top of the quality tree in Australia. It also produces small quantities of riesling and pinot noir for sale at the cellar door. Exports to all major markets.

**Shelmerdine Vineyards** (est. 1989) has dual residence in the Yarra Valley and Heathcote. It is the venture of Stephen Shelmerdine (and his wife), who has been a major figure in the wine industry for well over 20 years – like his family (which founded Mitchelton) before him – and has been honoured for his many services to the industry. The business has 130 ha of vineyard spread over three sites: Lusatia Park in the Yarra Valley, and Merindoc Vineyard and Willoughby Bridge in the Heathcote region. Substantial quantities of the grapes produced are sold to others; 10,000 cases of high-quality wine are made by Steve Webber at De Bortoli. Webber and Shelmerdine also have a joint venture label, PHI, which likewise produces wines of very high quality from selected rows of grapes at the Lusatia Park vineyard. Exports to the UK, Singapore and Hong Kong.

**Shepherd's riesling** was the original (and incorrect) name in the Hunter Valley for semillon.

**sherry** see apera.

**shiraz** is Australia's single most important red grape variety. Its plantings (43,417 ha in 2008, 44 per cent of the nation's red grape vineyards and 25 per cent of all plantings) and tonnage (441,900 in the 2008 vintage, 24 per cent of the total 2008 crush of 1,837,034 tonnes) are on a par with those of chardonnay. However, the whole world makes chardonnay, and it is suffering a certain amount of contempt borne of familiarity, whereas no other country has shiraz as old as Australia's, nor plantings anywhere near as large. As with many other of Australia's varieties, it was thanks to James Busby that 12 cuttings from the Hill of Hermitage in the northern Rhône Valley arrived in 1832, and were quickly propagated, with cuttings or rootlings soon planted in the Hunter Valley and elsewhere in New South Wales, and in many parts of South Australia.

The oldest planting in South Australia is a 2-ha block dating from 1843 which produces Langmeil's The Freedom Shiraz, and vines planted one or two years later at what is now the Turkey Flat vineyard in the Barossa Valley. In 1847 Joseph Gilbert planted it at his Pewsey Vale vineyard; Samuel Smith at Yalumba successfully planted a little over 5.5 ha in 1852; in 1860 Tahbilk planted a block of shiraz on a sandy knoll which is the oldest block without any younger vines introduced over the ensuing 150 years to replace those which had died; in the 1860s (the exact date is not known) the first vines on Henschke's Hill of Grace were planted; and isolated blocks of vines dating from the same decade survive in the Hunter Valley.

Australia has 62 Geographic Indications, and shiraz is present in every one of them. It has proved extraordinarily adaptable to the vast range of climate and soil, with a unique ability to reflect that climate and soil without losing varietal integrity. Thus the styles range from relatively low-alcohol (plus or minus 12.5% alc/vol), spicy, cherry-flavoured wines (which flourish when 5 per cent or less viognier is co-fermented with the shiraz) through to towering, monolithic Barossa Valley shiraz, alcohol sometimes exceeding 16% alc/vol. In between are the elegant, long-lived wines of Coonawarra, upon which Coonawarra made its reputation (not, as commonly assumed, cabernet sauvignon); the long-lived shiraz of the Hunter Valley, with moderate alcohol levels, starting life with distinctly leathery and earthy overtones and slowly but surely assuming a silky smoothness, with spicy notes developing; the luscious, layered black-fruited examples from Central Victoria, with Heathcote leading the way; the very spicy, peppery wines of Sunbury, home to Craiglee, the 1874 vintage surviving in a sunken part of the cellar until discovered in the 1960s, still alive and well, and with an alcohol of only 10.5% alc/vol; the increasingly important wines from both the Margaret River and Great Southern regions of Western Australia, the fruit generous but never heavy-footed, spice and pepper never far away; and vibrant cool-climate examples from the Mornington Peninsula, Yarra Valley and Geelong. Even here, one has barely touched the surface.

**Shoalhaven Coast,** gazetted 6 August 2002, in the South Coast Zone of New South Wales, stretches from Kiama in the north past Ulladulla in the south, hugging the coastline with its western boundary essentially falling on the eastern side of the Great Dividing Range, although the straight lines of the boundary deny any altitude or contour determinants. Most of the wineries have been established since the early 1970s, and all rely heavily on cellar door sales to tourists.

The principal threat to viticulture lies with unpredictable but sometimes substantial summer rainfall, a problem which diminishes somewhat as you move south. It is a situation with which the Hunter Valley and New South Wales' north coast wineries are thoroughly familiar, and fortunately it is far from insuperable. Nonetheless, it seems almost certain that vineyard holdings along the coast – and winery size – will remain small, and

that the major developments of the future will continue to take place on the interior (or western) side of the Great Dividing Range.

What is more, it is notable that the two most successful wineries, Cambewarra Estate and Coolangatta Estate (the latter with wonderful five-year-old semillons), rely on contract winemaking by experienced wineries in the Hunter Valley. Making small quantities of wine in isolated regions has never been easy unless the winemaker has both experience and technical qualifications. Yet here, more than in any other region, the key to success rests with the tourist trade. It is not that the central and southern coasts are especially desirable or suitable places in which to grow grapes – quite simply, they are not – but they are desirable places in which to market wine. It is generally accepted that the overall quality of wine made by the small winery of today is significantly better than that of 20 years ago. What is not clear is just how discerning the average tourist is about wine style and quality; good may be good enough for these wineries.

Growing season temperatures are especially moderate, with extremely high summer temperatures uncommon due to the strong maritime influence of the Pacific Ocean. High humidity also diminishes stress on vines and aids growth, but – together with summer rainfall – significantly increases the risk of downy and powdery mildew and botrytis. The soil varies in depth and consistency from the alluvial valleys to the hillsides, but most are red and brown earths which are well suited to viticulture and which promote good yields. Well-exposed, well-drained and ventilated slopes are best. The plantings are slanted to white varieties, although cabernet sauvignon, shiraz and chambourcin (the latter resistant to the summer rainfall) are also important.

LAT 36°40'S; ALT 10–70 m; HDD 1900; GSR 324 mm; MJT 22.1°C; HARV Mid-February to mid-March; CHIEF VIT. HAZARDS Vintage rainfall; mildew

**Sirromet Wines** (est. 1998) is Queensland's most important winery, established by the Morris family (with a large industrial construction business providing the funds) and marked by the building of a large and striking winery southeast of Brisbane, looking out over the Coral Sea. Partly for cosmetic reasons, 17 ha of vines (primarily chambourcin) were planted around the winery; infinitely more important are the 124 ha of vines in the Granite Belt planted to all the classic *vinifera* varieties. The quality of the wines is commendably consistent, and Sirromet exports to all major markets.

**Smart, Richard** (1945–) has the highest international profile of any Australian viticulturist, with a long and distinguished record in both research and practical spheres. He studied agricultural science at the University of Sydney before taking up his first appointment in 1965 in viticultural research at Griffith, New South Wales. His initial research interests were in irrigation, vine physiology and canopy microclimate. Subsequently he completed an MSc (Hons) degree at Macquarie University and a PhD degree at Cornell University of New York under Professor Nelson Shaulis, studying canopy microclimate effects on yield. From 1975 to 1981 he taught at Roseworthy Agricultural College in South Australia (now Roseworthy Campus of the University of Adelaide). In April 1980 he and fellow lecturer Dr Peter Dry published a very

detailed and groundbreaking comparison between the climates of 44 sites (or regions) in Australia with the climates of Montpellier in the south of France, Bordeaux, Burgundy, Alsace and Champagne. His ongoing studies resulted in an even more important publication in 1991, the handbook *Sunlight into Wine* (Winetitles of Adelaide), which has remained one of the standard texts for grapegrowers in Australasia. From this point on his consultancy work progressively expanded into Europe (particularly Spain), South America and North America. Before his theories and methods were adequately understood, he was able to walk into vineyards with poorly trained canopies and say (with truth), 'I can increase the yield of the vines and the quality of the grapes.' He also has a particular interest in climate change.

**Smithbrook** (est. 1988) is a major player in the Pemberton region, with over 60 ha of vines in production. It is owned by Petaluma/ Lion Nathan, but continues its role as a contract grower for other companies, as well as supplying Petaluma's needs and making wine under its own label. Perhaps the most significant change has been the removal of pinot noir from the range of products, and the introduction of merlot. Exports to the UK, Canada and Japan.

**smoke taint** of grapes has become a major problem in parts of Australia, South Africa and California in the first decade of this century. Expansion of vineyards into forested country, prolonged drought and associated extreme heat events have increased the risk of fires and attendant smoke. At the same time, there has been a steady increase in the understanding of the way smoke taint characters find their way into wine, of the chemical composition of key taint components, and of the concentration of those components that is sufficient to trigger sensory perception of taint in the berries, juice and wine. Growing awareness of the problem also shows that experienced tasters are becoming more sensitive to the taint, and able to detect it in ever-decreasing concentrations.

Major bushfire events in 2003, 2007 and 2009 in southeastern Australia have simultaneously added to research knowledge and awareness of the problem by grapegrowers and winemakers, but many questions remain unanswered. It is established that guaiacol and 4-methylguaiacol (4EG) are markers, and correlate with the perceived level of taint. The Australian Wine Research Institute has a commercial technique readily able to determine the concentration of each of these two substances in leaves, grapes, must and finished wine. However, as yet, there is no identification of the dozens, possibly hundreds, of other compounds that also play a role. To make matters more complicated, no two fires are the same, so the taint compounds will likely vary in relative concentrations.

Studies which began in 2003 show that the compounds are present in the skins, but not in the pulp of the grape, nor on its exterior. It is also known that the level of taint continues to increase for weeks, or months, after the fire event. Moreover, grapes are significantly more sensitive to taint pre-veraison than post-veraison. Efforts to reduce the taint by sophisticated washing of the berries have proved fruitless.

All this strongly suggests that the compounds are trapped on the leaves and are then translocated through the vine's system to ultimately reach the skins. In the absence of controlled experiments (exceedingly difficult, if not impossible) this remains a hypothesis, albeit a very convincing one. The one piece of good news is that there is no evidence that the compounds remain in the vine's system sufficiently long to compromise the crop of the following vintage.

The response for white wines is to hand-pick, chill the bunches overnight, whole bunch press in a bladder tank press, and separate the juice at around 400 litres per tonne (out of a total of a possible 700 litres). This necessarily presumes a high value in the finished wine, because the picking and handling costs are substantial.

The options for red wines are extremely limited. Hand-harvesting (and exclusion of leaves and leaf fragments) is the first step. Ignoring rosés for the moment, red wine colour comes only from the skins, as does a significant amount of flavour. Analysis of smoke-tainted red grapes, must and wine in 2003 showed that 25–33 per cent of the total guaiacol present in the grapes was extracted within 24 hours of crushing – in other words, before fermentation had commenced. The concentration of guaiacol increased in a near linear manner for the first three or four days of fermentation, and increased only slightly thereafter. Free-run, light and heavy press fractions all contained the same concentration of guaiacol and 4EG.

The consequence is that it is impossible to sidestep the taint if you are making red wine, and very difficult for rosés. Therefore, are there ways of removing the taint? There is some ongoing experimental work with the use of special yeasts and the addition of high levels of tannin (subsequently diminished by fining), but no published results exist (in Australia).

This leaves the magic of reverse osmosis. As at April 2009 the situation was that RO (as it is called for short) was effective in reducing the degree of taint by one-third, on the basis of chemical analysis. What is unknown is whether RO removed compounds other than guaiacol responsible for taint. Disconcertingly, there was no significant difference in sensory preference by the expert tasting panel between the treated and untreated samples.

Moreover, there are numerous verbally reported findings that, having initially been reduced (by sensory and scientific analysis), the taint reappears or increases as the wine ages in barrel. Guaiacol and 4EG are stable compounds, and there will in fact be no change in their analysed levels post-treatment. It appears that, as the intense primary fruit of a young red wine in barrel diminishes (which it always does), the taint becomes more obvious.

This is in turn consistent with findings that smoky characters in white juice intended for sparkling wine could be detected at 6–10 mg/l (micrograms per litre, or parts per billion), a level likely to be similar for (unoaked) semillon, riesling and pinot noir; at 15–25 mg/l in medium-bodied dry reds; and at 30–40 mg/l in full-bodied warm-region shiraz. There are those who suggest that the levels at which taint can be smelt and tasted are significantly lower than even these minute amounts.

The obvious question is how the taint characters are detected and described. At low levels, terms such as 'smoky', 'burnt' and 'ash' are used; at higher levels it is 'cigarette', 'ashtray' and 'acrid', with a 'hard', 'metallic' and

'persistently unpleasant' finish. The paradox is that concentrations of 20 mg/l are considered a highly positive outcome from the use of new oak barrels which are of medium toast (the most commonly used). This strongly supports the belief that there are unidentified compounds which are increasing the impact and adding to the unpleasant consequences of smoke taint.

soil is a small word encompassing a wide range of topics, albeit with different emphases in the New World from the Old World (and vice versa). In its simplest and most basic form it is the result of the breaking down of rock by climate and vegetation, the latter originally in microscopic form. In this narrow view it is rocks that have been reduced to small fragments and which have been changed chemically, together with the remains of plants or animals that lived in it or on it. This, however, does not take into account the all-important questions of soil structure, depth, fertility, nutrient status, texture and water-holding capacity.

For most New World grapegrowers and consultants, the most significant attributes are: permeability, allowing the vine roots to penetrate deep into the subsoil; balance between free-draining capacity and water-holding capacity; pH (acid soils inhibit vigour, alkaline soils promote vigour); and nutrient status, chiefly measured in the amount of organic compounds present. Within these parameters, one type of soil satisfying the criteria should be no better or worse than any other type of soil. Specifically, New World grapegrowers do not believe that there is any translocation of either mineral or organic substances in the soil into the grape berries.

For those holding this belief, climate has a greater impact on the flavour and quality of the wine ultimately produced.

In the Old World, soil is regarded as part of terroir, its importance indivisible from climate. Although most research scientists do not suggest that there is translocation of matter from the soil which can ultimately be found in the grapes, there is often an assumption, explicit or implicit, that this is so.

**solids** is a non-technical term which is mainly used in the context of white grape juice prior to fermentation and encompasses fine particles of skin and pulp in suspension in the juice. Makers of chardonnay and other barrel-fermented white wines may well deliberately leave a percentage of solids in the juice, thus gaining flavour complexity.

**sour** is a term denoting a wine with excessive acidity, often a by-product of unripe grapes, and usually manifesting itself on the back of the palate and in the aftertaste.

**South Burnett,** gazetted 8 December 2000, is the second of the two official Geographic Indications in Queensland. While the modern viticultural history of the South Burnett region dates back only to 1993, vines were first planted in the last years of the 19th century, and wine for home consumption was made from some of these vines. The great-grandfather of one of the modern-day vignerons planted shiraz in 1898, and the vineyard remained in production until 1970. As in the Granite Belt, table grapes were used both for winemaking and eating, and a small table grape industry has continued since that time.

The town of Kingaroy is the geographical centre of the region, which is basically defined by the Blackbutt, Brisbane and Coast Ranges in the east, the Great Divide to the southwest and west, and the Central Burnett and Burnett River to the north. The Stuart and Booie Ranges run south to north through the centre of South Burnett, with undulating, rolling landscape to the Stuart and Boyne river plain to the west and Barkers Creek in the east. The majority of wineries are clustered around Kingaroy or Murgon (to the north). So far the western half has no wineries. Vineyards compete with all manner of farms, from peanuts to orchards to pigs to grains and the remnants of once-dominant grazing. A feature of the region is the large Bjelke-Petersen dam, used extensively for boating and fishing in the holiday seasons.

South Burnett is subtropical, with long summers and mild winters; rainfall is spread throughout the year, with more falling in the growing season than in winter. The hottest months are December and January. During an average year, there are only 10 days where the temperature exceeds 32°C and one day when the temperature is over 38°C. So, while the area is hot, temperature variability is relatively low compared with other inland grapegrowing regions. Temperatures are comparable throughout the region except for a minor effect of elevation.

The soils are principally basalt and granite derived, with small areas of volcanic soils in northern parts of the region. At lower elevations sandy alluvial soils are common, and on slopes red soils of light clay, through to brown and black clay, dominate. The red, brown and black soils are quite fertile, and controlling vine vigour becomes an issue.

Mainstream varieties are the order of the day, with a bias towards red; in descending order they are shiraz, chardonnay, cabernet sauvignon, merlot, semillon and verdelho. The principal winery is Clovely Estate.

**LAT** 26°00'S; **ALT** 300–600 m; **HDD** 2500; **GSR** 490 mm; **MJT** 23.8°C; **HARV** End January to early March; **CHIEF VIT. HAZARD** Hail

**South Coast Zone** of New South Wales takes in (for obvious reasons) the Shoalhaven Coast, but for less obvious reasons the Southern Highlands, which physically has no connection to the coast, even if the climate is affected by summer rainfall in the same way as the coast.

**Southcorp** was the corporate head of a large number of very well known wineries, most obviously Penfolds, Lindemans, Wynns Coonawarra and Rosemount Estate, acquired by Foster's in 2005. For details of the wineries and brands see Foster's Wine Estates.

**Southern Eyre Peninsula** – and the Yorke Peninsula on the eastern side of the Spencer Gulf – is at an embryonic state viticulturally, although the two wineries on the Eyre Peninsula are over 20 years old. It seems remoteness, rather than lack of appropriate conditions for grapegrowing, has held back the rate of development. The strong maritime influence of the Spencer Gulf, combined with patches of terra rossa over limestone soils similar to Coonawarra, make the area particularly suited to full-bodied red wine production from shiraz, merlot and cabernet sauvignon; riesling and chardonnay have also performed quite well. Viticulture on the Yorke Peninsula has been slower to develop, although the climate and terra rossa sandy loams on its southeastern quadrant seem equally suited to quality grapegrowing. There are only two wineries in the region: Boston Bay and Delacolline Estate.

**LAT** 33°30'S; **ALT** 50–100 m; **HDD** 1655; **GSR** 161 mm; **MJT** 20°C; **HARV** Early March to April; **CHIEF VIT. HAZARD** Birds

**Southern Fleurieu**, gazetted 6 June 2001, is one of the newer wine regions of South Australia and one which, buffered as it is by the Southern Ocean, may assume more prominence if the worst fears of climate change do eventuate. This apart, as with Kangaroo Island, the vineyards and wineries are but one of numerous tourist attractions. The undulating slopes and gentle hills pose no limitations to viticulture, simply enhancing the beauty of the vineyards and the diversity of the scenery. This is quite distinct from any other part of the Fleurieu Zone, and the quality of the wines made to date will almost certainly lead to further plantings and developments.

Settlement began in the middle of the 19th century, and rapidly diversified into flour mills for locally grown wheat, a brewery and extensive grazing. Viticulture began with the arrival of Buxton Laurie (the ancestor of a distinguished wine family in the regions around Adelaide) in the 1860s. By 1876 his Southcote Vineyards near Port Elliot covered 180 ha; they were destroyed by massive bushfires in the 1890s. Other vineyards in the region escaped, although by the turn of the century activity had ceased. It was only reactivated after a gap of nearly 90 years.

The eminent viticultural climate researcher Dr John Gladstones has written, in *Viticulture and Environment* (Winetitles, Adelaide, 2002), 'At least in climatic terms, the lower Fleurieu

Peninsula has arguably the best conditions in all of mainland South Australia for table wine production.' That said, the best wines to date are the fragrant, elegant chardonnays, sauvignon blancs and semillon sauvignon blancs. The red wines share the same elegance, but – particularly in cooler vintages – can struggle with mid-palate vinosity and fruit sweetness. Merlot and shiraz seem the most likely to adapt as the vines mature; pinot noir is a late arrival of promise courtesy of Tapanappa.

The climate is Mediterranean, very strongly maritime-influenced by the expanses of water which surround the peninsula, in particular its southern end. Thus temperatures are 1–2°C cooler in summer than McLaren Vale, with an average summer maximum of only 25°C. The Mediterranean pattern means the rainfall is winter dominant and the minimal growing season rainfall makes irrigation essential. Spring frosts are simply not an issue, and the prevailing southerly winds seldom blow with sufficient force to inhibit growth. Overall, the climate is cooler than one envisages and it is reflected in the wine styles.

There are two soil types in the vineyard areas: a friable sandy to more clayey loam over a limestone subsoil, and a buckshot gravel, again over limestone. Both are suited to viticulture, and support moderately vigorous vine growth. The foremost wineries are Minko, Mt Billy and Vincognita.

LAT 35°33'S; ALT 250 m; HDD 1628; GSR 121 mm; MJT 19.6°C; HARV Mid-February to April; CHIEF VIT. HAZARD Mildew

**Southern Flinders Ranges**, gazetted 19 August 2003, is at the southern extremity of the Far North Zone (which takes in the whole of the remainder of South Australia), and its only region – the latter not a situation likely to change in the foreseeable future. The well-known Goyder's Line, drawn by surveyor George Goyder in the 19th century, runs east to west through the region, marking the northernmost limits of feasible agriculture. The Spencer Gulf marks the western edge of the region, which is sandwiched between the Peninsulas Zone to the west and the Mount Lofty Ranges Zone to the southeast. The beauty of the region attracts numerous campers and tourists – the Mount Remarkable National Park is one of its jewels. In geological terms, it has two parts, the ridgeline of the Flinders Ranges separating the Wild Dog Creek land system to the east from the coastal Baroota land system to the west. The soils of the former range from deep red loams to shallower stony loams on the slopes; those of the latter are deep sandy loams.

Most of the vineyards have been established on the slopes of the Flinders Ranges at a height of 350–550 metres; both the altitude and sea breezes from the Gulf temper the otherwise hot climate. The limitation on viticulture is the low annual rainfall of 450–650 millimetres, making irrigation nigh on essential during the establishment phase of the vineyards. While most of the mainstream varieties are planted, the focus is on shiraz, merlot and cabernet sauvignon. The major part of the grape production is sold to Barossa Valley makers, a minor part vinified for the handful of wineries in the region. The foremost producers in the region are Bartagunyah Estate, Belalie Bend, Bundaleer, Glenholme Vineyards and Remarkable View.

**Southern Highlands**, gazetted 25 March 2002, has been one of the fastest developing regions in Australia since 2000, if not the fastest. Admittedly, it has come from a low base, but the amount of investment in this fashionable weekend playground for Sydneysiders has been substantial. It has had a somewhat spotty history: the government records for 1886 show a wine-grape harvest of 4275 litres for the Berrima district, suggesting the first vineyards were planted in the 1870s. (Table grapes had been established earlier in that decade.) German vineyard workers from the Vogt family came from vineyards at Camden to establish plantings on Joadja Road in the 1890s; these remained in cultivation for a considerable time thereafter. Yet further vineyards were planted around the turn of the 19th century, leading to exports to Europe.

It was not until the 1950s that all commercial grapegrowing ceased; in 1983 it resumed with the establishment of Joadja Vineyards and Winery. It and Eling Forest Winery began wine sales in 1990, and development accelerated thereafter. By 2008 there were 19 wineries and vineyards.

When successfully seeking registration as a Geographic Indication, it was decided to use the boundaries of the Shire of Wingecarribee for the region, thus taking in the towns of Mittagong, Bowral, Moss Vale and Berrima. Southern Highlands sits astride the Hume and Illawarra Highways, along the spine of the Great Dividing Range, stretching west to the Wollondilly River and east to the escarpment overlooking Wollongong on the coast. It is rolling hill country, with abundant tree and vegetation cover, both native and exotic, which remains green for much of the year. After an

uncertain start, and notwithstanding some climatic challenges, its professionally run vineyards and wineries are providing some very impressive wines.

Centennial Vineyards has produced a succession of high-quality wines, partly through sourcing grapes from the Orange and Hilltops regions to supplement its 30 ha of estate plantings. Cuttaway Hill Estate has 38 ha on three sites, covering all major varieties and with varying soil, climates and mesoclimates, using skilled contract winemaking services in the Hunter Valley.

The overall climate is cool sub-temperate, with mild summers and cool, foggy, frosty winters. Rainfall is evenly distributed throughout the year; summer rainfall tends to occur during violent electrical storms, sometimes accompanied by heavy hail.

The altitude varies from 550 metres to a few high spots at 880 metres; most of the vineyards are within the 600–750 metres range. The main soil types are those derived from basalt (red and brown kraznozems and red earths) and shale (red and brown podzolics and brown earths). They are relatively free draining, but acidic clay increases at depth.

While in the long term the region is likely to focus more on white wines than red, the plantings in the middle of the first decade of the 21st century were split 60 per cent red and 40 per cent white. The leading wineries are Blue Metal Vineyard, Centennial Vineyards, Cuttaway Hill Estate and Pulpit Rock, supported by Howards Lane and Tertini.

LAT 36°27′S; ALT 600–750 m; HDD 1330; GSR 596 mm; MJT 18.9°C; HARV Late March to early May; CHIEF VIT. HAZARDS Vintage rain; hail

**Southern New South Wales Zone** takes in the Canberra District, Hilltops, Gundagai and

Tumbarumba regions, but leaves much of this mountainous area uncovered. The southern boundary is the New South Wales–Victoria border, the eastern and northern boundaries taking contour lines from the spine of the Great Dividing Range before more arbitrary lines in the flat country to the west.

**Southern Tasmania** had as its viticultural prophet Claudio Alcorso, who became the first person to establish a vineyard there for over 100 years. He chose a beautiful peninsula site on the Derwent River, founding Moorilla Estate in 1958. He did so not knowing that Jean Miguet (see Northern Tasmania) had beaten him by two years, but he shared with Miguet a scorn for the state Department of Agriculture and the difficulty of self-taught winemaking with no one to turn to for advice in the early years. It was not until the second half of the 1970s that Moorilla Estate realised the potential it had always had. (For the area's history prior to 1958, see Tasmania.)

The other 20th-century pioneer in the south was George Park, who, like Miguet, worked for the Hydro Electric Commission. Together with wife Priscilla, he planted a 0.5 ha vineyard at Campania in the Coal River area in 1973. Into this small area they crammed cabernet sauvignon, pinot noir, shiraz, zinfandel, riesling, traminer, sylvaner and four other varieties. Stoney Vineyard, as it was called, produced some lovely, long-lived wines (including a spicy, perfumed zinfandel), and showed that the very dry Coal River/Richmond area could easily accommodate late-ripening varietals.

Today the Stoney Vineyard is the kernel of a much-expanded Domaine A, where Swiss-born and -trained Peter Althaus and wife Ruth produce Tasmania's most distinguished cabernet sauvignon. The arrival of water for irrigation transformed the previously precarious business of grapegrowing in this part of Tasmania, which is now growing at a pace close to that of the north, albeit from a much smaller base. The dry climate is also conducive to organic and biodynamic viticulture, led by Frogmore Creek's Tony Scherer.

Moorilla Estate has long since passed out of the ownership of the Alcorso family, but Julian Alcorso continues his father's involvement in wine by running a highly successful and substantial contract winemaking service standing alongside that of Wellington Wines. Given the small size of many of the vineyard holdings, erecting an onsite winery was not a sensible economic or lifestyle decision for many of the island's vignerons. Wines made by the two contracting services have accumulated more trophies and gold medals since 2000 than all the other wineries of the state.

To the northeast is a string of four coastal or near-coastal wineries around Bicheno (the east coast), with the natural amphitheatre of Freycinet providing a local site climate which caused the eminent climate researcher Dr John Gladstones to shake his head in admiration when he visited in the 1990s.

Vineyards stretch up along the banks of the Derwent River to Meadowbank Estate. But they also extend down to the D'Entrecasteaux Channel country and the Huon Valley, 50 kilometres to the south of Hobart, and up into the nearby Hartz Mountains. Placenames such as Snug and Cygnet tell the tale of the usually placid and outrageously beautiful Channel Country, but not of the wild and savage scenery in and around the Hartz Mountains.

In viticulture and climate terms there are three distinct regions in the south – the Derwent Valley, the Huon Valley and Coal River/Richmond – and a fourth on the east coast in the Cranbrook/Bicheno area. They underline yet again the gross over-simplification of regarding Tasmania as a uniform 'region', but also point to the constantly changing backdrop, measured as much in the feel or atmosphere as in the more tangible scenic highlights.

Given Southern Tasmania's latitude, and with nothing between it and the Antarctic, it is not surprising that the statistics suggest the climate is colder than that of the north. In reality, some sites are, but others draw upon special local features (such as the much higher number of sunlight hours in the Coal River/Richmond area, or the Freycinet vineyard amphitheatre) to create notable exceptions to the rule.

The unifying feature of the topography is that there is none, so varied is it. The soils follow suit, from sandstone-based with some schist in the Derwent Valley, to the Coal River's similar weakly structured, sandy, low-humus soils in parts, and black peaty alluvial soils in others.

As with Northern Tasmania, the three principal varieties are pinot noir (which accounts for all but 10 per cent of the total red grape plantings across the state), chardonnay and riesling, with sauvignon blanc and pinot gris later arrivals but very unlikely to supplant any of the big three. Substantial amounts of pinot noir and chardonnay go to make sparkling wines which are the best in Australia, but not at the expense of a significant share of Australia's finest pinot noir. Although

Australian riesling is not a star in the court of public opinion, that of Tasmania equals the quality of the two mainland areas, the Great Southern of Western Australia and the Clare and Eden valleys of South Australia. The difference comes from the vibrant acidity which drives the long and piercing palate.

Zinfandel was once grown successfully at Coal River, and the colour and extract of the Tamar River red wines is extraordinary, hinting misleadingly at a warm to very warm climate. Instead, as noted in the Tasmania entry, the island's major producers have hitched their future to such cool-climate varieties as riesling, pinot gris, chardonnay and pinot noir (the latter two for both table and sparkling wine use). However, the possible effect of climate change – or at least, some warm vintages – has led recently to some impressive merlot, cabernet sauvignon and shiraz coming from the warmer sites of the Tamar River and the Coal River.

The leading southern and east coast wineries (from a total of 67) are Bream Creek, Coal Valley Vineyard, Craigow, Derwent Estate, Domaine A, 'ese Vineyards, Freycinet, Frogmore Creek, Home Hill, Meadowbank Estate, Moorilla Estate, Nocton Park, Observatory Hill Vineyard, Pooley, Puddleduck Vineyard, Spring Vale Vineyards, Stefano Lubiana, Tinderbox Vineyard and Winstead.

LAT 42°45'S; ALT 50–175 m; HDD 1013; GSR 360 mm; MJT 16.8°C; HARV April to early June; CHIEF VIT. HAZARD Spring frost

**South West Australia Zone** takes in the Margaret River, Great Southern, Blackwood Valley, Geographe, Manjimup and Pemberton regions. Viewed on a map of Australia, the zone may not appear large, but it in fact stretches 400 kilometres east to west, and 200 kilometres north to south.

**sparging**  is a process of introducing a stream of gas (oxygen, CO$_2$ or nitrogen are the most commonly used, each for a different purpose) from the bottom of a tank or vat so that it passes through the must or wine.

**sparkling wine**  can be made in several ways but all superior examples, most notably Champagne, involve the addition of a precise amount of sugar and yeast to a blend of still (base) wines immediately prior to it being bottled (tiraged). The second fermentation follows and then the spent yeast cells (lees) settle on the side of the bottle. Enzymatic processes (autolysis) break down the dead cells and the compounds released greatly add to the character of the wine after 12 to 18 months and beyond. After two or three years the lees are shaken (riddled) to the top of the now inverted bottle; the neck is then frozen, and the yeast lees are disgorged by the removal of the crown seal and the ejection of the frozen plug of lees and wine. A mixture (*liqueur d'expédition*) of older base wine and a small amount of sugar (dosage) is added to the bottle to achieve flavour balance and the bottle is then sealed with a cork and wire muselet.

**Spinifex**  (est. 2001) is a Barossa Valley winery established by Peter Schell and Magali Gely, a husband and wife team from New Zealand who came to Australia in the early 1990s to study oenology and marketing respectively at Roseworthy Agricultural College. Magali Gely's family has a long history of winemaking in the south of France near Montpellier, and both

Peter Schell and she worked four vintages in the region, developing a natural affinity for the southern French varieties and wine styles. They have brought that affinity to the Barossa Valley with particularly impressive skill, making wines which have a degree of elegance and silky softness not common in the valley. Open fermentation, basket pressing, indigenous yeast fermentations and long post-fermentation maceration are common enough in small, high-quality wineries, but are seldom used to better effect. Schell also makes the wines for a number of clients for whom he consults. Exports of part of the 3500-case production to the UK, the US, Canada and elsewhere.

**sporadic oxidation**  see random oxidation.

**Spring Vale Vineyards**  (est. 1986), on the east coast of Tasmania, was established by Rodney Lyne and family, initially with a planting of 1.5 ha each of pinot noir and chardonnay, followed by 0.5 ha each of gewurztraminer and pinot gris. It took a major step forward with the 2007 purchase of a nearby vineyard with 3 ha of pinot noir, 1 ha each of sauvignon blanc and riesling, and 0.5 ha of chardonnay. Exports to the UK, the US, Canada and Malaysia.

**spur**  is the name given to a cane which will produce grapes in the year following the winter pruning, and which typically will have two buds clear of the base of the spur where it joins old wood. In the following growing season it will produce two fruitful canes.

**stabilisation**  encompasses two winemaking procedures for white wines, both important from a visual (marketing) viewpoint.

Stabilisation using a specific form of clay called bentonite is used to remove protein haze from wine which may not be obvious at the time the procedure is carried out, but which will form if the wine is exposed to warm storage or transport conditions. Cold stabilisation is used to remove tasteless potassium bitartrate crystals, called wine diamonds by German winemakers. The process involves reducing the temperature of the wine to around 0°C, and keeping it at this temperature for between one and three weeks.

**standard drink**  is a serving of wine, beer or spirits which contains approximately 10 grams of pure alcohol. Because different drinks contain different concentrations of alcohol, the number of standard drinks in any given container will depend on the alcohol concentration of the drink. All packaged alcoholic drinks are required to clearly display on the label the number of standard drinks in the bottle. A 750-millilitre bottle of wine containing 12% alc/vol will have seven standard drinks. Counter-intuitively, perhaps, the lower the alcohol, the fewer the standard drinks; conversely, the higher the alcohol, the greater the number of standard drinks.

The National Health and Medical Research Council of Australia has long had guidelines suggesting that males should have not more than 28 standard drinks in a week, and, on average, no more than four standard drinks a day, with one or two alcohol-free days a week. The apparent anomaly in the numbers is solved by an allowance of up to six standard drinks a day for no more than three days a week. For females the recommendations are half those for males, except for the three-day allowance,

where females can have up to three standard drinks a day. Notwithstanding a vast body of epidemiological research (dating back decades) that supports these guidelines, as at 2008 there were suggestions that the recommended limits be reduced to two standard drinks a day, and that any consumption above that level be characterised as binge drinking.

**Stanton & Killeen**  (est. 1875) was founded by the long-lived Stanton family, which has had up to three generations actively involved in the business at various times. Timothy Stanton and his son John Lewis Stanton arrived in Australia from East Anglia, England, in the 1850s to search for gold, but turned instead to farming. They settled first at the picturesquely named Black Dog Creek near Rutherglen, before moving in 1875 to the property they called Park View, where they established a vineyard. Timothy and John Stanton carried on the winery until the death of Timothy in 1895; when phylloxera struck, Timothy's grandson John Richard Stanton replanted the vineyard, but it was sold to Campbells in the 1940s. Meanwhile, in 1925, fourth-generation winemaker John Charles Stanton had established Gracerray Winery on the site of a vineyard that had disappeared at the time of phylloxera. A winery had also been in existence there, and the new Gracerray Winery was built on the same site. It has been in continuous production ever since, and is still the Stanton & Killeen winery. During the 1930s the vineyards exceeded 40 ha, but by the 1950s they were back to 12 ha.

New plantings commenced at the Moodemere vineyard in 1968, and in 1977 a new vineyard, the Quandong vineyard, a kilometre away was commenced. It was named after the first Stanton winery, and is planted on the prized red loam soil which is dotted throughout the district. The vineyards now amount to 40 ha, roughly half given to the production of fortified wines, the other half to table wines, led by durif and shiraz. The fortified wines span the usual northeast Victorian muscats and tokays, using the rare/grand/classic/varietal hierarchy, but the most remarkable wines are the vintage fortified reds, with up to half of the blend fashioned from four Portuguese port varieties, the remainder from shiraz and durif. This was the special project of the late Chris Killeen, who died prematurely in 2008, but with his son Simon poised to carry on the tradition. The 20,000-case production is exported to the UK, the US and other major markets.

**Stefano Lubiana** (est. 1990) is the venture of the eponymous owner and winemaker, who moved from the Riverland to Southern Tasmania, where he set up a substantial contract sparkling wine making facility to help cover the costs of the move and the establishment of his new business. Over the years, Lubiana has steadily decreased the amount of contract winemaking, now focusing on his estate-grown wines from 18 ha of beautifully located vineyards sloping down to the Derwent River. Exports to Italy, Sweden, Korea, Indonesia and Japan.

**Stella Bella Wines** (est. 1997) has come a long way since its establishment, production now exceeding 50,000 cases of Margaret River wines mainly sold at premium to super-premium levels. It owns or controls more

than 80 ha of vineyards, primarily from the central and southern parts of Margaret River, and has moved into a 3000-tonne capacity winemaking facility at Karridale. The wines are released at three price points, the top being the somewhat eclectic Suckfizzle range, the bottom Skuttlebutt, with varietal releases in the middle. Its sauvignon blanc semillon, chardonnay, cabernet merlot and cabernet sauvignon are sophisticated and complex wines of high quality. Exports to the UK, the US, Canada, China, Hong Kong and Singapore.

**sterile filtration** is the most controversial form of what is a controversial subject at best, although the controversy is seldom created by winemakers; it is more frequently due to wine writers who have no practical knowledge of the subject. Once achieved by using very small pore size filters, it is increasingly carried out by cross-flow filtration.

**Stonehaven** (est. 1998) has fallen victim to CWA's move (in 2008) to aggressively reduce its regional winery and vineyard holdings. It has been closed down, but will presumably be sold at some future date. The brand, however, will continue, using grapes from the Padthaway region, including the 400 ha of estate plantings.

**Stoney Rise** (est. 2000) is the venture of Joe and Lou Holyman. While Joe Holyman's family had been involved in grapegrowing in Tasmania for two decades, Joe took time out to work in wineries in New Zealand, Portugal, France, Mount Benson and Coonawarra before returning to Tasmania to acquire the former Rotherhythe vineyard. Rotherhythe had been established in 1986, and had produced some outstanding wines, but was in need of restoration and a degree of replanting. It now has 3 ha of pinot noir and 1 ha of chardonnay. The pinot noirs have had exceptional show success, and there seems every reason to suppose they will continue to have that success. Exports to the UK.

**Stonier Wines**  (est. 1978) is one of the most senior wineries of the Mornington Peninsula, established by Brian Stonier and family. It became part of the Petaluma Group in a wholly amicable arrangement, with ultimate control passing to Lion Nathan when that company acquired Petaluma. Significant winemaking and management changes occurred in 2008, and it remains to be seen whether the chardonnay and pinot noir (in particular) produced from the 50 ha of estate vineyards will be as good in the future as they have been in the past. Exports to all major markets.

**Strathbogie Ranges**,  gazetted 25 March 2002, is a sparsely populated region in the Central Victoria Zone, without a single town of any significance other, perhaps, than Strathbogie itself. It is an open, windswept place, the original forest having been felled during the 19th century for large-scale grazing and thereafter to provide sleepers for the Melbourne to Sydney railway line. There is scant record of any early viticulture, the only exception being a vineyard established near Longwood in 1900 by the Tubbs family, which made table and fortified wine, and later disappeared without a trace. The modern era began tentatively in 1968 when local grazing family the Plunketts planted an experimental

vineyard of a little over a hectare with no less than 25 varieties. The first commercial venture was that of Dr Peter Tisdall, who, after extensive climatic research, in 1975 purchased the property which became Mount Helen. He planted 13 ha of chardonnay, 8 ha each of pinot noir and cabernet sauvignon, 6 ha of riesling, 5 ha of sauvignon blanc and 4 ha of gewurztraminer. The Tisdall empire flourished spectacularly but briefly, an unfortunate legacy being the introduction of phylloxera from the vineyards owned by Tisdall at Echuca.

The Plunkett family began planting a commercial vineyard in 1980; it grew to 120 ha in three locations. In 2008 the Fowles family, headed by Matt, acquired the large Dominion Winery from receivers, and the businesses of the two families were united under the Plunkett Fowles name. The contract winemaking business of the winery has a secure base, because grapes cannot be taken out of the Strathbogie Ranges to any of the surrounding regions which do not have phylloxera. Thus the 40-ha vineyard of Domaine Chandon planted to chardonnay and pinot noir can only take fermented wine back to its Yarra Valley base.

Given that vineyards are planted at altitudes between 160 and 600 metres, it is not surprising that there is substantial site variation. The region is at its warmest on its northwestern boundary with the Goulburn Valley, becoming progressively cooler as the elevation increases with the move east. In the lee of Mount Broughton and Mount Concord in the south, near the quaintly named town of Caveat, Antcliff's Chase is at an elevation of 600 metres, and the Mount Helen vineyard is between the 420- and 480-metre contour lines.

Elevation again plays a role, but most of the soils are derived from the granitic base rock of the surrounding mountains, mixed with sand, sandy loams, ironstone gravel and quartz, with a clay subsoil. All of these soils are moderately acidic and devigorating.

Chardonnay, riesling, sauvignon blanc, pinot noir, shiraz and cabernet sauvignon are the principal varietal wines from the region, shiraz and cabernet sauvignon doing well from warmer sites, and chardonnay, riesling and sauvignon blanc doing best in the cooler parts. The leading wineries are Maygars Hill and Plunkett Fowles, with Baddaginnie Run and Elgo Estate in support.

LAT 37°12'S; ALT 160–600 m; HDD 1460; GSR 320–80 mm; MJT 20.7°C; HARV Mid-March to mid-May; CHIEF VIT. HAZARD Frost

**stuck fermentation** describes a red wine or white wine fermentation which, contrary to the winemaker's wishes, finishes without converting all the grape sugar to alcohol. It is usually possible to re-start the fermentation by introducing new yeast strains and lifting the temperature to the extent necessary, but even if this is successful, telltale signs of the problem may remain, often described as attenuated ferment.

**subregion** see Geographic Indications.

**sultana,** known in California and elsewhere as Thompson Seedless, is in Australia regarded as a multipurpose grape, albeit of declining importance for the wine industry. Thus 65,907 tonnes were grown in 2008, but only 17,335 tonnes were used for winemaking – as a blend component in the cheapest white wines.

**Summerfield** (est. 1979) in the Pyrenees is a specialist red wine producer, the particular forte of which is shiraz. The red wines are luscious, full-bodied and fruit-driven, but with a slice of vanillin oak to top them off. Founder Ian Summerfield has handed over the winemaking reins to son Mark, who continues to make shiraz and cabernet sauvignon built for the long haul, and which richly repay cellaring. Exports to the US and the UK.

**sumoll** is a red grape variety and is one of the two parents of tyrian.

**Sunbury,** gazetted 10 December 1998, while a relatively small region, has a marvellously rich history, some of which has been miraculously preserved. In 1858 James Goodall Francis, a former Victorian premier, planted the first vines at Goona Warra – an Aboriginal name chosen long before Coonawarra was even a twinkle in John Riddoch's eye. He subsequently built a magnificent bluestone winery, and while winemaking ceased there in the early 1900s, the buildings were preserved. In 1982 Goona Warra was purchased by Melbourne lawyer John Barnier and family, and brought back to life with estate vineyards, a winery and a restaurant.

James S Johnstone followed quickly in the footsteps of Francis, establishing Craiglee in 1864. A fellow parliamentarian, he also established the *Argus* newspaper, and in 1872 made a shiraz which the author has been lucky enough to taste on several occasions – bottles from a cache long forgotten and unearthed in the 1950s. Still with remarkable life and vinosity, they were a powerful testament to the suitability of the region for the production of elegant but long-lived shiraz.

The four-storey stone winery remains at Craiglee, but in this instance public health bureaucracy has decreed that Pat Carmody (whose family purchased the property in 1961, 40 years after wine production had ceased, and re-established the vineyard in 1976) should make the wine in a new building. This, it must be said, has not prevented him from making the best and most consistent wines from the region, most notably the multi-trophy-winning Craiglee Shiraz.

Where the Macedon Ranges (with which Sunbury was once lumped) are hilly, indeed mountainous, Sunbury is almost, but not quite, flat. Situated 15 minutes past Melbourne Airport, and the closest wine region to the Melbourne CBD, it is not particularly well known. It can be a chilly place, at times downright forbidding, particularly when the wind blows hard from the north, sweeping the plain with frigid air drawn up from the Southern Ocean and circulated over the mountains to the north before rushing back whence it came. But Sunbury's proximity to Melbourne, its historic wineries and the quality of its wines are more than enough to compensate for these shortcomings.

The growing season climate, in particular, is much influenced by the wind which sweeps across the plain, further cooling an already cool region. The nearby Macedon Ranges to the north and the sea to the south each also exercise moderating though different influences; this is a cool climate, however measured. The soils are typically dark, and – except on old alluvial river terraces with free-draining sandy loams – not particularly fertile. Their depth and structure vary significantly from lower level plains to hillsides, ranging from alkaline to acidic.

The principal grape varieties, in descending order, are shiraz, chardonnay, pinot noir, cabernet sauvignon, sauvignon blanc and semillon. The leading winery is Craiglee, with Galli Estate, Goona Warra Vineyard and Wildwood all producing wines of particular merit.

LAT 37°45'S; ALT 275 m; HDD 1380; GSR 310 mm; MJT 19.2°C; HARV Late March to early May; CHIEF VIT. HAZARD Birds

**super zones**  see Geographic Indications.

**supple**  is a largely self-explanatory tasting term, most commonly used in the context of red wines, to describe a palate which is round and pliant, with no aggressive tannins.

**sur lie**  is a French expression normally used in conjunction with white wines which have been kept in contact with their lees, and, in certain circumstances, bottled direct from the barrel or tank without first being racked.

**Swan District**,  gazetted 10 December 1998, is one of the three regions making up the Greater Perth Zone, the other two regions being Peel and Perth Hills. It has a scattering of wineries of no great importance other than Paul Conti, its chief claim to fame being its sole subregion, the Swan Valley.

**Swan Hill**,  gazetted 11 June 1996, in the North West Victoria Zone, straddles the Murray River, and is thus partly within New South Wales and partly within Victoria. Swan Hill was so named by the explorer Major Thomas Mitchell in 1836 because of its abundance of swans and other water fowl.

Irrigated crops were established as early as 1880, but salinity and other problems caused the pioneer schemes to fail, and it was not until the 1930s that the present-day framework was established. Best's Wines is recognised as the pioneer; Frederick Thompson established Best's Lake Boga Vineyard and winery in 1930 (it was then named St Andrews).

RL Buller of Rutherglen began purchasing grapes from the region in the 1930s, and (after the interruption of World War II) bought the vineyard at Beverford, 14 kilometres north of Swan Hill.

As is the case in the Murray Darling region, the protracted drought in the first decade of this century has cast a long shadow over the future of the area. Innovative techniques to make efficient use of whatever limited water is available may provide a partial answer. The question remains whether more expensive water (at best) and lower yields will be economically viable.

The area is unambiguously hot and dry, with the low humidity keeping the threat of downy mildew and botrytis to an absolute minimum, which means it is a low-risk environment for grapegrowing (provided adequate irrigation water is available). The heat degree day summation is slightly lower than that of the Murray Darling, the rainfall slightly higher, with a slightly longer and slower ripening period. Harvest runs from February to mid-March, with no clear break between varietal maturity dates, placing maximum pressure on the wineries. The soils are a mix of lacustrine (lake), fluviatile (river) and aeolian (wind) derived sands and clays up to 90 metres deep. Irrigation from the Murray River was always regarded as absolutely essential through the dry summer months. While superficially dead flat, subtle rises and falls in elevation are of significance.

The principal grape varieties, 55 per cent white and 45 per cent red, are led by chardonnay and shiraz. The leading winery is Andrew Peace Wines, able to produce 400,000 cases of well-priced wines a year with a strong export focus.

LAT 35°20'S; ALT 60–85 m; HDD 2138; GSR 178 mm; MJT 23.6°C; HARV Early February to mid-March; CHIEF VIT. HAZARD Drought

Swan Valley, gazetted 6 January 2003, was populated by two waves of immigration by Yugoslavs, the first in the early years of the 20th century (principally from Dalmatia), and the second after World War II. These surges of new arrivals gave the Swan Valley two claims to fame. The first is that, most surprisingly, for a time it had more wineries in operation than either New South Wales or Victoria; the second is that, more obviously, it joined the Barossa Valley (German) and the Riverland (Italian) as a significant ethnically driven wine-producing region.

It was not always so. Viticulture was started by English settlers, most notably Thomas Waters, who dug the cellar at Olive Farm in 1830, thus giving this winery the distinction of being the oldest winemaking establishment in Australia to be in use at the start of the new millennium. Sadly, it has since been sold and decommissioned.

Another link with the past comes through the colonial surgeon Dr John Ferguson, who purchased part of a substantial land grant owned by three Indian army officers, the most senior of whom was Colonel Richmond Houghton. Even though Houghton never came to Australia, the property was named after him – likewise the Houghton winery of today (Western Australia's largest wine company).

The Swan Valley has always been a friendly place in which to grow vines and make wine. The completely flat, alluvial river plain provides soils which are immensely deep and well drained (or are so in the prime vineyard locations), and the hot, dry summer means that grapes ripen easily and quickly. This is an ideal climate for table grapes (huge quantities were produced for export markets in bygone years) and for fortified wines. It is likewise suited to the production of bulk table wine, which was once sold to a large but uncritical local clientele, many of whom were of Yugoslav origin, and who brought their own flagons, drums and sundry other containers to be filled up at their chosen winery.

Inevitably, the ethnic base of the Swan Valley winemaking changed steadily through the years, while the dominance of Houghton grew. After years of uncertainty, Sandalford was revived under new ownership and management. But it is no accident that both Houghton and Sandalford draw the majority of their grapes from the Margaret River, Great Southern, Pemberton and Manjimup, or that, at the other end of the scale, the self-effacing but brilliant John Kosovich has established a new vineyard at Pemberton. Other small wineries in the Swan Valley have looked to Margaret River, variously establishing vineyards there or buying grapes therefrom.

Just when it seemed that the smaller wineries would quietly fade away, the opposite has happened. New wineries have opened, older ones have revived, accommodation has been upgraded and restaurants have opened –

all driven by wine, food and lifestyle tourism within an hour's drive of the Perth CBD.

Whichever yardstick is used, the Swan Valley proper has an unequivocally hot climate. It has the highest mean January temperature of any significant Australian district. It has the lowest summer rainfall of any Australian region, the lowest relative humidity (47 per cent) and the most hours of sunshine per day. Its heat summation (HDD) almost comes as an anticlimax, at 2340. The Gin Gin/Moondah Brook area, well to the north of the Swan Valley, is somewhat cooler, and although still at the warm end of the climatic spectrum, has consistently demonstrated a surprising capacity to produce full-flavoured, full-bodied white wines. The Swan Valley proper is a flat alluvial plain flanked by the Darling Range and permeated by the tributaries of the Swan River. The best soils are brown or yellow-brown loamy sand surface soils passing gradually through lighter coloured (and slightly more clayey) subsurface soils and thence into porous sandy clay loam subsoils. This structure allows deep penetration by the vine roots to tap the reserves of the heavy winter rainfall.

Over 70 per cent of the grapes are white, with chenin blanc, chardonnay and verdelho leading the way. The principal wineries are Faber, Houghton, Jane Brook, John Kosovich, Lamont's, Moondah Brook, Oakover, Sandalford, Talijancich and Upper Reach.

LAT 31°50'S; ALT 45 m; HDD 2340; GSR 145 mm; MJT 24.3°C; HARV End January to end March; CHIEF VIT. HAZARD Excessive heat

**Symphony Hill Wines** (est. 1999). Ewen and Elissa Macpherson purchased what was then an old table grape and orchard property in the

Granite Belt, and in partnership with Ewen's parents, Bob and Jill Macpherson, developed 4 ha of vineyards, while Ewen completed his bachelor of applied science in viticulture (2003). The vineyard has been established using state-of-the-art technology; vineyard manager and winemaker Mike Hayes has a degree in viticulture and is a third-generation viticulturist in the Granite Belt region.

Between Hayes and Ewen Macpherson, a trial block of 50 varieties has been established, including such rarely encountered varieties as picpoul, tannat and mondeuse. The quality of the wines is excellent, superior to that of all other Queensland wineries with the exception of Boireann. Exports to Singapore and China.

**syrah** is a synonym for shiraz.

a b c d e f g h i
j k l m n o p q
r s t u v w x y z

Tahbilk, for much of its life known as Chateau Tahbilk, had a turbulent (and, in one view, accidental) birth in 1860. In January of that year an energetic and visionary promoter, RH Horne, sought to raise £30,000 via a prospectus to the public, which proposed that a large property named Noorilim be purchased from its owner, Andrew Sinclair. The prospectus waxed lyrical about the proposal, confidently asserting that wines better than those of the Rhine and Moselle [sic] would be equalled, and in some vintages surpassed by those of the Goulburn Valley, adding, 'Beside the commercial benefits, the best sanitary and moral results may be anticipated, because a wine-drinking population is never a drunken population.' There was a special irony in those words, for Sinclair suddenly disappeared, and his body was later discovered in the bush near the St Kilda seashore. RH Horne wrote, 'It appeared that he had wandered after having been hocused by some brandy he had drunk at one of the evil villas of the suburbs.' A new company was hastily established to purchase the adjoining property of 260 ha, known as the Tahbilk run. The money was duly raised, and the purchase was completed on 1 August 1860.

RH Horne was joined by a successful merchant, John Pinney Bear, who oversaw the rapid development of the property, purchasing 1 million vine cuttings, and successfully planting 700,000 of those cuttings. Somewhat improbably, Horne's accounts suggested that the cuttings produced grapes in the first year. By 1861, 80 ha were under vine, including a still-surviving block of shiraz, and development continued apace, a corporate reconstruction resulting in Hugh Glass and Bear having between them a controlling shareholding.

After a number of further changes, both ownership and management responsibility fell to JP Bear alone. Under his direction, and with François de Coueslant as winemaker and vineyard manager from 1877 until 1887, Tahbilk prospered mightily.

The 'old' cellars had been constructed at the end of the 1860s: 91.4 metres long, they were built of stone quarried on the estate and timbered with beams hewn from the massive gum trees which flourished in the region. The 'new' cellars were commenced at the end of 1875: the successful tenderer for the work was James Purbrick of Seymour, a third cousin of Reginald Purbrick, who ultimately acquired the property.

The period of prosperity was to be cut short by the arrival of phylloxera, which saw production steadily decline in the first years of the 20th century. It did not devastate Tahbilk as much as surrounding vineyards because some of the plantings were on sandy soils. It is on one particular knoll of sandy soil that the 1860 block of shiraz still stands, a unique planting because no younger vines have ever been introduced.

Following the death of Bear in October 1889, his wife and daughters, who were living in London, became the long-distance owners, and until her death there in 1925 at the age of 92, Mrs Bear corresponded at great length on management details. When English member of parliament Reginald Purbrick purchased the property in the same year, less than half of the 120 ha of vines established before the arrival of phylloxera remained. Noted viticulturist François de Castella was appointed consultant, and was adamant that Tahbilk could be brought back to its former glory with appropriate viticultural practices, not the least of which was the planting of grafted vines on the heavier soils.

In 1927 plantings began again, including 2 ha of marsanne, which produced a single bottling, the white wine equivalent of the 1860 Vines Shiraz. Other plantings on rootstock followed, but management still remained a long-distance affair until 1931, when Reginald Purbrick's son Eric, then aged 28, began the long job of rehabilitating the property. He had been born in Sydney and raised in Melbourne, then went to England with his family in 1921, studying law and history at Jesus College, Cambridge, graduating in 1925. He first visited Tahbilk after his father bought the property in that year, but returned to England to be called to the bar in 1929, spending some of his spare time in winter mountaineering in Switzerland.

Eric Purbrick was a remarkable man, with a superb sense of humour and a deep understanding of and appreciation for the fine arts, which was partly embodied in the house that was built on the property in 1936. It was designed by leading architect Sir Roy Grounds and incorporated a still-surviving room from the homestead built in the 1860s in one wing. The design of the 'new' house is timeless, merging imperceptibly with the old, and featuring such extraordinary items as concrete bricks (of the kind made popular in the 1970s) manufactured on site. Quarry tiles on the floor were another touch 40 or 50 years ahead of their time.

Well before Eric Purbrick's death in 1991, aged 88, grandson Alister Purbrick took control of the business. He has worked tirelessly and effectively ever since to turn

Tahbilk into a highly profitable business, with an exceptional range of wines built around the foundation stones of marsanne, shiraz and cabernet sauvignon at various price points, supported by riesling and viognier. Every one of the wines in the portfolio has had significant wine show success at one time or another. The jewels in the crown are the 1860 Vines Shiraz, the 1927 Vines Marsanne, the Eric Stevens Purbrick Shiraz and the Eric Stevens Purbrick Cabernet Sauvignon. The 120,000-case production is sold in various ways: through an active mailing list club and cellar door, conventional retail and substantial exports to all major markets.

It is one of the most beautiful of wineries and vineyards in Australia, oozing history from every pore of its National Trust–classified buildings with their white-painted walls and red roofs. Set among the winding billabongs which run off the Goulburn River, it is an oasis on the hottest day of summer, and a somehow secure port on a cold winter's day. A modern restaurant, with a verandah out over the Goulburn River, adds to the 'must visit' status of the winery.

**Taltarni** (est. 1972), in the Pyrenees region, was established by wealthy Californian businessman John Goelet, who ensconced Dominique Portet as winemaker manager there and elder brother Bernard Portet at Clos du Val in the Napa Valley. It has been a remarkably stable bi-country investment in two substantial businesses. Notwithstanding that stability, Taltarni has not ossified: there have been significant changes in the management of the 139 ha of estate vineyards; major upgrading of winery equipment and investment in new oak barrels; a long-term contract for the purchase of grapes from the Heathcote region; and the introduction of a flagship red wine, Cephas. It also owns Clover Hill, in Tasmania, a specialist producer of high-quality sparkling wine. The 80,000-case production is exported to all major markets as well as having significant distribution throughout Australia.

**Tamar Ridge**  (est. 1994), in Tasmania, has experienced many changes and grown prodigiously since its establishment by Josef Chromy. In 2003 it was purchased from Chromy by Tasmanian timber company Gunns Limited, which is embroiled in all the political and sustainability issues which surround logging and pulp mill activities; this has made an objective appreciation of the growth and achievements of the winery difficult. Since the purchase in 2003, Gunns has installed Dr Richard Smart as viticultural adviser. He has overseen the rapid expansion of its vineyards to 135 ha at Kayena and a further 83 ha at the White Hills site. In conjunction with chief winemaker Andrew Pirie, a $1.9 million micro-vinification winery is used both to run courses for PhD students and for research into clonal evaluation and canopy trials. Its mainstream wines are of unambiguously high quality, but experimental plantings have already paid dividends, with a promising albarino one of the first of many varieties under evaluation. The business grew further in 2005 with the acquisition of the Coombend property on the east coast, with 160 ha under vine (including albarino). The 75,000-case production is sold on the Australian mainland and to all export markets,

and – as with most Tasmanian wineries – has a healthy cellar door and domestic off-take.

**Tamburlaine**  (est. 1966) was the second winery to follow in the footsteps of the late Max Lake at Lake's Folly, appropriately enough under the guidance of another medical practitioner, Dr Lance Allen. In 1966 he purchased a 34-ha property fronting onto McDonalds Road, Pokolbin, in the Lower Hunter Valley; he commenced planting the following year. Later on he purchased a second block, part of the once-famous Caerphilly Vineyard, and extended the plantings. The first Tamburlaine wines were made in 1971, but it was not until 1974 that an on-site winery was established.

It had been Dr Allen's intention to hand the property over to his children, but that was not to be and, in 1985, the property was sold to a group headed by present-day winemaker Mark Davidson. Since that time the business has grown very substantially on the back of a remarkably successful mailing list to club members, part of the success resting on a sophisticated en primeur offer system which sees the wines held at Tamburlaine until such time as the member wishes to take delivery. The vineyards now extend to 12.5 ha in Pokolbin, 32 ha at Broke and 88 ha in Orange. There are thus two streams of wines, one from the Hunter, the other from Orange. Sales have risen to 80,000 cases a year as the quality and variety of wines on offer have blossomed. The vineyards have been intelligently planted, the styles produced from the two regions entirely appropriate, and very different from each other. Exports to the US, Japan, China and Sweden.

**tannat** produces a deeply coloured, rough and tannic red wine grown in Madiran, France; it was directly responsible for the development of the micro-oxygenation technique by a Madiran winemaker. The small plantings in Australia are on the increase, with 21 growers (and makers) spread from the Granite Belt in Queensland to the King Valley in Victoria and the Eden Valley in South Australia, with a number of regions in between. While used as a 100 per cent varietal wine, it is also blended, the latter use the most logical.

**tannins** are predominantly found in the skins and seeds of berries, and also in the stems; the amount in the pulp of the grape is insignificant. If, as in the case of red wines, the skins, seeds and (possibly) stems are involved in the fermentation process, there will be a greater extract of tannin in the resulting solution. By contrast, the skins, seeds and stems of white grapes are removed before fermentation commences. The one period of possible extraction for white grapes comes as the grapes are crushed and pressed; the longer the period between crushing and pressing, the more the extract. This is known as skin contact, and has been of particular use in the making of cheap, early-maturing chardonnay; it is excluded as far as possible in the making of riesling and semillon. The pigmented tannins of red wines result from the reactions of anthocyanins with catechins and tannins. They are of great importance to the colour, sensory properties and longevity of red wines.

There is considerable variation in the tannin content of red grapes, with cabernet sauvignon, shiraz and tannat notably high, and pinot noir notably low. The handling of the extraction of tannins in the red winemaking process is of critical importance. The amount and type of tannin extract varies significantly from the pre-fermentation maceration phase to the primary fermentation phase, where temperature plays a major role, and in the post-fermentation phase, which may be a matter of hours or weeks. In the pre-fermentation period, extract is achieved without the aid of alcohol, while in the post-fermentation period it is of course achieved in the presence of alcohol.

Deliberate pre-fermentation maceration, called cold soak in many parts of the world, came into popularity in the second half of the 1980s in Burgundy and elsewhere, due mainly to the work of Guy Accad. It was achieved by chilling the must to below 10°C and (if following the instructions of Accad to the letter) adding high levels of sulphur dioxide to prevent the onset of fermentation. The practice thus started with pinot noir, but has since spread to other red varieties.

In tandem with cold soak, a number of techniques have been developed to soften the tannins, or make them more complex. Traditionally this was achieved through post-fermentation maceration, a controlled form of oxidation. An even more sophisticated form of oxidation which has become widely used is micro-oxygenation.

Oak tannins also play a role in barrel-fermented wines and/or in simple barrel maturation. This, obviously enough, is the main source of tannins in white wines which have been barrel-fermented or -matured. An interesting side light was the traditional practice in Rioja, Spain, where white wines would be matured for years in American oak, but heavily egg white fined every six months or so to remove the oak tannins. In Australia, and most other parts of the New World, the winemaker controls the amount of tannins by the choice of smaller or larger oak barrels varying from new to five or more years of age.

Technically, tannins cannot be smelt or tasted, as they cause tactile sensations in the mouth, but no more. Nonetheless, experienced tasters develop a sixth sense, and have a shrewd idea from the aroma of a young red wine about the likely tannin content. The tactile sensations vary widely: terms range from silky to squeaky to supple, to round to firm, to hard, to dry and harsh. The last types of tannin often congregate on the inside of the upper lip.

As red wines age, tannins progressively polymerise, soften, and eventually fall out of solution in a dark red deposit at the bottom of the bottle.

Tapanappa (est. 2002) is a partnership of three high-profile wine families. The partners are Brian Croser (formerly of Petaluma), Jean-Michel Cazes of Chateau Lynch-Bages in Pauillac, and Société Jacques Bollinger, the parent company of Champagne Bollinger. The partnership has three vineyard sites in Australia: the 8-ha Whalebone Vineyard at Wrattonbully (planted to cabernet sauvignon, shiraz and merlot 30 years ago); 4.7 ha of Tiers Vineyard (chardonnay) at Piccadilly in the Adelaide Hills (the remainder of the Tiers Vineyard chardonnay continues to be sold to Petaluma); and the most recent, the 4-ha Foggy Hill Vineyard on the southern tip of the Fleurieu Peninsula (pinot noir), which seems likely to produce pinot noir of significant quality. Exports to all major markets.

tarrango is a red cross bred in Australia by the CSIRO in 1965. The parents are touriga nacional and sultana; the aim was to provide a grape with a highly aromatic profile, low tannins and high acidity, suited to Beaujolais-style wines, and which would thrive in the Riverland. Brown Brothers have been the major producers of the variety. The original enthusiasm seems to have declined substantially, the amount under vine decreasing from 201 ha in 2005 to 102 ha in 2008.

TarraWarra Estate (est. 1983) is one of the showpiece wineries of the Yarra Valley, established by clothing magnate Marc Besen and wife Eva. A noted art collector, he subsequently built what was then the largest privately owned art gallery in Australia, which houses the hundreds of major paintings he has acquired over the years. A fine restaurant completes the buildings, overlooking immaculately manicured lawns, gardens and vines. The quality of the wines produced from the 29 ha of estate plantings of sauvignon blanc, chardonnay, pinot noir, merlot and shiraz is exemplary, the principal focus on chardonnay and pinot noir. The 18,000-case production is exported to all major markets, albeit in small quantities, with domestic sales largely confined to the cellar door, mailing list and fine restaurants.

tartaric acid is the most important form of acid in grapes and wine; it is of critical importance because of the major part it plays in the taste of the wine, and in underwriting its stability and longevity. Curiously, of all the natural organic acids occurring in plants, tartaric is one of the rarer. The amounts of tartaric acid vary widely among varieties; in most instances the higher the natural level of tartaric acid, the better the quality of the grape, and the greater its ability to maintain balance in hot climates. The other principal acid in grapes is malic acid. While tartaric acid in wine is highly stable, malic acid is decomposed by the malolactic fermentation which virtually all red wines undergo. Malolactic fermentation is used with fuller bodied white wines such as chardonnay, but is seldom encountered in aromatic varieties such as riesling or semillon.

While malic, citric and tartaric acid can all be added to reduce pH where the need arises, tartaric is the most commonly used. It is highly preferable that the major additions be made before or during fermentation.

Tasmania (Zone) was one of the earliest grapegrowing colonies, but has been – and continues to be – the most reluctant to embrace the Geographic Indications legislation, declining to seek registration of any regions, or even divide north, south and east into regions. Its reluctance is well founded: the island has very effectively promoted itself as a premier wine, food, wildlife and scenic destination, and is sufficiently small to allow quick movement through and to its main districts. It elicits a high degree of recognition from other countries, and a strong case can be made to defer any thought of registration of regions until (say) 2020 or beyond.

That said, a diagonal northeast to southwest line would not create any anomalies, and segregates what are in loose terms often described as regions. Northern Tasmania encompasses the northeast region, immediately to the south of Devonport, and with Cradle Mountain to its south; the Tamar Valley, with numerous wineries spread along the Tamar River, then trickling southward past Launceston; and the Pipers Brook/Pipers River region that is due north of Launceston and approaches the northern coast of the island. The second quasi-region is the east coast, stretching from Freycinet to Bicheno, with five wineries (Apsley Gorge, Coombend Estate, Craigie Knowe, Freycinet and Spring Vale Vineyards) all in relatively close proximity to each other. The third is Southern Tasmania, encompassing Coal River/Richmond, the Derwent Valley and the Huon Valley/ Channel.

Yet Tasmania can claim to have founded both the Victorian and South Australian wine industries in the early decades of the 19th century. Wine was being commercially made and sold in Tasmania several years before vines were planted in either of those states, and it was the source of the first vines for those states. When William Henty sailed from Launceston to Portland (in Victoria) onboard the schooner Thistle in 1834, his personal effects included 'one cask of grape cuttings and one box of plants'. John Hack planted vines in South Australia (he is said by some authorities to have been the first to do so, but records are not conclusive) in 1837, followed by John Reynell in 1838; both men obtained their cuttings from Port Arthur in southern Tasmania.

Like their mainland counterparts, the Tasmanian settlers planted vines in much the same way that they planted other staple-food-producing plants. Many of these 'domestic' vines – dating from 1825 to 1850 – still survive in gardens all over the island. A number of these have been identified as chasselas, a variety which is regarded as a table grape in France but which in very cool areas – principally Switzerland – is used for making wine. It's no wonder that it adapted well to Tasmania, or that it has survived so long there.

The state's first commercial vineyard was planted by Bartholomew Broughton in 1823, and in 1827 he advertised that he had 300 gallons (1365 litres) of 1826 vintage wine for sale. By 1827 commercial nurseries were offering vine cuttings, and by 1865 the government garden at the Queen's Domain, an important source of cuttings, had 45 varieties available, including pinot noir, cabernet sauvignon, shiraz, malbec, pinot blanc and sauvignon blanc.

Ironically, that decade marked the sudden collapse of the industry, due in part to the gold stampede on the mainland, which drained Tasmania of labour. There was a brief flurry of activity in the 1880s when Diego Bernacchi obtained cuttings from St Huberts in the Yarra Valley, planting them on Maria Island, east of Hobart, and exhibited a wine at the Melbourne Centennial Exhibition of 1888/89. He subsequently sought investors, and is said to have attached artificial bunches to his vines and sailed past the island at night with potential investors, pointing to the vines with the aid of a lamp. They were unimpressed, and Bernacchi faded away.

By the middle of the 20th century the official view of the Tasmanian Department of Agriculture was that the island was unsuited to the commercial production of wine. Two men with a European background were the first to challenge that view: Jean Miguet in northern Tasmania, and Claude Alcorso on the Derwent River, on the northern outskirts of Hobart in the south. The story of these two pioneers is continued in the Southern Tasmania entry.

Development continued at a slow pace in both Northern and Southern Tasmania; as at 1984 there were only 53 ha of vines planted in the north, which was home to seven of the 12 wineries. Towards the end of the 1980s the rate of development increased somewhat. This continued through to 1997, when plantings reached 235 ha, supporting 24 wineries. By 2008 the plantings for the whole of Tasmania had reached 1507 ha, two-thirds in the north, and one-third in the south. The primary driver has been Tamar Ridge, owned by Gunns Limited, which alone has 240 ha of vines, with more planned.

At some point the wide spread of Tasmanian vineyards, and the marked differences in site climates and soils, may lead to a change of philosophy on the question of regions. For the flip side of the coin is that outside observers not only habitually exaggerate the extent of Tasmania's viticulture, but are oblivious to the diversity of terroir and climate in the island's extremely complex geography. There are sites which are both warmer and very much drier than southern Victoria (for example, the Coal River/ Richmond area northeast of Hobart, and, in terms of warmth, the Tamar River valley south of Launceston). The one clear pattern is that pinot noir finds itself at home in all parts of the state, with the qualified exception of parts of the Tamar River valley.

Tasmania is an exquisitely drawn cameo,

with travel time compressed from hours to minutes. The drive time from the southern end of the Mornington Peninsula to the Yarra Valley (over two hours) would get you more than halfway from Hobart to Launceston, and from the Huon Valley to Bicheno. With its wealth of stone buildings and houses, its towering forests, huge lakes and beautiful rivers, Tasmania is a tourist paradise.

A high level of corporate takeover activity around the turn of the millennium saw the emergence of some well-resourced medium-sized companies, and also investment by CWA. Tasmania no longer has a doll's house–sized industry, although happily many tiny producers continue to populate the scene.

Tatachilla (est. 1903), in McLaren Vale, was reborn in 1995 but has had an at times tumultuous history going back to 1903. Between 1903 and 1961 the winery was owned by Penfolds. It was closed in 1961 and reopened in 1965 as the Southern Vales Co-operative. In the late 1980s it was purchased and renamed The Vales but did not flourish; in 1993 it was purchased by local grower Vic Zerella and former Kaiser Stuhl chief executive Keith Smith. After extensive renovations, the winery was officially reopened in 1995 and won a number of tourist awards and accolades. It became part of Banksia Wines in 2001, in turn acquired by Lion Nathan in 2002. Exports to all major markets.

Taylors was established by the eponymous family in 1969. The Taylors had had a close association with the Clare Valley for over 20 years prior to their move to establish what they called Chateau Clare. Bill Taylor senior

and his two sons, John and Bill, were Sydney hoteliers and liquor wholesalers who since World War II had purchased substantial quantities of wine from the district, chiefly from the Clarevale Cooperative, and this had brought them into contact with Jim Barry. So it was to Barry they turned when they purchased their 300-ha property at Auburn, at the bottom end of the valley. In a decision nigh-on identical to that of Rothbury Estate, established at the same time, there were to be just two wines: a cabernet sauvignon and a hermitage. (Rothbury had one white and one red, the varieties not even specified on the front label.) The cabernet sauvignon was to be the standard bearer, the wine which would make Chateau Clare as well known and respected in Australia as Chateau Mouton Rothschild in France, the label design a less than subtle hint of their aspirations.

The venture started with an appropriate fanfare, and with enough wine show success to keep the momentum up for some time. Of even greater importance was the strong distribution system the family had in New South Wales. Through the 1970s to the 1990s various winemakers were appointed, each with new ideas, but – in the end – unable to lift the profile of the winery out of the ordinary. Varietal plantings in the vineyards came and went, a massive move into chardonnay yielding few dividends.

Then, in the mid-1990s, a number of major changes were made both in the vineyard and in the winery, followed five or so years later with the establishment of the Jaraman label allowing cross-regional blending. French oak replaced American for the top wines, and two icon labels emerged: St Andrews Riesling and

St Andrews Cabernet Sauvignon, released when four to five years old. Its vineyards now extend to 550 ha, and production has leapt to 580,000 cases. Very substantial exports have been established, under the Wakefield Wines label in the UK following objections by the Portuguese port firm Taylors.

**TCA** see trichloranisole.

**tears** (as in tear drops, also called 'legs') are especially obvious in white wines which have been swirled in a wine glass. Sometimes called 'legs', the phenomenon is observed by irregular streams of wine adhering to the side of the glass, and slowly moving down the side like tiny, slow-moving rivers. Contrary to widely held belief, they are not the result of glycerol, and thus are not a measure of viscosity. The chemical and physical activities which cause the tears to form are very complex, but essentially turn on the difference in evaporation rates of alcohol and water. Just to add complexity, even German wines with alcohol of 8% alc/vol or less can give rise to tears as readily as wines with much higher alcohol. The message is to observe them, enjoy them if you will, but not regard them as any indicator of quality.

**Temple Bruer** (est. 1980) was in the vanguard of the organic movement in Australia and was the focal point for the formation of an association known as Organic Vignerons Australia. Based in Langhorne Creek, it has 19.2 ha of vineyards; part of the production is for its own label, part sold. Winemaker/owner David Bruer also has a vine propagation nursery, likewise run on an organic basis. Exports to the US and Japan.

**tempranillo** is the most important red grape variety of Spain, its greatest expression coming in Rioja, where it adds structure and spine to grenache. Like sangiovese in Italy, it also blends well with cabernet sauvignon, a blend made famous by the Vega Sicilia winery. In 2008, 386 ha were planted by 198 producers, up from the 312 ha in 2005. It is being grown in every possible climate, but its early-ripening classification strongly suggests that the best results will come from cooler regions. Because the plantings are new, final judgements on the worth of the grape in Australia cannot be made, but it holds as much promise as sangiovese, and distinctly more than nebbiolo.

**Ten Minutes by Tractor** (est. 1999) is a Mornington Peninsula winery established by three vineyard owners who found the maximum distance between each was 10 minutes by tractor. The catchy name was complemented by equally clever label designs, but it was not until Martin Spedding acquired the business in early 2004 that it really blossomed. Spedding entered into long-term leases of the three original vineyards, thus having complete management control over grape production. A fourth vineyard was added on the site of the then new cellar door and restaurant; this vineyard has been managed organically since day one, and is used to trial various organic viticulture practices which will ultimately be employed across all the plantings.

Spedding, with a wine science degree from Charles Sturt University, is responsible for the winemaking alongside Richard McIntyre (the latter as a mentor) at Moorooduc Estate, where the wines are made.

**terroir** is a French word which cannot be adequately translated into any single English word, simply because it covers a multitude of factors. Bruno Prats, the former proprietor of Chateau Cos d'Estournel in the Medoc, explained it thus:

> The very French notion of terroir looks at all the natural conditions which influence the biology of the vinestock and thus the composition of the grape itself. The terroir is the coming together of the climate, the soil, and the landscape. It is the combination of an infinite number of factors: temperatures by night and by day, rainfall distribution, hours of sunlight, slope and drainage, to name but a few. All these factors react with each other to form, in each part of the vineyard, what French wine growers call a terroir.

The late Peter Sichel, former president of the Grand Crus de Bordeaux, put it even more succinctly when he said, 'Terroir determines the character of a wine, man its quality.'

It lies at the heart of the French appellation system, itself built up by 1000 years of practical experience and observation. This system has led to a most precise and detailed delineation of quality, to the identification of a limited number of grape varieties considered to be especially suited to the terroir (and the climate) in a particular area, and to the exclusion by force of law of all others. It has led also to the prescription of pruning methods, and to the specification of maximum yields (but with such a dose of pragmatism as to render the restraints largely meaningless) and of minimum alcoholic strengths (again blurred by the use of chaptalisation).

History shows that the vineyards of France were originally planted by default, in terroir which was too deficient to support other forms of horticulture or farming. In Bordeaux there is a saying: 'If these soils were not the best in the world, they would be the worst.' But that in no way diminishes the validity of the subsequent matching of grape and soil, nor of the identification of those microscopic dots on the face of the earth which produce wines of the ineffable majesty of Chateau Petrus (Bordeaux), Romanée-Conti and Le Montrachet (Burgundy) and their ilk.

Australian vignerons may be denied the extraordinary prestige and marketing power of the top French producers, but there are compensations: they are free of the rigidity and constraints of the appellation system, and can (and do) prove that fine wine can be made in a far wider range of circumstances than the French would ever admit.

It may well be that ignorance was bliss, but the average Australian vigneron of the recent past made little attempt to correlate specific soil types with particular grape varieties and, outside certain broad parameters, made almost no attempt to link soil type and quality. (Such linkage as did occur was between climate, variety and quality.) Those broad parameters define an ideal soil as a sandy loam, preferably interspersed with gravel or small, fragmented rock. It should be deep, free-draining and of low to moderate fertility. There should be no mineral element deficiencies and it should have sufficient water-holding capacity to supply enough moisture to the vines to prevent premature senescence and defoliation.

Conversely, the most frequently encountered problems in Australian vineyard soils are excess clay and excess acidity. Heavy clay drains poorly, holding too much water after rain or irrigation, and is frequently associated with dense and hard subsoils that roots cannot penetrate. Excessively acid subsoils are far more widespread in Australia than is commonly realised, and they have a significant adverse impact on vine health and vigour. The vine's roots cannot tolerate the aluminium toxicity which is associated with high acidity (low pH), which forces them to remain in the shallow topsoils (usually less acid), making the vine much more susceptible to drought, even though the local rainfall may in theory appear adequate.

Correct moisture supply to the vine is all-important and, apart from anchorage and nutrients, is the principal function of soil in determining growth. During early shoot growth until flowering (early November to late December, depending on region and variety) vines should be well supplied with moisture. By the time the fruit starts to ripen (January to February) available water should tail off, causing vegetative growth to stabilise, and the vine to focus its attention on ripening the grapes by sugar accumulation. (The photosynthetic activity of the vine's leaves causes carbohydrates stored in the system to be converted to sugar in the grapes.)

Another problem for Australian winemakers is that a large proportion of grapes are grown by farmers who sell to winemakers. Some winemakers (often with large companies) may have never visited the vineyard and thus lack any intimate knowledge of variation in vine growth within its confines.

By contrast, the French winemaker will typically know every vine, every tiny variation in soil. Moreover, that observation will have been repeated over many centuries and handed down through the generations, whereas in Australia experience in winemaking is typically confined to one or two generations. But such experience does exist in the small estate, and is very probably one of the reasons why the small Australian winery can produce top-quality wine to rank with the best the big winery can produce.

All observers are agreed that the future of Australian winemaking lies in the vineyard, and, as a consequence, attitudes and practices are changing significantly. Cutting-edge technology is being used: airborne sensing via electromagnetic radiation (EMR) directed at the soil, the EMR device measuring the amount of energy reflected back. Together the radio wave emissions, radar and laser-imaging radar and near-infrared radiation data collected by the EMR device can provide detailed images of the soil structure (and vine growth and cropping levels) on areas of 100 square metres.

The changes in attitude are also epitomised by the 'distinguished site' concept devised and promoted by Brian Croser. This can be applied both to existing vineyards and (equally importantly) to sites and soil being evaluated for their suitability for plantings. The soil may be physically examined by excavation on a grid pattern as small as 5 metres. Overnight, a large company can acquire intimate knowledge of its plantings; Wynns Coonawarra Estate is one example of a large producer using these techniques to selectively harvest the crop and make replanting decisions.

To summarise, the supply of moisture – neither too much nor too little, made available at the right times – is crucial for quality grapes. If the correct supply can be achieved naturally through the soil's moisture retention, so much the better. In France, for example, it is provided by the alluvial gravel and clay mix of Bordeaux, and the limestone marl (a mix of limestone and clay) of Burgundy. But in both Australia and France, identification of the best terroir (in the broadest sense of that term) is (or was) of paramount importance. In France, the search concluded centuries ago; in Australia, it has only just begun.

**texture** is a tasting term which overlaps with mouthfeel and structure, but which does not concern itself with flavour elements, and is chiefly discerned and evaluated on the mid-palate of the wine, structure extending to the finish **and** aftertaste.

**The Islander Estate Vineyard** (est. 2000) was established by French flying winemaker Jacques Lurton on Kangaroo Island. He has established 11 ha of close-planted vineyard to an eclectic mix of semillon, viognier, grenache, malbec, shiraz, cabernet franc **and** sangiovese, and has built a substantial winery. The 5000-case production is exported to many countries including the US and France, with on-premise distribution in Australia the major domestic sales base.

**thiols,** or mercaptans, are a group of chemical compounds most commonly encountered with red wines formed by yeast reacting with sulphur in the lees after the primary fermentation. It is a common occurrence,

usually rectified by aeration (that is, deliberately exposing the wine to oxygen), by splash racking or sparging, or by the addition of a small amount of copper sulphate, followed thereafter by racking. Mercaptans in this concentration and form have unpleasant smells, variously described as rotten egg gas, burnt rubber or similar, and the need to treat them is obvious. More sinister are very low levels, which may go unnoticed, and which if not treated become bound before or after the wine is bottled. Untreated thiols are likely to be the precursors of the reduced aromas which will develop in screwcapped bottles. It should be emphasised, however, that the problem lies with the wine, and not the screwcap. If properly checked and treated prior to bottling, reduced aromas will not occur regardless of the type of closure used. Conversely, wines with mercaptans can develop reduced characteristics under any closure.

**Thistle Hill** (est. 1976) is the family-owned venture of Lesley Robertson and her children, who decided not to sell the Mudgee winery and vineyard after the untimely death of husband David. The 11 ha of riesling, chardonnay, pinot noir, cabernet sauvignon, shiraz and muscat hamburg are NASAA-certified organic, and the wines are made in the on-site winery.

**Thomas Wines** (est. 1997) is the venture of Andrew Thomas and wife Jo. Thomas moved to the Hunter Valley from McLaren Vale to join the winemaking team at Tyrrell's, and it was 13 years before he left Tyrrell's to start Thomas Wines. To provide additional income, he rented space in another winery and began to establish a now very successful contract winemaking business, in addition to making the wines of his own label. The wines contract-made by him have enjoyed significant show success, claiming many trophies and gold medals. Thomas Wines' releases focus on individual vineyard semillons and shirazs, and are of impeccable quality. Exports to Canada and Singapore.

**Thorn-Clarke Wines** (est. 1987), in the Barossa Valley, is the highly successful business of David and Cheryl Clarke (née Thorn) and son Sam, the latter managing director. The Clarkes began assembling their vineyards in 1987. There are now four, totalling 270 ha, with all the main varieties planted; petit verdot, nebbiolo, mammolo and aglianico are recent additions. Although production has rapidly increased to 80,000 cases, there is still a substantial surplus of grapes sold to other Barossa Valley wineries – in many instances the best blocks are left for the Thorn-Clarke label. It is for this reason, no doubt, that it has had an imposing run of gold medal and trophy success in wine shows across Australia, including the National Wine Show. Their particular strength lies with red wines, but extending well beyond the Barossa staple of shiraz. Exports to all major markets, and significant domestic distribution.

**tinta amarella** is widely grown in Portugal's Douro Valley, where it is regarded as a good (rather than very good) red grape variety. In the early part of the 1990s there were about 30 ha in South Australia, usually called Portugal. To add further confusion, some plantings of 'malbec' were in fact of tinta amarella. Its prospects are not particularly good. Only two growers remain.

**tinta barocca, tinta cao, tinta roriz** are Portuguese red grape varieties of varying degrees of importance. All are grown by Stanton & Killeen in Rutherglen for use in vintage port styles, and are also used by Seppeltsfield; likewise in the Yarra Valley. Tinta cao is grown in other regions on a limited basis, by a total of eight growers.

**titratable acidity** see total acidity.

**tokay** see topaque.

**Tomboy Hill** (est. 1984) is the venture of former schoolteacher Ian Watson, who seems to be following the same path as Lindsay McCall of Paringa Estate (also a former schoolteacher) in extracting greater quality and style than any other winemaker in his region, in this case Ballarat. Since 1984 Watson has slowly and patiently built up a patchwork quilt of small plantings of chardonnay and pinot noir. In the better years, single-vineyard wines of chardonnay and/or pinot noir are released; Rebellion Chardonnay and Pinot Noir are multi-vineyard blends, but all 100 per cent Ballarat. Exports to the UK and Canada.

**Toolangi Vineyards** (est. 1995) was established by Garry and Julie Hounsell when they acquired a property in the Dixons Creek subregion of the Yarra Valley, adjoining the Toolangi State Forest. The 10,000-case production is heavily biased in favour of chardonnay, with three price points, reserve at the top, estate in the middle, and varietal at the bottom level. Unusually, the wines have different contract winemakers, all prominent, none more so than Rick Kinzbrunner of

Giaconda and (formerly) Tom Carson, then of Yering Station. A much smaller amount of estate-grown shiraz is made, and pinot noir is made from purchased grapes. The quality of the chardonnays has taken Toolangi to a strong position.

**topaque** is the name adopted by Australia in January 2009 to replace tokay; the reasons for the change appear in the apera entry. To complicate matters, there has been no necessity for any change in the use of the name muscat, nor the retention of the word 'tawny' (without the word 'port' appended); thus, for topaque, muscat and tawny, the three most important fortified wine categories, there will be four categories of ascending quality and age: Australian, classic, grand and rare.

**Torbreck Vintners**, in the Barossa Valley, dates back to 1994, when David Powell established it with his wife. In the wake of their divorce, Torbreck was completely re-capitalised, with Powell continuing as the hugely talented winemaker, but with a minority shareholding. In 2008 the financial partners who had come to his aid were (amicably) bought out, and Torbreck is now owned by the Powell interests and Peter Kight of Quivira Vineyards & Winery in California's Dry Creek Valley. Through this period of at times stressful corporate change, the style and quality of the wines, primarily based on old shiraz vines, have remained of the highest order. Exports to all major markets.

**Torzi Matthews Vintners** (est. 1996), in the Eden Valley, was established by Domenic Torzi and Tracy Matthews, who searched for a number of years before finding a 6-ha block at Mount McKenzie. The block they chose is in a hollow and the soil is meagre, and they knew it was frost-prone, but they were in no way deterred. The result is predictably low yields, concentrated further by drying the grapes on racks and reducing the weight by around 30 per cent (the Appassimento method is used in Italy to produce Amarone-style wines). Four wines are made, two under the Frost Dodger label, and two under the Schist Rock label. Exports to the UK, the US and elsewhere.

**total acidity** is one of the four most commonly used wine measurements, the other three being alcohol, pH and residual sugar. While the process of measurement is simple enough, in Australia, the US, Italy, South Africa, New Zealand and the UK it is recorded as if all acids were tartaric. In France, and most of Europe, it is recorded as if the acid is sulphuric, even though the amount of this acid in wine is minuscule. Thus if an Australian wine is said to have a total acidity of 6.5 grams per litre, the French will describe the same wine as having 3.9 grams per litre. To complicate the matter further, Germany uses an altogether different system.

**touriga nacional** is the red grape cornerstone of Portuguese vintage port which, after centuries of use for this purpose alone, is now also being used in the production of high-quality Portuguese table wines as a blend component. Deeply coloured, thick-skinned and tannic, a small percentage in a blend makes a major impact. In 2007 there were 53 ha of touriga in Australia, 28 ha being grown in South Australia (some used by

Seppeltsfield). Since that time it has spread across Victoria (Bendigo, Goulburn Valley and Rutherglen), into New South Wales (Hunter Valley, Mudgee and Canberra District), and thence into Queensland. It is used both in table wines and in vintage fortified styles, and grown by 36 producers.

**Tower Estate** (est. 1999), at Pokolbin in the Lower Hunter Valley, was founded by the late Len Evans, with the five-star Tower Lodge accommodation and convention centre part of the development. Since his death there has been no change in the day-to-day management of either Tower Estate or Tower Lodge by the remaining owners. Semillon, verdelho, chardonnay and shiraz all come from the Hunter Valley; Adelaide Hills provides sauvignon blanc and a second chardonnay; Barossa Valley a second shiraz; and Tasmania pinot noir. Exports to the UK, Canada, Asia and Russia.

**trebbiano** is a high-yielding white grape variety widely grown in Italy to produce anonymous white wines, and in France as the most important base wine for cognac. In both countries its high natural acidity is its principal virtue. As recently as 1997 there were over 850 ha planted in Australia, mainly in the Riverland. Since that time plantings have decreased, falling to 341 ha by 2005 and 219 ha by 2008. There are scattered plantings across Glenrowan, Rutherglen, Mudgee, the Pyrenees and Geelong, but it is most unlikely that it will make a return to popularity.

**Trentham Estate** (est. 1988) is owned by the Murphy family, with Anthony (Tony) Murphy chief winemaker and CEO. It was established on the family's property on the Murray River at Trentham Cliffs; Murphy's winemaking skills quickly became apparent as he was able to produce a range of wines with more clearly defined varietal character and better balance and length than most of the other producers using similar grape sources. When the long-term future of the Murray Darling became uncertain, he began to look elsewhere (in Victoria), expanding the winery portfolio to include Mornington Peninsula pinot noir, Yarra Valley chardonnay and Heathcote shiraz (the first vintage of which won a major international trophy in the UK in 2008). Exports to the UK, Canada and elsewhere.

**trichloranisole** (more correctly, 2, 4, 6-trichloranisole or, in the vernacular, TCA) is a compound created when chlorine reacts with organic phenols to form chlorophenols, which in turn react with mould in the presence of moisture to form TCA. It is detectable by the human nose in minute proportions; indeed, there was a time when scientific analysis was less sensitive. The detection threshold is as low as five parts per trillion (equivalent to one second in 64 centuries). While TCA can affect any wood (including barrels, wooden pallets and structural wood in a winery), its role in tainting corks is by far the most significant. The great problem with TCA is that its level of contamination varies greatly; even an amateur can recognise a grossly corked bottle of wine, but as the level of contamination reduces, so does the effect. Winemakers are resigned to the fact that a significant number of their wines will be found wanting by consumers who do not realise that the faint bitterness they taste in the wine is in fact a cork taint. Decades of denial of the problem by the Portuguese cork makers so frustrated Australian winemakers that they began to move en masse to screwcaps at the end of the 20th century. It is ironic that at the same time Portuguese cork makers finally acknowledged the problem, and introduced major changes to the way cork is harvested and to the subsequent manufacturing processes. Had the Portuguese been more proactive, the even bigger issue of random oxidation might not have come into such clear focus; it is this, rather than TCA, which has pushed the rapid adoption of screwcaps.

Troncais is one of the three oaks loosely grouped under the centre of France banner, the other two being Nevers and Allier.

Tuck's Ridge (est. 1985) in the Mornington Peninsula has changed focus significantly since selling its large Red Hill vineyard. Estate plantings are now an eclectic mix of chardonnay (2 ha), pinot noir (1.2 ha) and albarino (0.7 ha), and contract grape purchases have been reduced. Quality, not quantity, is the key. Exports to the US, Germany, the Netherlands and Hong Kong.

Tulloch (est. 1895) is part of the fabric of the Hunter Valley, in continuous production over three centuries. However, the chain of ownership was first fractured when, in 1969, the UK-based Reed Consolidated purchased Tulloch from the family; five years later Reed onsold Tulloch to Gilbys Australia, who in turn passed ownership to the Allied Vintners Group. In 1985 Penfolds acquired Allied Vintners, the ultimate ownership of Tulloch thus changing yet again. Wine production did not cease, and Jay Tulloch was for much of this time involved in a managerial role. In 2002 the winery was sold to Poole's Rock, and the brand separately sold to a partnership of Jay Tulloch and family, Two Rivers and Angove Family Winemakers. The physical location for the Tulloch business moved along the same road (De Beyers), where a lavish cellar door has been established. The wines are made by a local contract winemaking business, and the quality is unimpeachable. Exports to Belgium, Canada, the Phillipines, Singapore, Hong Kong, Malaysia, Japan and China.

Tumbarumba, gazetted 10 December 1998, in the Southern New South Wales Zone, is one of the most remote wine regions in Australia. The first vines were established by Ian Cowell at Tumbarumba and by Frank Minutello at Tooma in the Maragle Valley, 18 kilometres southeast of Tumbarumba, in 1982 and 1983. The first harvest from Ian Cowell's vineyard was sold to Rosemount Estate for sparkling wine, and the majority of the pinot noir and chardonnay grown in the region is still put to the same (sparkling wine) use. Between 1983 and 1992 the pace of development was slow. At the end of that period, there were eight vineyards established with 78 ha in total. By 1997 there were over 25 vineyards with a total of 309 ha, thanks to a major planting program in 1994, and there have been continuing plantings thereafter.

Foster's, CWA, Hungerford Hill, Chalkers Crossing and McWilliam's (the largest purchaser) take a large part of the annual production, but only Foster's owns a vineyard here, understanding only too well the marginal nature of grapegrowing. The ability of the region to produce table wine (as opposed to sparkling wine) is dependent on two things: seasonal conditions and site altitude. The margin for error is small, the need for first-class viticultural management high. The region can and does produce outstanding chardonnay, with a major cool-climate impact giving the wines great finesse and length.

With a mean January temperature of 19.3°C, Tumbarumba's climate may not seem so cool. But there is also a number of other mutually counterbalancing factors: high sunshine hours with brilliant light, cold summer nights and a late start to the growing season. Frost is the chief viticultural threat, and dictates careful site selection and management. Night-time temperature inversion – the propensity of cold air to sink and warm air to rise – can play tricks, but elevation is significant in determining varietal choice.

Tumbarumba generally has typical high mountain soils, derived from decomposed granite and basalt, with a gritty/grainy texture; there is also red sand over clay soils in parts. The choice of viticultural site is chiefly determined by aspect (north- and northeast-facing preferred, south-facing nigh on impossible) and slope (sufficiently steep to promote good air drainage at night and thus minimise the risk of frost).

Chardonnay and pinot noir together make up almost 80 per cent of the total plantings, chardonnay the senior partner. Sauvignon blanc (for table wine) and pinot meunier (for sparkling) make up the rest. The production of the six wineries is small; most of the grapes are transported out of the region by non-resident purchasers.

LAT 34°36′S; ALT 300–800 m; HDD 1010; GSR 375 mm; MJT 19.3°C; HARV Early March to early May; CHIEF VIT. HAZARD Frost

**Turkey Flat** is one of the foremost family-owned wineries in the Barossa Valley. On one view the establishment date is 1990 (or even 1992), but most proprietors would choose 1870, when the Schultz family purchased the Turkey Flat vineyard, or even 1847, when the vineyard was first planted to the very old shiraz which still grows today alongside 8 ha of equally old grenache. It is owned by Peter and Christie Schulz, and shares with Rockford a philosophy which is at the very heart of the best attributes of the Barossa Valley. The wines are made skilfully, with maximum emphasis on the combination of terroir and old vines; the Schulzes do not favour late-picked, high-alcohol wines laced with an abundance of new oak. Turkey Flat has three vineyards: the home vineyard at Tanunda of 21 ha, 18 ha in the Stonewell area, and 13 ha in the Koonunga Hill area. The attention to detail in the modern winery puts the finishing touches to bespoke winemaking. Exports to the UK, the US and other major markets.

**Two Hands Wines** (est. 2000) was established by successful South Australian businessmen Michael Twelftree and Richard Mintz, and has come a long way in a short time with a carefully thought-out business plan focused primarily on the US market. While all but a small handful of the wines are made from shiraz, grapes are purchased each year from the Barossa Valley, Padthaway, Clare Valley, Langhorne Creek and Heathcote (Two Hands does not own any vineyards). A cabernet sauvignon is the other top-end wine in the portfolio. The wines place utmost importance on sweet fruit and soft tannin structure, with elevated alcohol levels a consequence. Exports to the UK and elsewhere as well as the US.

**Two Rivers** (est. 1988) is a significant part of the viticultural scene in the Upper Hunter Valley, with over 160 ha of vineyards established, involving a total investment of around $7 million. Part of the fruit is sold under long-term contracts, and part is made for the expanding winemaking and marketing operations of Two Rivers, the chief brand of Inglewood Vineyards, with the emphasis on chardonnay and semillon. It is also a partner in the Tulloch business, together with the Tulloch and Angove families, and supplies much of the grapes for the Tulloch label. A contemporary cellar door has opened, adding significantly to the appeal of the Upper Hunter Valley as a wine-tourist destination.

**tyrian**, like tarrango, is a CSIRO-bred cross of cabernet sauvignon and the obscure Spanish variety sumoll, taken into commercial production by McWilliam's. It produces a very deeply coloured red wine.

**Tyrrell's**, arguably the pre-eminent winery in the Hunter Valley, traces its origins back to March 1847, when the Archbishop of Canterbury wrote to the rector of the insignificant parish of Beaulieu in Hampshire, England, offering William Tyrrell (the rector in question) the bishopric of the newly founded city of Newcastle, New South Wales. Tyrrell accepted the offer, and arrived in Australia to be installed as bishop on 30 January 1848.

In 1850 three of his nephews arrived in Australia to further their education under his guidance. One was Edward Tyrrell, who was 15 at the time. His father was Frederick Tyrrell, a surgeon at St Thomas' Hospital in London and William's older brother. Within a few years of his arrival, and while still a teenager, Edward moved to Singleton and started a dairy farm. It was not a success, and when in 1858 Edward Tyrrell heard that selections suited to vinegrowing at Pokolbin were available, he applied for and was granted one of the last available.

As luck would have it, the 134-ha grant, nestling under the lee of the Brokenback Range, contained some of the finest red basalt soil in the district, with a limestone subsoil. First Edward Tyrrell had to clear by hand the spotted gums (not so hard) and ironbark (very hard) which forested the land, and then work up the soil for planting. Even in these days of bulldozers and tractors that is regarded as hard work, a notion that he would find highly amusing.

He produced his first vintage in 1864 from the first few acres of vines. By 1870 he had planted 12 ha of vines, half to aucerot (which the locals regarded very highly and which they pronounced 'ocka'), and the rest to semillon and shiraz. In the meantime he had built (in 1858) the one-room slab hut which stands diminutively but proudly in the forecourt of today's winery complex, a building beyond price. The first stage of the winery was completed just in time for the 1864 vintage; it, too, stands today at the core of the subsequent extensions, most of which look to be very nearly as old.

The second of the 10 children of Edward and his wife Susan (née Hungerford), Edward George Young Tyrrell, was born in 1873. He and his youngest brother, Avery, were to assume responsibility for the vineyard and winery following the ill health of their father in 1888. Edward George (known to all as

Dan, and eventually as Uncle Dan) assumed that responsibility immediately, although he was only 15 years old. His ensuing 70 vintages as a winemaker (he was forced to suspend winemaking activities in 1958 when he fell off a ladder) certainly stands as an Australian record, and can have few parallels in wine history.

Not content with making the wine and managing the estate (Avery eventually assumed responsibility for viticulture) at Tyrrell's, Dan Tyrrell also took over the day-to-day winemaking operations of Doyle's Kaludah Winery at Lochinvar. This brought him into contact with Philobert Terrier, a winemaker born and trained in France who had been in charge at Kaludah before moving across the road to commence his St Helena Vineyard and winery.

Under Dan Tyrrell's stewardship all the estate-grown grapes were made into wine, wine which gradually gained a reputation among wine merchants and other wine companies still operating in and out of the region. From the 1930s, Maurice O'Shea of McWilliam's became a regular customer, to the point where most of Tyrrell's best wines were bought by O'Shea. These were either blended with other wines from the district (including those made by O'Shea himself) or kept separate and released under the name Mount Pleasant Richard Hermitage.

Dan Tyrrell died of a heart attack at the age of 89 in April 1959, and Murray Tyrrell – who had spent several years in the winery after World War II learning the trade – came back from his cattle business to take over Tyrrell's Ashmans Winery. Even at this time, virtually all Tyrrell's wine was sold in bulk. Anne Tyrrell (now Anne Ellis) recollects that in the late 1950s, at the age of eight or nine, she became a child typiste. The odd person who called at the winery to purchase wine in bottle was as often as not cheerfully accommodated by means of syphoning the desired wine direct from the vat into bottles. Anne would then type up the necessary labels by inserting 'claret' or 'burgundy', and the year, under the maroon coat-of-arms design.

Murray Tyrrell did not have much of an opportunity to change things immediately, for 1959 saw virtually the entire vintage wiped out by hail, and in 1960 the after-effects were such that only 2730 litres, or two casks, of wine were made. Hail struck again in 1961, and only three casks of wine were made that year. So 1962 was the first year nature gave Murray a chance, and he took it with both hands. Vat 5 of 1962 won a gold medal at the Sydney Wine Show, and caused such a storm that the committee sent Hector Tulloch and the local police sergeant around to the winery to check – first that the show wine was indeed a Tyrrell wine, and second that the quantity made was sufficient for the show entry.

After the death of Murray Tyrrell in 2000, son Bruce Tyrrell took over management of what was by then a very large business. He was responsible for the inspired move in 2003 to sell its Long Flat brand (and stocks) for a price reported to be in excess of $10 million, allowing Tyrrell's to focus on its premium, super-premium and ultra-premium wines, led by a magnificent portfolio of single-vineyard semillons released when five to six years old, and the Winemaker's Selection Four Acres Shiraz, a single-vineyard wine made from vines planted in 1879. Vat 47 Chardonnay, the first chardonnay to be sold and labelled as such in the Hunter Valley in 1971, is another flagship. Tyrrell's has extended its estate vineyards and hence regional wines with 42 ha in McLaren Vale, 30 ha in Heathcote (going to make the Rufus Stone brands), and 42 ha in Coonawarra, all adding to the 185 ha in the Pokolbin district and the Upper Hunter Valley. Needless to say, exports to all major markets.

a b c d e f g h i
j k l m n o p q
r s t u v w x y z

**ullage** refers to the space between the upper surface of wine in a barrel, cask or bottle, and the stopper or bung used to close the container. Also called the head-space, it may be present from the outset, or be wholly or partly formed as the result of evaporation of the wine, or seepage through the container or its stopper. In the context of wine bottles, where the term is most commonly encountered, it is the distance between the bottom of the cork and the level of the wine in the bottle when it stands upright. Unless the wine has been subjected to extreme heat, or there is a defect in the cork, ullage will develop slowly, starting approximately 1 centimetre below the cork and over a period of 20 to 30 years increasing to 3 centimetres or more below the cork. Once the level falls to 4 centimetres or more, prudence would suggest that the wine should be professionally recorked, having first been tasted to ensure it is sound, and topped up to the original level with the same or a similar wine. Bottles with greater ullage are usually oxidised and not really suitable for drinking, unless the age is extreme and it is approached as a piece of living history. Occasionally, and for no apparent reason, a bottle with large ullage may turn out to be largely unaffected. The colour of the wine in the bottle before the cork is removed may provide some advance information: if the wine is bright in colour there is cause for hope. The whole subject will become of decreasing importance in future decades as screwcaps progressively replace cork.

**Upper Goulburn,** gazetted 14 October 2003, is in the Central Victoria Zone, on the western prolongation of the Great Dividing Range. It encompasses the headwaters of the Goulburn River, and Lake Eildon, the latter one of Melbourne's major water storage dams. It was originally proposed that the Upper Goulburn and Strathbogie Ranges regions form a region to be called Central Victorian High Country, but the decision to split the two regions was clearly correct. This is a seriously cool area, with mountains up to 1800 metres, and vineyards planted as high as 800 metres (and as low as 250 metres). It is one of the few Victorian regions without a history of 19th-century viticulture: it may well have seemed to be too cold.

The scenery is always beautiful and varied, with alternating areas of dense forest, grazing pasture and – increasingly – vineyards. Delatite offers spectacular views towards the Australian Alps, snow-clad in winter and (sometimes) well into spring. Mount Buller, one of Victoria's foremost skiing destinations, is accessed through Mansfield. Lake Eildon is in the eastern half of the region, and the Goulburn River runs east to west through its centre. The continuing links with its past are grazing (sheep, dairy cattle and beef cattle), timber logging and (on a small scale) gold mining. Wine has added to the tourism attractions of the region: boating on Lake Eildon, trout fishing in the lake and the numerous streams in its borders, and Delatite itself, which is on the road to Mount Buller's ski slopes.

While the winter–spring rainfall (and snow) is normally substantial, most vineyards use drip irrigation in summer. This is in turn mainly supplied by surface dams which fill readily; drought excepted, water is not the limiting force here that it is in other parts of Central Victoria.

Both rainfall and growing season temperatures are strongly influenced by altitude. Likewise, north-facing slopes receive more effective heat and light than do south- or southwest-facing slopes. Both soil and topography are varied, with valleys and slopes running in many different directions. The region as a whole is geologically described as the East Victorian Uplands, with volcanic origins. The soils are most commonly clay and loam, but with sandstone, siltstone, granite, shale, limestone and dolomite all represented.

The plantings are roughly split between white and red (the latter 55 per cent of the total): chardonnay and riesling, with a fast-increasing amount of sauvignon blanc, lead the white wines; shiraz, cabernet sauvignon and merlot lead the red wines, with pinot noir also planted. The leading wineries are Cheviot Bridge, Delatite, Mount Cathedral Vineyards, Mount Terrible and Rocky Passes Estate, supported by Jean Pauls Vineyard, Sedona Estate, Tallarook and Terra Felix.

**Upper Hunter Valley** does not officially exist; for inexplicable reasons it was decided that there would be a Hunter Valley Zone, with a single region called Hunter, further distinction between the Lower and Upper Hunter to be achieved through subregions. Given the distances involved, the very different nature of the countryside, the wine styles and the climate, the only rationale is or would be the ability of wineries in the Lower Hunter Valley to buy grapes from the Upper Hunter without any indication on the label that this had taken place. The very different history of the two regions is another reason for treating them differently. Notwithstanding that a young German settler named Carl Brecht had planted vines in 1860 at the junction of Wybong Creek and the Goulburn River, and had gone on to make wines that won gold medals at international shows throughout the 1870s, viticulture ceased in the region between 1900 and 1910. The 1958 decision by Penfolds to sell its Dalwood winery in the Lower Hunter Valley and establish Wybong in the Upper Hunter Valley, after a gap of 48 years, was initially seen as a success, and Max Schubert was an enthusiastic supporter of the venture.

It is true that with appropriate management, site and varietal selection, grapegrowing in the Upper Hunter is economically viable – more so, indeed, than in many Lower Hunter locations. Thus, Lower Hunter wineries have become important stakeholders, either owning vineyards or as grape purchasers. But neither approach has given the Upper Hunter much focus or personality, something underlined by the continued dearth of small wineries and also by the decision not to seek recognition as a subregion under the Geographic Indications legislation. The Upper Hunter seems to lie at the end of a vinous road that heads nowhere, and is thus rarely travelled. Arguably, this pretty area deserves better.

The all-important difference from the Lower Hunter is the lower rainfall: 620 millimetres compared with 750 millimetres. As in the Lower Hunter, January and February are the two wettest months, with rain ever likely to interfere with vintage. The heat summation (at Muswellbrook) is even greater than that of the Lower Hunter, reflecting the lack of the afternoon sea breezes which slightly temper the latter district. The well-drained and moderately fertile black silty loams, overlying alkaline dark clay loam, are the key to the success of the region from a viticultural standpoint. This is first and foremost white wine country, with chardonnay, semillon and verdelho the leading white grapes. The wineries are Arrowfield, Penmara, Polin & Polin, Pyramid Hill and Two Rivers. Rosemount disappeared from the scene with the closure of its winery in 2009.

LAT 32°15'S; ALT 150–250 m; HDD 2170; GSR 400 mm; MJT 22.3°C; HARV Mid-January to early March; CHIEF VIT. HAZARDS Vintage rain; mildew

a b c d e f g h i
j k l m n o p q
r s t u v w x y z

**varietal** is a descriptive term for a wine named after the dominant grape variety from which it is made. The term emanates from the New World, California the trailblazer from the 1950s onwards. To qualify for varietal labelling in Australia, the wine must contain not less than 85 per cent of the specified variety. For more information see labels.

**Vasse Felix** (est. 1967) was established by Perth cardiologist Dr Tom Cullity, making him the father of viticulture in Margaret River. That said, Cullity always gave full credit to the work done by Dr John Gladstones in so accurately pinpointing the Margaret River, and the grapes it was suited to. The Holmes à Court family company, Heytesbury Holdings, acquired and transformed it over the ensuing decades. The most controversial of the changes was the establishment of 150 ha of estate vineyards in the Jindong area in the northern part of the Margaret River; the principal concern was that the soils would be too fertile. Whether or not that was correct, the flagship wines come from the 15 ha of 40-year-old vines in Cowaramup, but a major part of the 150,000-plus cases produced under the Vasse Felix label come from Jindong, and, in good vintages, it is hard to fault these wines. Exports to all major markets.

**vat** is a generic term for any large container used for fermentation or maturation of wine. Oak was the traditional medium, but in the late 19th and early 20th centuries slate and wax-lined concrete vats made their appearance, followed by epoxy resin; mild steel with an enamel coating followed, and, in the second half of the century, stainless steel became the most widely used construction material. In the early years of the 21st century, oak vats started to appear again in New World countries for the fermentation of highest quality wines – not for the purpose of introducing oak flavour, but for a more gentle fermentation process.

**veraison** is the minutely altered English word from the French *véraison*, which denotes the beginning of the rapid growth in and colour change of individual grape berries. At the beginning of veraison, the berries are hard and green, the colour little different whether they are white or red grape varieties. Paradoxically, cell division stops at the onset of veraison, which means that the eventual size of the grape is largely fixed by then. It is for this reason that many quality-conscious viticulturists withhold water prior to veraison, and apply however much is needed post-veraison, knowing it will not unduly enlarge the berries. This, too, is the reason why most viticulturists prefer to delay bunch-thinning until veraison, to prevent the vine transferring enzymes and carbohydrate to the remaining bunches, thus increasing berry size and bunch weight, and partially defeating the purpose of bunch-thinning. Finally, if bunch-thinning takes place during veraison, the bunches which are still hard and green can be selectively removed, ensuring even ripening of all of the remaining bunches.

**verdelho** was an early white grape arrival in Australia, probably brought to Western Australia from the Cape district of South Africa. Its passage to New South Wales – and, in particular, to the Hunter Valley – is less clear, as it does not appear on the list of varieties brought to Australia by James Busby.

Contemporary records in the Hunter Valley show that it was highly regarded at the end of the 19th century, but for whatever reason kept only a toehold in the Hunter Valley until it began its rapid growth from 1990 onwards. The rate of growth slowed significantly at the end of the planting boom between 1996 and 2004, but nonetheless increased from 1603 ha in 2005 to 1761 ha in 2008. Most Australian verdelho comes from the Margaret River and Swan Valley regions of Western Australia, and the Hunter Valley in New South Wales, with the Granite Belt an outpost in Queensland. Its generous fruit salad flavour, evident from the conclusion of fermentation, needing neither bottle age nor oak, has doubtless contributed to its massive growth.

**verduzzo** is one of Italy's ancient white grape varieties, primarily grown in Friuli, and used to make both dry and sweet wines. In either case, the wine is full-bodied, with considerable extract (which needs to be carefully managed). Plantings are minuscule, with only four producers, including Pizzini in the King Valley and Bianchet (the pioneer) in the Yarra Valley.

**vermentino** is the principal white grape of Corsica, and is grown in Italy along the Tuscan coast where its quality has led to the creation of a new appellation, Vermentino di Gallura DOCG (DOCG is the top quality classification in Italy). Jancis Robinson (*The Oxford Companion to Wine*) notes it is variously called pigato, favorita, rolle, rollo and malvoisie de Corse in various parts of Italy, France and Corsica. Its European track record suggests it is capable of producing wines with abundant character, and that as at 2005 demand in Italy

far exceeded supply. In Australia it is grown in 11 vineyards, notably in the King Valley. Producers of note include Banrock Station, Buller, Chalmers, Foxeys Hangout, Politini, Trentham Estate and Yalumba. Although all of the plantings are young, it is already performing with distinction in Australia.

**vertical spur positioning** see pruning.

**Vincognita** (est. 1999) has been developed by vigneron/owner Peter Belej, who moved from Ukraine as a boy with his family, and grew up on the family vineyards at Gol Gol in New South Wales. After 40 years he decided to move to the Fleurieu Peninsula. Here he has planted 40 ha on the Nangkita Vineyard, with 14 ha of shiraz, 8 ha each of cabernet sauvignon, merlot and sauvignon blanc, 2 ha of gold medal–winning viognier and one row of zinfandel. Daughter Carolyn (Carrie) Belej is a winemaker with Foster's, but directs the winemaking at Vincognita on a consultant basis. The sheer consistency of the quality of the wines is as impressive as the modest price tags.

**vinegar fly** (known in the UK and the US as fruit fly) is correctly called *Drosophila melanogaster* and is given its common name because of its ability to produce acetic acid in wine. The population over winter falls dramatically; as summer comes the population increases, and by the time of vintage can increase by a factor of 2000 or more. It has only a two-week life cycle, but breeds prolifically when conditions are favourable.

**Vine Pull Scheme** was legislated by the South Australian Government in 1987, compensating growers who removed old vines or unwanted varieties, and left their land unplanted. It came in the wake of five years of grape surpluses and very low prices. In 1982 the surplus of 9000–10,000 tonnes of red grapes led to the uprooting of 400–500 ha of vines, and the continued top-grafting of grenache and mourvedre to chardonnay (a grafting program which had begun the previous year). In 1984 Penfolds vintage notes said it was likely that 500 ha of vines would be removed in the winter of 1984 from the Barossa Valley, Clare Valley and Angle Vale areas. In 1985 shiraz brought $275 per tonne, grenache $190 per tonne, chardonnay $420 per tonne and riesling $385 per tonne. It was these sub-economic prices, and the distortion between white and red grape prices, that led to the introduction of the Vine Pull Scheme. It resulted in a reduction in the overall plantings in the Barossa of 9 per cent; the greatest loss was the destruction of old shiraz vines which, 10 years later, were bringing prices in excess of $3000 per tonne from Penfolds. By 1989 the price of shiraz had risen to $800 per tonne, cabernet sauvignon to $1220 per tonne and chardonnay to an astonishing $1590 per tonne (largely unwanted 20 years later), while riesling slipped backwards.

**viognier** had a near-death experience in its home in the northern end of the Rhône Valley in 1968, when the plantings of this white grape variety had shrunk to a mere 14 ha. Its tenuous hold on life was in Condrieu, and the minuscule 1.6-ha Chateau Grillet Appellation Contrôlée, plus interplanted vines in Côte-Rôtie. The reasons for its near-disappearance were its extremely unreliable fruit set and its sensitivity to powdery mildew. It has been saved as the wines of the northern Rhône Valley became increasingly well known, thanks in no small measure to the exceptional skill and dedication of Marcel Guigal, and the subsequent discovery and adoption of his wines by Robert Parker Jnr.

James Busby collected syrah from the Hill of Hermitage, together with marsanne and roussanne, but makes no mention of viognier, which nonetheless ultimately found its way into the massive collection of vines at the CSIRO division of horticulture at Merbein in Victoria, under the care of the late Allan Antcliff. It was from Antcliff that Baillieu Myer of Elgee Park obtained the first vines for a single-vineyard planting on his Mornington Peninsula vineyard in 1972, around the same time as the late Dr Bailey Carrodus interplanted a small number of viognier vines with shiraz at Yarra Yering. In the 1990s Yalumba began an intensive program of experimentation in both vineyard and winery to try to unlock the best characteristics of the grape as expressed in the finished wine. (It now rates its Virgilius Viognier as its most distinguished wine, white or red.) It was not until 2003 that its plantings were sufficiently large to rate mention in the Australian Bureau of Statistics figures. In that year 268 ha were in bearing, with another 273 ha planted but yet to come into bearing, for a total of 541 ha. By 2005 the total had risen to 927 ha, reaching 4391 ha by 2008, with 468 growers. The compound rate of growth over the 2005 to 2008 period was greater than that for any other variety.

Making a table wine with clear varietal character but which avoids excess phenolics is very difficult; Yalumba is one of the few to have consistently mastered the art. It is arguable that the demand for the grape does in fact stem from the practice of co-fermenting 5 per cent of viognier with shiraz, aping the wines of Côte-Rôtie in the northern Rhône Valley. It is a remarkable union, increasing the vibrancy of the colour, and substantially lifting the aromatic qualities of the shiraz. The pioneer (other than Yarra Yering) was Tim Kirk of Clonakilla in the Canberra District, and it has become clear that the marriage works best in moderately cool to cool climates.

**Virgin Hills** (est. 1968) was the creation of the highly unconventional, larger-than-life figure of Tom Lazar. Lazar came to Australia from Hungary via Paris, where he spent three years studying sculpture at the École des Beaux Arts. He first made his presence felt in Melbourne, establishing the Little Reata as the ultimate lunch spot for the affluent in the mid-1960s and, later, Reata. These were the days of success for Tom Lazar, and in 1968 he ventured to Virgin Hills, acquiring the timber-clad property for $74 per hectare on the strength of a most favourable report from the Victorian Department of Agriculture. This was despite the fact that there had been no previous history of winegrowing in the hill country above Kyneton, where the vineyard was duly established.

Though this was and is a seriously cool part of the Macedon Ranges, Lazar elected to plant cabernet sauvignon, cabernet franc, malbec, merlot and shiraz, with a sideways look at gewurztraminer and chardonnay, which quickly disappeared from the scene. Having selected the site and started to establish the vineyard, Lazar taught himself to make wine by reading textbooks and by spending the 1971 vintage with Owen Redman at Coonawarra. The first vintage was made in 1973, and immediately a legend was born. Lazar designed a label which simply said 'Virgin Hills 1973'; from minute print at the bottom one learnt that the wine was produced in Australia at Kyneton, Victoria, by Tom Lazar. He also procured the longest corks ever to find their way into an Australian wine bottle – 60 millimetres long, compared with today's rarely used maximum of 49 millimetres, they were extravagantly and needlessly long, but a pointed comment on the parsimony of others. He was greatly assisted in the early vintages by the Knight family at Granite Hills, and it is generally known that a significant amount of Granite Hills shiraz found its way into the early vintages. Be that as it may, the wines he made in 1974, 1975 and 1976 were undeniably great, still capable of providing enjoyment 30 years later.

But almost before the first wine was on the market, problems started to beset Lazar. He made a fateful decision to sell his restaurant and to turn Virgin Hills into a gastronomic and oenological mecca. Just as was the case at Mitchelton, the expected crowds stayed away and the losses mounted. The most crushing blow came when the large restaurant he had built burnt down; it has never been re-erected. A mortgagee's sale was averted at the last moment when Melbourne businessman Marcel Gilbert and his wife, Renata, bought Virgin Hills; Lazar stayed on for a number of years as winemaker.

The Gilberts fiercely defended the quality and style of the Virgin Hills wines, but in 1988 were persuaded by their winemaker to move to sulphur-free winemaking (on top of organic grapegrowing). At the time, the experiments seemed to work well, but a longer timeframe has exposed the frailty of such wines. At the turn of the 21st century the Gilberts were persuaded to sell to a short-lived public company. This was a time of considerable distress for all concerned, but within another year Virgin Hills had been purchased by Michael Hope of the Hunter Valley, and stability had returned; it was then agreed to abandon the four- or five-grape blend, and produce only a cabernet sauvignon and a shiraz malbec.

**virtual winery** is the expression used for a standalone wine producer which has neither winery nor vineyards, buying grapes (often from many regions) and having the wine contract-made in various locations.

**virus diseases** made their first appearance in vines in Europe about 1890, when American rootstocks were used to control phylloxera. This entailed grafting the desired varietal scion onto the rootstock, which doubled the risk of virus spread, as viruses chiefly gain a foothold when cuttings are taken from a vine for propagation. They are mainly spread by taking cuttings from infected plants, but can also be spread by nematodes and insects. The most common virus is leafroll, which can be present in rootstocks which show no sign of the infection, but impact on the scion material once grafted, delaying ripening and reducing yield. Australia has a stringent protocol on imported vines, designed to reduce the likelihood of virus infection.

**volatile acidity** (commonly shortened to VA) is caused by the interaction of bacteria (known as *Acetobacter*) with the alcohol of the wine and oxygen to produce acetic acid. It is far more commonly encountered in dry red wines than dry white wines, and has a maximum legal level in Australia of 1.5 grams per litre, almost twice the taste threshold level (0.8 grams per litre). The twist in the tail is that acetic acid itself does not have the sharp (at high levels, vinegary) smell, but its accompanying ethyl acetate does. Ethyl acetate is usually produced concurrently with acetic acid and in the same relative proportion, and has no legal limit. Some *Saccharomyces* yeasts produce significant levels of acetic acid, but almost no ethyl acetate; thus, the wine may have a high level of volatility by analysis, but this is not apparent on the palate. Recent advances in reverse osmosis allow the reduction of acetic acid from wine without significant downsides.

**Vosges** oak comes from the mountains west of Alsace and is thus distinct from the centre of France oaks.

**Voyager Estate** (est. 1978) is the Margaret River winery of iron ore magnate Michael Wright and family. It was originally established by West Australian viticulturist Peter Gherardi, just to the north of Leeuwin Estate. Michael Wright acquired it in 1991. He had never drunk wine at the time and held the view that wine should be marketed in much the same way as Coca Cola. Both he and Voyager Estate have come a long way since. The estate plantings have been increased to 110 ha, on some of the best soil in the region, and a new winery has been constructed, featuring the same Cape Dutch architecture as the striking cellar door. The production of around 35,000 cases of the wine styles for which Margaret River is most famous (chardonnay, sauvignon blanc semillon, cabernet sauvignon and cabernet merlot) means that only the best grapes are retained; the balance is sold to other local wineries. In turn, the wines have unusual depth and intensity of flavour while retaining finesse. Exports to the UK, the US and other major markets.

a b c d e f g h i
j k l m n o p q
r s t u v w x y z

**Waite Precinct** was established in 1924 following a bequest – of Urrbrae House and 120 ha of surrounding land. It has developed into an integrated research and teaching precinct that has been presented as a model for agricultural research institutions. It has the largest concentration of expertise in the southern hemisphere in the areas of plant biotechnology, cereal breeding, sustainable agriculture, wine and horticulture, and land management. In all 1000 staff and postgraduate students work at the Waite, the annual research expenditure for all the institutional partners being more than $110 million. Among other things, it functions as the Waite Campus for the University of Adelaide, offering education and training through undergraduate, graduate diploma, masters and PhD programs. It is home to the Australian Wine Research Institute and to the oenology campus of the University of Adelaide, thus absorbing what was once Roseworthy Agricultural College.

**Wantirna Estate** (est. 1963) sits roughly halfway between the Yarra Valley proper and the Melbourne CBD, a bare 20 minutes' drive from the latter. It was established by Reg and Tina Egan in the same year that the late Max Lake first planted vines at Lake's Folly. Wantirna took rather longer to release wines, and even then planted a near-psychedelic mix of crouchen, pedro ximinez, grenache, malbec and mataro before ultimately converting to the long-term plantings of 2 ha (in total) of cabernet sauvignon, cabernet franc and merlot, and 1 ha each of chardonnay and pinot noir. Reg Egan was a self-taught vigneron, commuting to Melbourne to carry on his practice as a

lawyer – first as a solicitor, and thereafter as a barrister – but made it seem easy. It has become easier still since daughter Maryann Egan (co-owner of one of Melbourne's great restaurants, Becasse) gained an oenology degree and worked at various wineries, most significantly Domaine Chandon, before coming back to become executive winemaker in her spare time. Production is a mere 800 cases of pinot noir, chardonnay, cabernet merlot and cabernet franc merlot, exported to Asia and sold through a mailing list and to leading Melbourne restaurants.

**Warren, Roger** (1905–60) enrolled at Roseworthy Agricultural College in 1924. He obtained honours in chemistry and surveying, and in an obscure fashion this enabled him to become a woolclasser, but in 1929 former fellow student Colin Haselgrove, a winemaker and manager with Thomas Hardy & Sons, persuaded him to join the firm. For two hours a night, three times a week, Haselgrove became a one-on-one tutor to Warren, teaching him the principles of winemaking and of the wine business generally; meanwhile, Warren became Haselgrove's understudy at Hardys.

Haselgrove, a major figure in the wine industry in his own right, chose well. Roger Warren was promoted to senior technical officer in 1938. In 1953 he joined the Hardys board of directors, and succeeded Haselgrove as technical director, becoming in effect chief winemaker. Over the intervening decades Warren's exceptional gifts had become apparent. He had an excellent palate and memory for wines, which were the foundation of his skill as a blender. Thus he made regular trips to the Hunter Valley, to northern and

Central Victoria, and to all the winegrowing districts of South Australia, purchasing wines for the blends. This led to his development of Cabinet Claret, St Thomas Burgundy and Old Castle Riesling, three of the most important wines of the 1950s. There was a plethora of special bottlings of the red wines with back labels often completed in handwriting giving a bin number, which could then be linked to the blend books in the Hardys cellars. He thus forged a reputation as South Australia's answer to Maurice O'Shea of the Hunter Valley and Colin Preece of Great Western.

**Wendouree** is one of the brightest jewels in the crown of Australian wine. It was born in 1892 when Alfred Percy Birks and his brother planted a 0.2-ha block of cabernet sauvignon, and made a few gallons of wine from grapes purchased from other growers in the Clare Valley district. An additional 1.2 ha of shiraz were planted in 1893 and both of these plantings, together with a further 0.5 ha of shiraz planted in 1896, remain in production. By 1903 the Birks brothers had built a small winery and storage area. They were unable to turn all their grapes into wine, but made 4550 litres and sold both them and their surplus grapes to the Stanley Wine Company. For the next 20 years Stanley remained their sole customer, either reselling the wine to the London market, or using it to bolster some of their own lighter bodied wines.

In 1914, with production around 18,000 litres a year, Alfred Birks decided the time had come to build a proper wine cellar and expand production. The first stone section of the cellars, which remains in use virtually unaltered to this day, was constructed. A large basket press was installed on rails set in cement running between the newly built open fermenters. In 1917 failing health caused Alfred Birks to hand over winemaking responsibilities to his son Roly Birks, who then started a winemaking career which was to span 65 vintages. Under Roly's direction, Wendouree's vineyards were almost immediately expanded. What became known as the Eastern Vineyard was purchased and planted over the winters of 1919 and 1920. Part of this survives: two large blocks of shiraz of 1.6 and 0.8 ha respectively, and 0.2 ha of bush-pruned mourvedre (still called mataro in 2009, and unlikely ever to change). The remaining two blocks have been grafted to cabernet sauvignon and malbec respectively, but the 1920 rootstocks remain.

The cellars were once again extended, and equipment was upgraded with one of the first must pumps in the district. In 1925 Roly Birks and his brother decided it was time to start establishing their own markets for their ever-increasing production. They would load up a truck with casks and kegs of varying sizes (never bottles) and set off on a round trip selling to hotels. In the years up to World War II output stayed roughly constant, at half full-bodied dry red and half fortified wine. In the years after the war Wendouree built up a surprising business in supplying substantial quantities of base wine for the then-infant sparkling wine production of Wynns. By the early 1950s this had grown to between 55,000 and 65,000 litres a year.

The 1950s also marked the appearance of the respected Melbourne wine merchant WJ Seabrook & Son. The late Doug Seabrook began purchasing substantial quantities of

Wendouree wines, making a specialty of Birks' 'pressings' red. Absolutely immense wines, they nonetheless had sufficient fruit and acid to balance the tannin, and soon became one of Seabrook's most important house labels. Although the wines were bought in cask by Doug Seabrook and matured for a period of time before bottling, the maker was always specified on the label.

In 1970, aged 77, Roly Birks decided to sell Wendouree, but unfortunately found a purchaser who had neither the capital nor the winemaking knowledge to do anything other than rapidly run down the business to the point where, in 1974, only 10 tonnes of grapes were crushed. The properties were then split up and offered for sale by the mortgagee. The two principal vineyard blocks (which included the old house and winery) were purchased by Sydney businessman Max Liberman, and son-in-law, Tony Brady, together with wife Lita, were installed as managers. Brady was an Adelaide lawyer who, in his own words, barely knew how to spell the word 'grape', but he nonetheless tackled the project with enthusiasm. Roly Birks was retained as a consultant, and a close and enduring friendship was forged between the Bradys and the Birks.

Right from the outset, the Bradys regarded it as their duty to rejuvenate the old vineyards, preserving wherever possible the oldest plantings, and removing or grafting only those established to inferior varieties. That attitude has continued through to the 21st century. There are now 12 ha of vineyard planted to cabernet sauvignon, malbec, shiraz, mataro and a little muscat gordo blanco, most with different blocks of different ages. Production

seldom exceeds 60 tonnes a year, and is often less. Even at its maximum this is only 2 tonnes per acre. At the other end of the spectrum, only 18 tonnes were picked in the drought and bushfire year of 1983.

For several decades the wines have been made by Stephen George, who is also the owner/winemaker of Ashton Hills in the Adelaide Hills. The contrast in style between the elegant and delicate wines of Ashton Hills and the extraordinarily powerful wines of Wendouree could not be greater. Even when 20 years old, the Wendouree reds are apt to drink as if they had only recently been bottled. However, they are always balanced, and it is not altogether surprising that many are consumed long before they have a chance to show all their glory. The wines are sold almost entirely through a mailing list, always with a limit on the number of bottles of each wine that may be purchased. There is, in turn, a lengthy waiting list for those wishing to get, as it were, on to the A-list. Nor is it a question of first in, best dressed: all the orders are stockpiled for several months to enable those regular customers who are travelling to place their orders. The wines of Wendouree may or may not be the greatest in Australia, but no others have as much heart, soul and terroir in their make-up.

**West Australian South East Coastal Zone** has an impressively long name, and covers an even more impressively large area, but boasts only one winery, Dalyup River Estate, established in 1987. This tiny winery came from the clouds when it won the trophy for best wine of show at the Qantas Wine Show of Western Australia in 1999 with its shiraz.

**West Cape Howe Wines** (est. 1997) was founded by Brenden and Kylie Smith in the Denmark subregion of the Great Southern region of Western Australia. After a highly successful seven years, they moved on, selling the business to a partnership including Gavin Berry (until that time, senior winemaker at Plantagenet) and viticulturist Rob Quenby. As well as pre-existing fruit sources, West Cape Howe had the 80-ha Lansdale Vineyard, planted in 1989, as its primary fruit source. Production had risen to 55,000 cases, and the previous contract winemaking side of the business had been significantly curtailed to allow full focus on the winery brands. These are uniformly good, covering all the main varieties at often enticingly low price points, and it is not surprising that there are exports to the UK, the US, and other major markets. But it was a major surprise when in February 2009 CWA announced that it had sold the 7700-tonne capacity Goundrey winery (though not the brand) plus the Langton, Windy Hill, Omrah and Fox River vineyards to West Cape Howe, but with an ongoing contract to purchase the grapes from those vineyards. This will mark the arrival of a major new force in the south of Western Australia, and rebuild the contract winemaking business of West Cape Howe.

**Western Plains Zone** of New South Wales abuts the Northern Slopes and Central Ranges zones on its eastern boundary, and extends all the way to the South Australian boundary in the west, and the Queensland boundary in the north. It thus covers more than a third of the state, and its handful of wineries are in fact all congregated around Dubbo, on the eastern side of the zone. They are Boora Estate, Canonbah Bridge, Glenfinlass, Lazy River Estate, Macquarie Grove Vineyards, Red Earth Estate Vineyard, Seplin Estate, Tombstone Estate and Wattagan Estate.

**Western Range Wines** is the larger of the two wineries in the Perth Hills (the other is Millbrook) which have changed the wine landscape of the region, taking it from small-scale, do-it-yourself weekend wineries to a region which can and does produce significant quantities of quality wine (judged by national standards). Between the mid-1990s and 2001, several prominent West Australians, including Marilyn Corderory, Malcolm McCusker, and Terry and Kevin Prindiville, established approximately 125 ha of vines (under separate ownerships), with a kaleidoscopic range of varietals. The next step was to join forces to build a substantial winery. This is a separate venture, but takes the grapes from the individual vineyards and markets the wine under the Western Range brand. The wines are made and sold at four levels: Lot 88, Goyamin Pool, Julimar and Julimar Organic, the label designs clear and attractive. Exports to an eclectic range of countries.

**Western Victoria Zone** extends from Cape Otway in the southeastern corner to the South Australian border in the west, Horsham in the centre of the northern boundary and Ballarat (directly north of Cape Otway) just within the eastern boundary. The positioning of Ballarat is significant: it has a particularly cool climate, and has a number of small wineries capable of producing high-quality pinot noir and chardonnay. There is another group of wineries directly south on the interior of the Otway Range. All of these fall outside the eastern boundaries of the adjoining Henty, Grampians and Pyrenees regions, and there is every reason to suppose this eastern sector will infill the remainder of the eastern side of the zone with its fourth region.

**whole bunch** is, in part, self-explanatory, but has different implications for white wines and red wines. Wineries in Champagne do not have crushers or crusher-destemmers. All three of its varieties – chardonnay, pinot noir and pinot meunier – are placed as whole bunches in the specially designed champagne presses. The purpose is to minimise extraction of tannins or other phenolics from the skins and pips of the grapes, although some minor extraction from stems is a necessary trade-off. The result is very clear juice with pristine varietal fruit flavour, albeit at the acidic end of the spectrum. In Australia, and other parts of the New World, whole-bunch pressing of chardonnay, semillon and riesling has become common for the best wines made from those three varieties.

With red varieties, the application is very different. Here it refers to the practice of fermenting whole bunches, either as part of each batch, or, less commonly, as the whole of each batch. Beaujolais (notably), Burgundy and the Rhône Valley are the chief practitioners in France; the technique is not used in Bordeaux. The rationale for the use of whole bunches turns on intra-cellular fermentation, which is not precipitated by yeast, but by enzymes in the berries. When a bunch is cut from the vine it remains alive, in the sense that it can, and does, initiate enzyme-triggered changes in its chemical composition. The first change

is the consumption by the berry of its stored $CO_2$, which it needs to stay alive. Enzymes then attack the sugar in the berry, turning it to alcohol and producing more life-sustaining $CO_2$ in the process. If $CO_2$ is readily available from the surrounding atmosphere, the berry may also absorb it from this source. The fermentation which thus occurs within the individual cells bears no relationship to normal fermentation. Over a period of days, or up to two weeks at lower temperatures, up to 2 degrees of alcohol accumulate inside the berry, at which point the alcohol effectively kills the berry, and the intra-cellular fermentation ceases. During that fermentation period, however, glycerol, methanol, ethyl acetate and acetaldehyde will have been produced in significant quantities, along with a range of amino acids. It is these substances which give wines made using whole-bunch/ carbonic maceration their characteristic lifted bouquet.

**Wignalls Wines** (est. 1982) was one of the two pioneers of viticulture in Albany, established by Bill Wignall. It very quickly earnt a reputation for pinot noir. It remains focused on sauvignon blanc, chardonnay and pinot noir, but its 16 ha also include cabernet sauvignon, merlot, shiraz and cabernet franc. It produces 9000 cases a year. The assumption of the chief winemaker and CEO role by son Rob Wignall has also signalled a return to form for the pinot noir, which had various problems, partly associated with excess vine vigour and overcropping, and partly with contract winemaking elsewhere. The construction of an on-site winery in 1998 was a turning point for the better. Exports to Denmark and Asia.

**Wild Duck Creek Estate** (est. 1980) was established in Heathcote by David and Diana Anderson. The original 4.5-ha vineyard produced tiny quantities of wine from 1986 until 1991, which marked the first commercial vintage. Thereafter the vineyard was extended to 9.5 ha of cabernet sauvignon, merlot, malbec, shiraz, cabernet franc and petit verdot, and, as production increased, exports to the US began. A forgotten block on the vineyard became super-ripe, was picked as an afterthought, and was irreverently labelled Duck Muck in the winery. It was blessed by Robert Parker Jnr, and to the surprise and embarrassment of the Andersons became an icon wine. The range of red wines made outside Duck Muck have alcohol levels ranging between 13.5% alc/vol to a high of 15.5% alc/vol, and David Anderson prefers wine in the lower end of the scale. Annual production is in the region of 4000 cases. Exports to the UK, the US and other major markets.

**wild yeasts**, an expression used inter-changeably with indigenous yeasts, are derived from the vineyard environment and come into the winery on the grapes, but may also be permanently resident in the winery. These yeasts are made up of many different genera (as different from each other as mice and whales) and include both *Saccharomyces* and non-*Saccharomyces* species. At the beginning of fermentation the non-*Saccharomyces* yeasts play their part, and add to the complexity of the wine. There are four other genera which may be involved: *Hansenula, Klöckera, Pichia* and *Torulopsis*. These are intolerant of sulphur dioxide and of alcohol, and most will start to expire once the alcohol rises above 2–3% alc/vol. Moreover,

they will not populate in sufficient numbers prior to this time to prevent *Saccharomyces* from taking control of the fermentation. *S. cerevisiae* is the main species, but *S. bayanus* and others may be involved.

To complicate matters, both Yalumba and the Australian Wine Research Institute have been able to establish that some yeasts other than those belonging to the *Saccharomyces* genus remain viable until the end of fermentation. Moreover, research suggests that a combination of all the yeasts in the wild category has the advantages of slower and cooler fermentation, increased flavour complexity, increased texture, increased longevity, better colour in whites (more greens), better oak integration and less alcohol hotness. The problem is that, as at 2009, insufficient research had been done to determine which yeasts are responsible for which effect.

**Wilkinson, W Percy** delivered a paper to the Royal Geographical Society of Australasia at the Athenaeum Hall, Melbourne, on 13 December 1918, when he was director of the Commonwealth Laboratory. The paper was entitled 'The Nomenclature of Australian Wines in Relation to Historical Commercial Usage of European Wine Names, International Conventions for the Protection of Property and Recent European Commercial Treaties'. In printed form, the paper runs to 54 pages, and it is in a small typeface; it must have been a long night. He laboriously built to the finale, which was to propose wine names:

which may be claimed to possess the el-ement of distinctiveness in a sufficiently marked degree to serve adequately for

distinguishing wines of Australian production, from corresponding kinds or
types of European wines, and they may
also be claimed to be easy to remember,
euphonious, and affording at once a clue to
the at-present used European wine name
by the retention of the initial syllable.

He went on to disclose that he had put in place
applications for trade marks for each name
(these were ultimately successful) and that he
would make the names available at no cost to
the Australian wine industry.

    The system he proposed was simplicity
itself. For Burgundy, Burgalia; for Chablis,
Chabalia; for Champagne, Champalia; for
Claret, Claralia; for Hermitage, Hermalia;
for Hock, Hockalia; for Muscat, Muskalia;
for Port, Poralia; for Sauternes, Sautalia; for
Sherry, Sherralia; for Shiraz, Shiralia; and for
Tokay, Tokalia. If there is any extant record of
the commercial use of any one or more of these
names, the author has not heard of it.

**Willow Bridge Estate**  (est. 1997) was
established in the Geographe region by the
Dewar family. Sixty hectares of sauvignon
blanc, chenin blanc, semillon, chardonnay,
cabernet sauvignon, merlot, shiraz and
tempranillo have been planted on a spectacular
180-ha hillside property. While production
remains around 40,000 cases, there is potential
both from the vineyard and in the winery for
considerable expansion. The quality of the
wines has been consistently excellent. Exports
to the UK, the US and other major markets.

**Willow Creek Vineyard**  (est. 1989) is
a significant presence in the Mornington

Peninsula area, with 12 ha of vines planted
to cabernet sauvignon, chardonnay, pinot
noir and sauvignon blanc. The grape intake is
supplemented by purchasing small, quality
parcels from local growers. The Willow Creek
wines rank with the best from the peninsula,
the 7000-case production allowing limited
exports.

**Wine Grape Growers' Australia**,  established
in 2005, is the peak industry body for
Australia's wine grape growers. WGGA
enumerates its mission as representing the
political and economic interests of the national
wine grape sector through advocacy and
dialogue with government and with other wine
industry bodies; the development and delivery
of policies and programs that enhance the
profitability and sustainability of Australia's
wine grape growers; and providing services
to its members – particularly wine grape
market information and industry data that
supports timely commercial decision-making
by growers.

**Winemakers' Federation of Australia**  was
established in 1990, and is the peak industry
body representing Australia's wineries on all
national and international issues. It is funded
by annual membership fees calculated on the
size of the annual crush of the subscriber,
but membership is voluntary. Its ongoing
activities revolve around minimising tax
and regulation, facilitating access to export
markets, encouraging better environmental
performance, being strongly proactive in
response to health issues and, in particular,
responsible wine consumption, developing
winery tourism activities, monitoring

research and development proposals to ensure relevance, protection from and management of vine diseases, managing changes in bottling and packaging protocols, ensuring technical proficiency and flexibility in wine production, and, of the greatest importance, advocating for the interests of the wine industry in the halls of power in Canberra. Its most recent activity has been the development of an Australian Wine Industry Code of Conduct, promulgated in December 2008. Annual or biennial activities include the Wine Industry Outlook Conference, the Wine and Food Tourism Conference and Wine Australia. It has also played the lead role in the formulation of Strategy 2025, and the ensuing reviews and directions strategies.

**winepress**, see press.

**Wirra Wirra**  (est. 1969) stands tall as one of the most successful, high-quality family-owned wineries in Australia, its 150,000-case production coming principally from its home base of McLaren Vale, but also drawing grapes from the Adelaide Hills. It exists in its 21st-century form because of the vision of the late Greg Trott (known to all as Trott or Trottie) and the stoicism of brother Roger.

Truth being stranger than fiction, Wirra Wirra was built in 1894 by Robert Strangeways Wigley, who was every bit as eccentric as Trott. Photographs show his eyes pointing in different directions, which did not stop him from becoming a state cricketer (cricket being also one of the many passions of Trott). Nor did it stop him commandeering a horse and cart from the Adelaide City Council and riding it through the city streets at full gallop, resulting in a fine which he later paid by riding his horse into the Adelaide Town Hall.

To avoid further scandals he was sent to McLaren Vale, where he became a vigneron. He began building his house at the same time, abandoning four starts before finally deciding on its precise location. He never married; his home was run by an Irish housekeeper who was able to cope even when, in stormy weather, he would take to his bed in coat and hat, refusing to leave until the weather turned fine.

He died intestate in 1924, and the vineyards were sold by his family, the winery coming into the ownership of Vern Sparrow, the son of Wigley's foreman, Jack Sparrow. By 1936 it had fallen into disuse, and only two walls and some fermenting tanks remained when Greg and Roger Trott purchased it in 1969.

Greg Trott and an enthusiastic band of friends spent the ensuing five years rebuilding the winery: Trott shared with the late Len Evans the love of collecting things large and small, useful or useless, and incorporating them into buildings (a $450,000 pipe organ remains to be installed in either the winery or the new cellar door complex completed in 2004).

Trott was not a winemaker, but engendered loyalty, bordering on love, from all those who worked at Wirra Wirra. It was inevitable that this would result in great wines, and that whenever a position became vacant in the team, it would be filled by winemakers who did not wait for an advertisement, simply offering their services.

Its Angelus Cabernet Sauvignon and RSW Shiraz (named in honour of Robert Strangeways Wigley) have won countless trophies and gold medals in many parts of the world, and it was no surprise that current winemaker, New Zealand–born former lawyer Samantha (Sam) Connew, should have received the award of international red winemaker of the year in 2007 from the International Wine & Spirit Competition in London. This was no flash in the pan, as all of the wide range of wines, covering many price points, are made with the same care and attention as the flagbearers. Nor is it just a red wine producer: all the major white wine styles form an important part of the mix. Exports to all major markets.

**Wise Wine**  (est. 1986), headed by Perth entrepreneur Ron Wise, has been a remarkably consistent producer of high-quality wine. The vineyard adjacent to the winery in the Margaret River is supplemented by contract-grown grapes from Pemberton, Manjimup and Frankland River. The estate plantings are (in descending order) shiraz, cabernet sauvignon, chardonnay, sauvignon blanc, merlot, verdelho, cabernet franc and zinfandel. Exports to the UK, the US and other major markets.

**Witches Falls**  (est. 2004) is the venture of Jon and Kim Heslop, and former Brisbane lawyer turned winemaker Richard Abraham. Abraham's conversion was more recent than that of Jon Heslop, who had 12 years' experience in the wine industry, the first three as a sales representative for Orlando, before realising he wanted to make his own wine, rather than sell someone else's. His career began as a cellarhand with Richmond Grove. He then moved to the Hunter Valley as a winemaker at Tamburlaine, and says, 'I was

influenced by Rod Kempe of Lake's Folly, PJ Charteris of Brokenwood and Andrew Thomas of Thomas Wines,' which is an impressive trio. In 2004 he moved back to Queensland with his wife to establish Witches Falls, and was joined in 2005 by Richard Abraham, who undertook a degree in applied science (oenology) at Charles Sturt University, a degree which Jon Heslop also has under his belt. The only estate plantings are of durif; the other wines are made from contract-grown grapes.

**Wolf Blass Wines**  (est. 1966) started life as the standalone company which propelled its eponymous founder to fame and fortune. The foundation had been laid when, over three successive years, commencing with 1974, Wolf Blass Wines won the Jimmy Watson Trophy at the Royal Melbourne Show, a feat unequalled either before or since, and overshadowing the even more extraordinary achievement of winning the Montgomery Trophy at the Royal Adelaide Wine Show for six consecutive years from 1978 to 1983. It hardly need be said that gold medals and trophies cascaded on all of the top red wines from other capital city shows, and when on 9 May 1984 Wolf Blass Wines Limited issued its prospectus, the share issue valued the company at just under $16 million. Success followed success, leading to the acquisition of Mildara to create Mildara Blass, then a decade or so later Beringer Blass. While the company which Wolf Blass built is now simply part of a corporate aggregation wholly owned by Foster's, it has kept its separate identity courtesy of the massive winery built in the Barossa Valley in March 2000. Exports to all major markets.

**Woodlands** (est. 1973) was founded by David Watson and wife Heather in the Wilyabrup area of the Margaret River, the initial plantings being around 6.8 ha of cabernet sauvignon. It was a weekend and holiday operation, the Watsons commuting from Perth to the Margaret River, and the development was leisurely. Finally, he bottled a cabernet sauvignon from the 1981 vintage, which proceeded to win the Trophy for Best Wine of Show at Mount Barker in 1982. Urged on by chairman of judges Brian Croser, he entered it in the Canberra National Wine Show, where it once again was a trophy winner. The 1982 vintage, too, had great show success. But thereafter things went a little pear-shaped, and Woodlands faded from sight.

In the latter part of the 1980s and early 1990s, no wine was made, the grapes being sold to other Margaret River wineries. Winemaking resumed in a small way in 1992, and over that decade the vineyard was extended with the planting of merlot, malbec, cabernet franc, pinot noir and chardonnay. In the first few years of the new millennium Woodlands returned to its glory days of the early 1980s, with a stellar array of small-volume single-lot varietals, a reserve cabernet merlot and a larger volume standard cabernet merlot which has been of exceptional quality given its price and volume. The quality of the wines has been underlined by annual tasting pitting the Woodlands Margaret Reserve Cabernet Merlot against the might of Bordeaux from the same vintage; Woodlands consistently emerges either at or near the top in the blind tasting format. Exports to the UK.

**Woodside Valley Estate** (est. 1998) has been developed by a small syndicate of investors headed by Peter Woods. In 1998 they acquired 67 ha of land at Yallingup, in the Margaret River, and have now established 19.4 ha of chardonnay, sauvignon blanc, cabernet sauvignon, shiraz, malbec and merlot. The experienced Albert Haak is consultant viticulturist and, together with Peter Woods, took the unusual step of planting south-facing in preference to north-facing slopes. In doing so they indirectly followed in the footsteps of the French explorer Thomas Nicholas Baudin, who mounted a major scientific expedition to Australia on his ship *The Geographe* in 1800, and defied established views and tradition of the time in (correctly) asserting that the best passage for sailing ships travelling between Cape Leeuwin and Bass Strait was from west to east. The quality of the wines is impeccable. Exports to the UK, the US, Singapore, China and Japan.

**Wrattonbully's registration** as a Geographic Indication within the Limestone Coast Zone of South Australia, finally achieved on 5 July 2005, had been delayed for many years because of bitter infighting – over the name, not the boundaries. The name 'Koppamurra' was the obvious choice, but it would have involved special arrangements to accommodate the particular position and needs of Koppamurra Wines. This winery made wines not only from estate-grown grapes, but also from grapes grown outside the putative Koppamurra region. This would have necessitated Koppamurra's use of a second label for non-regional or blended wines, a label that made no reference to Koppamurra. At the last moment, a commercial agreement to resolve the problems fell over. In the outcome the 'Rat 'n Bully' derivative was adopted by default. The ultimate irony is that the Koppamurra Vineyard has been purchased by the Brian Croser-headed Tapanappa, and the Koppamurra name has fallen into disuse, thus ending the dilemma.

After a slow start (the Koppamurra Vineyard was established in 1973), the pace of development accelerated dramatically during the 1990s. There are now over 10 major vineyard developments and 2000 ha of vineyards. As in the case of Padthaway, much of the production is used by major wine companies (notably CWA, Foster's and Yalumba) in blended wines, but Yalumba's Smith & Hooper range is regionally identified. In 1998 a large contract crush and winery was constructed. Its primary purpose was to service the needs of the major grape (and bulk wine) buyers from the region. In 2001 the winery was leased to Orlando and is now called Russet Ridge.

The climate is poised between that of Coonawarra and Padthaway, warmer than the former and cooler than the latter, although there is surprising variation across the region. Relative humidity and rainfall (and hence the risk of disease) are slightly lower than in the other two regions, and the risk of frost is significantly less. Irrigation is essential, but there is sufficient underground water of appropriate quality (salinity is not a problem) to irrigate 10,000 ha of vines in the region if no other irrigated agriculture is carried on.

The Naracoorte Range is the last in a series extending from the coast, and has permitted the establishment of vineyards at an elevation of 75–100 metres above sea level on gently undulating slopes. The vineyards are almost exclusively planted on the so-called terra rossa soils made famous in Coonawarra, deriving from the ancient coastal dunes and seabed formations which give the Limestone Coast its name. Technically known as non-cracking, subplastic clays, they are very friable and free-draining. The region is overwhelmingly a red wine producer, with cabernet sauvignon monopolising the plantings, supported by shiraz and merlot, and a limited amount of chardonnay. The principal wineries (or brands) are Redden Bridge, Russet Ridge, Stone Coast and Tapanappa.

LAT 40°45'S; ALT 75–150 m; HDD 1468 (Struan), 1535 (Naracoorte); GSR 205 mm (Struan), 232 mm (Naracoorte); MJT 19.4°C (Struan), 20.5°C (Naracoorte); HARV Mid-March to mid-April; CHIEF VIT. HAZARD Frost (though moderate)

**Wynns Coonawarra Estate** spent the first 60 years of its life fighting for survival: William Leonard (Bill) Redman arrived as a 14-year-old in 1901, and secured a vintage job at John Riddoch's winery. John Riddoch died on 15 July that year, in the middle of the rapid expansion of the business. Bill Redman worked at the winery for six years, rising to the position of head cellarman (aged 19) in 1907. Over those six years he had watched as the mini-empire built up by John Riddoch was sold off piece by piece. Much later he made the celebrated one-line summary: 'From 1890 to 1945 you can write "failure" across Coonawarra.'

Wine production in the Riddoch cellars continued, even though there was almost no market, the winery running out of storage capacity, and forced to store additional casks in the vast Katnook shearing sheds (where wine is once again being made today). The only solution the executors could come up with was to install a pot still, and tens of thousands of gallons of fine, aged Coonawarra claret were turned into brandy. Its quality caught the eye of Chateau Tanunda, which bought the winery and vineyards towards the end of World War I and expanded the planting. But it soon learnt that the low alcohol content of the wine made distillation disconcertingly uneconomic. Within two years it had sold out to the Adelaide distillers Milne & Company, who ran the winery and vineyards making nothing but brandy until 1946. Through this time the only winery in continuous winemaking production in Coonawarra was that of Bill Redman; HBH Richardson established Coonawarra Winery in the 1930s, but, in the absence of any market for the wine, it closed down. Redman was able to stay in business because he had established a market for his wine first with Tolleys, and thereafter with Colonel Fulton of Woodley Wines.

At the end of 1945 it became clear that Milne & Company wished to dispose of its Coonawarra interests. JL Williams, a long-time lecturer in viticulture at Roseworthy Agricultural College, wrote to Samuel Wynn on Christmas Eve 1945 proposing a fifty–fifty joint venture for the acquisition of the Milne interests. He concluded his proposal by observing that Coonawarra was 'extremely good for the production of grapes for dry-winemaking, in fact I consider it is destined to become Australia's premier dry-wine area … Milne's vineyards and distillery have been shockingly managed but could be made into an excellent proposition with proper attention.'

Wynns decided not to go ahead, concentrating instead on the development of its Modbury Estate vineyard. Woodley Wines was very much more interested; it had of course purchased all of Redman's production for more than 20 years, and needed no persuasion about the potential of the district. Tony Nelson, having acquired control of Woodley, formed Chateau Comaum and purchased the winery, the 58 ha of vineyard and 8 ha of unplanted land for the sum of $18,000.

Bill and his son Owen Redman had already agreed that they would run the winery for Nelson and make the wine. The first task confronting the Redmans was to restore the winery to a condition adequate for making table wine. Williams had not exaggerated when he said that it had been shockingly managed – the concrete tanks were coated with thick layers of acetic acid crystals, which meant that the wine was thoroughly acetified by the end of fermentation. While this would not have helped the quality of the spirit ultimately distilled, it was not as critical for Milne as it would have been for Woodley.

The winery restored, the Redmans divided their attentions between their own winery and that of Chateau Comaum. They continued to sell most of the production from their own winery to Nelson, and for a few years the arrangement worked well enough. Strains then began to emerge, and the Redmans announced that they were not prepared to continue running the Riddoch Winery for Chateau Comaum. On the other hand they were still prepared to make the wine for Chateau Comaum at their own winery. At one stage Tony Nelson sought to dispose of the old Riddoch Cellars to the Woods and Forest Department of South Australia. When this and other proposals came to nothing, Nelson put the property on the market for sale.

In 1951 an advertisement appeared in the *Australian Brewing and Wine* journal, and this time Wynns took a more careful look. David Wynn commissioned a report from JL Williams (who had in the meantime joined Wynns and was to take the opposite view from the one he had put forward in 1945), and from winemakers Ken Ward and Ian Hickinbotham. In a coldly realistic report, the committee argued that the property should be valued not as a vineyard, but as an agricultural property suited to wool and dairying. The authors observed:

> In view of the difficulties of management and labour associated with vine growing in the area, together with the hazards of frost and downy mildew, the property cannot be considered as suitable for viticulture. The justification for this argument lies in the fact that the property has had three or four owners. They have all (except the present owners) contributed something to the way of improvements not derived from the property itself, and none has managed to survive the battle against adverse conditions.

David Wynn was not deterred: on 19 July 1951 Tony Nelson accepted S Wynn & Company's offer of £22,000 on a walk-in, walk-out basis. David Wynn's father, Samuel Wynn, was overseas at the time; when David informed him of his decision to proceed his father sent a telegram saying simply, 'Admiring your courage.'

The decision of David Wynn to buy Chateau Comaum and rename it Wynns Coonawarra Estate was one for which lovers of Australian wine should be forever grateful. It was a decision taken 10 years before its time, and in the face of a market that as a whole displayed little or no interest in the fine claret styles at which Coonawarra excelled. Certainly the major wine companies appreciated the quality of these wines, but used them only for blending; the consumer had no idea that many of the top reds of the day had a Coonawarra component in them.

The first thing David Wynn did was to commission Richard Beck to design the classic woodcut front and back labels that adorned the Wynns Coonawarra Estate wines. True, so-called marketers have been unable to resist the temptation to update the label insidiously, so it has lost some of the simplicity and purity of its original design, but the concept remains. Next Wynn embarked on an advertising campaign in such unlikely magazines as *Quadrant* and *Meanjin*, it being always intended that the wines from Coonawarra Estate would be positioned at the very top end of the market.

Penola's newspaper, the *Pennant*, of 29 April 1954 records a visit by David Wynn to Coonawarra in which he explained the aims and philosophies of Wynns to local growers. His company hoped to increase its crush from 300 to 1000 tonnes within a few years. Wynn was reported as saying, 'My prime aim is an extensive advertising campaign in Melbourne to make Coonawarra famous. People, when thinking of claret, would then naturally think of Coonawarra. Even in a depression there would always be a demand for claret, as it is of such high quality.'

But before he did all this Wynn had sent Ian Hickinbotham to take charge at Coonawarra, the first formally qualified winemaker to work in the district since Ewen McBain. Hickinbotham had graduated from Roseworthy Agricultural College in 1950; his first job was with Wynns at their Melbourne offices. He had inherited from his father, Alan Hickinbotham, a deep interest in the workings of malolactic fermentation, a fermentation of particular significance for Coonawarra. Ian made the first two vintages (1952 and 1953), and pioneered the use of far lower than traditional sulphur levels to encourage the malolactic fermentation.

Although 1952 was a miserable vintage, some great wine was made in 1953. In 1954 Norman Walker took over winemaking responsibilities; that year also saw the first vintage of Wynns Coonawarra Estate Cabernet (which almost certainly had a substantial shiraz component). The year 1955 was historic: not only did Wynns plant the first riesling in the district (and commence an expansion of its then tiny cabernet sauvignon plantings), but it also produced a range of quite magnificent wines. The most exceptional of these was the 1955 Michael Hermitage, a freak wine which seemingly gained much of its character from the second-hand fortified-wine cask in which it was matured. Repeated tastings of the 1955 Michael Hermitage between 1970 and 2008 emphatically underline what an extraordinary wine this is. Fortune smiled when the corks were obtained, for tainted or oxidised bottles were few and far between, and the wine continues to show amazing tenacity.

In June 1970 the Wynn family made the decision to convert the business into a public company listed on the stock exchange. Less than two years later, in May 1972,

Allied Vintners of the UK made a successful takeover offer. Then followed a period of considerable disquiet on the part of the senior winemakers at Seaview and Wynns, and there was almost relief when Penfolds acquired Wynns and Seaview. Nonetheless, contemporary viticultural practices, involving total mechanisation and minimal pruning, impacted significantly on the potential quality of the red wines. On the other side of the coin, winery practices changed with the arrival of John Wade and the introduction of the super-premium John Riddoch Cabernet Sauvignon, and, later on, the rebirth of Michael Hermitage. By the end of the 20th century there had been a complete change in viticultural management, with many millions of dollars spent in rehabilitating (and in some instances replanting) vineyards mutilated by extreme mechanisation. Prior to the 2008 vintage, an entirely new winery-within-a-winery was built to enable winemaker Sue Hodder to maximise the quality of the best grapes coming from the 1800 ha of estate vineyards. The release of individual vineyard wines preceded the construction of the small-lot winery, and if the quality of these is lifted further by the new opportunities, Wynns Coonawarra Estate, with wine production spanning three centuries, will show just what it is capable of.

**Wynn, David, AO** (1915–95) made major contributions to the Australian wine industry across an extraordinarily broad range of commercial activities. It is a matter of argument whether his innovative marketing and packaging ideas, which led to the development of the flagon and the wine cask, are more important than his decision to buy Chateau Comaum (now known as Wynns Coonawarra Estate) despite a report commissioned by him which recommended that the purchase should not proceed (for further details see the previous entry). David Wynn was the recipient of the Maurice O'Shea Award in 1993.

a b c d e f g h i
j k l m n o p q
r s t u v w x y z

**Xanadu Wines** was founded in 1977, but overreached itself in 2005 against a background of wine surpluses, and the business was acquired by the Rathbone Group, completing the Yering Station (Yarra Valley), Mount Langi Ghiran (Grampians), Parker Coonawarra Estate and Xanadu (Margaret River) structure. It is a tribute to the business acumen of CEO Doug Rathbone that there is no overlap of wine style, and each winery has depth to its premium and ultra-premium offerings. Xanadu has 130 ha of vineyards, and a 65,000-case winery, exporting to all major markets.

a b c d e f g h i
j k l m n o p q
r s t u v w x y z

**Yabby Lake Vineyard** (est. 1998) is the venture owned by Robert and Mem Kirby, who have been land owners in the Mornington Peninsula for decades. In 1998 they began the planting of 40 ha of vineyard on north-facing slopes, capturing maximum sunshine while also receiving sea breezes. The plantings are 21 ha of clonally selected pinot noir, 10 ha of clonal chardonnay, 5 ha of pinot gris and 2 ha each of shiraz and merlot. An exceptionally experienced and highly skilled winemaking team manages Yabby Lake and Heathcote Estate. As the still youthful vineyards gain greater vine age, even greater wines can be expected in the future. Yabby Lake has taken the bold step of establishing its own cellar door outlet in Beijing, China, with similar outlets in Shenzhen and Shanghai planned.

**Yalumba** is the chief brand name of Samuel Smith & Sons, the corporate name honouring a remarkable family history. Samuel Smith was clearly no ordinary man: he was 35, with a wife, five children and a successful career as a brewer when he decided to leave the security and comfort of England to make a new home in Australia. Evidently he was then of modest means, for on his arrival in South Australia he moved to Angaston, which was then being created by George Fife Angas. He worked for Angas by day establishing gardens and orchards; by night he began the establishment of a small vineyard on the 12 ha of land he had purchased and called Yalumba, an Aboriginal word meaning 'all the country around'.

In 1852 Smith and his 15-year-old son followed the rest of Australia's male population to the Victorian goldfields. After sinking 15 barren shafts, they struck gold on the 16th attempt and returned to Angaston with enough money to purchase a further 32 ha, a plough, two horses and a harness, and had some money left in the bank to finance the erection of a new house and wine cellars. By the time Smith died in 1889 Yalumba was a thriving business, with markets established both in Australia and England, and medals in international shows and exhibitions to its credit. Samuel's son Sidney built upon the base his father had left, building the imposing two-storey winery and clock tower of blue marble that stand today as part of the vast complex of buildings which are set in the spacious grounds. In 1903 the vintage produced 810,000 litres, and Yalumba was established as one of the principal producers in the region.

Expansion continued steadily through the first decades of the 20th century: in one particularly bountiful year excess port was stored in the in-ground swimming pool, protected only by a coating of liquid paraffin wax. Yalumba made limited quantities of white and red table wine, but it was primarily a fortified wine producer, venturing into significant brandy production shortly before World War II. It was also at this time that it established a substantial distribution business of wines and spirits, principally imported. But even at this time Yalumba was going where others feared to tread. Sidney Hill Smith, one of those tragically killed in the Kyeema air crash of 1938, was responsible for introducing riesling into the Eden Valley, and employed German-trained Rudi Kronberger as winemaker. Kronberger made some remarkable rieslings, introducing early bottling 20 years before it became common practice.

When Sidney Hill Smith was killed,

28-year-old Wyndham was peremptorily summoned back from Perth and shared the management responsibilities with his brother Donald, in due course becoming managing director. Windy, as he was universally known, was one of the great characters in the wine industry, following in the footsteps of his father, Walter Hill Smith. Walter was known as Tiger, in recognition of his passion for big-game hunting and travel, making Yalumba port a well-known brand in India and the East. Wyndham's dual passions were cricket and horse-racing. His uncle was none other than Test player Clem Hill, and Windy himself played cricket at both interstate and international level. In the 1970s horse-racing became a major interest, leading to a brief but extremely popular series of racehorse ports, each taking the name of a famous racehorse.

In 1972 Wyndham handed over the role of managing director to his nephew, Mark Hill Smith, and in due course Mark's cousin (and Wyndham's son) Robert Hill Smith became managing director. He has been an inspired CEO, steering the company through difficult financial days in the early to mid-1980s, selling the fortified wine business at precisely the right time and certainly for the right price, setting the stage for the vibrant company of the 21st century. As well as its highly successful Pewsey Vale, Heggies Vineyard and Hill Smith Estate, anchored in the hills of the Eden Valley, he had the foresight to develop the very large Oxford Landing brand at Qualco, with 260 ha in production. (Yalumba's other vineyard holdings are 150 ha in the Eden Valley; 35 ha in Coonawarra; 170 ha in Wrattonbully, for the Smith & Hooper brand; 50 ha at Angaston; 70 ha in the Barossa Valley proper; and 24 ha

in Tasmania, for the Jansz Tasmania sparkling wine.) Oxford Landing has given Yalumba the critical mass to enable it to develop a wide range of premium, super-premium and ultra-premium wines, sold throughout the world. In best Yalumba tradition, the viticultural team at Oxford Landing began a five-year trial in 2008 to ascertain whether vines could survive and produce a crop using only 10 per cent of normal irrigation water. This has in turn allowed the development of Nautilus Wines in Marlborough, New Zealand, and a major and very successful import business under the Negociants title.

**Yarrabank** (est. 1993) is a highly successful joint venture between the French Champagne house Devaux and Yering Station. Until 1997 the Yarrabank Cuvee Brut was made under Claude Thibaut's direction at Domaine Chandon, but thereafter the entire operation has been conducted at Yarrabank. There are 4 ha of dedicated 'estate' vineyards at Yering Station; the balance of the intake comes from other growers in the Yarra Valley and southern Victoria. Wine quality has consistently been outstanding, frequently with an unmatched finesse and delicacy. Exports to all major markets.

**Yarra Burn** (est. 1975) is the brand of CWA's very substantial Yarra Valley operations, centring on the large production from its Hoddles Creek vineyards. The new brand direction has taken shape; all the white and sparkling wines are sourced from the Yarra Valley; the shiraz viognier is a blend of Yarra and Pyrenees grapes. Exports to the UK and the US.

**YarraLoch** (est. 1998) is the ambitious project of successful investment banker Stephen Wood. He took the best possible advice, and did not hesitate to provide appropriate financial resources to a venture which had no exact parallel in the Yarra Valley or anywhere else in Australia. Twelve hectares of vineyards may not seem so unusual, but in fact he assembled three entirely different sites, 70 kilometres apart, each matched to the needs of the variety or varieties planted on that site. The 4.4 ha of pinot noir are on the Steep Hill Vineyard, with a northeast orientation, and a shaley rock and ironstone soil. The 4 ha of cabernet sauvignon were planted on a vineyard at Kangaroo Ground, with a dry, steep northwest-facing site and abundant sun exposure in the warmest part of the day, ensuring full ripeness of the cabernet. Just over 3.5 ha of merlot, shiraz, chardonnay and viognier were planted at the Upper Plenty vineyard, 50 kilometres from Kangaroo Ground. This has an average temperature 2°C cooler and a ripening period two to three weeks later than the warmest parts of the Yarra Valley. Add the winemaking skills of Sergio Carlei (of Carlei Estate) and some sophisticated (and beautiful) packaging, and there was a fine recipe for success. The 4500-case production is sold by mailing list, to fine wine retailers and to top-end restaurants.

**Yarra Valley**, gazetted 30 October 1996, was first settled by grazier William Ryrie, who arrived in the valley in 1837, having travelled overland from Arnprior Station in the Monaro, and set up a large grazing run extending well towards Melbourne. His brother, Donald, recorded the planting of the first vines in 1838. He wrote:

They were taken from Arnprior and were the Black Cluster or Hamburg and a white grape, the Sweet Water. We afterwards had sent from Sydney other vines taken from MacArthur's vineyard at Camden. The first wine was made in March, 1845; a red wine resembling Burgundy and a white wine resembling Sauterne, and both very good. Dardel, a Swiss (afterwards at Geelong) used to come to prune the vines. He also put us in the way of making the wine.

The Swiss connection was soon further cemented: Paul de Castella left Gruyères in Switzerland in 1849 and landed in Victoria later that year. He purchased Yering Run from Ryrie and inherited the 0.4-ha vineyard. Impressed with the quality of the wine it made, he arranged for a consignment of vine cuttings to be obtained from Europe; 20,000 cuttings, chiefly taken from Chateau Lafite, arrived in 1854 or 1855. They were packed in moss for the journey, and the vast majority survived. A plant nursery was quickly established, and in 1857 the bulk of the 40-ha Yering vineyard was planted. The vineyard development was carried out by Samuel de Pury, brother of Guillame de Pury, the founder of Yeringberg.

Yering soon gained a reputation for its red wines. Because of the frequent misspelling of cabernet as carbinet, de Castella shortened the name to Yering sauvignon. In 1861 it was awarded a 100-guinea gold cup offered by the *Argus* for the best Victorian wine; in 1889 it won a grand prix at the Paris Exhibition, the only southern hemisphere wine to receive such an award, and one of only 14 given to wine entries at the exhibition.

In 1862 Charles Hubert de Castella purchased a portion of Yering from brother Paul's creditors and established St Huberts, and Yeringberg was founded the following year. Curiously, there were relatively few other vineyards. Samuel de Pury planted Cooring Yering, between Coldstream and Lilydale, in the late 1850s; he returned to Switzerland in 1868, and the purchaser of the property uprooted the vineyard in 1870.

While the de Castella and de Pury families ultimately established the largest viticultural enterprises in the Yarra Valley, neither had any prior viticultural experience, and both families initially intended to graze sheep. The family that did have viticultural experience was the Deschamps, headed by Joseph Clement, who arrived in the Yarra Valley in January 1854. His family had been vignerons in Beaujolais, France, for 12 generations, and he was employed by Paul de Castella to develop the Yering vineyard, working there until 1860.

In that year land around the present Lillydale (*sic*) township was opened up, and Deschamps (by then 48 years old) was able to acquire the land for, and supervise the layout, draining and planting of, three vineyards for his three sons: Auguste's Pine Grove of 14.2 ha in Anderson Street; Louis' Olinda, 7.3 ha in Cave Hill Road; and Clement's Market Street Vineyard of 12.1 ha in Cemetery Road.

Subsequently, in 1894, grandsons Rudolph and Louis planted 10 ha at Yeringa, not far south of Yering on St Huberts Road. Both were in their early 20s, but died while very young (in 1902 and 1904 respectively), and the vineyard was bought by Melbourne negociants Alexander & Patterson, who offered the wine under the Yeringa label. The vines disappeared

around the time of World War I, but have been re-established by Alan and Louise Johns under the Yering Farm Wines label.

Coldstream was planted by David Mitchell (Dame Nellie Melba's father) in the 1890s, and produced some wines which François de Castella described as 'worthy of the district', but the vineyard was uprooted in 1921, by which time St Huberts (which Mitchell had purchased in 1902) was abandoned. A similar fate befell Chateau D'Yves, which had been established in the hills near Emerald in the 1880s by Belgian bacteriologist and chemist Auguste de Bavay, a contemporary of Louis Pasteur who revolutionalised the yeast culture and fermentation techniques of the Foster Brewing Company in Melbourne. De Castella said that 'Recurring frosts were the cause of abandonment of this vineyard, which produced some wines recalling French medoc in a remarkable manner.'

The Yarra Valley flickered briefly in the early 1890s when the government of the day announced its intention to fund the erection of a cooperative winery, encouraging many of the farmers to plant grapes. A change of government, and a new premier who preferred milk to wine, saw the promise revoked. Yeringberg and David Mitchell's Coldstream continued until 1921, when, in François de Castella's words, 'The Yarra Valley fell to the cow.'

Vines returned in the second half of the 1960s with a sudden surge of plantings by Peter Fergusson at Fergusson's (1968), at St Huberts by the Cester family (who had bought the property) in the same year, by the late Dr Bailey Carrodus at Yarra Yering in 1969, and by Baron Guillaume (universally known as

Guill) de Pury at Yeringberg in the same year. Kellybrook had been established by Darren Kelly in 1966, initially with an emphasis on true cider making, vineyards coming onstream a little later. Dr Peter McMahon purchased the Seville Estate property in 1970, and the late Dr John Middleton Mount Mary in 1971. He had been growing grapes on an experimental basis in the backyard of his house in Chirnside for almost a decade before moving to Mount Mary. Other early movers were Warramate (1970); Chateau Yarrinya (now De Bortoli, Yarra Valley, 1971); Bianchet (1976); Diamond Valley (1976); Lillydale Vineyards (1976); Yarra Burn (1976); Oakridge (by the Zitzlaff family at Seville, and having no relationship to the present-day Oakridge, 1978); and TarraWarra Estate (1981). When Coldstream Hills was founded in 1985, it became the 35th winery. By 2009 the number had risen to 140.

It is a region of almost infinite beauty; most of the wineries are on hillsides, some gently rising, some very steep, some smaller, some larger. The Great Dividing Range runs along its northern border, the lower hills sometimes shrouded in mist, sometimes assuming an intense blue colour which fascinated the early Swiss settlers. The innumerable side valleys afford ever-changing vistas, accentuated by the major difference in the soils and ambience of the northern part of the valley (the eastern part constituting much of the Yarra Ranges National Park) and the southern portion, which has part of the Dandenong Ranges National Park in its confines. The most distinctively different part is in the southeast, from Launching Place to Warburton and in the hills south of the Warburton Highway. Here the red soil and massive mountain ash trees which escaped logging dominate the landscape.

Given the considerable variation in altitude throughout the Yarra Valley, and the significance of aspect (that is, north or south) on the many hillside vineyards, it is not surprising that there is substantial variation in mesoclimate. However, even the warmest sites are, comparatively speaking, cool; the mean January temperature at Healesville is 19.4°C, which is lower than at Bordeaux or Burgundy. There are two radically different soil types: grey-brown sandy clay loam with a mixed rock and clay subsoil, deriving from ancient sandstone of the Great Dividing Range, and a much younger, vivid red soil of volcanic origins, very deep and well drained. The grey soils are on the Maroondah and Melba highways (northern) sides of the valley, the red soils on the Warburton (southern) Highway.

Pinot noir and chardonnay dominate the region's plantings; shiraz, sauvignon blanc and pinot gris plantings are increasing; cabernet sauvignon and merlot are static. The wineries of note (other than those already mentioned) are Carlei Estate and Carlei Green Vineyards, Domaine Chandon, Dominique Portet, Gembrook Hill, Giant Steps/Innocent Bystander, Hillcrest Vineyard, Killara Estate, Labyrinth, Mayer, Oakridge, PHI, Punch, Stuart Wines, Toolangi Vineyards, Wantirna Estate, Wedgetail Estate, Yarra Yarra, Yarrrabank, YarraLoch and Yering Station.

LAT 37°49'S; ALT 50–400 m; HDD 1250–1352; GSR 400 mm; MJT 17.9–19.4°C; HARV Early March to early May; CHIEF VIT. HAZARDS Birds; mildew

**Yarra Yarra** (est. 1979) was established in the Steels Creek district of the Yarra Valley by Ian Maclean, who planted the first 2 ha of vines.

He focused on cabernet sauvignon blends and semillon sauvignon blanc blends in the style of red and white Bordeaux respectively, and soon established a considerable reputation for his wines. This led to the progressive increase in plantings to 9.5 ha, the last extension with modest plantings of shiraz and viognier, offering a third style. Yarra Yarra was hit hard by the 2009 bushfires, but the winery is being rebuilt and re-equipped, and the vineyard rehabilitated. The wines are sold direct, through top-end restaurants in Melbourne and to a few specialist retailers. Exports to the UK and Singapore.

**Yarra Yering** (est. 1969) was established by the late Dr Bailey Carrodus (a doctor of philosophy in plant physiology, not medicine, like so many of his confrères). He died in September 2008 leaving a legacy which deserves that much over-used epithet, unique. The labels for and the names of his two major red wines sounded an immediate alert: hand-drawn, and featuring laurel leaves in honour of his long-term partner Laurel and the enigmatic Dry Red No. 1 and Dry Red No. 2 (never did a back label besmirch a Yarra Yering wine) was all the information that customers were given. Particularly persistent enquiries would reveal that No. 1 was a Bordeaux blend, with cabernet sauvignon the dominant variety, and No. 2, a shiraz-dominant wine, with some viognier interplanted (the first such in Australia) and the possibility of other unspecified varieties, perhaps including a splash of pinot noir. The pinot noir itself was conventionally named, as was the chardonnay, but not the Dry White No. 1, a white Bordeaux-style blend with semillon and sauvignon blanc its principal

components. Even the vineyard plantings were a matter of mystery: a written question asking for the make-up of the vineyards, with hectares by variety, brought the response, 'Oh dear, total 12 ha.'

For several decades he alone made the wine, eschewing any vintage help (other than Laurel). To achieve this, he had constructed square fermentation vessels, with stainless steel lining a half-tonne box looking rather like a tea chest, which could then be tipped into a basket press with a capacity of half a tonne, and thence to barrel. To the end he denied ever having to add acid to the magnificently deeply coloured red wines, and likewise refused to have analysis done, except when it was needed for export approval and, when the law changed, to state alcohol on the label.

In the 1990s he purchased two adjacent properties, one already planted and fronting Maddens Lane, which gave rise to Underhill Shiraz, and the other, on the opposite side of the vineyard, a vacant block which he contour-planted to the Portuguese port varieties, fulfilling a long-held ambition to make a vintage port-style wine, which he labelled Portsorts (since changed to Potsorts). The white wines defied conventional analysis and were counter-cultural to the trend towards finer and more elegant chardonnay made in other parts of the Yarra Valley, but Dry Red No. 1 and Dry Red No. 2 (and, not infrequently, Underhill Shiraz) were in many ways the Yarra Valley's answer to Wendouree. They are wines of great complexity, depth and texture, and very long-lived.

Most of the wine is sold to faithful recipients of the annual mailing list, but Yarra Yering has the habit of popping up in the most unexpected places around the world, usually top-end restaurants.

**yeast** is a one-celled organism without which wine would not exist, nor food staples such as bread. It is ironic that the New World's current fascination with natural or wild fermentation (the rule rather than the exception in the Old World) should come at a time when the scientific understanding of and research into yeasts is expanding exponentially.

Pride of place must still go to Louis Pasteur, who demonstrated that this organism was the trigger for the conversion of grape juice to wine. Pasteur was the father of the science of microbiology, and it is fitting that yeast was the first eukaryotic organism whose genome was sequenced in 1997. Yeast has become the model organism for studying human diseases such as cancer; yeast scientists Paul Nurse and Lee Hartwell received the Nobel Prize for Physiology in Medicine in 2001.

The yeast population has served humankind since the dawn of civilisation. The member of overwhelming importance to winemaking is *Saccharomyces cerevisiae*. It best meets all of the requirements for fermentation: ability to tolerate a low pH medium, significant amounts of sulphur dioxide, steadily rising levels of alcohol and relatively high fermentation temperatures. Unless stressed, it does not produce undesirable side-effects, and its use extends (via lees) well after its death.

There is a vast number of different strains or types of *S. cerevisiae* sold around the world under different commercial names: one of the best known is EC1118, or Prise de Mousse, sold by Lalvin. In the last 20 years

5538 genes have been identified in yeasts, and, in a significant number of instances, the effect of a given gene identified. Some genes are thoroughly undesirable if overexpressed; thus the ATFI gene results in a wine with an overpowering ethyl acetate (nail polish) aroma. Others are highly desirable.

The conversion of grape juice to wine is a complex, multistage process, resulting in a liquid that is 83–89 per cent water, 10–15 per cent alcohol, 0.4–1 per cent glycerol, and 0.5–1.5 per cent acid. Only a fraction of the remaining 1 per cent (or thereabouts) constitutes the volatile flavour compounds that give wine its aroma and flavour. It is here that the specific action of different strains of yeast becomes critical, particularly given that grape juice (of any given variety) has much less fruit aroma than the wine it makes.

It is also necessary to distinguish between, first, grape flavour compounds which are present in both grapes and wines and are not altered and liberated by yeasts; second, grape-derived flavour precursors which are altered by yeast; and, third, yeast-derived flavour compounds probably produced as general side-reactions of primary yeast metabolism.

Esters are biosynthesised by the yeast, and confer a range of distinctive fruit aromas, including strawberry, apple, banana, peach, berry and pineapple. Quite why these esters should be produced is not understood, as they do not appear to have any metabolic function. But they most certainly explain why wine writers use such terms. The precursors for some esters, called higher alcohols, are themselves potent aroma compounds, ranging from fresh-cut grass to roses to nail polish. Then there are the volatile acids, mainly acetic acid, also biosynthesised by yeasts. These acids are always present – at low levels beneficial to wine quality, at high levels destructive.

Here choice and consequence become particularly stark. Some yeast strains release volatile thiols, whereas others do not. Jan H Swiegers, of the Australian Wine Research Institute, who has published a lengthy paper on yeast modulation of wine flavour with Professor Isak Pretorius (*Advances in Applied Microbiology*, volume 57), puts the thiol impact into perspective thus: 'One milligram of a certain volatile thiol is enough to flavour almost a million litres of wine.' Thiols originate from the grape as aroma-bound, non-volatile, amino acid–bound precursors. Through the process of fermentation, yeast enzymes split the volatile thiols away from the amino acid, releasing them into the wine. Here they create box-tree, passion fruit, guava, gooseberry and (at higher concentrations) sweaty aromas. Once again, wine writers can take comfort.

At present, the most effective thiol-release yeast strain can unbind only about 5 per cent of the volatile thiols from their precursors. Writes Swiegers (in a separate, unpublished paper): 'There is a huge, untapped aroma potential remaining in the grape (and ultimately in the wine that we drink!).' Together, Pretorius and Swiegers become even more poetic when they conclude their yeast modulation paper:

The infinite number of flavour profiles of bottled wines results from the synergy be-tween grapes and yeast … The blending of the precise amounts of different flavour compounds to produce the distinct flavours of different wines is akin to the blending of the sounds of many instruments [in an orchestra] … When in perfect balance, all the flavour compounds … result in a sat-isfactory sensory experience that the wine connoisseur will declare to be a symphony in a bottle.

Expressed thus, science becomes art. The artist, however, will have to be careful not to make the painting too colourful. If this technology comes to full flower, it will be most useful with cheap wines made from high-yielding, warm-region vines. These often lack varietal character; enhancement of this would prima facie be beneficial. It is an altogether different question with, say, the great wines of Burgundy.

Given the present and future ability to dial up flavour numbers by the use of highly specific yeast strains, where does this leave wild yeast fermentations (however called), and where do they fit in the choice-and-consequence scheme of things? Well, for a start, most of these yeasts are not found on grape skins, common belief to the contrary notwithstanding. Rather, they are airborne and are carried around vineyards and wineries by the wind and by such vectors as fruit flies.

The yeasts responsible for initiating spontaneous fermentations usually belong to four genera different from *S. cerevisiae*: *Hansenula*, *Klöckera*, Pichia and *Torulopsis*. These four have a number of things in common: they are intolerant of sulphur dioxide, they are intolerant of alcohol and most will start to expire once the alcohol reaches 2–3% alc/vol. They will not populate in sufficient numbers prior to this time to prevent other yeasts (most notably *S. cerevisiae*) from growing.

On the other side, possible disadvantages are higher alcohol conversion from the same sugar level, and less acidity at the end of the ferment. But all ferments complete their course, and there is no greater sulphide production, nor 'off-barrels'.

Research carried out with the assistance of the AWRI since 2000 has confirmed that in the first week of ferment four to five different groups of non–*S. cerevisiae* yeasts were identified each day, with around 17 groups in total. After the *S. cerevisiae* yeasts took over, there was only one group of non–*S. cerevisiae* yeast which continued through to the end of fermentation.

Yalumba has also studied the effect of using eight inoculated yeasts outside *S. cerevisiae*; this gave rise to different flavours, textures, and chemical analyses. In many cases, these fermentations were preferred to that of the *S. cerevisiae* control fermentation, but in no case were they better (in sensory terms) than the wild yeast control fermentation.

It seems highly probable that over a period of time the winery-resident population of yeasts will stabilise, particularly where the pomace is returned to vineyards near to the winery. The idea that a more distant vineyard may bring a particular character attribute to a specific wild yeast (or yeasts) has little scientific support, but the possibility cannot be ignored.

**Yeringberg** (est. 1863) was established by Baron Guillaume de Pury, one of the foremost members of the influential and wealthy Swiss families who were responsible for the establishment of the Yarra Valley wine industry. In 1862 he purchased part of the vast Yering vineyard from Paul de Castella,

and named it Yeringberg, in recognition of the fact that much of it was located on a large hill which looked out over the main bulk of Yering. It was on top of this hill that the first winery was built, and likewise the house. The property has never passed out of the hands of the family, the present owners being Guillaume de Pury, grandson of the founder, and his wife, Katherine.

Much of the production of Yeringberg was destined for export: by the late 1860s almost 30 ha of vineyard were established, and these were subsequently expanded. The first winery has long since gone, but the one erected in 1885 still stands in near-new condition. The striking two-storey wooden building, with some passing similarities to the architecture of Tahbilk, must have been a showpiece of technological design in its day. The grapes were carried to the top storey in a hydraulic lift and then crushed into railway trucks which ran along the top storey on a miniature railway line. From hereon the winery operated entirely on gravity. The red grapes would be deposited from the trucks into the open wooden fermenters; the whites into the press, thence into barrels or vats for fermentation. At the conclusion of fermentation the red wine would be drained into the oak casks in the large stone cellars underneath the wooden structure.

The original vineyard was planted to shiraz, pinot noir, marsanne, trebbiano, verdelho, pinot gris, pinot blanc and gouais. It was for the marsanne that Yeringberg was most famous. François de Castella commented that, 'Yeringberg has produced some of the finest white wines ever grown in the southern hemisphere.' A few bottles of the wine made in the last decade of the 19th century and the first two decades of the 20th were part of a small museum stock at the winery and, tasted at various times between 1985 and 2000, all had exceptional freshness and youth.

When in 1969 Guill de Pury (as he prefers to be known) was persuaded by friends to re-establish a tiny portion of the vineyard on the exact spot planted by his grandfather 100 years earlier, the first grape chosen was marsanne. The varieties also included shiraz, which was uprooted after the 1981 vintage because no one wished to buy it. The 1980 and '81 vintages were and are superb wines, and the wheel of fortune has turned sufficiently for shiraz to now once again form part of the patchwork quilt of the 3-ha vineyard. The varieties planted are chardonnay, marsanne, roussanne, pinot noir, cabernet sauvignon, merlot, malbec, cabernet franc and petit verdot (plus shiraz). Since none of the plantings exceeds half a hectare, the quantity of each wine is of course limited. Two very much larger blocks have been planted on the 483-ha property, one (of 11 ha) leased to Domaine Chandon until 2013, the other (a 20-ha block) with a long-term grape sale agreement to CWA. Ultimately, full operating ownership will revert to de Pury ownership, and children Sandra de Pury (winemaker) and David de Pury (viticulturist) stand to inherit one of the finest vineyards in the Yarra Valley. The wines are primarily sold by mail order (no cellar door sales) and through limited fine wine retail and restaurant venues in Sydney and Melbourne.

**Yering Station** today is established on part of the Yarra Valley property acquired by Paul de Castella in 1850. It was purchased in 1966 by the Rathbone family, who built a large winery into the side of small slope, sitting underneath the substantial restaurant and administration area. The 60,000-case production of table wines does not include the Yarrabank sparkling wine made as a joint venture with French Champagne house Devaux. The grapes for the Yering Station table wines come primarily from 115 ha of estate vineyards in the Yarra Glen, Coldstream and Lilydale areas of the Yarra Valley. Winemaker Tom Carson was in charge of winemaking until moving to Yabby Lake in July 2008. In his 10-year tenure he established Yering Station as one of the outstanding wineries in the Yarra Valley, in the latter years having the most successful shiraz viognier in Australian wine shows (Clonakilla does not enter) to supplement the chardonnay and pinot noir (both in varietal and Reserve form) which are the spearheads of the portfolio. Cellar door sales are through one of the original sandstock brick buildings, dating from the de Castella days, and the wines are, of course, served at the restaurant, which is open seven days a week and offers outstanding cuisine. The wines have fine wine distribution throughout Australia, and are exported to all major markets.

**yield** is most commonly (and, some would argue, crudely) expressed as tonnes per hectare. (Just as people in Australia still express height in terms of feet and inches, so do many vignerons express yield in tons per acre.) In Europe it is commonly expressed as hectolitres per hectare, which is equally crude. One tonne per acre is roughly 16–17 hectolitres per hectare: roughly, because the conversion depends not only on the weight of the bunches harvested, but also on the amount of juice extracted from those bunches. The many factors which both of these measures ignore include the planting density, the size of the bunches and berries, the number of the bunches, the architecture of the vine canopy, whether the yield was arrived at naturally or as a result of shoot- and/or bunch-thinning, the health of the vine, the nature of the soil and the age of the vine. Thus some prefer to talk in terms of yield per vine; others in terms of the sunlit leaf area per unit of land; others still in terms of the ratio between yield and the dry pruning weight of the canes removed in winter. Since some of these factors cancel each other out, tonnes per hectare (or the equivalent hectolitres per hectare) is still accepted as a generally reliable expression of yield.

a b c d e f g h i
j k l m n o p q
r s t u v w x y z

**Zema Estate** (est. 1982) is one of the last outposts of hand-pruning in Coonawarra, with Demetrio Zema and his wife, Francesca, and sons, Nick and Matt Zema, still tending the 61-ha vineyard (planted progressively since 1982 with care and pride). It is in the heart of Coonawarra's terra rossa soil, and, if ever there was an example of great wines being made in the vineyard, this is it. The quality of cabernet sauvignon, shiraz, merlot and Cluny (a Bordeaux blend) is always impressive, the Family Selection Shiraz and Family Selection Cabernet Sauvignon at the top of the pyramid. Exports to all major markets.

**Zilzie Wines** (est. 1999) is owned by the Forbes family, which has been farming Zilzie Estate since the early 1990s; it is currently run by Ian and Ros Forbes, and sons Steven and Andrew. A diverse range of farming activities now include grapegrowing, with 700 ha of vineyards in the Murray Darling region. Having established a position as a dominant supplier of grapes to Southcorp, Zilzie formed a wine company in 1999 and built a winery in 2000. It has a capacity of 16,000 tonnes, but is designed so that modules can be added to take it to 35,000 tonnes. The business includes contract processing, winemaking and storage, although the recent expansion may face problems given the state of the Murray Darling Basin. Exports to all major markets.

**zinfandel** arrived in the US in the early 19th century. DNA profiling has shown that it is in fact the same as primitivo, a red grape grown with considerable success in southern Italy. In some ways it parallels Australian shiraz, for it responds to an extraordinarily wide range of climate and terroir. In the US this means from the Sierra Nevadas to Lodi in the Central Valley, thence to Russian River in the Sonoma Valley: in other words, from very warm to distinctly cool. As is the case with shiraz, the flavour and structure of the wine changes dramatically as you move from warm to cool, but all the manifestations have easily understood appeal.

From a viticultural viewpoint, it is unique. Any given apparently ripe bunch at harvest time will have some bright green, totally unripe berries spotted throughout, without rhyme or reason, and more than likely a similar number of raisined berries. Conventional methods of assessing ripeness are virtually useless; the most successful makers rely on a sixth sense they have developed through observing the vine and making the wine for many years.

It might be seen as appropriate, therefore, that Sutter Home developed Blush, which is often labelled White Zinfandel (although it is, of course, made from black zinfandel). Blush is a slightly pink, more or less dry and largely tasteless wine which swept across the US like a tidal wave in the 1980s. Blush has no counterpart in Australia, nor is it ever likely to do so: it is one of the less appealing forms of wine to have been made in recent times.

Cape Mentelle pioneered plantings in Australia in the early years, doubtless due to David Hohnen's time in California before founding Cape Mentelle in Margaret River. The wine produced has always been interesting, the quality varying from good to excellent. The only other growers to follow over the next decades were Wilson Vineyard in the Clare Valley and Kangarilla Road in McLaren Vale. (This is ignoring a tiny planting in what is now Domaine A in the Coal River district of Tasmania, which produced remarkable zinfandel.) It is now grown with success in the Hilltops region, and in the Adelaide Hills as well as the Margaret River, McLaren Vale and Clare Valley to generally good effect. Plantings in the Riverland, too, have been moderately rewarding. Nonetheless, it is still not grown in sufficient quantity to be recorded in the generally available statistics, which, given the apparent mania for obscure varieties, is mildly surprising.

**zones** see Geographic Indications.

Complete List of Entries by Subject

## KEY FOR REGIONAL ENTRIES

**Lat** Latitude
**Alt** Altitude
**HDD** Heat degree days
**GSR** Growing season rainfall
**MJT** Mean January temperature
**Harv** Harvest
**Chief vit. hazard** Chief viticultural hazard

palomino
pedro ximinez
petite sirah
petit meslier
petit verdot
pinot gris
pinot meunier
pinot noir
primitivo
riesling
roussanne
ruby cabernet
sangiovese
saperavi
sauvignon blanc
savagnin blanc
semillon
Shepherd's riesling
shiraz
sultana
sumoll
syrah
tannat
tarrango
tinta amarella
tinta barocca, tinta cao, tinta roriz
touriga nacional
trebbiano
tyrian
varietal
verdelho
verduzzo
vermentino
viognier
zinfandel

## Viticulture

alternative varieties
ampelography
anthracnose
Appellation Contrôllée
Australian Wine Research Institute
biodynamic viticulture
Bordeaux mixture
botrytis
bush-pruned vines
canopy management
climate
climate change
clonal selection

clone
continental, continentality
cordon cut
cross, cross-breeding, or crossing
dead fruit
DNA profiling
double pruning
downy mildew
fungicides
genetic modification
hand-picking
heat degree days
hybrid
irrigation
lacasse
late harvest
layering
leafroll virus
machine-harvesting
Medieval Warm Period
mesoclimate
microclimate
Murray Darling River System
National Association for Sustainable Agriculture Australia
nematodes
New World
noble rot
oidium
organic viticulture
pH
phylloxera
planting density
powdery mildew
pruning
rootstock
scion
Scott Henry
Smart, Richard
smoke taint
soil
spur
tannins
terroir
veraison
vertical spur positioning
Vine Pull Scheme
virus diseases
Wine Grape Growers' Australia
yield

## Winemaking

acetaldehyde
acetic acid
acid
additives
alcohol
aldehydic oxidation
amontillado
amoroso
anthocyanins
apera
ascorbic acid
assemblage
Australian Wine Research Institute
autolysis
back-blending
barrel
baumé
biodynamic viticulture
botrytis
*Brettanomyces*
brine
brix
brut
bung
cap
carbonic maceration
cepage
chaptalisation
citric acid
clarification
clonal selection
cold soak
cold-settle
cordon cut
corks
Croser, Brian, AO
cross-flow filtration
crusher
crusher-destemmer
crust
dead fruit
destemmer
Diam®
disgorgement
Ditter, Don, OAM
esters
extract
extraction
fermentation
filtration
fining
flying winemakers

Fornachon, John
fortified wine
free-run
fumé blanc
gassy
glycerol
Grange
gross lees
header boards
heat exchanger
Hill of Grace
hydrogen sulphide
indigenous yeast
intra-cellular fermentation
Jordan, Dr Tony
lactic acid
late harvest
lees
lees stirring
Limousin
maceration
malic acid
malolactic fermentation
Mann, Jack, MBE
marc
mercaptans
metallic
methode champenoise
micro-oxygenation
must
native yeast
New World
noble rot
oak
oak chips
oak staves
oloroso
organic viticulture
O'Shea, Maurice
oxidation
pH
phenolics
pigeage
polymerisation
port
post-fermentation maceration
Potter fermenters
Potter, Ron
Prass, Guenter, AM
Preece, Colin
pre-fermentation maceration
press

pressings
punch-down
rack and return
racked
rancio
Rankine, Dr Bryce, AM
recorking
reduction
residual sugar
resveratrol
reverse osmosis
rosé
saignée
Schubert, Max, AM
screwcaps
Seppelt 100 Year Para
  Liqueur
sherry
smoke taint
solids
sparging
sparkling wine
stabilisation
sterile filtration
stuck fermentation
sur lie
tannins
tartaric acid
tears
terroir
thiols
titratable acidity
tokay
topaque
total acidity
Troncais
ullage
varietal
vat
vinegar fly
virtual winery
volatile acidity
Vosges
Warren, Roger
whole bunch
wild yeasts
yeast

## Personalities

Accad, Guy
Antcliff, Allan
Beckwith, Ray, OAM
Blass, Wolf, AM
Buring, Leo
Busby, James
Chaffey, George and
  William
Croser, Brian, AO
de Castella, Charles
  Hubert
de Castella, Francois
de Castella, Paul Frederick
Ditter, Don, OAM
Evans, Leonard Paul,
  OBE, AO
Fornachon, John
Gladstones, Dr John
Hardy, Thomas
James, Walter
Johnson, Hugh
Jordan, Dr Tony
Mann, Jack, MBE
Murphy, Hazel, AM
O'Shea, Maurice
Parker Jnr, Robert
Potter, Ron
Prass, Guenter, AM
Preece, Colin
Rankine, Dr Bryce, AM
Robinson, Jancis, OBE,
  MW
Schubert, Max, AM
Smart, Richard
Warren, Roger
Wilkinson, W Percy
Wynn, David, AO

## Climate

climate
climate change
continental
maritime
microclimate

## Education

ampelography
Charles Sturt University
  Winery
Len Evans Tutorial
Options Game, The
Riverina College of
  Advanced Education

Roseworthy Agricultural
  College
Wiate Precinct

## History

All Saints Estate
Angove Family
  Winemakers
Baileys of Glenrowan
Beckwith, Ray, OAM
Best's Wines
Bleasdale
Brand's Laira Coonawarra
Brown Brothers
Buring, Leo
Busby, James
Chaffey, George and
  William
Chambers Rosewood
Craiglee
de Castella, Charles
  Hubert
de Castella, Francois
de Castella, Paul Frederick
Forest Hill Vineyard
Grange
Hardy, Thomas
Hardys
Henschke
Hill of Grace
Houghton
Kyeema
Lake's Folly
Leasingham
Leo Buring
Lindemans
McWilliam's
McWilliam's Mount
  Pleasant
Mann, Jack, MBE
Maurice O'Shea Award
Medieval Warm Period
Minchinbury
Moorilla Estate
Murray Darling River
  System
oak
Orlando
O'Shea, Maurice
Penfolds
Peter Lehmann Wines
phylloxera

planting density
post-fermentation
  maceration
powdery mildew
Preece, Colin
Providence Vineyards
rootstock
St Huberts
Saltram
Schubert, Max, AM
Seppelt
Seppelt 100 Year Para
  Liqueur
Seppeltsfield
Sevenhill Cellars
Tahbilk
Tyrrell's
Vine Pull Scheme
Virgin Hills
Warren, Roger
Wendouree
Wilkinson, W Percy
Wirra Wirra
Wynn, David, AO
Wynns Coonawarra Estate
Yalumba
Yeringberg

## Labelling laws

additives
alcohol
amontillado
amoroso
apera
Appellation Contrôllée
labels
oloroso
port
sherry
standard drink
tokay
topaque

## Organisations

Australian Wine and
  Brandy Corporation
Australian Wine Research
  Institute
Charles Sturt University
  Winery

Grape and Wine Research
and Development
Corporation
National Association for
Sustainable Agriculture
Australia
Riverina College of
Advanced Education
Roseworthy Agricultural
College
Waite Precinct
Wine Grape Growers'
Australia
Winemakers' Federation
of Australia

## Research

DNA profiling
Fornachon, John
genetic modification
Gladstones, Dr John
Grape and Wine Research
and Development
Corporation
heat degree days
indigenous yeast
micro-oxygenation
native yeast
random oxidation
resveratrol
sporadic oxidation
TCA
trichloranisole
Waite Precinct
wild yeasts

## Tasting terms

aftertaste
aroma
aroma wheel
astringency
bitterness
body
breathing
*Brettanomyces*
broad
buttery
cassis
character
classic

clean
cloying
coarse
condition
decant
deep
developed, development
dry
dull
earthy
fading
finesse
finish
firm
flabby
flat
fleshy
flowery
fresh
fruity
green
hard
harmony
harsh
hollow
honeyed
jammy
line
maderised
mousy
mouthfeel
nose
nutty
oily
palate
sappy
sour
supple
texture

## Vine diseases

anthracnose
Bordeaux mixture
downy mildew
fungicides
lacasse
leafroll virus
nematodes
oidium
phylloxera
powdery mildew
virus diseases

## Wine faults

acetaldehyde
acetic acid
aldehydic oxidation
*Brettanomyces*
corked
fault
glycerol
hydrogen sulphide
mercaptans
metallic
mouldy
mousy
oxidation
oxidised
phenolics
random oxidation
recorking
reduction
smoke taint
sporadic oxidation
TCA
trichloranisole
vinegar fly

## Wine styles

amontillado
amoroso
apera
cepage
fortified wine
fumé blanc
Grange
Hill of Grace
oloroso
port
rosé
Seppelt 100 Year Para
Liqueur
sherry
sparkling wine
tokay
topaque

## Wineries

Abbey Creek
Alkoomi
All Saints Estate
Angove Family
Winemakers

Annie's Lane
Arrowfield
Ashbrook Estate
Ashton Hills
Baileys of Glenrowan
Balgownie Estate
Balnaves of Coonawarra
Bannockburn Vineyards
Banrock Station
Barossa Valley Estate
Barringwood Park
Barwang Vineyard
Bass Phillip
Bay of Fires
Belgravia
Bellarmine Wines
Best's Wines
Bindi Wine Growers
Bleasdale
Bloodwood
Blue Metal Vineyard
Borrodell on the Mt
Brand's Laira
Coonawarra
Brangayne of Orange
Bream Creek
Bremerton
Brokenwood
Brookland Valley
Brown Brothers
Buller
By Farr
Caledonia Australis
Capel Vale
Cape Mentelle
Capercaillie
Carlei Estate and Carlei
Green Vineyards
Casella Wines
Cassegrain
Castagna
Castle Rock Estate
Centennial Vineyards
Chalkers Crossing
Chambers Rosewood
Charles Melton
Charles Sturt University
Winery
Chatto
Cheviot Bridge
Clonakilla
Clovely Estate
Clover Hill
Coldstream Hills

Constellation Wines
  Australia
Coriole
Craiglee
Craigow
Crawford River
Cullen Wines
Cumulus Wines
Curlewis Winery
Curly Flat
Cuttaway Hill Estate
CWA
Dalrymple
Dalwhinnie
d'Arenberg
Deakin Estate
De Bortoli
De Bortoli, Yarra Valley
De Iuliis
Delatite
Devil's Lair
Diamond Valley
  Vineyards
di Lusso Wines
Domaine A
Domaine Chandon
Dominique Portet
Duke's Vineyard
Dutschke Wines
Eden Hall
Elderton
Eldridge Estate of Red
  Hill
Evans & Tate
Faber Vineyard
Ferngrove
Fonty's Pool Vineyards
Forest Hill Vineyard
Foster's Wine Estates
Frankland Estate
Frogmore Creek
Frog Rock
Garlands
Gemtree Vineyards
Geoff Merrill Wines
Geoff Weaver
Giaconda
Giant Steps
Gibson BarossaVale
Gilberts
Glaetzer Wines
Goundrey
Gralyn Estate
Grampians Estate

Granite Hills
Grant Burge
Greenstone Vineyard
Grove Estate Wines
Haan Wines
Hackersley
Hanging Rock Winery
Hardys
Hardy, Thomas
Harewood Estate
Harvey River Bridge
  Estate
Hay Shed Hill Wines
Heathcote Estate
Heggies Vineyard
Helm
Henschke
Hewitson
Houghton
Howard Park
Huntington Estate
Jacob's Creek
Jansz Tasmania
Jasper Hill
Jim Barry Wines
John Duval
K1 by Geoff Hardy
Kaesler
Kalleske
Katnook Estate
Kay Brothers Amery
  Vineyards
Keith Tulloch Wines
Kilikanoon
Kingston Estate
Knappstein
Kominos
Kooyong
Lake Breeze Wines
Lake's Folly
Lamont's Winery
Langmeil Winery
La Pleiade
Lark Hill
Larry Cherubino
Leasingham
Leconfield
Leeuwin Estate
Leo Buring
Lindemans
Lion Nathan
McGuigan Wines
McHenry Hohnen
  Vintners

McWilliam's
McWilliam's Mount
  Pleasant
Main Ridge Estate
Majella
Mayfield Vineyard
Meadowbank Estate
Meerea Park
Millamolong Estate
Millbrook Winery
Minchinbury
Miramar
Mistletoe Wines
Mitchell
Mitchelton
Mitolo Wines
Montalto Vineyards
Moondah Brook
Moorilla Estate
Moorooduc Estate
Morris
Moss Wood
Mountadam
Mt Billy
Mount Horrocks
Mount Langi Ghiran
  Vineyards
Mount Mary
Mount Trio Vineyard
Mr Riggs Wine
  Company
Murdock
Narkoojee
Norfolk Rise Vineyard
Oakridge
Old Kent River
O'Leary Walker Wines
Orlando
Padthaway Estate
Paringa Estate
Parker Coonawarra
  Estate
Patina
Paulett
Paxton
Peel Estate
Penfolds
Penley Estate
Pepper Tree Wines
Petaluma Wines
Peter Lehmann Wines
Pewsey Vale
PHI
Phillip Island Vineyard

Picardy
Pierro
Pikes
Piper's Brook Vineyard
Pirie Estate
Pirramimma
Plantagenet
Plunkett Fowles
Polleters
Pondalowie Vineyards
Poole's Rock
Pooley Wines
Port Phillip Estate
Primo Estate
Prince Hill Wines
Printhie Wines
Providence Vineyards
Pyramid Hill
Pyramids Road
Redman
Richfield Estate
Robert Channon Wines
Robert Oatley Vineyards
Robinvale
Rosemount Estate
Rothbury Estate
St Hallett
St Huberts
St Leonards Vineyard
Salitage
Salomon Estate
Saltram
Sandalford
SC Pannell
Scotchmans Hill
Seppelt
Seppeltsfield
Setanta
Sevenhill Cellars
Shadowfax
Shaw & Smith
Shelmerdine
Sirromet Wines
Smithbrook
Southcorp
Spinifex
Spring Vale Vineyards
Stanton & Killeen
Stefano Lubiana
Stella Bella Wines
Stonehaven
Stoney Rise
Stonier
Summerfield

Symphony Hill Wines
Tahbilk
Taltarni
Tamar Ridge
Tamburlaine
Tapanappa
TarraWarra Estate
Tatachilla
Taylors
Temple Bruer
Ten Minutes by Tractor
The Islander Estate
Thistle Hill
Thomas Wines
Thorn-Clarke Wines
Tomboy Hill

Toolangi Vineyards
Torbreck Vintners
Torzi Matthews
 Vintners
Tower Estate
Trentham Estate
Tuck's Ridge
Tulloch
Turkey Flat
Two Hands Wines
Two Rivers
Tyrrell's
Vasse Felix
Vincognita
Virgin Hills
Voyager Estate

Wantirna Estate
Wendouree
West Cape Howe
Western Range Wines
Wignalls Wines
Wild Duck Creek Estate
Willow Bridge Estate
Willow Creek Vineyard
Winemakers' Federation
 of Australia
Wirra Wirra
Wise Wine
Witches Falls
Wolf Blass Wines
Woodlands
Woodside Valley Estate

Wynns Coonawarra
 Estate
Xanadu Wines
Yabby Lake Vineyard
Yalumba
Yarrabank
Yarra Burn
YarraLoch
Yarra Yarra
Yarra Yering
Yeringberg
Yering Station
Zema Estate
Zilzie Wines

Published in 2009
by Hardie Grant Books
85 High Street
Prahran, Victoria 3181, Australia
www.hardiegrant.com.au

National Library of Australia Cataloguing-in-Publication data:
Halliday, James, 1938–
   The Australian wine encyclopedia / James Halliday.
   ISBN 9781740667746 (hbk.)
   Includes index.
   Wine and wine making –Australia – Encyclopedias.
641.2203

Design by Sandy Cull, gogoGingko
Typeset by Prowling Tiger Press
Jacket photographs by Getty Images
Printed and bound in Australia by McPherson's Printing Group

*Every effort has been made to incorporate correct information
and statistics. The author and publisher regret any errors and
omissions and invite readers to contribute up-to-date or relevant
information to Hardie Grant Books.*

10 9 8 7 6 5 4 3 2 1

t Southern, the name coming from a winter creek running alongside the vineyard, and a view of The Abbey in the St
eslings have had significant show success. Accad, Guy came to prominence in Burgundy in the mid-1980s, advocatir
e onset of fermentation, which in turn gave rise to the concept of pre-fermentation maceration, commonly known a
Oregon for the International Pinot Noir Celebration. In Australia cold soak is often used, but in lieu of high levels of
in liberating colour (which has particular relevance for pinot noir), and the extraction of all anthocyanins in an aq
ome winemakers in fact use both pre- and post-fermentation techniques. acetaldehyde is the most common form o
cessarily part of table wine, but at high concentrations it is a major fault. The wine will be described as aldehydic, den
dition of appropriate sulphur dioxide. acetic acid is present in all table wines, but normally at low levels. It is this v
gal limit is 0.8 mg/l for white wine and rosé, 1.2 mg/l for red wine and 1.5 mg/l for botrytised wine. acid is present
e amounts of citric acid. Where the acid is too low, any one of the three acids may legally be added to wine to bring i
ises the chance of oxidation. additives to wine are controlled by the Australia New Zealand Food Standards Code
cannot be added, even if it is in no way harmful. One example of the latter is sorbitol. It is widely used in the fruit
ere is the curious situation that as one travels north across the equator, acid becomes the work of the devil; as one cr
r substance if they believe the quality of the wine will be improved by the addition. On the other hand, they shoul
us. For a full list of permitted additives see Standard 4.5.1 of the Australia New Zealand Foods Standards Code.
o dissolve additives such as fining agents including casein and bentonite. It is also recognised that small amounts of
r simply to reduce the alcohol level; Californian winemakers, by contrast, are able to add up to 10 per cent of wat
Mount Lofty Ranges Zone, yet is a bare 30 minutes' drive from the CBD of Adelaide. A flourishing region in the 1
n in 1971, but the arrival of Brian Croser and his founding of Petaluma in 1976 were the pivotal events. If there is a
emost producers in the region are Ashton Hills, Bird in Hand, Deviation Road, Fox Gordon, Geoff Weaver, Hah
ma, Pike & Joyce, Romney Park, Setanta, Shaw & Smith, Tilbrook and Wicks Estate. The common themes of the
metre contour line, but the ever-twisting and turning hills, valleys and rivers within the region provide a large ran
climate to that of Adelaide throughout much of the summer has to be experienced to be believed. The veritable ma
Adelaide Hills has an unequivocally cool climate; it is not until one reaches the northern extremity of the region, ar
and sauvignon blanc, and into terrain which satisfactorily ripens cabernet sauvignon and shiraz. The Adelaide Hill
kly structured soils of lesser quality. Fertility varies, tending to be higher in the southern and central areas. Lat 34
de Plains, gazetted 25 March 2002, is the most dramatic proof of the lack of meaning to the grouping of regions w
ent Gulf of St Vincent is unable to provide any significant cooling. It is warmer than the Hunter Valley and its gr
Vale, leaving Ceravolo, Diloreto and Domenic Versace to provide some respectability. Shiraz, cabernet sauvigno
of southeastern Australia, with alkaline subsoils and free limestone at deeper levels. These are excellent viticultura
clay soils which are strikingly different in structure, but once again tend to be alkaline rather than acidic, and once
ch; Chief vit. hazard Nil Adelaide Zone is a so-called super zone which encompasses the Mount Lofty Ranges, Fle
es and regions in its purview, and simply label them 'Adelaide'. The only problem is that very few winemakers have
ith a back label affirmation of 'Wine made in Australia'. aftertaste is experienced after the wine has been swallowe
incipal variety used in Falernian, the most famous of all Roman wines). Its current champion in Italy is Mastrobera
ery late ripening variety will surely be more widely commercially propagated if temperatures continue to rise. Albar
curiosities of history that, when Great Britain formally claimed ownership of the western part of Australia on Chris
st and west was used for grazing and wheat farming, Albany became famous for whaling, which continued until 197
r perhaps Vancouver – itself named by Captain George Vancouver, the 1791 explorer of Albany and thereafter of B
re planted by the Sippe family at Redmond Vineyard in 1975, using cuttings of riesling supplied by Forest Hill Vine
on were made at Plantagenet; for some time thereafter the vineyard was neglected, but now it forms the core of Pl
on. Self-evidently, Albany's climate is maritime, strongly shaped and moderated by the Southern Ocean; the sta
al, and moderate humidity in summer assists ripening by reducing stress on the vines. The hills and valleys make th
r of an infallible guide to the best soils for grape vines: lateritic gravelly, sandy loams or sandy loams derived directly
z, cabernet sauvignon and merlot do best further away from the coast. The principal wineries are Kalgan River W
ljt 19°C; Harv Mid-March to end April; Chief vit. hazard Birds albarino is a native white grape of Spain, and seen
y. Its source, so it appeared, was impeccable: the nursery vineyards of the CSIRO at Merbein, Victoria. Doubts en

y Creek Vineyard (est. 1990) is the family business of Mike and Mary Dilworth in the Porongurup subregion of the G
e. The 1.6 ha vineyard is equally split among riesling, pinot noir and cabernet sauvignon planted in 1990 and '93. Th
f very high levels of SO2 in red must prior to the commencement of fermentation. The effect was to significantly dela
He spoke at two major conferences, one in 1987 and one in 1990, one in the UK for the Masters of Wine, the other
must is chilled below 10°C, and it is this temperature which prevents the onset of fermentation. It is extremely effec
on is quite different from that in an alcoholic environment. Thus, post-fermentation maceration has a different rol
ical compounds known as aldehydes, which are produced at the last stages of fermentation. At low concentrations it i
of fruit aroma and flavour not unlike the effect of oxidation. In barrel or tank, the problem is easily treated with th
es volatile acidity, which results in a pungent, sharp odour and flavour when present at levels of 0.6 mg/l or above. Th
s in various forms. The most important is tartaric acid, followed by malic acid at slightly lower concentration, with t
ce. The other acid added to white wines (though not red) is ascorbic, which, in conjunction with sulphur dioxide, m
gulations thereunder. The regulations list a series of substances which may be added, and any substance not on that
try, and gives the wine a softer and (arguably) more pleasant taste and mouthfeel – but it is an illegal additive. Finall
e opposite direction, sugar becomes the work of the devil. Good winemakers anywhere should not hesitate to add e
v the herd, seeking to rely instead on achieving balance in the vineyard so that the addition of either becomes super.
it has been legal to add up to 7 per cent of water to either the must or the finished wine, chiefly where water is neede
be incorporated with wine during bulk transfer by pump from one vessel to another. However, it is not legal to add
oration of fermentation problems. Adelaide Hills, gazetted 9 February 1998, is the coolest of the three regions in th
530 ha of vines, it declined into obscurity before the last vines disappeared, which was in the 1930s. Planting began a
y which marks the region, it is sauvignon blanc, however important chardonnay, pinot noir and shiraz may be. The
K1 by Geoff Hardy, Longview Vineyard, Mount Torrens Vineyard, New Era Vineyards, Ngeringa, Paracombe, Pet
ced are elegance and clarity of varietal expression.The southern and eastern boundaries are determined by the 40
climates. Altitude is the key to the climate: Mount Lofty and the Piccadilly Valley are at 500 metres, and the contra
s and sub-valleys means there is much mesoclimatic variation, making generalisations hazardous. However, most of
facing slopes, that one moves out of a climate suited principally to early-ripening varieties such as chardonnay, pinot
minantly grey, grey-brown or brown loamy sands and clay loams; there are also patches of much sandier and more v
00–500 m; hdd 1270; Gsr 310 mm; Mjt 19.1°C; Harv Mid-March to late April; Chief vit. hazard Poor fruit set Ad
, in this case the Mount Lofty Ranges Zone. This is a dead flat and hot region with an altitude of 20 metres; the ac
n rainfall is on a par with that of the Swan Valley. Its most highly rated winery, Primo Estate, has moved to McLa
che are the main varieties. There are two soil types. First, the ubiquitous red-brown loamy sands found through so n
n readily support the typically high yields of the region. Then there are also smaller patches of heavier loam and crack
ote vigorous vine growth. Lat 34°41'S; Alt 20 m; Hdd 2081; Gsr 130 mm; Mjt 23°C; Harv Mid-February to early N
Barossa zones. One of the ostensible reasons for this larger zone was to allow the blending of wines from the quality
tage of this somewhat dubious proposition. Even Penfolds Magill Estate is content with the vineyard name, couple
rst breath thereafter has been taken. aglianico is a red grape much admired by the Greeks and the Romans (it was the
e Taurasi is based on aglianico. It is propagated by Chalmers Nurseries at Mildura, with two clones available, and as
gion of the Great Southern region of Western Australia, its focal point being the town of the same name. It is one of
n 1826, the point of possession relied on was Albany rather than Perth. While the surrounding country to the north
luted bays and granite outcrops make this beautiful region (and, in parts, atmospheric town) seem like a mini Seattl
nbia. Albany's whaling museum is the largest in the world and is justifiably a major tourist attraction. The first vines
ernet sauvignon was also planted.) The first two crops of grapes were sold, but in 1981 a riesling and cabernet Sauv
k Estate. However, the present emphasis is more on chardonnay and pinot noir than on riesling and cabernet sau
iption is that it is Mediterranean, with moist, cool winters and warm, dry summers. Diurnal temperature range is mi
tive enough, but when ocean views are added, and huge marri or karri eucalypts soar skywards, it takes on the chara
te and gneissic rocks. The region is best suited to chardonnay. Sauvignon blanc and (in some vintages) pinot noir, s
gomery's Hill, Oranje Tractor, Phillips Brook Estate and Wignalls. Lat 35°02'S; Alt 75 m; Hdd 1495; Gsr 303 mm
many advantages in the Australian climate; its small plantings proliferated rapidly in the opening decade of this cen